Tromsø,
17 September
2014

Jo Marion,

Thank you for your contribution to the conference Demons and witches in Tromsø, 11–13 September 2014.

Best wishes,

Siv

Witches of the North

Studies in Medieval and Reformation Traditions

The titles published in this series are listed at brill.com/smrt

Witches of the North

Scotland and Finnmark

By

Liv Helene Willumsen

BRILL

LEIDEN • BOSTON
2013

Cover illustration: A Laplander, a Latvier, a Scot. Detail of Fig. 12, p. 347. StB Ulm

Library of Congress Cataloging-in-Publication Data

Willumsen, Liv Helene, 1948–
   Witches of the North : Scotland and Finnmark / by Liv Helene Willumsen.
     pages cm. — (Studies in medieval and reformation traditions ; 170)
   Includes bibliographical references and index.
   ISBN 978-90-04-25291-2 (hardback : alk. paper) — ISBN 978-90-04-25292-9 (e-book)
     1. Witchcraft—Scotland—History. 2. Witchcraft—Scotland—Orkney—History. 3. Witchcraft—
Scotland—Shetland—History. 4. Witchcraft—Norway—Finnmark fylke—History. I. Title.

   KJC7964.W58W55 2013
   345.411'0288—dc23

                                                                                      2013014249

This publication has been typeset in the multilingual "Brill" typeface. With over 5,100 characters
covering Latin, IPA, Greek, and Cyrillic, this typeface is especially suitable for use in the
humanities. For more information, please see www.brill.com/brill-typeface.

ISSN 1573-4188
ISBN 978-90-04-25291-2 (hardback)
ISBN 978-90-04-25292-9 (e-book)

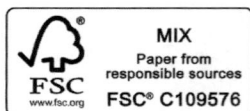

MIX
Paper from
responsible sources
FSC
www.fsc.org   FSC® C109576

                                                    Printed by Printforce, the Netherlands

To Terje, Tomas and Johannes

CONTENTS

CONTENTS

PART IV

CLOSING

ACKNOWLEDGEMENTS

I would first like to thank Julian Goodare, University of Edinburgh, for fruitful discussions on the topic witchcraft trials in Scotland and Finnmark. Then I would like to thank Peter Graves, University of Edinburgh and Brian P. Levack, University of Texas at Austin, for constructive comments. I would also like to thank the editor-in-chief of the Brill series Studies in Medieval and Reformation Traditions, Andrew Colin Gow, for valuable comments on the manuscript. My thanks also go to Brill Publisher's anonymous reviewer, whose suggestions have been of great help for me.

I would like to thank Brian Smith at Shetland Museum and Archives, Lerwick, for good help with the Shetland sources. I am grateful to John and Wendy Scott, Gardie House, Bressay, Shetland, for letting me use trial records in their possession. I would like to thank the staff at the Orkney Library and Archive, Kirkwall, for help with the Orkney sources. I would like to thank Diane Baptie for help with the old Scottish tongue. I am grateful to Lorna Pink for help with old Scots and to Ronald Black and Andrew Jennings for help with old Gaelic words and folklore. I would like to thank Arne Kruse, University of Edinburgh, for interesting discussions on place names. For professional help with Scottish archival sources I would like to thank the staff at the National Records of Scotland, Edinburgh. I would also like to thank the staff at the National Library of Scotland, Edinburgh, for good help.

I would like to thank Solbjørg Ellingsen Fossheim, Tore Sørensen and Arne Gunnar Edvardsen at The Regional State Archives of Tromsø, Norway, for good and professional help with the Norwegian archival sources. I would also like to thank Knut Johannessen, The National Archives of Norway, for comments on my transcriptions of Norwegian primary sources. I would like to thank Katjana Edwardsen for her work with the translation of Norwegian court records into English. For help with etymological questions I would like to thank Tor Guttu. I am grateful to Jørn Øyrehagen Sunde, Aage Thor Falkanger, Jens Chr. Johansen and Hans Eyvind Næss for help with questions related to seventeenth-century legislation in Denmark-Norway. For discussions on witchcraft trials I would like to thank Rita Voltmer, Rune Blix Hagen, Randi Rønning Balsvik, Einar Niemi, Bente Alver, Gunnar W. Knutsen, Ellen Alm, Per Sörlin, Reidun

Laura Andreassen, Ole Lindhartsen, William Moore, Raisa Maria Toivo, Marko Nenonen, Rolf Schulte, and Linda Burnett.

I would like to thank the Department of History and Religious Studies, University of Tromsø for research leave 2011–2012, making it possible to complete this book. I would like to thank the School of History, Classics and Archaeology, University of Edinburgh, for a good working place during my time as Academic Scholar spring 2012. I would like to thank Duncan and Elaine Stewart for making my stays in Edinburgh very good.

I would also like to thank my husband, Terje, and my sons, Tomas and Johannes, for good support throughout the years of this work.

Edinburgh, 18 June 2013
Liv Helene Willumsen

LIST OF ABBREVIATIONS

AF	Amtmannen i Finnmark [Regional Governor of Finnmark]
APS	*The Acts of the Parliaments of Scotland*, eds. T. Thomson and C. Innes, 12 vols. (Edinburgh, 1814–75)
BL	British Library, London
DDD	Database Documentation and Description
DOST	W. A. Craigie, *Dictionary of the Older Scottish Tongue*, 12 vols. (Chicago, 1931)
Fasti	H. Scott, *Fasti Ecclesiae Scoticanae: the Succession of Ministers in the Church of Scotland from the Reformation*, 8 vols. (Edinburgh, rev. edn., 1915–50)
HP	J. R. N. Macphail (ed.), *Highland Papers*, 4 vols. (SHS, 1914–34)
LF	Lagting for Finnmark [Court of Appeal Finnmark]
Lil.	H. H. Lilienskiold
LrV	Lensregnskap for Vardøhus len [District Accounts Vardøhus District]
MC	Marwick Collection
NLS	National Library of Scotland, Edinburgh
NRS	National Records of Scotland, Edinburgh
OLA	Orkney Library and Archive, Kirkwall
OPR	Orkney Presbytery Records
RA	Riksarkivet [National Archives of Norway], Oslo
RLC	Royal Library, Copenhagen
RMS	*Registrum Magni Sigilli Regum Scotorum* (Register of the Great Seal of Scotland), eds. J. M. Thomson et al. (Edinburgh, 1882–)
RPC	P. H. Brown et al. (eds.), *The Register of the Privy Council of Scotland*, 38 vols. (Edinburgh, 1908–70)
SATØ	Statsarkivet i Tromsø [Regional State Archives of Tromsø]
SAT	Statsarkivet i Trondheim [Regional State Archives of Trondheim]
SBSW	*A Source-Book of Scottish Witchcraft*
SF	Sorenskriveren i Finnmark [The Magistrate of Finnmark]
SHR	*Scottish Historical Review*
SHS	Scottish History Society
SMA	Shetland Museum and Archives, Lerwick
SPR	Shetland Presbytery Records

SRS   Scottish Record Society
SS   Stair Society
SSW   Survey of Scottish Witchcraft
Thott Thott's collection

LIST OF FIGURES, MAPS AND CHARTS

Figures

Maps

Charts

CHAPTER ONE

INTRODUCTION

The Topic

Not more than four centuries ago, alleged witches were burned in fire at the stake throughout Europe. They were persecuted of practising witchcraft, thus breaking the laws, and were brought before the court and tried in criminal cases, alongside with persons accused of murder, theft and other crimes. This book deals with women and men who were formally accused of witchcraft in two European areas which suffered severe persecution, Scotland and the district of Finnmark, Northern Norway. People could also be brought before the court because of seeking witches' advice or to have collaborated with witches.[1] The European witchcraft persecution is a historical phenomenon, taking place within a restricted period of time. The witchcraft trials in the two areas dealt with in this book took place from the late sixteenth century until early eighteenth century. For the whole of Europe, persecution of alleged witches took place from the 1420s until 1782, with the most intensive period from 1580 until 1630. Also the period from 1630 until 1675 experienced severe witchcraft persecution, particularly in Scotland, Scandinavia and Eastern Europe. The period from 1675 to 1750 was a time of decline and protraction in the persecution of alleged witches.[2]

The persecution started in the areas near the Alps and spread to other European areas rather quickly, with Trier in Germany and Scotland as areas which suffered severe early trial waves.[3] Protestant as well as Catholic

---

[1] Næss, H. E., *Trolldomsprosessene i Norge på 1500–1600-tallet. En retts- og sosialhistorisk undersøkelse* [Witchcraft trials in Norway during the sixteenth and seventeenth centuries. A legal- and socioeconomic study] (Oslo, 1982), 7; Sogner, S., 'Trolldomsprosessene i Norge på 1500–1600-tallet [Sixteenth- and seventeenth-century witchcraft trials in Norway], *Norveg*, no. 25 (1982), 155–182, at p. 155.

[2] Willumsen, L. H., *Seventeenth-Century Witchcraft Trials in Scotland and Northern Norway*, Ph.D. thesis, University of Edinburgh, (Edinburgh, 2008), 54–55; Levack, B., *The Witch-Hunt in Early Modern Europe*, 3rd edn. (London, 2006), 207, 209.

[3] Voltmer, R., 'Hexenverfolgungen im Maas-Rhein-Mosel-Raum', in F. Irsigler (ed.), *Beziehungen, Begegnungen und Konflikte in einem europäishen Kernraum von der Spätantike bis zum 19. Jahrhundert* (Trier, 2006), 153–187.

areas were involved. In Richard M. Golden's four-volume *Encyclopedia of Witchcraft. The Western Tradition* (2006), Robert Muchembled states in the foreword: 'The heartland of witchcraft persecutions lay mostly in parts of west-central Europe, which were sharply disputed between Protestants and Catholics between 1560 and 1630, and there were later prolongations in Eastern Europe during the post-1560 Catholic reconquest and in a few overseas colonies such as New England'.[4] This geographical outline pays particular attention to West Europe as the core area of witchcraft persecution. With regard to witchcraft geography, Marko Nennonen argues that the Western European paradigm has dominated witchcraft research so far, and that reconsideration is needed as for Eastern Europe.[5] The intensity of the European witchcraft persecution will in this book be understood as the proportion of executed individuals in relation to the population in an area. To get a picture of the intensity, Richard M. Golden has looked at the number of trials compared with the population in Europe at the time of the witch-hunt. The estimated population in Europe in *c.* 1600 was between 92 and 95 millions.[6] Golden's estimated numbers executed in Europe as a whole were between 40,638 and 52,738. Among other witchcraft researchers the estimated number of executions during the European witchcraft trials varies from 40,000 and 60,000.[7] This represents about 0.5 per thousand in *c.* 1600. Together with certain areas of Central Germany, the two areas studied in this book, Scotland and Finnmark, are among the worst hit European areas with regard to witchcraft persecution.[8]

---

[4] Muchembled, R., 'Foreword', in R. M. Golden (ed.), *Encyclopedia of Witchcraft. The Western Tradition*, 4 vols., i, (Santa Barbara, 2006), p. xxvii.

[5] Nennonen, M., 'Witch Hunts in Europe: A New Geography', *Arv, Nordic Yearbook of Folklore*, lxii (2006), 168–72, 182; Levack, *The Witch-Hunt in Early Modern Europe*, 209.

[6] Golden, R. M., 'Satan in Europe: The Geography of Witch Hunts', in B. P. Levack (ed.), *New Perspectives on Witchcraft, Magic and Demonology*, 6 vols., ii: *Witchcraft in Continental Europe* (New York, 2001), 2–33.

[7] Nenonen, 'Witch Hunts', 165; Behringer, W., *Witches and Witch-Hunts* (Cambridge, 2004), 156; Voltmer, R., 'Vom getrübten Blick auf frühneuzeitlichen Hexenverfolgungen—Versuch einer Klärung', *Gnostika. Zeitschrift für Wissencahft und Esoretik*, no. 11 (2006), 66; Levack, B. P., *The Witch-Hunt in Early Modern Europe* (3rd edn., London, 2006), 23; Toivo, R. M., *Witchcraft and Gender in Early Modern Society* (Hampshire, 2008), 9. Toivo takes 30,000–40,000 as the lower limit.

[8] See Golden, *Encyclopedia*, for an overview of the European witchcraft trials. In Scotland the rate of execution was at least 67%, ref. Willumsen, *Seventeenth-Century Witchcraft Trials*, 66. The rate of execution during the witchcraft trials in Finnmark was the same, ref. Willumsen, *Seventeenth-Century Witchcraft Trials*, 100. The Prince-Abbey of St Maximin, situated just outside the city walls of Trier suffered extreme witchcraft persecution, 500 persons were executed out of 2200 persons living in St Maximin, which is 22.7% of the population.

Witchcraft, Sorcery and Magic

The concept of witchcraft is a wide one. Randi Rønning Balsvik says: 'Witchcraft is close to the terms "magic" and "sorcery", the concepts refer to the ability that some have to make supernatural powers interfere in the lives of fellow human beings to the detriment of their welfare. The forces used are invisible and used to cause bad luck, sickness and even death'.[9] I would like to take a closer look at the terms magic, sorcery, and witchcraft, and make clear how the these words are understood and used in this book. The term magic, which has as its origin the word *magia*, includes all magical practice; black magic as well as white magic. The former has an evil intention and the latter a good intention.[10] Thus the term is a categorization of all performances of magic, whatever its intent or effect.[11] Bente Gullveig Alver says that according to the magical way of looking upon the world, there was a power of a special kind, which could take residence in particular places, objects and living beings, and which humans could actualize and make use of in certain situations and related to certain acts. Different explanations exist when it comes to how these persons got their powers. As a rule there is the conception among the populace that people who possess such powers have got contact with a spirit. Such a spirit may lead to practice of good or evil deeds. Usually such a contact was obtained by the person's own effort.

There were several means to get access to magical powers. One could get it through a person, who possessed it on beforehand, as a rule an elderly person, who taught this art to a younger person. Such powers could also be conveyed through an object, or it could be passed on hereditary from parents. The fact that the powers could be used both in a negative and a positive way, led to an ambivalent view on those who were alleged to possess these powers. One was careful in mixing with such persons and tried to make use of their positive side. Whether this use or these acts were experienced as good or evil, was dependent upon the context these

---

[9] Balsvik, R. R., 'Religious beliefs and witches in contemporary Africa', in R. L. Andreassen and L. H. Willumsen (eds.), *Steilneset Memorial. Art, Architecture, History* (Stamsund, 2013).

[10] Edvard Bever distinguishes between 'malefic magic' and 'beneficent magic', the latter often called 'benevolent magic' or 'white sorcery'. Bever, E., *The Realities of Witchcraft and Popular Magic in Early Modern Europe* (Basingstoke, 2008), xiv.

[11] Bever, *The Realities of Witchcraft and Popular Magic in Early Modern Europe*, 1.

acts were performed within and from which position the acts were seen.[12] Because their practice could be for good or for evil, there was an uncertainty associated with such people.

Acts of white magic have as its purpose 'to bring about some benefit to oneself or another'.[13] It is concerned with the healing arts, with prophecy, finding lost objects, supply of love potions, and with performances and rituals designed to counter black witchcraft.[14] White magic may be used to heal sickness, often sickness that it difficult to explain. It may be used for the benefit of fishermen, to improve their catch. It may be used for the benefit of farmers, who would like their harvest to be prosperous and their livestock to have good luck. It may be used for the benefit of women's fertility, their ability to bear children. It may be used to prevent storms and accidents to occur. It may be used to bring justice to its end, as stolen goods might be found. Even if some of these activities, like supply of love potions, could be considered good for some and bad for others, the intention of white magic most often is for the good of people. It is overall a kind of magical practice with positive results. In this book, the term white magic will be used synonymously with beneficent magic.

Black magic has, in contrast to white magic, as its intention to perform harmful deeds. It can be related to human sickness or death, storm and bad weather, and other catastrophes hitting individuals or local communities. Acts of black magic often had disastrous outfall, which could lead to an accusation of witchcraft.[15] Black magic, as if was practised in the early modern period, comprised two types of witchcraft: *maleficium* and diabolism. *Maleficium* is by Brian P. Levack defined as 'the performance of harmful deeds by means of some sort of extraordinary, mysterious, occult, preternatural or supernatural power.'[16] The result of *maleficium* was most often sickness or death related to humans and animals, but could also lead to misfortune, poverty or impotence.[17] *Maleficium* could be performed

---

[12] Alver, B. G., *Mellem mennesker og magter. Magi i hekseforfølgelsernes tid* [Between human beings and forces. Magic in the time of witchcraft persecution] (Bergen, 2008), 37.

[13] Levack, *The Witch-Hunt in Early Modern Europe*, 6.

[14] Larner, C., *Enemies of God. The Witch-Hunt in Scotland* (Oxford, 1981), 9.

[15] Bever, *The Realities of Witchcraft and Popular Magic*, xiv. See also Schulte, R., *Hexenverfolgung in Schleswig-Holstein, 16.–18. Jahrhundert* (Heide, 2001) 13.

[16] Levack, *The Witch-Hunt in Early Modern Europe*, 4.

[17] Monter, W., 'Witch Trials in Continental Europe 1560–1660', in B. Ankarloo, S. Clark, and W. Monter (eds.), *Witchcraft and Magic in Europe. The Period of the Witch Trials* (London, 2002), 1–52, at p. 48; Goodare, J., 'Scottish Witchcraft in its European Context', in J. Goodare, L. Martin and J. Miller (eds.), *Witchcraft and Belief in Early Modern Scotland* (Basingstoke, 2008), 26–50, at pp. 26–30; Briggs, R., *Witches and Neighbours. The Social and Cultural Context of European Witchcraft* (Oxford, 2002), 10; Schulte, *Hexenverfolgung*

also due to the alleged witch's general power to perform harm or by an internal act, meaning that an evil glance or an evil wish would be sufficient for harm to happen. In this book, *maleficium* will be used in the same meaning as sorcery, about harmful ritual magic, an acquired skill performed on an individual basis. It includes casting of spells, the use of words and actions to generate supernatural power. According to Christina Larner it is usually necessary to establish that the mobilization of powerful ill will has been attempted by using for instance 'cursing, gnomic utterance, or scarcely audible mumbling'.[18] In addition to spells, physical objects can be used to obtain the intended effect.[19] The meaning of *maleficium* is slighter broader than sorcery as the former does not necessarily require audible or visible techniques used.

Diabolism, worship of the Devil, is the other type of black magic performed in the early modern period. Diabolism differed from *maleficium* in several ways. This type of witchcraft, which was considered to be very serious on the part of the legal authorities, had the Devil as its core, and a pact between the alleged witch and the Devil as the central element. By entering such a pact, the witch got power from the Devil to perform evil deeds, and she or he agreed to become the Devil's secret servant and should contribute to introducing the Devil's kingdom on earth. The witch was tempted by the Devil to enter such a pact, and was often offered something in return for her service. There was a ritual connected to the entering of the pact, where the witch renounced her Christian faith and promised to serve the Evil One. According to this perception of witchcraft a suspected person's ability to do evil was based on the Devil's pact, and witches' meetings as well as shape-shifting was included. This type of witchcraft was frequently performed on a collective basis, including elements like witches' sabbaths and collective witchcraft operations. A cumulative concept of witchcraft emerged, with the Devil, the pact with the Devil, the Sabbath, the witch's flight through the air and shape-shifting as ingredients.[20] Witchcraft of this kind was related to the learned

---

in Schleswig-Holstein, 13; Rummel, W. and Voltmer, R., *Hexen und Hexenverfolgung in der Frühen Neuzeit* (Darmstadt, 2008), 2–5; Kallestrup, L., *I pagt med Djævelen. Trolddomsforestillinger og trolddomsforfølgelser i Italien og Danmark efter Reformationen* (København, 2009), 53, 70, 80, 82, 85, 89, 102–103.

[18] Larner, *Enemies of God*, 9.

[19] Alver, *Mellem mennesker og magter*; Alver, B. G., *Heksetro og trolddom* [Witch belief and sorcery] (Oslo, 1971); Willumsen, *Seventeenth-Century Witchcraft Trials*, 107; C. Larner, *Enemies of God*, 10.

[20] Levack, *The Witch-Hunt in Early Modern Europe*, 32–51.

European doctrine of demonology, a doctrine which got foothold throughout Europe from fifteenth until seventeenth century due to a rapid spread
of demonological works.[21] Demonological ideas entered into the laws and
into religious scriptures by early seventeenth century, and oral transfer of
such ideas to the populace had its origin in church preaching and local
sessions of witchcraft trials.

Bente Gullveig Alver argues that it is possible in the seventeenth
century to distinguish between an old and a new understanding of the
witchcraft. The old concept of witchcraft was based on the idea that some
persons have supranormal powers and have the ability to get in contact
with a supernatural world.[22] This view changed in the course of the fifteenth century. A new understanding of witchcraft appeared in Europe
just before the intense witchcraft persecution started. According to this
concept the witch was perceived only in a negative way, as a completely
evil and destructive person. This new concept of witchcraft was of great
importance for the development of the historical witchcraft trials.[23] Alver
sees strategies and counter-strategies during the witchcraft trials in
the light of common people's understanding of magic versus the elite's
understanding of the same. While the elite saw common people's magical
practice as evil and ungodly, common people saw the world as magical.
Persons with particular magical abilities and knowledge in the local communities were regarded as a medium between supernatural forces and
human beings.[24]

The practices of magic, sorcery and witchcraft have in common
attempts to manipulate mysterious and supernatural forces. There seems
to be a division line between white magic on one side and black magic on
the other, the last denoting evil intentions on the part of the practitioner.
Still, sometimes this line is blurred, as there exist grey zones where the
intention might be good for some people and bad for others. However, all
types of magic were exposed to legal persecution during the early modern
period, seen as ungodly and devilish practice, performances breaking the
law. During the period of witchcraft trials, white magic as well as *maleficium* and diabolism were activities forbidden by law in Scotland as well
as Denmark-Norway, and might lead to a criminal trial. The sentences
for practising white magic were usually milder than for practising black

---

[21] Willumsen, *Seventeenth-Century Witchcraft Trials*, 8–11; 68–78; 101–104; 246–248.
[22] Alver, *Heksetro og trolddom*, 19.
[23] Larner, *Enemies of God*, 7, 9.
[24] Alver, *Heksetro og trolddom*; Alver, *Mellem mennesker og magter*.

magic. However, in Denmark-Norway there was for a period death penalty for performance of white magic.[25] Certain differences appear for the entire period of witchcraft persecution with regard to how serious the various types were considered by the legal authorities. As has been seen, the word witchcraft, as it was used in early modern Europe, comprises a specter of meanings. When it comes to my use of the term in this book, I include all cases of witchcraft, sorcery and magic accusations brought before the court during the witchcraft trials. Thus the term witchcraft will be understood in a pragmatic way, which is also in accordance with Walter Rummel and Rita Voltmer's use.[26] Also Jørn Øyrehagen Sunde has a broad understanding of witchcraft, sorcery and magic treated within the early modern courts, including all types of metaphysical forces which can influence the destiny of human beings.[27] Hence the various ways of practising witchcraft are covered in this study, at the same time as all the cases constituting my corpus of sources have been captured.

The Impact of Demonology

A central notion in this study is the cumulative concept of witchcraft, also called the demonological witchcraft construct.[28] This construct implied that several persons together met with the Devil and performed witchcraft. Thus the accused person's confessions of witches' meetings and collective witchcraft operations led to denunciation of several new suspects,

---

[25] White magic was made a capital offence in the diocese of Stavanger in Norway in 1584. In 1593 this local criminal law was extended all over Norway. Ref. Næss, H. E., 'Norway: The Criminological Context', in B. Ankarloo and G. Henningsen (eds.), *Early Modern European Witchcraft. Centre and Peripheries* (Oxford, 1993), 368–369. See also Toivo, R. M., "Marking (dis)order: witchcraft and the symbolics of hierachy in late seventeenth- and early eighteenth-century Finland", in O. Davies and W. de Blécourt (eds.), *Beyond the witch trials. Witchcraft and magic in Enlightenment Europe* (Manchester, 2004), 9–25, at pp. 9–13.
[26] The authors include 'aller Verfolgungen von Schadenzauberei (ob mit oder ohne ausdrücklich genanntem Teufelspakt) sowie diabolisher Hexerei nach 1400'. Ref. Rummel and Voltmer, *Hexen und Hexenverfolgung*, 81.
[27] Sunde, J. Ø., *Speculum legale—rettsspegelen* [Speculum legale—the mirror of the law] (Bergen, 2005), 184.
[28] See Levack, *The Witch-Hunt in Early Modern Europe*, 29–49. In German called 'kumulatives Hexereidelikt' or 'Das dämonologische Hexereikonstrukt', see Rummel and Voltmer, *Hexen und Hexenverfolgung*, 4–5; Voltmer, R., 'Die Hexenverfolgungen in Raum des Erzbistums Trier (15.–17. Jahrhundert)—Strukturen und Deutungen', in B. Schneider (ed.), *Kirchenreform und Konfessionsstaat 1500–1800*, vol. 3 in M. Persch and B. Schneider, *Geschicte des Bistums Trier*, (Trier, 2010), 709–749, at p. 714; Schulte, *Hexenverfolgung in Schleswig-Holstein*, 14.

who were brought before the court in their turn. The confessions corresponded to a fear among legal and clerical officials of an ungodly, hidden
army of the Devil's accomplices existing on earth. The demonological concept of witchcraft is by several researchers seen as the core of the European witchcraft persecution, as it contains central features constituting
the contents and influencing the development of the most severe trials.[29]
Naming of accomplices resulted in panics, successive witchcraft trials during a concentrated period of time.[30] As witchcraft in many forms were
practised before, during and after the period of historical witchcraft trials,
persecution of witches must be seen in relation to factors which could
possibly be of importance for the initiation and continuation of witchcraft trials in the actual period of witch-hunts. Central for the start and
development of the European witchcraft trials are the ideas forming the
demonological doctrine. Therefore I will argue that the cumulative concept of witchcraft is an important element when it comes to explaining
the historical witchcraft trials, a view supported by several scholars.[31] As
for terminology, in this study demonological witchcraft is a term prefera-
bly used about the concept of witchcraft related to the doctrine of demonology, while the word demonic will be used in the constellation demonic
pact, interchangeable with Devil's pact. Diabolism is first and foremost
characterized by the accused person giving a Devil's pact confession.[32]

---

[29] Rummel and Voltmer, *Hexen und Hexenverfolgung*, 38–53, 94; Larner, *Enemies of God*,
134–203; Levack, B. P., *Witch-hunting in Scotland. Law, Politics and Religion* (New York, 2008),
81–113; Schulte, *Hexenverfolgung in Schleswig-Holstein*, 35–42; L. H. Willumsen, *Trollkvinne
i nord* [Witch in the North] (Tromsø, 1994), 23–45, 68–73; Willumsen, *Seventeenth-Century
Witchcraft Trials in Scotland and Northern Norway*, 8–11, 246–248; Schulte, *Hexenverfolgung
in Schleswig-Holstein*, 14, 19–24; Dillinger, J., *"Evil people". A comparative study of witch hunts
in Swabian Austria and the electorate of Trier* (Charlottesville/London, 2009), 3.
[30] Rummel and Voltmer, *Hexen und Hexenverfolgung*, 5; Willumsen, *Seventeenth-
Century Witchcraft Trials*, 8–10; Willumsen, L. H., *Trollkvinne i nord i historiske kilder og
skjønnlitteratur* [Witch in the North in historical sources and literature] (University of
Tromsø, Master's thesis, 1984), 28–44; Larner, *Enemies of God*, 107, 193; Levack, *The Witch-
Hunt in Early Modern Europe*, 161–62.
[31] Larner, *Enemies of God*, 17, 18, 24; Levack, *Witch-hunting in Scotland*, 7, 10, 77;
Willumsen, *Seventeenth-Century Witchcraft Trials*, 246–48; Rummel and Voltmer, *Hexen
und Hexenverfolgung*, 24; Schulte, R., *Hexenverfolgung in Schleswig-Holstein 16.–18. Jahrhundert* (Heide, 2001), 16–34.
[32] For 'diabolic magic', see Monter, 'Witch Trials in Continental Europe 1560–1660',
48; for 'diabolism' see Hagen, R. B., *Dei europeiske trolldomsprosessane* (Oslo, 2007), 10–11,
73–74; Larner, *Enemies of God*, 17, 18, 24, 26; Kieckhefer, R., *European Witch Trials. Their
Foundations in Popular and Learned Culture, 1300–1500* (London, 1976), 6, 13–26, 73–88;
Knutsen, G., *Servants of Satan and Masters of Demons. The Spanish Inquisition's Trials for
Superstition, Valencia and Barcelona, 1478–1700* (Turnhout, 2009), 1–3; Bever, *The Realities
of Witchcraft and Popular Magic*, 65.

However, all European witchcraft trials were not centred round demonology, neither did they occur in panics. Marko Nenonen, Raisa Maria Toivo,
Marie Lennersand and Linda Oja are among those who have emphasized
that a substantial number of witchcraft trials had to do with isolated trials
of non-demonological type.[33] Robin Briggs has suggested that the panics,
or linked trials, only touched the lives of a tiny fraction of Europeans.[34]
He argues that the witchcraft trials were patchy chronologically as well
as geographically and considers the witch-persecution in early modern
period as 'a relative failure, which only gained momentum in relatively
few exceptional instances'.[35] It is true that witchcraft persecution had a
very uneven pattern with regard to frequency and geographical distribution. Witchcraft trials in general had a stochastic or accidental character,
as will be seen for both areas in question in this study. Some years were
intense, other years were calm. Hence it is correct to say that witchcraft
trials chronologically varied a lot in each country. However, in my view
the severity of witchcraft trials also have to be taken into consideration,
understood as a percentage of the number of executed in relation to the
number of accused persons. This severity had to do with demonological
trials. Even if the panics in total lasted few years, the rate of execution
during panics years was very high. Therefore the panics must be reckoned
as much more severe than the periods in between, and it is still relevant to
see the panics and the influence of demonology as the strongest markers
of historical witchcraft trials. In addition to number of persons touched by
witchcraft trials, geographical variation matters, as Briggs and Nenonen
point to. There might be intense trial activity in one local community, and
no trials in the neighbouring community. However, the reason for this is
an unsolved question among witchcraft scholars, as it has not so far been
possible to state a distinct triggering factor for the outbreak of trials neither calming factors for the areas with no witchcraft trials.

White magic, *maleficium* and diabolism are all activities mentioned
in the legal documents underlying my study. These acts resulted in two
types of trials occurring during the witchcraft persecution in Scotland and

---

[33] Nenonen, 'Witch Hunts', 168–72, 182; Toivo, *Witchcraft and Gender*; M. Lennersand
and L. Oja, 'Vitnande visionärer. Guds och Djävulens redskap i Dalarnas häxprocesser',
177–184 in H. Sanders (ed.), *Mellom Gud og Djævelen. Religiøse og magiske verdenbilleder i
Norden 1500–1800* [Between God and the Devil. Religious and Magical Images of the world
in the Nordic Countries 1500–1800] (København, 2001).
[34] Briggs, R., *Witches and Neighbours: The Social and Cultural Context of European
Witchcraft* (Oxford, 2002), 343–411.
[35] Briggs, *Witches and Neighbours*, 346.

Northern Norway. On one hand there were isolated trials, where one person at a time was brought before the court accused of practising witchcraft. This type of trial was mostly based on the perception of sorcery and witchcraft as an evil act.[36] It should be mentioned, though, that also performance of beneficent magic was brought before the court during the period of witchcraft persecution.[37] On the other hand there were panics, based on demonology. Its aim was basically to identify the Devil's secret accomplices on earth and bring these to punishment. To this end teachings centred round the means to recognise witches and to learn what they could accomplish were important. All over Europe, a large number of books laying out the tenets of demonology were published at the same time as witchcraft trials took place.[38]

Studies in Magic and Witchcraft

Related to Scotland, the interest in studies of magic and witchcraft has been great the later years. An anthology edited by Julian Goodare, Laureen Martin and Joyce Miller contains a variety of articles on witchcraft and belief in early modern times.[39] This volume include studies of witch belief among the two ethnic groups the Highlanders and the Lowlanders, presentation of the appearance of the Devil in witchcraft discourse as well as demonic possessions, analyses of cunning-folk and charmers, as well as discussion of traditional patterns of belief in Scotland within a European context.[40] A book on fairy belief in Scotland, with most of the source material fetched from witchcraft records, is written by Lizanne Henderson and Edward B. Cowan.[41] Witchcraft in the Highlands has been dealt with

---

[36] See also Schulte, *Hexenverfolgung in Schleswig-Holstein*, 13.
[37] See Toivo, R. M., 'Marking (dis)order: witchcraft and the symbolics of hierachy in late seventeenth- and early eighteenth-century Finland', in Davies and Blécourt, *Beyond the witch trials*, 9–25, at pp. 9–13.
[38] Clark, S., *Thinking with Demons: the idea of witchcraft in early modern Europe* (Oxford, 1997); Clark, S., 'Witchcraft and Magic in Early Modern Culture', in Ankarloo, Clark and Monter, *Witchcraft and Magic in Europe*, 122–169; Schulte, *Hexenverfolgung in Schleswig-Holstein*, 16–34; Rummel and Voltmer, *Hexen und Hexenverfolgung*, 24–33; Willumsen, *Trollkvinne i nord*, 20–22; Willumsen, *Seventeenth-Century Witchcraft Trials in Scotland and Northern Norway*, 9, 205, 212.
[39] J. Goodare, L. Martin and J. Miller (eds.), *Witchcraft and Belief in Early Modern Scotland* (Basingstoke, 2008).
[40] Goodare, 'Scottish Witchcraft in its European Context', 26–50.
[41] Henderson, L. and Cowan, E. B., *Scottish Fairy Belief: A History* (East Linton, 2004).

by Ronald Hutton.[42] Shamanism related to a Scottish case has been studied by Emma Wilby.[43] Joyce Miller has made research on the topic of Scottish magic, folk medicine and folklore.[44] P. G. Maxwell-Stuart has among other books on Scottish witchcraft written about the magical aspects.[45] In total these studies show the variety of witchcraft beliefs and a wide scope of approaches among the researchers.

For Norway, witchcraft and magic is a field which primarily has been studied by Bente Gullveig Alver. In 1971 she published the book *Heksetro og trolddom* [Belief in witchcraft and sorcery] and in 2008 *Mellem mennesker og magter. Magi i hekseforfølgelsernes tid* [Between human beings and forces. Magic in the time of witchcraft persecution]. Ørnulf Hodne has in 2011 written about magic and beliefs in more general terms in the book *Mystikk og magi i norsk folketro* [The mystical and magical in Norwegian folk belief]. The same author has in 2012 written *Kjærlighetsmagi: folketro om erotikk, forelskelse og ekteskap* [Love magic: folk belief related to erotic, love and marriage]. Going back to the time before the witchcraft trials, Stephen A. Mitchell is the author of *Witchcraft and Magic in the Nordic Middle Ages* published in 2011.

Leaving Scotland and Norway, taking a glance at Europe in general, a number of studies and source editions about witchcraft beliefs in early modern times have been published during the last two decades. Mention should be made of a collection of articles edited by Jonathan Barry, Marianne Hester and Gareth Roberts, *Witchcraft in Early Modern Europe*.[46] The book contains articles on witchcraft beliefs in Austria, Germany, Switzerland, France, England and America. It has a clear inter-disciplinary approach, taking into account history, religion, Renaissance fiction, as well as the social environment. In a collection of essays edited by Bengt Ankarloo, Stuart Clark and William Monter, *Witchcraft and Magic in Europe*, Stuart Clark deals with the cultural aspects of witchcraft and magic in early

---

[42] Hutton, R., 'Witch-hunting in Celtic societies', *Past and Present*, 212 (2011), 43–71.
[43] Wilby, E., *The Visions of Isobel Gowdie: Magic, Witchcraft and Dark Shamanism in Seventeenth-Century Scotland* (Eastborne, 2010).
[44] Miller, J., *Cantrips and Carlins: Magic, Medicine and Sociey in the Presbyteries of Haddington and Stirling, 1600–1688* (University of Stirling, Ph.D. thesis, 1999); Miller, J., 'Devices and directions: folk healing aspects of witchcraft practice in seventeenth-century Scotland', in J. Goodare (ed.), *The Scottish witch-hunt in context* (Manchester, 2002) 90–95; Miller, J., *Magic and Witchcraft in Scotland* (Musselburgh, 2004).
[45] Maxwell-Stuart, P. G., *Satan's Conspiracy: Magic and Witchcraft in Sixteenth-Century Scotland* (East Linton, 2001).
[46] (Cambridge, 1996), reprinted 1998, 1999.

modern culture; popular magic, demonology and intellectual magic.[47] His essays comprise popular magic as cultural constructions as well as printed demonological literature. Another collection, *Beyond the Witch Trials. Witchcraft and Magic in Enlightenment Europe*, edited by Owen Davies and Willem de Blécourt, is focusing on the period after the witch hunts, when witchcraft was decriminalized.[48] This volume includes witchcraft research from Finland, Sweden, Italy, Spain, Holland and Germany.

A broad view with regard to source material and an interdisciplinary approach to understand the shades of early modern beliefs with regard to witchcraft, sorcery and magic characterizes this widespread recent research. For my purpose, however, it is necessary with a narrower range of source material to work with. Hence my sources, and thus the basis of my analyses, will be restricted to the court records in the two areas focused in my study, Scotland and Finnmark, Northern Norway.

Comparison

The object of this book is the historical witchcraft trials, and the comparative perspective will throw light on how these trials developed in two European areas throughout the seventeenth century. When these two areas are chosen, it has to do with certain similarities at first sight, mentioned by Marc Bloch in an article from 1928 as one of the main criteria for choice of objects in a comparative study.[49] The most important similarity, and one which will be paid close attention to throughout this study, is of ideological character; the occurrence of demonological notions in the confessions the accused persons' gave before the court. This feature is pointed out by Christina Larner in 'Crimen Exceptum' from 1980 and *Enemies of God* from the 1983.[50] For Finnmark, my study *Trollkvinne i nord*

---

[47] Clark, 'Witchcraft and Magic in Early Modern Culture', 97–169.

[48] (Manchester, 2004).

[49] Bloch, M., 'Towards a Comparative History of European Societies' in F. C. Lane and J. C. Riemersma (eds.), *Enterprise and Secular Change. Readings in Economic History*, (London, 1953), 494–521, at p. 496. Bloch's article is a written version of a lecture given at a History Conference in Oslo in 1928. The article, first published in French, has later been translated into German and English. For a German version, see Bloch, M., 'Für eine vergleichende Geschicte der europäischen Gesellschaften', in P. Schöttler (ed.), *Aus der Werkstatt des Historikers. Zur Theorie und Praxis der Geschichtswissenschaft* (Frankfurt, 2000), 122–167.

[50] Larner, 'Crimen Exceptum' in B. Lenman, G. Parker and V. A. C. Gatrell (eds.), *Crime and the law: the Social History of Crime in Western Europe since 1500* (London, 19780) and *Enemies of God*.

[Witch in the North] from 1984 was the first one to emphasize the strong influence of demonology during the witchcraft trials. It was also the first study pointing to the close resemblance between Scotland and Finnmark when it comes to the contents of accused persons' confessions.[51]

In this study, demonological notions will be seen as central for the initiation and development of historical witchcraft trials. Other similarities have to do with the severity of the witchcraft trials with regard to execution rate, the variation in frequency of trials during the period of persecution, the majority of trials held in local courts, the use of circumstantial evidence during the trials, the use of torture during the trials, a majority of women among the accused and executed, a population with two ethnic groups living side by side, and communities characterized by orality. In addition, both areas had a rural settlement consisting mainly of peasants and fishermen.

The object of research in this study will be court records and interpretation of these. The study is structured in the following way: The witchcraft trials will be analyzed by quantitative and qualitative methods. A set of component elements is the analytical framework for the comparison of the two areas. This framework is defined according to ten factors; the demonological element, the role of the state, the role of the local courts, the role of the church, ethnicity, neighbourhood disputes, the spoken word, folk belief, the superstitious north, and the personal factor, meaning the person or persons in position to influence the trials. These factors will constitute the analytical framework and will be activated during comparison. On one hand they have to do with similarities in the contents of the witchcraft trials. On the other hand the factors have to do with the context, the complex of features establishing a milieu surrounding the witchcraft trials, the phenomenon in focus.

My aim is not an analysis of the witchcraft trials in all their aspects. Instead I have chosen a simplified analytical reference around the main object, consisting of the mentioned set of factors. This analytical reference makes it possible to compare the two areas. A description of the analytical framework will make possible references to parallel conditions in the areas chosen. The analytical framework include major influential and inter-dependent factors pushing and supporting witch-hunt, namely the spread of demonological ideas, and pressure for the persecution of witches from the state, the courts, the church and the local community.

---

[51] Willumsen, *Trollkvinne i nord i historiske kilder og skjønnlitteratur*, 73.

Firstly, the demonological element is considered to be an important factor as for comparison. This factor plays a central role in the urge for persecution because of the impact such notions had on law, politics and religion. Demonological notions entered into official laws and religious scriptures, upon which preaching in the churches relied. Secondly, the role of the state is a major factor in the comparative framework. Both areas to be compared were located to the north of a strong central power at the time when witchcraft trials started, the kingdom of Scotland to the north of the kingdom of England and the district of Finnmark in the northern periphery of a united kingdom of Denmark-Norway. The areas had strong monarchs in power, who also were eager witch-hunters at the time of the most severe witch-hunts; James VI in Scotland and Christian IV in Denmark-Norway.[52] Thirdly, the local courts played a crucial role in the persecution of witches in both areas, as for the functioning of the judiciary, the legal apparatus, the laws, the administration of the court and the legal practice. The structure and functioning of the secular courts was to a large extent similar in the two areas in question.[53] In both countries, the legal apparatus consisted of central courts and local courts. The local courts were the main arenas for witchcraft trials, as the bulk were carried out there. Fourthly, the role of the church with regard to witchcraft trials is interesting to examine, as demonological notions by the seventeenth century had crept into religious literature, and influenced the preaching of the church and the image of the Devil portrayed in sermons. The church was in both areas a post-Reformation one, with a change between Presbyterianism and Episcopalianism in Scotland and Protestantism in Denmark-Norway. Fifthly, ethnic conditions in the two areas will be compared. Both areas had two ethnic groups with separate languages and separate cultures living side by side; in Scotland the Lowlanders and the Highlanders, in Finnmark the Norwegians and the Samis.[54]

---

[52] In 1603 King James VI of Scotland became also King James I of England. Norway and Denmark were in a personal union from the end of the fourteenth century until 1536, after that Norway was considered a province of the Danish kingdom. In 1660, absolutism was introduced in Denmark-Norway. This union lasted until 1814.

[53] For legal structure in Scotland see Goodare, J., 'Witch-hunting and the Scottish state', in J. Goodare (ed.), *The Scottish witch-hunt in context* (Manchester, 2002), 122–45; Levack, *Witch-hunting in Scotland*, 15–33. For legal structure in Finnmark see Næss, *Trolldomsprosessene i Norge på 1500–1600-tallet. En retts- og sosialhistorisk undersøkelse.*

[54] Willumsen, *Seventeenth-Century Witchcraft Trials*, 8; Granquist, K., 'Thou shalt have no other Gods before me (Exodus 20:3). Witchcraft and Superstition trials in 17th- and 18th century Swedish Lapland' in P. Skiöld and K. Kram (eds.), *Kulturkonfrontation i Lappmarken* (Umeå, 1998), 13–21.

This factor to a certain extent relates to practice of witchcraft. Sixthly, neighborhood disputes have frequently been connected to the first step of a witchcraft trial. Such disputes relates to the local community and the social sphere: the social position of women in the communities, women's quarrels and the growth of witchcraft reputations over time. Seventhly, the spoken word will be paid attention to during the comparison, as this is a factor essential for the transmission of ideas about witchcraft from the court and the church into the local communities, as well as dissemination of witchcraft notions among the populace. Society at this time was mainly oral, and demonological notions were fused with traditional oral narratives through a process of assimilation. What eased this process was use of the same form, structure and stylistic devices as narratives known from folklore. Narratives containing demonological concepts were transmitted rapidly from person to person, and became part of the mentality sphere. Eightly, folk belief is a field wherein witchcraft notions were flourishing. Popular beliefs in Scotland and Finnmark at the beginning of the seventeenth century are difficult to get hold of, even if a few written Scottish sources from late seventeenth century exist.[55] In fact, much of what we know about country folk's beliefs in the seventeenth century comes from witchcraft confessions in court records.[56] To what extent the confessions were influenced by folk belief is a question to be discussed and compared between the two areas. Ninthly, the superstitious north is a most interesting comparative factor. Most Europeans were convinced that particular conditions were connected to the north as a wild area on the margin of Europe. Moreover, the ethnic groups of Samis and Highlanders were believed to be exotic. Certain characteristics related to magic and folkloric motifs have been attributed to them, and this may have influenced the witch-hunters' approach to these groups. Tenthly, the personal factor has to be taken into consideration. I will argue that the personal factor is important for the introduction and spreading of demonological ideas. When such ideas first were introduced into a community, it is unlikely that they could exist for a long time on different 'levels' without merging

---

[55] See Hunter, M., *The Occult Laboratory: Magic, Science and the Second Sight in Late 17-th Century Scotland. The Secret Commonwealth and Other Texts* (Woodbridge, 2001).

[56] What has been written down from popular belief mostly derives from the nineteenth century, and was an activity related to the Romantic movement. In Germany, the Grimm brothers started to publish *Kinder- und Hausmärchen* in 1812. In Norway, P. C. Asbjørnsen and J. Moe collected traditional tales and published them first in small pamphlets, later in books in the 1840s. In Scotland, Walter Scott published *Minstrelsy of the Scottish Border* in two volumes in 1802.

with traditional folk beliefs. The above mentioned factors will define the structure of the study and make a systematic comparison possible. To examine various parallels as for political, judicial, clerical and social conditions, as well as mentalities, has the potential to give fruitful results.

The ten factors will form the structural backbone of the comparison to be performed. Together, this framework will permeate the quantitative as well as the qualitative analyses, and will be taken up again for discussion in the final chapter of the book. Some factors will be dealt with in greater detail than others, due to the nature of my primary sources and the alleged explanatory potential with regard to witchcraft trials. The analytical framework will indicate and clarify how quantitative and qualitative analyses of the primary witchcraft sources may offer new knowledge about the early modern witch-hunt. I will argue that the activity of witchcraft trials quickly progressed because of the interplay between legal, religious and ideological influences. An important feature of this picture is the introduction and transmission of demonological notions from the learned elite, as well as the reception of these ideas on the part of peasants. My assumption is that these factors as a complexity created particular fertile ground, well suited for the outbreak of severe witchcraft trials.

As the title of this book, *Witches of the North*, suggests, the study deals with northern areas of Europe, more accurate a geographical room divided by the North Sea, the Norwegian Sea, and the Barents Sea. Finnmark borders to the latter. The size of the two areas Scotland and Finnmark is about the same. In the seventeenth century the structure of settlement was to a large extent similar in the two areas.[57] I have concentrated on regions that easily can be described in necessary detail for a comparative study. The archipelagos Orkney and Shetland will be treated in a separate part of the book. The reason for this division is partly historical, as will be discussed in further detail later, and partly geographical, as the islands form an intermediate area in the North Sea between Scotland and Norway. At the time period covered by this study, these islands had many features in common with Norway. Even if these islands formally belonged to Scotland from the 1400s onwards, their geographical location and their historical tight ties to Norway make it interesting to examine them as

---

[57] For Scotland, see Rogers, C., *Social Life in Scotland. From Early to Recent Times*, 3 vols. (Edinburgh, 1886). For Finnmark, see Niemi, E., *Vadsøs historie* [The history of Vadsø], i (Vadsø, 1983); Balsvik, R. R., *Vardø. Grensepost og fiskevær 1850–1950* [Vardø. Border post and fishing village], (Vardø, 1989).

regions of their own with regard to witchcraft persecution.[58] When the district of Finnmark, and not the whole of Norway, has been chosen as a counterpart to Scotland in this study, this has to do with features in the Finnmark witchcraft trials that have parallels in the Scottish trials. These features make Finnmark differ from the rest of Norway. Particularly the marked impact of demonology is a feature which led to more severe persecution in Finnmark than in other parts of Norway.

Theoretical Works on Comparison

Historical comparison has been an active field of research throughout the twentieth century, partly inspired by Marc Bloch's article mentioned above. Bloch defines historical comparison in this way: the historian 'selects two or more phenomena which appear at first sight to be analogous and which occur in one or more social milieus. He finds out how these phenomena resemble or differ from one another, traces their evolution, and, as far as possible, explains the similarities and differences.'[59] The emphasis on the phenomenon in focus as well as the surrounding milieu is further elaborated: 'In order to have historical comparison, two conditions must be fulfilled: a certain similarity or analogy between observed phenomena— that is obvious—and a certain dissimilarity between the environments in which they occur'.[60] This definition of Bloch points to central criteria for my choice of areas to be compared. My comparison aims at understanding the development of witchcraft persecution in two areas. Included in this is also the discovery of the uniqueness of these different societies and the observation of differences. For the relation between regional studies and more general overviews, Bloch on one hand points out that preliminary local studies are necessary in order to make a comparison, 'Over-all comparison can only come afterward.'[61] On the other hand, 'monographs become important only because the comparative method can elicit from the chaotic multiplicity of circumstances those which were generally effective—the real causes'.[62] He underlines that any historian who cites

---

[58] Anderson, P. D., *Black Patie* (Edinburgh, 1992); Anderson, P. D., *Robert Stewart. Earl of Orkney, Lord of Shetland* (Edinburgh, 1982); Donaldson, G., 'The Scots Settlement in Shetland', in D. J. Withrington (ed.), *Shetland and the Outside World 1469–1969* (Oxford, 1983), 8–19.
[59] Bloch, 'Towards a Comparative History', 496.
[60] Bloch, 'Towards a Comparative History', 496.
[61] Bloch, 'Towards a Comparative History', 506.
[62] Bloch, 'Towards a Comparative History', 506.

purely local factors for explanations, will certainly make mistakes. Such 'local pseudo-causes' are insufficient for explanation, and since 'a general phenomenon must have equally general causes', comparison undermines the purely local explanations.[63] Thus the general conclusions would over-rule elements and structures of the compared areas. Interestingly, Bloch several times refers to the humanities, specifically comparative linguistics, as fields of research having taking comparison on board as a fruitful method.

As his first step, Bloch states the discovery of the phenomena to be focused.[64] He also stresses 'the need to use comparison to overcome the national particularism built into European historiography'.[65] It is possible by comparison to detect errors and inadequacies in hypothetical prerequisites, which would seem unimpeachable if viewed in one single historical and geographical setting. Bloch's second use of the comparative method is to discover the uniqueness of the different societies.[66] There has to be a certain variation in order to give an explanation. Placing a study in a comparative framework both singles out those phenomena which are genuine peculiarities of the locality, and which will have to be explained by local conditions, but also invalidates purely local explanations for what are in fact general phenomena. The third use is the possibility of formulating problems for historical research. Bloch points to the fact that sometimes the comparison in itself raises questions to be explained, using as example ways of dividing property in France and England in the Middle Ages, pointing to the problem how borders were drawn at the time. Here Bloch discovered analogy by using examples from the enclosure movement during the fifteenth to seventeenth centuries.[67] Because the two countries had similar patterns of agricultural organization, it was discovered that France had an enclosure movement. Only comparison established that there was something to be explained. Bloch drew attention to the fact that the comparative method could help to determine real causes, not only causes on the local level, and he saw in the comparative method a procedure for allowing the specificity of particular processes to emerge more clearly.

---

[63] Bloch, 'Towards a Comparative History', 505; Sewell, W. H., 'Marc Bloch and the Logic of Comparative History', *History and Theory*, vol. 6, no. 2 (1967), 208–218, at p. 210.

[64] Bloch, *Aus der Werkstatt*, 127.

[65] Grew, R., 'The Case for Comparing Histories', *The American Historical Review*, vol. 85, no. 4 (1980), 763–778, at p. 770.

[66] Sewell, 'Marc Bloch', 210.

[67] Bloch, 'Towards a Comparative History', 498–501.

The importance of a broad historical context when working with comparison has been underlined by for instance Theodor Schieder, Heinz-Gerhard Haupt and Jürgen Kocka, Chris Lorenz and Johannes Dillinger.[68] Theodor Schieder emphasizes the historical context and warns against static and mono-causal studies, as they are bound to their historical time and complex reality.[69] Haupt and Kocka underline that for historical comparison it is required that the context's dependency of culture should be taken seriously and that a connection to cultural and social history should be made.[70] Haupt and Kocka take as an outset Bloch's definition. However, they have broadened it.[71] Chris Lorenz has a profound discussion of historical comparison, which he, pointing to John Stuart Mill for its original logical structure, calls the 'third road' as explanatory model besides positivism and hermeneutics.[72] Lorenz deals with Mill's suggested terms the method of agreement and the method of difference.[73] In addition he takes up problems of competing causal explanations, continuity, and the relationship between persons and structures in historical explanation. He discusses the consequences of history and social sciences as increasingly more close disciplines, emphasizing the methodological challenges therein.[74] Contributions from Raymond Grew and William H. Sewell are also of great value in the debate of historical comparison. Grew maintains

---

[68] Schieder, T., 'Möglichkeiten und Grenzen vergleichender Methoden in der Geschichtswissenscahft', in *Geschicte als Wissenscahft* (München, 1968), 195–196, 217–219; Haupt, H.-G. and Kocka, J., 'Historischer Vergleich: Methoden, Aufgaben, Probleme. Eine Einleitung', in H.-G. Haupt and J. Kocka (eds.), *Geschicte und Vergleich. Ansätze und Ergebnisse international vergleichender Geschichtsschreibung* (Frankfurt, 1996), 37–39; Lorenz, C., *Konstruktion der Vergangenheit. Eine Einführung in die Geschictstheorie* (Köln, 1997) 231–321; Dillinger, J., *"Böse Leute". Hexenverfolgungen in Swäbish-Österreich und Kurtrier im Vergleich* in G. Franz and F. Irsigler (eds.), Trierer Hexenprozesse. Quellen und Darstellungen, vol. 5 (Trier, 1998); Also discussed more briefly in Dillinger, J. *"Evil people"* (Charlottesville, 2009), 8–12.

[69] Schieder, 'Möglichkeiten und Grenzen', 217.

[70] Haupt and Kocka, 'Historischer Vergleich', 19, 39.

[71] According to Werner Daum, Günter Riederer and Harm von Seggern. Ref. Daum, W., Riederer, G. and von Seggern, H., 'Fallobst oder Steinschlag: Einleitende Überlegungen zum historischen Vergleich', in H. Schnabel-Schüle (ed.), *Vergleichende Perspectiven. Perspectiven des Vergleichs*, (Mainz, 1998), 1–21, at 6.

[72] Lorentz, C., 'Kausale Erklärungen in der Geschictswissenschaft (3): Das vergleichende Erklärungsmodell', in *Konstruktion der Vergangenheit. Eine Einführung in die Geschictstheorie* (Köln, 1997), 231–284. Orig. *De constructie van het verleden. Ein inleiding in de theorie van de geschiedenis* (Amsterdam, 1987), new editions 1990, 1994.

[73] 'Die Methode der Überstimmung und die Methode der Unterschieds'. Ref. Lorentz, *Konstruktion*, 268.

[74] Also Knut Kjeldstadli points to John Stuart Mill when discussing comparison. Ref. Kjeldstadli, K., *Fortida er ikke hva den engang var* [The past is not was it once used to be] (Oslo, 1999), 264, 266.

that comparison can help historians at four stages of their work; in asking
questions, in identifying historical problems, in designing the appropriate
research and in reaching and testing significant conclusions.[75] He underlines that the validity of any comparison rests on the careful definitions
against which the elements compared must be systematically tested.[76]
Sewell argues for a comparative perspective, 'that is, viewing historical
problems in a context broader than their particular social, geographical
and temporal setting'.[77] He points to the fact that most historians, when
they use the term comparative history, mean 'comparative history as subject matter: that is, studies which make systematic comparisons between
two or more societies and present their results in a comparative format.
Of course nearly all such studies use comparative method and perspective, but it is important not to restrict the term to so confined a use.'[78] This
viewpoint is interesting related to the more recent field of research *histoire croisée*, with contributions from among others Michael Werner and
Bénedicte Zimmermann.[79] This direction focuses on 'empirical intercross-
ings consubstantial with the object of study, as well as on the operations
by which researchers themselves cross scales, categories and viewpoints'.[80]
Bringing new importance to the question of reflexivity, emphasis is placed
on what, in a self-reflexive process, can be generative of meaning. Discussions are carried out over comparative approaches such as transfers
and socio-cultural interactions, for instance the process of historicization,
defined as 'articulating the essential aspect of reflexivity and the multiple
time frames that enter into the construction of an object to the extent
that it is envisaged as a production situated in time and space'.[81] Also
mentioned are the categories of analysis and the relationship between
researcher and object. This urge to articulate various dimensions and set
them in motion, instead of an analytical model, contributes to avoid a
static view. It is a challenging way of analysis, and very much influenced
by French continental thinking, in contrast to the 'harder' American

---

[75] Grew R., 'The Case for Comparing Histories', *The American Historical Review*, 85,
nr. 4 (1980), 769.
[76] Grew 'The Case for Comparing Histories', 765.
[77] Sewell W. H., 'Marc Bloch and the Logic of Comparative History', *History and Theory*,
6, nr. 2 (1967), 218.
[78] Sewell 'Marc Bloch and the Logic of Comparative History', 218.
[79] Werner, M. and Zimmermann, B., 'Beyond comparison: *Histoire croisée* and the challenge of reflexivity', *History and Theory* 45 (2006), 30–50.
[80] Werner and Zimmermann, 'Beyond comparison', 30.
[81] Werner and Zimmermann, 'Beyond comparison', 45.

empiricism. It provides rethinking about the relationship between observation, object of study and analytical instruments used in a comparison,
and might, even if not used to its full extent, give inspiration to any historical comparison carried out.

Several theoretical contributions on historical comparison go in
favour of developing typologies, for instance Charles Tilly, Anton van
der Braembussche and Thomas Welskopp.[82] Tilly attempts to arrive at
a satisfactory typology that allows for the diversity of historical practice.
He points to four principal types of comparison; the individualizing, the
generalizing, the inclusive and the universalizing. They are all ideal types,
abstracted from historical practice. Only a combination of two or more
types might account for parallels and differences.[83] According to van der
Braembussche, the inclusive type of comparative history enjoys a special status. In this type, the cases examined are located at varying points
within the same system.[84] A typology of comparative history can offer
a relevant framework within which the question of the relative advan-
tages and disadvantages of the different types can be formulated and discussed.[85] Welskopp has suggested that the only claim to a comparative
study is two equally weighted social contexts, reconstructed according to
the research questions posed and communicating with each other over
a common reference point.[86] He claims that history becomes analytical
when typological criteria and typical patterns are constructed and that
these are the basis of a true comparison.[87] Welskopp underlines that the

---

[82] Tilly, C., *Big structures. Large processes. Huge comparisons* (New York, 1984), 118–19,
144–47; Welskopp, T., 'Stolpersteine auf dem Königsweg: methodenkritische Anmerkungen
zum internationalen Vergleich in der Gesellschaftsgeschichte', *Archiv für Sozialgeschichte*,
35 (1995), 339–367, at 346, 351.

[83] Tilly, C., 'Big Structure, Large Processes, Huge Comparisons', Ann Arbor, University of Michigan, CRSO Working Paper 195 (1983). In his book with the same title, published 1984, Tilly uses the terms individualizing comparisons, universalizing comparisons,
variation-finding comparisons, and encompassing comparisons. Ref. Tilly, *Big structures*
(1984), 145.

[84] Braembussche, A. von der, 'Historical explanation and comparative method: towards
a theory of the history of society', *History and theory* (1989), 1–24, at p. 14.

[85] Braembussche, 'Historical explanation', 15.

[86] Orig., 'dass das einzige methodologische Spezificum komparativer Gesellschaftsgeschichte ihre Konstruktion als erklärende Interpretation eines historischen Phänomens in
mindestens zwei über ein *tertium comparationis* miteinander kommunizierenden sozialen
Kontexten ist, die möglichst gleichgewichtig auf die jeweilige Fragestellung hin zu rekon-
struiren sind'. Welskopp, 'Stolpersteine', 345.

[87] Welskopp, 'Stolpersteine', 366; Welskopp, T., 'Vergleichende geschicte', in Europäische
Geschicte Online (EGO), Mainz European History Online, published by the Institute of
European History (IEG), Mainz 2010-12-03.

causal principle which is characterized by narrative structures, is typical for analytic history writing.[88] Michel Espagne claims that historical comparison should at least be complemented with research into cultural transfers and the reciprocal effects studied.[89]

The discussion on historical comparison has also included the borders between regional history and historical comparison, with several contributions related to witchcraft research. Eva Labouvie has discussed some of the questions arising here, pointing to the possibilities when it comes to bringing together analyses of sources from different regions within a framework of more general and critical methodology.[90] Labouvie is pointing to an international and interdisciplinary openness as a fruitful way to follow when it comes to research questions, perspectives and themes, as well as the positive effects of the closeness between history and social sciences, particularly anthropology and ethnology. Wolfgang Behringer says, using the expression 'comparative regional studies', that when different regional studies are compared, particular results from these studies may be integrated in the ongoing research and contribute to modification.[91] Gerd Schwerhoff maintains, based on a study of witchcraft, gender and regional history, that it is necessary to see isolated regional witchcraft studies in a systematic way within general explanatory patterns.[92] Thus regional studies increasingly tend to be framed by researchers in the light of ongoing international research, which in fact implies comparison.

Even if these theoretical viewpoints differ when it comes to models for historical comparison, it is basically seen by historians as a possible fruitful approach that could be pursued. A question is raised whether a comparison should contain two or three areas or fields. While Bloch's definition implies two areas, for the sake of creating a typology it has been suggested

[88] Welskopp, 'Stolpersteine', 351.

[89] Dillinger, *"Evil people"*, 8.

[90] Labouvie, E., 'Hexenforschung als Regionalgeschichte. Probleme, Grenzen und neue Perspektiven', in G. Wilbertz, G. Schwerhoff, and J. Scheffler (eds.), *Hexenverfolgung und Regionalgeschichte. Der Grafschaft Lippe im Vergleich*, Studien zur Regionalgeschichte, vol. 4 (Bielefield, 1994), 45–60.

[91] Orig. 'Vergleichende Regionalstudien'. Behringer, W., 'Zur Geschichte der Hexenforschung', in S. Lorenz (ed.), *Hexen und Hexenverfolgung in deutschen Südwesten*, Aufsatzband, Volkskundliche Veröffentlichungen des Badischen Landesmuseums Karlsruhe, b. 2 (Ostfildern, 1994), 93–146. Also mentioned in Dillinger, *"Böse Leute"*, 19–20.

[92] Schwerhoff, G., 'Hexerei, Geschlect und Regionalgeschicte', in Wilbertz, Schwerhoff, and Scheffler (eds.), *Hexenverfolgung und Regionalgeschichte. Der Grafschaft Lippe im Vergleich*, 325–353, at p. 329.

at least three fields.[93] Alan Macfarlane has argued for three points in a comparison, saying that the positing of for instance two geographical areas does not represent a comparison, instead it is merely a pinpointing of a subject and it's opposite. Therefore we ought to have a third point of reference to make a true comparison.[94] However, I do not think this is necessary. In my case, I have chosen two areas for comparison—two categories with sufficient degree of difference and which are not overlapping. Hence they are regarded as areas suitable for comparison. I have chosen to follow Bloch's model, claiming that in-depth studies of these two areas will provide sufficient fundament for comparison.[95] My comparison will then be close to what Sewell calls 'comparative perspective', as mentioned above. My areas for comparison are geographical neighbours and contemporaries, which again make the comparison easier, as many similarities are given from the beginning due to closeness in space and time. I will pay attention to Grew's criteria, which I believe could function in a positive way, 'obviously comparison is most enlightening when the choice of what to compare is made in terms of general and significant problems, the elements compared are clearly distinguished, and attention is paid to the intricate relationship between the elements compared and the particular societies in which they are located'.[96] This structure is similar to a clear-cut and good model for comparative studies presented by Georg Z. Bereday, consisting of the four main elements: description, interpretation, juxtaposition and comparison.[97] For the outline of my study, I will lean on these points as well.

In this book my aim is explanation of particular events, namely witchcraft cases, as the first step, then afterwards an attempt to explain the witch-hunt as a general phenomenon. The witchcraft trials as an object of research are suitable for such a method, as the sources are well preserved and accessible with regard to various detailed methodological approaches. In addition, a contextual analytical framework, similarly found in the two areas to be compared, is possible to define. Such a positive assumption with regard to the fruitfulness of a comparison on witchcraft trials is supported

---

[93] See Haupt and Kocka, 'Historischer Vergleich', 17.

[94] Macfarlane, A., 'To Contrast and Compare', *Social Dynamics and Complexity. Working Papers Series*, Institute for Mathematical Behavioral Sciences, University of California (Irvine, 2006).

[95] Sewell, 'Marc Bloch', 214.

[96] Grew 'The Case for Comparing Histories', 773.

[97] Bereday, G. Z. F., *Comparative Method in Education* (New York, 1964), 28.

by other researchers.[98] Gunnar W. Knutsen argues that the similarities in
witchcraft trials are quite striking, because they have in common the content of the accusations as well as the historical uniqueness of diabolical
witchcraft. In addition there are similarities with regard to the time frame,
to laws, literature and 'to purpose and self-understanding as Christians
saw themselves fight off Satan's onslaught'.[99] I am well aware of the fact,
pointed out among others by Grew, that some common institutions, like
church or party or bank, may perform quite different functions in different societies or at different times.[100] This will be born in mind during my
study. Still, my analyses of witchcraft trials in Scotland and Finnmark are
not simply case-studies of a European phenomenon, but display general
similarities within a number of fields. Thus the fruitfulness of a comparative study will come to the fore in the possibility of seeing patterns and
establishing focal points when it comes to investigating witchcraft trials
on a more general basis. It is possible to draw general conclusions. The
results of my study may be generalized beyond Scotland and Finnmark, as
the comparisons will pose questions and topics relevant for further international witchcraft research. I suppose that new attention to the details of
individual cases and to local studies can contribute to ongoing witchcraft
research. Therefore my study is rooted in the sources and the concern
for detailed accuracy. I agree with Grew in his statement, 'The search for
patterns implies comparison by seeking regularities in the behaviour and
issues common to a certain set—a kind of group, institution, or form of
social organization—or common to a certain process.'[101] Through parallel descriptions and common features of the two areas and the connections between these related to synthesis and causal explanatory patterns,
formulations toward generalisations will be attempted. The main question is, what kind of constellations of common features and differences
in the various aspects of the investigated phenomenon will be possible
to answer.[102] An openness towards the importance of paying attention
to results on micro- as well as macro-level will be fundamental. As Grew
puts it: 'To call for comparison is to call for a kind of attitude—open,
questioning, searching—and to suggest some practices that may nourish
it, to ask historians to think in terms of problems and dare to define those

---

[98] Dillinger, *"Böse Leute"*, 23; Knutsen, *Servants of Satan*, 2–3.
[99] Knutsen, *Servants of Satan*, 3.
[100] Grew 'The Case for Comparing Histories', 765.
[101] Grew 'The Case for Comparing Histories', 777.
[102] See Welskopp, 'Stolpersteine', 362.

problems independently, and to assert that even the narrowest research should be conceived in terms of the larger quests of many scholars in many fields'.[103]

Comparative Witchcraft Studies

Comparative studies within witchcraft research have not been frequent so far. Johannes Dillinger, Louise N. Kallestrup, Gunnar W. Knutsen and myself are the authors of four comparative Ph.D. theses on witchcraft from different areas of Europe. Johannes Dillinger's research is related to Swabian Austria and the Electorate of Trier in Germany, an in-debt study of witchcraft cases against two male accused at the end of the sixteenth century. It claims to be a holistic comparison, 'a comparison that takes account of the phenomena in the entirety of their respective elements, aspects, and changes over the course of time'.[104] Kallestrup's study is a comparison between 50 persons tried for witchcraft before the Roman inquisitor in Ortobello in Italy and 50 persons tried for witchcraft at Viborg District Court, North Jylland in Denmark in the seventeenth century.[105] Both men and women are represented in the Italian sources, in the Danish sources only women. The study shows clear differences between the two countries, one Catholic and one Protestant, as for legal procedure, contents of confessions and execution rate. Knutsen's study is a comparison of trials for superstition before the Spanish Inquisition's tribunal in Valencia and Barcelona during the period 1478–1700. The cases display differences between accusations of witchcraft and accusations of sorcery. In the Barcelona tribunal, 287 cases are studied, of them 52 for witchcraft. In the Valencia tribunal, 356 cases are studied, of them 10 for witchcraft. Both women and men were involved in the trials in both areas.[106] There were clear differences between the outcomes of the trials in the two areas, among other with regard to acquittals. In my doctoral thesis, the comparison between Scotland and Finnmark focuses on how witchcraft trials, with particular attention paid to the influence of demonology, developed with similarities and differences. For Scotland, more than 3000 cases are included in the study, for Finnmark, 135 cases are studied. Both women

---

103   Grew 'The Case for Comparing Histories', 776.
104   Dillinger, "Evil people", 11.
105   Kallestrup, I pagt med Djævelen, 227–230.
106   Knutsen, Servants of Satan, 66, 70.

and men were tried for witchcraft in both areas.[107] Of these four Ph.D. theses mentioned, only two have their sources from areas with different languages, namely Kallestrup's and my own. All the four studies are ground-breaking in the sense that they display careful close-readings of primary sources. Even if in some of these areas witchcraft studies have been performed earlier, the four above mentioned theses no doubt, by using a comparative approach, are opening up new venues for research.[108]

Methodology

I see comparison as a perspective where, when it comes to the factual analyses, other methodological approaches must be implied.[109] In my view, it is the research position I undertake, in terms of choice of method towards the phenomena to be investigated, which will decide the various strategies for comparison. An important research question is to examine how the demonological ideas gained influence in the two geographical areas in question and what impact this had on witchcraft trials. For this aim I need a methodology, which in my case is a combination of quantitative and qualitative methods, namely statistical research in addition to close-readings of court records from a narratological angle.

Both Scotland and Finnmark have good surveys of primary sources, and archival conditions which allow access to primary sources. The amount of primary source material for the two areas Scotland and Finnmark is manageable. For Scotland, an on-line documentation project, the Survey of Scottish Witchcraft (SSW), led by Julian Goodare, updates references to source material for all known Scottish witchcraft trials, and is invaluable

---

[107] Willumsen, *Seventeenth-Century Witchcraft Trials*, 39, 94.

[108] For earlier studies from the Spanish area, see Henningsen, G., *The Witches' Advocate. Basque Witchcraft and the Spanish Inquisition* (Nevada, 1980). For the Trierer area, see Voltmer, 'Hexenverfolgungen im Maas-Rhein-Mosel-Raum'. For the Danish area, see Johansen, Jens Chr. V., *Da Djævelen var ude... Trolddom i det 17. århundredes Danmark* (Viborg, 1991) and Birkelund, M., *Troldkvinden og hendes anklagere* (Århus, 1983). For the Scottish area, see Larner, *Enemies of God*; Levack, *Witch-hunting in Scotland*; Goodare, *The Scottish Witch-hunt in context*.

[109] Several historians have commented upon this. Dillinger argues that while 'a historical method is a specific way to approach and evaluate a particular kind of data (...) historical comparisons deal with and correlate multiple phenomena. The comparative method never specifies the nature of its objects, the questions posed, or the way in which we might try to answer these questions.' Ref. Dillinger, *"Evil People"*, 8.

for Scottish witchcraft research.[110] References to all known original sources are given in SSW. For Scotland, complete court records of witchcraft trials are only partly preserved. Transcribed court records of witchcraft trials have been published in collections of criminal trials as well as in volumes of various historical texts published by historical societies.[111] For Finnmark, very good court records from the period of witchcraft persecution are preserved.[112] Several source editions have been published. Court records for the period 1620–33 were published in 1987.[113] Recently the Finnmark witchcraft sources for the period 1620–1692 have been edited by myself and published in an English volume, *The Witchcraft Trials of Finnmark, Northern Norway*.[114] This text-critical edition is also published in Norwegian.[115]

For statistical analyses, all known trial records from both areas are used in this study. For qualitative analyses, I have chosen a sample of court records. The sample reflects the diversity of trials from early and late period of witchcraft persecution, male and female accused persons, and linked witchcraft trials as well as single trials. Bloch once said that 'human capacity being what it is, primary studies must not be of too great geographical or chronological scope'.[116] This statement has been born in mind and helped to limit the number of sources qualitatively examined, as close-readings require accuracy and is time demanding.

Statistical Methods

My chapters based on statistical research refer to findings in my doctoral thesis on Scottish and Finnmark witchcraft trials.[117] I have chosen in this book to minimize the amount of figures and tables and rather refer to the results in a running text. Thus, for more detailed tabulation and statistical

---

[110] www.arts.ed.co.uk/witches, SSW project by Julian Goodare, Lauren Martin, Joyce Miller and Louise Yeoman, (archived January 2003, accessed February 2007).

[111] For instance R. Pitcairn's three volumes of *Criminal Trials* in Scotland 1488–1624 (Edinburgh, 1831–33).

[112] Court records from local courts are kept in the Regional State Archives of Tromsø, and court records from the Court of Appeal for the district of Finnmark are kept in the Regional State Archives of Trondheim.

[113] H. Sandvik and H. Winge (eds.), *Tingbok for Finnmark 1620–33* (Oslo, 1987).

[114] The translation is by Katjana Edwardsen.

[115] Willumsen, L. H., *Trolldomsprosessene i Finnmark. Et kildeskrift* (Bergen, 2010).

[116] Bloch, 'Towards a Comparative History', 518.

[117] Willumsen, *Seventeenth-Century Witchcraft Trials in Scotland and Northern Norway*.

analysis, the reader should consult my thesis, where particularly the documentation of a great number of statistical analyses is found. For the Scottish sources, SSW has been used to provide information about the trials and references to the trials. The database is very detailed, and my thesis describes the procedures used for statistical studies. For the source material from Finnmark, the quantitative analyses are based on my own transcriptions and data registration of the Finnmark seventeenth-century court records.

The data being the background of this book is well suited for standard social science statistical methods as most of the variables and concepts used can be analyzed as categorical variables. I have used some robust statistical methods, variants of correlation analysis. Particularly, the Chi-square test is often used to test if frequency of observations strongly deviates from what could be expected. Thus, the null-hypothesis is normally used to test that no correlations or influences of the variable under study exist. To illustrate with an example: women are far more frequently accused of witchcraft than men. There is a gender bias. No need to test that. However, in a few years there are far more trials than in remaining years. One research question is then: Is the gender bias different in years with many witchcraft trials compared to years with few witchcraft trials? The null-hypothesis could be that the gender bias is the same. I find relatively more women accused in years with many trials compared with years with few trials. By statistical methods (primarily the Chi-square test), we can also conclude whether this is a significant difference, or if it can be attributed to random effects. When interpreting the results of the many statistical tests, I have generally been cautious of interpreting statistically significant findings as a proof of cause-effect relationships. For me it is important to make a clear distinction between causality on one hand, and correlation on the other. If there is causality between two variables, there must be significant correlation, but not the other way around. Correlation between two or more variables may very well exist without any causation. From a scientific point of view, establishing, or refuting, causation is normally the most interesting finding. In some cases, which I will return to, we may, based on earlier studies and logical deductions, present a hypothesis that there is a cause-effect relationship. One example is the use of torture to extract confessions. The line of reasoning may be the following: use of torture may lead to confession, and the case normally ends in execution. If torture is correlated with execution rate, we may be inclined to interpret this as a proof of cause-and-effect. In other cases we may resort to the time-line argument. Events happening in sequence cannot have a cause-effect relationship in reverse sequence, even if correlation is found. However, in many tests a statistical significant correlation may only be established. In those cases, my study may be interpreted as explorative. That means something interesting has been observed. This is not due to random effects, but is a real pattern. The findings I have thus documented may open up for more inquiries, research and formulation of new theories. These new theories may eventually be tested, and the tests may confirm, or refute, my findings later on in the research process.

Narratological Approach

To perform the qualitative analyses, a narratological approach to close-reading of text has been used, which pays careful attention to the language and the way of telling. My methodology is based on Gérard Genette's influential study *Discours du récit* from 1972.[118] Genette's two following works, *Narrative Discourse Revisited* and *Fiction and Diction*, expands his original narratology and incorporates a discussuion of the boundaries between fictional and factual narratives.[119] Genette has been particularly known for his methodological handling of the voices of the different persons in a narrative.[120] He is frequently referred to in narratological studies, and his methodological approach has been applied in witchcraft research for studying stylistic and rhetorical textual mechanisms.[121] Narratology is defined as the study of structures in narrative texts—an exploration of the narrator's function.[122] Genette uses for non-fictional texts the terms diction and factual narratives, stating that 'it is unlikely to exempt us from having to undertake a specific study of factual narrative (...) Such a study would require a large-scale inquiry into discursive practices such as those

---

[118] Genette's main work, a study developing a narratological methodology through the analysis of a fictional work, Marcel Proust's *A la recherché du temps perdu*, 7 volumes published during the years 1913–1927, is published in English with the title *Narrative Discourse. An Essay in Method* (Ithaca, 1980).

[119] The original titles are *Nouveaux Discours du Recit* (Paris, 1983) and *Fiction et diction* (Paris, 1991). The English editions were published in Ithaca, 1988 and Ithaca, 1993.

[120] Onega, S. and Landa, J. Á. G., Introduction to Gérard Genette: 'Voice', in S. Onega and J. Á. G. Landa (eds.), *Narratology* (London, 1996), 172–173; Ferraiuolo, A., 'Pro exoneratione sua propria coscientia: magic, witchcraft and church in early eighteenth-century Capua', in Davies and de Blécourt, *Beyond the witch trials*, 26–44.

[121] See for instance D. Herman (ed.), *Narratologies. New Perspectives on Narrative Analysis* (Ohio, 1999), 390.

[122] The narrator is seen as an absolutely necessary textual device. Cf. Genette, *Narrative Discourse Revisited*, 101.

of *history*, biography, personal diaries, newspaper accounts, police reports, *judicial narratives' [My italics].*[123] When it comes to interpretation of factual narratives, the importance of an interpretation related to the historical context of the document is underlined. This point is of uttermost importance when analyzing historical documents as texts, as the historical background has to be paid serious attention to. While a close-reading of the historical document might give access to shades of meaning that would otherwise have been overlooked, it is imperative that this analysis has to be placed in a historical context for further interpretation. When analyzing historical source material, the principle of text autonomy—making the text in itself the sole object of the analysis—is not alone satisfactory. In addition, it is necessary to consider the historical context in order to understand the meaning of the text. Hence the historical context as well as extra-textual features will add important information to a text-immanent analysis and is of absolute necessity for an interpretation of a historical phenomenon.

In order to interpret court records from the seventeenth century, it is important to remember that the life conditions for people at that time were different from today. Therefore they have looked upon the existence in ways uncustomary several centuries later.[124] This might have been influential in witchcraft cases more than in other criminal cases because common people's wievs on witchcraft deviated from that of the governmental officials. Still, there is reason to consider the persons accused of witchcraft, who were mostly peasants, as average representatives of the local communities in which they lived, and interpret their voices in the courtroom as a possible way of gaining insight in the contemporary mentality.[125]

When working with original documents, the historian meets texts and has to interpret texts. In my view, the variety and richness of the sources will be taken care of in a fruitful way by close-readings inspired by narratology. The researcher wishes to examine not only *what* a text means, but *how* it means.[126] It should be emphasized that an analysis based on narrative structures does not deal only with the formal structures of a text; semantics is implied as well. The manner in which a text is expressed is

---

[123] Genette, *Fiction and Diction*, 55–56.
[124] Sogner, S., 'Rettsprotokollene som kilde til mentalitet og kultur i europeisk historieforskning', in L. Mathinsen (ed.), *Tingboka som kilde* [Court proceedings as sources] (Oslo, 1990), 7–18, at p. 12.
[125] Sandmo, E., *Tingets tenkemåter* (Oslo, 1992), 21.
[126] Fludernik, M., *The fictions of languages and the languages of fiction: the linguistic representation of speech and consciousness* (London, 1993), 13.

of the greatest importance with regard to the contents conveyed.[127] The
extra insight which a narratological approach gives, is the understanding
of how specific qualities characterize the rendered courtroom discourse.
Singling out and getting close to the specific voices give a possibility of
broadening the understanding of the verbal interaction taking place.
Such an approach is to a certain extent similar to the one taken by Laura
Gowing in her study of narratives of slander litigation in Early Modern
London.[128] Also Garthine Walker's study of narratives of violence in Early
Modern Chesire focuses on narrative conventions used by women in
the legal courtroom.[129] However, while Gowing and Walker concentrate
on narrative skills characterizing the discourse of a group of women, a
narratological approach methodologically gets closer in touch with the
separate voices in rendered court records, whether it is the voice of the
accused, the witnesses, the scribe, or the law. In that respect, a narratological approach may get closer to the spectre of meanings entangled in a
complex discourse situation, due to the attempt to uncover personalized
narrative strategies. Another close-reading of a historical witchcraft narrative is performed by Emma Wilby. She tries to reconstruct in great detail
the interrogation and confession of a single witchcraft trial, as well as
analyzing shamanistic and demonological elements.[130] The study draws
on a wide range of knowledge from different subject fields, rather than
regarding the discourse interaction in itself as the aim. Wilby's analytical
arguments are not restricted to contemporary historical conditions, as she
encounters timeless and global elements for interpretation.

The narrative aspect of court records has attracted attention among
historians. This might be seen for instance in Alison Rowland's study
of German witchcraft trials 1561–1652,[131] Raisa Maria Toivo's studies

[127] Willumsen, L. H., "Narratologi som tekstanalytisk metode" [Narratology as text-analytical tool], in M. Brekke (ed.), Å begripe teksten [To understand the text] (Kristiansand,
2006), 69.
[128] Gowing, L., Domestic Dangers. Women, Words and Sex in Early Modern London
(Oxford, 1996), 232–276; Gowing, L., "Language, power and the law: women's slander litigation in early modern London", in J. Kermode and C. Walker (eds.), Women, crime and
the courts in early modern England (London, 1994), 26–47.
[129] Walker, G., "Crime, Gender and Social Order in early Modern Chesire", Ph.D. Diss.,
(University of Liverpool, 1994), 46–74; Walker, G., "Women, theft and the world of stolen
goods", in J. Kermode and G. Walker (eds.), Women, crime and the courts in early modern
England (London, 1994), 95–97.
[130] Wilby, E., The Visions of Isobel Gowdie. Magic, Witchcraft and Dark Shamanism in
Seventeenth-Century Scotland (Eastbourne, 2010).
[131] Rowlands, A., Witchcraft narratives in Germany: Rothenburg, 1561–1652 (Manchester,
2003).

of Finnish witchcraft trials,[132] Per-Anders Östling's studies of Swedish Blåkulla witchcraft trials,[133] Malcolm Gaskill's studies of testimonies in England and New England,[134] and Natalie Zemon Davis's study of pardon tales in sixteenth-century France.[135] They all emphasize the importance of a cultural and contextual interpretation. Davis also keeps her eye open for a more structural approach: 'But I will also be conceiving of "structures" existing prior to that event in the minds of the sixteenth-century participants: possible story lines determined by the constraints of the law and approaches to narrative learned in past listening to and telling of stories derived from other cultural constructions'.[136] This is an important point with regard to dissemination of demonological ideas within the oral sphere of the community, as the narratives about the Devil have features that might easily attach to tales in oral tradition. I consider it important to take the archival text as well as the wider cultural context into consideration. Throughout my study, all performed qualitative analyses of primary sources will be placed within a relevant historical context for comparison.

The awakening interest among literary scholars for reading witchcraft documents from a linguistic perspective has resulted in several studies during the 1990s and 2000s, among them studies by Marion Gibson and Diane Purkiss.[137] Purkiss' study comprises historical documents and literature. She draws attention to textuality and the way in which things are said—questions related to narration and genre.[138] Gibson works with English witchcraft pamphlets, and emphasizes that since they are only representations of events, 'they need to be studied structurally, with traditional literary inquiries into their construction, as well as considered in

---

[132] Toivo, *Witchcraft and Gender in Early Modern Society*; Toivo, R. M., 'Marking (dis)order'; Toivo, 'Discerning voices and values in the Finnish witch trial records', *Studia Neophilologica*, 1 (2012).

[133] Östling, P.-A., 'Blåkulla Journeys in Swedish Folklore', in A. B. Amundsen (ed.), *Arv. Nordic yearbook of Folklore*, vol. 62 (2006), 81–122.

[134] Gaskill, M., 'Witches and Witnesses in Old and New England', in Clark, *Languages of Witchcraft*, 55; Gaskill, M., 'Reporting murder: fiction in the archives in early modern England', *Social History*, vol. 23, no. 1 (1998), 1–29.

[135] Davis, N. Z., *Fiction in the Archives. Pardon Tales and their Tellers in Sixteenth Century France* (Cambridge, 1987).

[136] Davis, *Fiction in the Archives*, 4.

[137] Purkiss, D., *The Witch in History* (London, 1997); Gibson, M., *Early Modern Witches* (London, 2000), *Reading witchcraft* (London, 1999), *Witchcraft and society in England and America, 1550–1750* (New York, 2003), *Women and witchcraft in popular literature, c. 1615–1715* (Aldershot, 2007).

[138] Purkiss, *The Witch in History*, 74.

a more historical way as databases of "facts" '.[139] She interprets the writing of witchcraft pamphlets as a multiple authorship, with the court clerk representing only one of several layers of input in a given account, alongside with victim, questioner, witch, shorthand writer, author, editor and printer.[140] Gibson's studies are valuable because they underline the complexity of the text. However, in several respects pamphlets differ from court records. Some of the layers of input mentioned by Gibson, like author, editor and printer, came into play because the pamphlets are printed material, and would not appear for primary sources.[141] As the interpretation of voices heard in a witchcraft document hinges on the importance of the scribe in the process of writing down the event, I will focus more clearly on the possible influence of the scribe in the act of recording. The entire recorded trial might be seen as a narrative and the function of the scribe similar to that of the narrator, being the device which structures and keeps together the text.[142] This holds true for court records as well as minutes from church sessions, which often document the first stages of a witchcraft trial. The voices of the various participants during the trial are filtered through the scribe's recording. The confession of the accused person may in narratological terms be described as an embedded narrative within the larger narrative of the entire trial.

The role of the scribe in the study of court records has attracted considerable attention among witchcraft researchers, linguists, orality scholars, law historians, and general historians. Elizabeth S. Cohen has written several articles on discourse analysis in court records from the Italian early modern period.[143] She emphasizes these documents' position between oral and written text and the necessity of double modes of reading. On one hand, they are documents 'to be read as "fairly" straightforward descriptions of the world; on the other, they are constructed texts conceived strategically to represent their speakers and negotiate more complex meanings'.[144] Through close-readings that engage both modes,

---

[139] Gibson, *Reading Witchcraft*, 7.

[140] Gibson, *Early Modern Witches*, 3, 5.

[141] Gibson, *Reading Witchcraft*, 22.

[142] Willumsen, 'Narratologi som tekstanalytisk metode', 61–64.

[143] Cohen, E. S., 'Back Talk: Two Prostitutes' Voices from Rome *c.* 1600', *Early Modern Women: An Interdisciplinary Journal*, vol. 2 (2007), 95–126; Cohen, E. S., 'Between Oral and Written Culture: The Social Meaning of an Illustrated Love Letter', in B. Diefendorf and C. Hesse (eds.), *Culture and Identity in Early Modern Europe (1500–1800): Essays in Honour of Natalie Zemon Davis* (Michigan, 1993), 181–201.

[144] Cohen, 'Back Talk', 95.

Cohen underlines individualized features in the voices of two accused women: 'Not only do they speak, but they tell, assert, complain, argue, and correct'.[145] The agendas of the two women are common. They talk back against their vulnerable positions, at the same time they resist marginalization, claim legitimacy and seek, 'within the bounds of law and convention, a greater measure of respect and security'.[146] Cohen's applied close-readings and interpretations are of great interest to my application of narratological method, as for her focus on the records' intermediate position between oral and written culture, as well as the personalization of voice.

Studies from different areas of Europe and the United States have been carried out, focusing on courtroom discourse and the scribe's influence on the records. Because there are several uncertain factors, it is not possible to say exactly how seventeenth-century court records were written.[147] There is consensus among scholars that court records in several respects were influenced by the scribe, for instance related to precision, errors or shortcuts, and possible changes introduced by interventions.[148] However, when it comes to the important question *to what extent* the scribe has influenced the court records, the meanings differ. Barbara Kryk-Kastovsky and Kathleen L. Doty maintain that courtroom records reflect the language spoken in a given historical period more faithfully than other sources, depending on the degree of orality. In addition, it is possible to assume that the language recorded in trial proceedings

---

[145] Cohen, 'Back Talk', 95.

[146] Cohen, 'Back Talk', 96.

[147] For instance in Norway there is a written decret that records from Court of Appeal should be written directly in protocols during the trials, not on loose paper. However, it is uncertain whether this decision was followed during trials in local courts. Ref. Sogner, S., 'Rettsprotokollene som kilde til mentalitet og kultur i europeisk historieforskning' [Court records as source to mentality and culture in European witchcraft research], in L. Marthinsen (ed.), *Tingboka som kilde*, 7–18; Næss, H. E., 'Forbrytelse og straff', in Marthinsen, *Tingboka som kilde*; Næss, H. E., 'Sorenskriverenes tingbøker fra 1600–1700-tallet som historisk kildemateriale' [The seventeenth and eighteenth-centuries Magistrates' court records as historical sources], *Heimen* no. 4 (1981), 781–795; Næss, H. E., 'Lagtingsprotokoller—gullgruber med feller [Court records from the Court of Appeal—gold mines with traps], *Heimen* no. 1 (1984), 59–67; Sandvik, H., Tingbøker. Avskrivning og registrering (Oslo, 1989); Sandvik, H., 'Tinget i Finnmark 1620–33' [*The court in Finnmark 1620–1633*], *Heimen* no. 4 (1987), 232–242.

[148] Kryk-Kastovsky, B., 'Historical courtroom discourse', *Journal of Historical Pragmatics*, 7:2 (2006), pp. 213–245; Doty, K. L., 'Telling tales. The role of scribes in constructing the discourse of the Salem witchcraft trials', *Journal of Historical Pragmatics*, vol. 8, no. 1 (2007), 25–41, at pp. 26, 27, 39.

provide rich historical and socio-cultural information.[149] These findings are based on analyses of historical courtroom discourse, fathoming
wider than witchcraft trials.[150] When it comes to interrogation in witchcraft trials, researchers who have carried out studies on material from
southern Germany, maintain that the confessions recorded in interrogation protocols are constructed by the scribe.[151] Peter Rushton maintains
that the type of narrative we hear in witnesses' testimonies in English
witchcraft cases 'depends on a number of shared understandings', all
intended to persuade about signs of the diabolical.[152] Rushton argues that
' "bewitchment" is constituted in the depositions themselves, we cannot
go behind the testimonies to find another source'.[153] In that respect the
suspects and witnesses would be essentially inaudible to us.

  This point of view has been challenged by among others Malcolm Gaskill.
In a study of depositions, Gaskill argues that the way they were structured
allowed access to the mental and psychological worlds of the people who
made them, not just the expectations of those who demanded them or
wrote them down.[154] The historical importance of depositions 'lies not just
in what they tell us about crime and the law, but how they can help us to
recover popular mentalities in general'.[155] Gaskill is pointing to historical

---

[149] Kryk-Kastovsky., 'Historical courtroom discourse', pp. 167–68; Kryk-Kastovsky, B.,
'Representations of Orality in Early Modern English Trial Records', *Journal of Historical
Pragmatics* vol. 1, no. 2 (2000), 201–230; Kryk-Kastovsky, B., 'How bad is "bad data"? In
search for the features of orality in Early Modern English legal texts', *Current issues in
unity and diversity of languages. Collection of papers selected from the CIL 18, held at Korea
University in Seoul on July 21–26, 2008* (Seoul; The linguistic society of Korea); Doty, 'Telling
tales', 27.
[150] The questions related to court recording in general, would also hold true for the
production of other types of written documents relevant for witchcraft trials, like pre-trial
dittays (endictments) and minutes from church sessions and presbytery.
[151] Macha, J., 'Redewiedergabe in Verhörprotokollen und der Hintergrund gesprochener
Sprache', in S. Krämer-Neubert and N. R. Wolf (eds.), *Bayerische Dialektologie. Akten der
Internationalen Dialektologischen Konferenz 26.–28. Februar 2002*, Schriften zum Bayerischen Sprachatlas 8, (Heidelberg, 2005), 171–178; J. Macha, E. Topalovic, I. Hille, U. Nolting and A. Wilke (eds.), *Deutsche Kanzleisprache in Hexenverhörprotokollen der Frühen
Neuzeit*, Auswahledition 1 (Berlin, 2005); Topalovic, E., ' "Ick kike in die Stern vndt versake
Gott den Herrn". Versprachligung des Teufelspaktes in westfälishen Verhörprotokollen
des 16./17. Jahrhunderts', *Augustin Wibbelt-Gesellschaft. Jahrbuch 20*, 69–86.
[152] On structural grounds, it is argued, these linguistic findings tend to create a pattern. Ref. P. Rushton, 'Texts of Authority: Witchcraft Accusations and the Demonstration
of Truth in Early Modern England', in S. Clark (ed.), *Languages of Witchcraft. Narrative,
Ideology and Meaning in Early Modern Culture* (New York, 2001), 31.
[153] Rushton, 'Texts of Authority', 35.
[154] Gaskill, M., 'Witches and witnesses in New and Old England', in Clark, *Languages
of Witchcraft*, 56–58.
[155] Gaskill, M., 'Reporting murder: fiction in the archives in early modern England', 2.

narratives as complex texts, with possibilities for semantic interpretation based on sources behind the documents themselves. I agree with this. As I see it, obviously source-critical questions like who is the speaker as well as the intention and motivation of the narrative contextualised in a legal frame, will be central during the process of analysis of court records. However, one has to distinguish between form and contents. The influence of legal conventions when it comes to the rendering of discourse in the courtroom has to mostly do with form. With regard to the contents of the confessions, it is the knowledge of the accused person which is decisive. It is not likely that the scribe changed the contents of utterances given. And, as pointed out by Gaskill, an official 'could not distort what was not said in the first place'.[156]

The interpretation of courtroom discourse is closely connected to the question how close the scribe's recording was to the actual speech, in other words whether he was able to render individualized voices.[157] In my view, a confession before the court gives access to the language of the accused person, because the reported speech has preserved features of orality. The words taken down by the scribe reflects what was actually expressed in the courtroom. The scribe was a professional person. This is the reason why in-depth studies of the various voices in witchcraft trials may be performed. The close-readings performed in this study rest on the conviction that the voices rendered in the records relate to what different persons said and may be analyzed as such. Several in-depth studies of voices in witchcraft cases, for instance Raisa Maria Toivo's studies of Finnish sources, rely on the assumption that it is possible to get hold of mentalities of the common populace through studying legal documents.[158] The same is seen in Elizabeth Cohen's studies, where the voices are interpreted as

---

[156] Gaskill, 'Reporting murder', 3.

[157] Willumsen, *Seventeenth-Century Witchcraft Trials*, 28–33; Willumsen, L. H., 'Witches in Scotland and Northern Norway: two case studies', in A. Kruse and P. Graves (eds.), *Images and Imaginations. Perspectives on Britain and Scandinavia* (Edinburgh, 2007), 35–66; Willumsen, 'Narratologi som tekstanalytisk metode', 39–72; Willumsen, L. H., 'A Narratological Approach to Witchcraft Trials: A Scottish Case', *Journal of Early Modern History*, 15 (2011), 531–60; Willumsen, L. H., 'Barn anklaget for trolldom i Finnmark— en narratologisk tilnærming', *Heimen* vol. 48 (2011), 257–78; Willumsen, L. H., 'Children accused of witchcraft in 17th-century Finnmark', *Scandinavian Journal of History*, vol. 38, no. 1 (2013), 18–41.

[158] Toivo, *Witchcraft and Gender in Early Modern Society*; Toivo, 'Discerning voices and values in the Finnish witch trial records'.

personalized and differentiated, according to the scribe's professionism.[159] Similarly, that personal testimonies gives insight in hidden and imaginative worlds, is maintained in Alison Rowlands' study of German witchcraft narratives.[160] Also Lyndal Roper's studies based on German witchcraft cases are characterized by an individualized approach.[161] The tendency towards personalization is seen as well in Jari Eilola's study of children's voices in Swedish witchcraft trials.[162] For these studies it holds true that the recorded speech has been considered an appropriate object for close-reading. With reference to Rothenburg testimonies, Alison Rowlands says: 'Through them we can explore communal and domestic disharmony; perceptions of honour; experiences of motherhood, childhood, marriage, illness and war, and beliefs about magic and religion'.[163] So, while caution should be taken on text-critical grounds, my view is that court records are suitable for fruitful analyses of form as well as contents.

Historiography European Witchcraft Research

I would here like to give some brief comments on the historiography of European witchcraft research in general. This area has been expanding rapidly during the last decades, and it will only be possible to mention a few works here. A broad picture of ongoing research at the time is found in *Early Modern European Witchcraft. Centres and Peripheries*, edited by Bengt Ankarloo and Gustav Henningsen, first published in 1990.[164] This collection of essays gives an impression of the wide geographical scope and the many aspects focused in witchcraft research; studies related to law and theology, to the origins of the witches' Sabbath and to the witch-hunting in peripheries of Europe, namely Scandinavia, Iceland, Portugal, Hungary and Estonia. It presents an essay on comparison, by Peter Burke, as well as an essay on Scandinavian witchcraft in Anglo-American perspective,

---

[159] Ref. Cohen, 'Back Talk: Two prostitutes' Voices from Rome *c.* 1600', Cohen, 'Between Oral and Written Culture: The Social Meaning of an Illustrated Love Letter', 181–201.

[160] Rowlands, *Witchcraft narratives in Germany*, 2.

[161] Roper, L., *Witch Craze. Terror and fantasy in Baroque Germany* (New Haven, 2004); Roper, L., ' "Evil Imaginations and Fantasies": Child-Witches and the End of Witch Craze', *Past and Present*, no. 167 (2000), 107–139.

[162] Eilola, J., 'Lapsitodistajien kertomukset Ruotsin noitatapauksissa 1668–1676' [Child witnesses' stories in witchcraft trials in Sweden 1668–1676], E-journal *Kasvatus and Aika*, 3 (2009).

[163] Rowlands, *Witchcraft narratives in Germany*, 2.

[164] (Oxford, 1990).

written by E. William Monter. The volume is based on a centre-periphery model of European witchcraft trials, which has later proved to be a fruitful model, although with modifications. Of other works from the 1990s could be mentioned *Witchcraft in early modern Europe. Studies in culture and belief*, edited by Jonathan Barry, Marianne Hester and Gareth Roberts.[165] The volume contains essays on the crime of witchcraft, witchcraft and religion, as well as essays related to the making of a witch and the social environment as background for accusations. The volume also has two essays focusing on the decline of witchcraft. After the turn of the new millennium Richard M. Golden's four volumes *Encyclopedia of Witchcraft. The Western Tradition* appeared in 2006.[166] This encyclopedia has a broad spectre of short, updated, articles from all of Europe and New England.[167] The following year, in 2007, a *Witchcraft historiography*, edited by Jonathan Barry and Owen Davies, was published.[168] The volume shows the interdisciplinary approaches to witchcraft studies and includes new research from a number of countries. The development of witchcraft research shows an increasing focus on witchcraft accusations coming 'from below', from common people in the villages.[169] At the same time, the interest in witchcraft trials as legal operations has been emphasized.[170] There has been a strong tendency towards interdisciplinary studies, from the fields of social science, sociology, anthropology, ethnology, religious studies and linguistics.[171] In-depth studies of witchcraft persecution in Germany, Switzerland, France, Spain, and Anglo America have been carried out.[172] A variety of regional witchcraft studies have been carried through, not least for

---

[165] (Cambridge, 1996).

[166] (Santa Barbara, 2006).

[167] US—a region in the northeastern corner of the United States consisting of the six states of Maine, New Hampshire, Vermont, Massachusetts, Rhode Island, and Connecticut.

[168] (Hampshire, 2007).

[169] This was first pointed out by Walter Rummel for the Central German area. Ref. Rummel. W., 'Hexenprozesse in Raum von Untermosel und Hunsrück. Raumkulturelle und Soziokulturelle Dimensionen', in K. Freckmann (ed.), *Prozesse in Raum*, Sobernheimer Gesprache I (Bonn, 1993), 83–92.

[170] Among others by Brian P. Levack and Hans Eyvind Næss. Ref. Levack, B. P. *The Witch Hunt in Early Modern Europe*, 3 edn. (London, 2006); Næss, H. E., 'Norway: The Criminological Context', in Ankarloo and Henningsen, *Early Modern European Witchcraft*.

[171] Works by John Demos, Gary K. Waite, Robert Thurston and Thomas A. Fudge point to these widely different perspectives.

[172] From Germany, witchcraft studies have been carried out by Franz Irsigler, Rita Voltmer, Wolfgang Behringer, Rolf Schulte and Johannes Dillinger, to mention some. In addition, Alison Rowlands and Lyndal Roper have made research based on German sources. For France, Robin Briggs has studied the Lorraine area. For Spain, Gunnar W. Knutsen has compared Valencia and Barcelona. For the Anglo-American area there has been active

Germany.[173] For the Scandinavian countries, witchcraft research has been an active area, and particular attention had been given to the Blåkulla trials in Sweden and the Finnmark witchcraft trials in the very north of Norway. In the summer of 2011 the Steilneset Memorial was opened in Vardø, Northern Norway, commemorating the Finnmark witches.[174] For Eastern Europe, there has been a steady increase in witchcraft studies.[175] The perspective of gender has been focused on in several books, not least has the interest for male witches been increasing, as seen for instance in Laura Apps and Andrew Colin Gow's book *Male Witches in Early Modern Europe*, as well as in books by Rolf Schulte and Alison Rowlands. The last contains articles by among others Rita Voltmer, Sarah Ferber, Jonathan Durrant, Malcolm Gaskill and Julian Goodare.[176] There has also been an increased interest in single trials, in contrast to linked trials, as well as trials that led to acquittals.[177] Mention should also be made of the recently

research resulting in frequent publications during this period, as seen by the references to literature mentioned above.

[173] Among these are Behringer, W., *Hexenverfolgung in Bayern, Volksmagie, Glaubenseifer und Staatsraison in der Frühen Neuzeit* (München, 1987); Schulte, *Hexenverfolgung in Schleswig-Holstein vom 16.–18. Jahrhundert*; Labouvie, E., *Zauberei und Hexenwerk. Ländlicher Hexenglaube in der frühen Neuzeit* (Frankfurt am Main, 1991); Lambrecht, K., *Hexenverfolgung und Zaubereiprozesse in den schlesischen Territorien* (Köln, 1995); Rummel, W., *Bauern, Herren und Hexen. Studien zur Sozialgeschichte sponheimischer und kurtrierischer Hexenprozesse* (1574–1664 (Göttingen, 1991); Voltmer, R., 'Hexenverfolgungen im Maas-Rhein-Mosel-Raum'.

[174] Steilneset Memorial consists of three components: Art, Architecture and History. The French-American artist Louise Bourgeois has contributed with an art installation, the Swiss architect Peter Zumthor is the architect, and the exhibition texts are written by Liv Helene Willumsen.

[175] Nenonen, 'Witch Hunts in Europe: A New Geography', 168–172; Kivelson, V. A., 'Witchcraft in Russia', in G. N., Rhyne and J. L. Wieczynski (eds.), *The Modern Encyclopedia of Russian and Soviet History*, vol. 55 Supplement: Witchcraft in Russia (Zvenigorod, 1993); Ryan, W. F., 'The Witchcraft Hysteria in Early Modern Europe: Was Russia an Exception?', *The Slavonic and East European Review*, vol. 76, no. 1 (1999); Worobec, C. D., *Possessed. Women, and Demons in Imperial Russia* (De Kalb, 2001).

[176] Apps and Gow's book was published in Manchester and New York, 2003. See also A. Rowlands (ed.), *Witchcraft and Masculinities in Early Modern Europe* (Hampshire, 2009), containing Voltmer, 'Witch-Finders, R., Witch-Hunters or Kings of the Sabbath? The prominent Role of Men in the Mass Persecutions of the Rhine-Meuse-Area (Sixteenth-Seventeenth Centuries)', 74–99; Durrant, J., 'Why Some men and Not Others?', 100–120; Gaskill, M., 'Masculinity and Witchcraft in Seventeenth-Century England', 171–190; Ferber, S., 'Possession and the Sexes', 214–238; Goodare, J., 'Men and the Witch-Hunt in Scotland', 149–170, Schulte, R., *Man as Witch. Male Witches in Central Europe* (Basingstoke, 2009).

[177] Toivo, *Witchcraft and Gender in Early Modern Society*, 15; Lennersand, M., 'Rättvik', in Lennersand, M. and Oja, L., *Livet går vidare: Älvdalen och Rättvik efter de stora häxprocesserna 1668–1671* (Gidlund, 2006), 375–596; Davies, O. and Blécourt, W. de, 'Introduction: beyond the witch trials', in Davies and de Blécourt, *Beyond the witch trials*, 1–8.

published *Oxford Handbook of Witchcraft in Early Modern Europe and Colonial America*, edited by Brian P. Levack, which gives updated articles on witchcraft research until 2013. All in all it must be said that witchcraft research in Europe certainly is a flourishing area.

Outline

Witches of the North is a fourpartite study, focusing on mainland Scotland in Part I, Orkney and Shetland in Part II, Finnmark in Part III, and Comparisons and Conclusions in Part IV. The respective parts will contain background information about the area in question. Parts I–III will have three chapters each, the first of which dealing with the context of the witchcraft trials, the next giving factual information about the witchcraft trials based on quantitative analyses, and the last presenting close-readings of separate court records. In the first of the three chapters, effort will be paid to describe the backdrop of the witchcraft trials in the two regions in question, by giving a brief survey of the political, juridical, clerical and social background. In the second, facts about the trials will be presented related to statistical analyses, with regard to chronology, frequency, gender, type of trial, contents of confessions, use of torture, verdict and sentence.[178] This factual information points to trends in the source material as a whole. The last of the three chapters will contain close-readings of selected court records. These textual analyses of witchcraft documents are in-depth studies. The main focus is on the voices of the accused persons and the confessions given by them. These close-readings are interpreted in relation to a wider historical context. Finally, in part IV, Comparisons and Conclusions, the various findings will be discussed related to the comparative analytical framework sketched above, and the conclusions of the entire study will be formulated.

---

[178] Primarily Liv Helene Willumsen's thesis *Seventeenth-Century Witchcraft Trials in Scotland and Northern Norway* (2008) is consulted for results here.

PART I

MAINLAND SCOTLAND

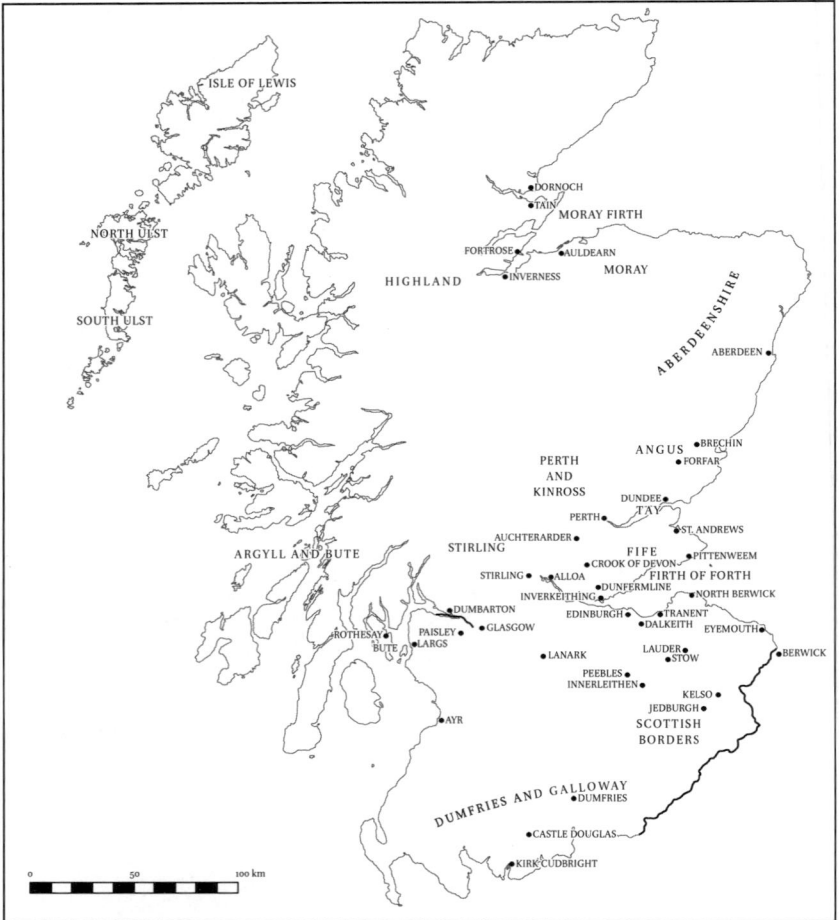

Map 1: Mainland Scotland with principal places mentioned in the text. Made by
Tomas Willumsen Vassdal.

CHAPTER TWO

MAINLAND SCOTLAND—HISTORICAL BACKGROUND

This chapter will deal with the general historical background of the witch-craft trials in Scotland mainland, giving some pieces of information about the political, juridical, clerical and social conditions for the period in question. As the following two chapters will contain analyses of the witchcraft documents carried out according to my analytical framework, this chapter will give information about the context of the trials—how society functioned on levels important for the witchcraft persecution. As the state was heavily involved in the witchcraft trials, some knowledge of the political conditions is necessary. With legal documents being the main sources analyzed, information about the seventeenth-century courts and judicial procedures is essential. As witchcraft trials were almost a post Reformation phenomenon, it is important to touch upon the development of the church in Scotland, usually written kirk, after the Reformation. A glimpse of social conditions during the seventeenth century, including demographical facts and information about ways of living for common people, is important, as most of those accused in witchcraft trials were peasants.[1] The chapter will thus prepare the ground for the analyses of witchcraft trials to follow as well as for the comparison between the two geographical areas in question in the final chapter. In an article on the English perspective on early modern Scotland, K. E. Wrightson gives this synopsis:

> The period between the Scottish Reformation and the Union of 1707, was clearly of vital importance in the making of modern Scotland. It witnessed a strengthening of royal authority and the associated development of Scotland's distinctive legal institutions. It saw the establishment and spreading influence of the reformed Kirk, with all the implications which that great watershed had for the creation of the distinctive texture of Scottish culture; the genesis of the national educational system and the Scottish poor laws; the beginning of the transformation of agriculture and rural society; the nascent phase of Scottish industrial development. And yet on the other hand, the same period witnessed Scotland's political marginalisation, the removal to London of the apex of the political and social

---

[1] Christina Larner maintains that 95% of the accused in Scotland were peasants. Ref. Larner, *Enemies of God*, 1.

order, and Scotland's eventual absorption as a junior partner in the larger
political unit of the United Kingdom. Similarly, Scotland was increasingly
incorporated into a larger economic and social system in which the centre
of gravity lay far to the south. Whatever Scotland's particular achievements,
they were increasingly overshadowed by, harnessed to, or submitted within
those of a bigger, more powerful, more confident neighbour.'[2]

The Scottish witchcraft trials differed substantially from the English ones
in contents as well as number, a fact that might be related to the historical background, and underlined by among others Christina Larner.[3] Seen
in that light, a sketch of the historical background of Scotland might be
useful as a back-drop for the trials.

Demography and Ways of Living

Mainland Scotland has an area of *c.* 76000 square kilometres and had a
population of about 1 million *c.* 1600. Around the turn of the century four
towns had universities; Aberdeen, Edinburgh, Glasgow and St Andrews.
This manifestation of knowledge was of importance for the intellectual
climate, not least the spread of new, learned European ideas about witchcraft. Across the countryside, Scotland's people were more evenly distributed than would be the case later. Until the middle of the eighteenth
century, half of the population may have lived north of an imaginary line
stretching from Tay to Dumbarton. More than one third was located in
the Highlands and Islands. Nevertheless, there was a marked internal
movement and population redistribution. By first half of the eighteenth
century the signs of future migration trends had been established, the
main one being the flow of people to the western Lowlands.[4] Population
growth in the sixteenth and early seventeenth centuries was substantial,
and a major force for change in settlement pattern.[5]

During the period 1500–1800 many towns grew rapidly. By the fifteenth
century two groups of burghs had emerged, royal burghs and burghs of

---

[2] Wrightson, K. E., 'Kindred adjoining kingdoms: An English perspective on the social
and economical history of early modern Scotland', in R. A. Houston and I. D. Whyte (eds.),
Scottish Society 1500–1800 (Cambridge, 1989), 245–60, at p. 250.

[3] Larner, *Enemies of God*, 198–201.

[4] Foyster, E. and Whatley, C. A., *A History of Everyday Life in Scotland, 1600 to 1800*
(Edinburgh, 2010), 4.

[5] Calculations based on the 1691 hearth tax returns give a population for Scotland
at this date of 1.234.575. Ref. Whyte, I. D., *Scotland before the Industrial Revolution* (Essex,
1995), 113.

barony and regality.[6] In the fifteenth and sixteenth centuries the royal burghs consolidated their system of trading monopolies which was strong by European standards. They became a more homogeneous group and their ability to define and pursue common interests gave them great unity and solidarity.[7] The gulf in urban society was between burgesses and the unfree inhabitants, not between merchants and craftsmen.[8] The merchant guilds in larger towns contained men of widely varying status and wealth, and often craftsmen were as wealthy as the merchants. A feature of the period was greater social segregation according to wealth and status.[9] In 1500 below 2 per cent in Scotland lived in towns with more than 10,000 inhabitants. As for level of urbanisation, Scotland at this time had more in common with Scandinavia and Ireland than with England, the Low Countries and Italy. During the seventeenth century from 3.0 till 5.3% of the population lived in towns, which meant that towns had an increase from 30,000 till 53,000 inhabitants during this period. Edinburgh, the capital, had around 12.000 inhabitants by 1560 and the double by 1640.[10] By c. 1600 the Scottish capital was dominant in size. In the 1690s Edinburgh was twice the size of the second city, Glasgow. In addition there existed major regional centres, for instance Aberdeen, which doubled its population during the same period. By 1750 Scotland was already highly urbanised.[11] Therefore the seventeenth century is often called a century in transition.

During the period of witchcraft persecution, most people lived in villages, with farming as the main way of living. Everyday life was closely connected with the land, with the rhythms of the seasons of vital importance. Throughout Scotland agriculture was organized using a form of open-field farming. In many regions oats and bere, a hard variety of barley, were the only grain crops sown. In the Highlands, despite the unsuitable environment, arable farming was important. Almost all farms in Scotland were mixed with sheep farms and dairy cattle, in the Highlands goats were kept in addition. Scottish agriculture suffered from stagnation

---

[6] A burgh was an autonomous corporate entity in Scotland and North England. This type of administrative device existed at the time of King David I of Scotland, a twelfth century ruler, who created the royal burghs. A royal burgh paid a tax to the king each year.

[7] Whyte, *Scotland before the Industrial Revolution*, 170.

[8] Lynch, M., *The Early Modern Town in Scotland* (London, 1987), 26.

[9] Foyster and Whatley, *A History of Everyday Life in Scotland*, 6.

[10] Whyte, *Scotland before the Industrial Revolution*, 113.

[11] Scotland was then more highly organized than France, Germany or Iberia, and rapidly catching up with England. Ref. Whyte, *Scotland before the Industrial Revolution*, 172.

and decline until they switched to net grain exports *c.* 1620. Economic
and social conditions favoured widespread agricultural change.[12] When
the transformation of the rural economy and society began in earnest, the
process was extremely rapid, a true agricultural revolution which altered
Lowland agriculture and rural society within a couple of generations.[13] In
addition to agriculture, fishing was an important economical factor, with
cod and herring fished at sea and salmon fished in rivers.

Throughout the period of the witch-hunt, landowners dominated
Scotland's political life, society and economy. The stability of the greater
landowning families and their estates was a notable feature of Scottish
society over long periods. The most marked change in the rural landscape
in the later seventeenth and early eighteenth centuries was the creation
of blocks of enclosures mainly confirmed to land close to and surrounding the homes of landowners. Seventeenth-century improvement largely
took the form of enclosing fields, draining and planting trees. For more
than a century after 1600 it was common for burgesses and others to grow
crops, and own and graze livestock either on their own plots or on common land. Farming methods altered little until well into the eighteenth
century. However, there were marked regional differences. Advance was
most apparent in the Lothians, where most enclosing activity in the seventeenth century had taken place.[14] Throughout the period, fairs for the sale
of and hiring workers were regular features of urban life, especially in the
smaller towns and villages.

Scotland lacked a large landless class. Social stratification most likely
became more sharply defined during the later sixteenth and early seventeenth centuries. Feudal relationships, derived from the holding of land
in exchange for service or labour, were weaker in Scotland than in other
parts of Europe. Still, the power which proprietors had over the inhabitants of their estates should be noted. In a country where rural settlement
was dispersed it is difficult to define those structures which bound the
rural population into communities. However, the parish provided a grow-
ing focus from the later sixteenth century. Below the landowners, the ten-
ant farmers formed the most important social group in terms of wealth
and status.

---

[12] A series of acts passed by the Scottish Parliament from 1661 till 1695 represent an
effort of encouraging improvement on a large scale.
[13] Whyte, *Scotland before the Industrial Revolution*, 136.
[14] Foyster and Whatley, *A History of Everyday Life in Scotland*, 8.

Over most of the countryside settlement was dispersed, often in hamlets. In the Lowlands the parish church generally provided the focus for a larger hamlet, the kirktoun. In the Highlands such locations were less common and it was more usual to find churches and chapels in isolated locations.[15] Along the coast fishing villages reflected a distinctive way of life that was often quite separate from neighbouring agricultural communities. They were particularly characteristic of the north east from Angus to the Moray Firth. In the Highlands settlement expansion, which may have been linked to the growth of both population and demand, often involved the permanent colonisation of shielings, small stone huts in the hills.[16]

Those at the lower levels of society just survived beyond the margins of subsistence. In the Lowlands life in this regard was tolerable, and by the end of the seventeenth century there was an adequate supply of a narrow range of basic foodstuffs. But in the Highlands and islands of the north and west, where as much as one third of the population was found prior to the middle of the eighteenth century, life was lived with a lingering spectre of crop failure in the most challenging of natural environments. Health conditions were bad, and death was a frequent visitor in early modern Scotland.[17] There was no co-ordinated effort to deal with the problem of poverty until an Act of Parliament in 1575.[18] However, the structure of legal authority in Scotland was not suited for enforcing this act. The reformed church and its kirk sessions took over poor relief, officially from 1592.

Women formed a major element in the labour force, which mostly consisted of tenants or cottars or their wives. A range of tasks including all but the heaviest labouring were undertaken by the women. They also worked in the coal mines. When married they had to undertake a wide range of household tasks as well as employment which brought in additional cash such as spinning linen yarn. The wages of women, for those who had them, were most often inferior to men's. Also women's rights regarding property were restricted. The right to land was stronger, especially

---

[15] Whyte, *Scotland before the Industrial Revolution*, 132.
[16] The shielings were built for summer grazing on the hillside, in which the farm communities lived during the few weeks in summer when the animals could benefit from the lush pastures in the hills. Dairy products, butter and cheese, were made there in summer time.
[17] Foyster and Whatley, *A History of Everyday Life in Scotland*, 14.
[18] This act was confirmed with minor changes in 1579. It was copied from the English statute of 1572 which set up the Elizabethan poor law.

for widows. Women were excluded from politics and from church government, even at the level of the kirk session, though the church recognized them as independent moral individuals. In law, however, they were
not accepted as independent criminals or reliable witnesses, except in
witchcraft trials. They were also disadvantaged educationally, resulting in
higher levels of illiteracy than among men.

Political Conditions

From 1560 until the Act of Union in 1707 Scotland experienced very
unstable political conditions. From the last years of Queen Mary during
the reigns of James VI and I, Charles I, Charles II, James VII, William and
Mary, and Queen Anne, upheavals, executions and abrupt changes often
took place in the political sphere. After James VI departed to England in
1603, Scotland was administered by the Privy Council for several years.
Many of the turbulent events had to do with religion and changing dog-
matic directions within the church. Jenny Wormald argues that the pres-
tige of the monarchy was weakened by the last years of Mary's rule, and
that it was further damaged by the civil war that followed. 'The minority
government of the infant James VI was less clearly a government than a
party: the king's party, as opposed to the queen's.'[19] The 1560s and the
1570s were turbulent years. The Earl of Moray, regent from 1567 until 1570,
was killed, and his successor, Lennox, was killed after a year in office. Also
the successor, Mar, was regent for only a year, even if he died of natural causes. The nation was divided politically. The developing idea of the
nation-state strengthened the power of the secular ruler, as heads of individual states and leaders of reform or defenders of the old faith.[20] King
James, a well educated person, argued for the theory of divine right in his
academic treatise from 1598 and in his practical manual of king-craft from
1599.[21] With regard to temperament, he was a man who saw kingship in
its highly academic ad highly personal guise.[22] James was successful as a
Protestant king, and economically and politically he developed contacts
with the Baltic and Spain. During his reign, Scottish government started to

---

[19] Wormald, J., *Court, Kirk, and Community. Scotland 1470–1625* (London, 1981), 145.
[20] Wormald, *Court, Kirk, and Community. Scotland 1470–1625*, 145.
[21] *The Trew Law of Free Monarchies* (1598) and *Basilikon Doron* (1599).
[22] Wormald, *Court, Kirk, and Community. Scotland 1470–1625*, 155.

develop some state bureaucracy, with several lawyer-administrators, and magnates involved in central government.

Three forms of seventeenth-century state power in Scotland have been emphasized by Julian Goodare—ideological, economical and military.[23] The period after James VI and I was characterized by several landmarks: the creation of a new government by the covenanters in 1638–40; the English occupation in 1651; the Restoration of 1660; the Glorious Revolution of 1689; the Union of 1707. As for state structure, there were broadly two models: the absolutist state, dominant in the reigns of James VI and I and his Stewart successors, and the covenanting and parliamentary state of the 1640s and 1690s. The regimes of James VI and Charles I relied on a powerful monarchy, a powerful landed nobility with hierarchically organized client networks, a system of regulated trade and industry in corporate towns, and a rent-paying peasantry. These regimes were characterized by respect for hierarchy and tradition. The crown began to come into conflict with parliament and conventions of estates. The absolute state needed a compliant nobility. The royal court gathered and reconstructed nobility around itself, using nobles to promote central policies. Parliaments began to contain opposition groups, hostile to taxation and religious innovation.

The covenanting state was reversing this system. It had no court, the monarchy being eliminated in all but name. It was parliament which governed. In opposition to James VI and I, the covenanting state firmly established ascending principles of authority in both church and state, where members of the nobility could exercise leadership. In contrast, the Restoration regime based its claims to authority on its return to the governmental system of the 1630s. It was the last period of dominance for the ideology of the divine rights of kings. The absolute partnership between the crown and nobility was one of the most important 'restorations' of 1660. Nobles could not survive without office. The nobles became parliamentarians. A fully parliamentary regime, with a firmly constitutional monarch, was once more established in 1689. The union of 1707 continued this. From 1689 politics was primarily the art of parliamentary management. Goodare maintains that in the positions of crown, parliament and nobility, the Restoration state was once more an absolutist state. The royal court regained control of policy, and readmitted nobility to the spoils of office.[24]

---

[23] Goodare, J., *State and Society in Early Modern Scotland* (Oxford, 1999), 338.
[24] Goodare, *State and Society in Early Modern Scotland*, 327.

By the events of the 1640s, the sovereignty of parliament had been established, and the monarchical element curtailed. In 1689 the ideology of the
divine rights of kings was buried. Parliament was now sovereign; judiciary
as well as parliament increased their independence from the crown, religion came under parliamentary control, and taxation required parliamentary consent. Religious ideology declined in political importance during
the second half of the seventeenth century. The regime of the 1690s based
itself on moderate Presbyterianism and religious pluralism. The different
religious dissenter groups did not threaten the state in the same way as a
single broad Presbyterian movement had been able to do.

The fiscal power of the state witnessed some forward leaps after 1625.
The covenanting revolution was such a leap, because it established an
unprecedented system of state finance. It was formed by land tax and
excise, taxing a wide variety of commodities. These two fiscal pillars
continued to be a model for more than a century. The fiscal differences
between the absolute state and that of the covenanters were striking. The
absolutist state had inherent weaknesses through its reliance on a nobility with financial difficulties. This state was not able to secure a fiscal
base. James VI and I had moved from taxation of land towards taxation
of commerce. This was reversed after 1638. The covenanting fiscal system
was continued and extended under the English occupation in the 1650s.
The Restoration of 1660 intended to restore a cheap civilian state, and
there was a fiscal decline. Land tax was abolished. The regime wanted
to lighten the burden of the nobility. It based itself of the power of large,
landed proprietors, who were able to direct the tax burden elsewhere. In
1678 a land tax returned, and in 1690 revenue was based on both landed
property and commercial wealth. Both 1640 and 1690 were significant fiscal turning-points, in England as in Scotland, with substantial increases
in the revenue. The major turning-point in Scotland probably came with
the covenanting revolution, since the regime of the 1690s was essentially
reviving the fiscal system of the 1640s. The Union of 1707 enabled Scotland
to tackle the task of fiscal catching up, with vast increased taxes.

The exercise of military power is an important part of state power. The
covenanting regime created the first modern armies in Scotland. They
were not so numerous, but had modern equipment and campaigned for
long periods. At the Restoration, a standing Scottish army was established,
the first regular peacetime army of the Scottish state. After 1660 there was
a military decline. In 1689 the Highlands demonstrated that they could
mount an armed challenge to the regime of William. With the establishment of Fort William in 1690, the idea of garrisoning the Highlands was

realized. Gradually the Scottish and English army command structures were merged, and Scottish regiments became units of the English army. The Scottish state thus displayed threefold convergence with England during the seventeenth century, and particularly in the decade after 1689: in the way it deployed military power; in its ideological trappings, and in the fiscal structure which underpinned it. At the end Scotland built its own state. This state, however, might best be seen as a union of states than one of nations.[25] It took the route towards a parliamentary state with limited monarchy and a limited role for territorial nobility. The Union of 1707 was a union of 'sovereign parliaments in which the monarchical element had been heavily curtailed—while maintaining the separation of most of the old ones—especially laws and churches'.[26]

Judicial Conditions

The Scottish legal system was to a large extent decentralized in the seventeenth century. Much of the law of early modern Scotland had evolved from within communities, rather than being imposed from above. According to Ian D. Whyte, much of the administration of justice was in the hands of local landowners through a mosaic of franchise courts within which the interpretation of justice depended on local custom rather than statute law.[27] The different courts seem to have integrated well with each other, as each level of the judicial system had a defined role and disputes over jurisdictions were uncommon. The jurisdictions of regality and barony courts became permanent once they were created by a royal grant. They were hereditary, and the size of the territories could vary. The regalities could try all crimes except treason and witchcraft. Some baronies had the power of 'pit and gallows', the right to imprison and even execute offenders.[28] By the seventeenth century, the secular franchise courts were reinforced by church courts. In addition to the criminalization of sins, like adultery, fornication, blasphemy and other moral offences, kirk sessions could also deal with crimes, like assaults. Presbyteries were formed by ministers and, after 1638, by ruling elders elected from each parish. They monitored the activities of group of parishes. In addition to controlling the preaching of their

---

[25] Goodare, J., *The Government of Scotland 1560–1625* (Oxford, 2004), 307.
[26] Goodare, *State and Society in Early Modern Scotland*, 325.
[27] Whyte, *Scotland before the Industrial Revolution*, 210.
[28] Larner, *Enemies of God*, 37; Whyte, *Scotland before the Industrial Revolution*, 211.

ministers they handled difficult cases passed on from the kirk sessions. They could impose excommunication upon accused persons. Sheriff court, an Anglo-Norman institution, had been introduced in Scotland in the twelfth century. Sheriffs were local agents of the crown, and they were supervised by central government. They often worked together with franchise courts and kirk sessions within their jurisdiction. Much of the business was carried out by sheriff deputes. Burgh courts, being the urban counterparts of the rural franchises, worked closely with local kirk sessions. The Court of Justiciary, from 1672 called the High Court of Justiciary, formed the upper level of the Scottish criminal system. The court dealt with particularly difficult cases, among those occasionally witchcraft.

Even if there was a variety of decentralized and franchise courts, the state had a strong influence on the legal arena. As for witchcraft trials, this influence may be marked by laws passed, the decision for a criminal trial to be held, and the actual witchcraft trials held. In Scotland, the witchcraft statute of 1563 brought witchcraft within the jurisdiction of the secular courts, whereas punishment for witches before the Reformation was carried out by church courts. The most important option was to have a commission of justiciary appointed. To get such a commission, a delegation from a community would arrive 'complaining of witches in their community, and ask for a commission that would provide the authority to try them. They would then be given a commission'.[29] Most witchcraft trials in local courts were held by virtue of such commissions. A commission of justiciary was a document issued by the Crown, normally under the signet, empowering the recipient to hold a criminal trial for a specific crime. Such a judicial commission granted by the king or Privy Council to local elites who then held trials in the local community, was the easiest and cheapest way of trying a witch.[30]

Scottish witch-hunting may be seen as a centralized operation due to the Privy Council's close to monopoly position with regard to appointing commissions for trying witches in local courts.[31] The Privy Council of Scotland, which was a central institution, had authority to issue a com-

---

[29] Wasser, M., 'The Privy Council and the Witches: The Curtailment of Witchcraft Prosecutions in Scotland, 1597–1628', *The Scottish Historical Rewiev*, vol. LXXXII, 1, no. 213 (2003), 22.

[30] Goodare, J., 'The framework for Scottish witch-hunting in the 1590s'; J. Goodare, "Witch-hunting and the Scottish state," in Goodare, *The Scottish Witch-Hunt in Context*, 122–145.

[31] Levack, *Witch-hunting in Scotland*, 15–33; Goodare, 'The Framework for Scottish Witch-Hunting in the 1590s', 240, 248; Goodare, 'Witch-hunting and the Scottish state', 122, 124–25, 139.

mission in order to try suspected witches in local courts. Most commissions were to try named individuals. There has been a debate on whether
or not general commissions were established. A general commission was
limited as to geographical area and time period, but 'could try as many
accused witches as they wished without any further consultations with
higher authorities'.[32] In this respect the local court became important for
the outfall of a witchcraft trial. Additional options were found for individuals or local officials who wished to prosecute a crime. One option was
to ask the lord advocate, the chief judicial officer of the Crown, 'to draft
an indictment of the defendant and prosecute the person in the justiciary
court, which was the central criminal court in Edinburgh. The powers of
the lord advocate were greatly enhanced by the judicial reforms enacted
during the reign of James VI in 1587'.[33]

With regard to the accusatorial approach to judicial procedure, the initiative lay in the hand of the plaintiff and the judge assumed a passive
role. The trial took on the character of a private settling of accounts with
the defendant, and was not effective enough in fighting crime. In large
parts of Europe it was replaced or influenced by the inquisitorial procedure. This procedure was invented by the Papacy and began to be applied
during the Middle Ages related to heretics. It was used by both ecclesiastical and secular courts.[34] The term 'inquisitorial' suggests the fundamental difference between the two systems: unlike the older, accusatorial
approach, the courts were now supposed to be actively involved in the
search for truth.[35] In Germany, the old 'Volksrecht' had been replaced by
the Carolina in 1532. From then on torture, which was considered as 'Köni-
gin der Beweismittel', was permitted in witchcraft trials to enforce the
confession.[36] Standards of evidence were taken from Roman law, and efforts
to enhance legal security were made. For conviction in serious crimes,
an admission of guilt or testimonies from two witnesses was required.
However, to obtain such a confession on the part of the accused person,
various means of coercion were used, among them torture, which was

---

[32] Goodare, J., 'Witchcraft in Scotland', in Levack, *The Oxford Handbook*, 304–305;
Wasser, 'The privy council and the witches', 22.

[33] Levack, *Witch-hunting in Scotland*, 19.

[34] Rummel and Voltmer, *Hexen und Hexenverfolgung*, 34–41; Sörlin, P., *'Wicked Arts'.
Witchcraft and Magic Trials in Southern Sweden, 1635–1754* (Leiden, 1999), 46; Trusen, W.,
'Der Inquisitionsprozess: Seine historische Grundlagen und frühen Formen', *Zeitschrift der
Savigny-Stiftung für Rechtsgeschichte* 105, Kanonische Abteilung 74 (1988), 168–230.

[35] Sörlin, *'Wicked Arts'*, 46.

[36] Schulte, *Hexenverfolgung in Schleswig-Holstein*, 35.

not prohibited in Scotland until 1708, by an Act of the British Parliament. It has been pointed out that the provisions of the 1587 Act marked the introduction of an important element of inquisitorial procedure in Scotland.[37] According to Levack, 'the hallmarks of inquisitorial procedure were the elimination of the replacement of the private accuser by an officer of the court (known variously as a public prosecutor or fiscal) and the prosecution of the crime by officials rather than individuals acting in a private capacity.'[38] Even if Scotland did not adopt all the features of inquisitorial procedure, the new approach to prosecuting harm marked a significant modification of accusatorial procedure.

Clerical Conditions

Compared to many other European countries, the Scottish Reformation, which took place in 1560, was rather late.[39] In 1559–60 there was a sudden change of pace from the slow growth of Protestant support to the widespread adoption of the new faith. Reformation started in May 1559 by a riot following a sermon by John Knox, a priest who had broken with the established church. The sermon took place in Perth, a town characterized by sharp economic and social tensions with a tradition of anti-clericalism. The riot snowballed into a rebellion and by October Mary of Guise had been deposed. The towns played a key role as centres of protestant support in the early days of the revolution, among them several burghs north of the Forth. However, the Reformation could never have succeeded if it had been a purely urban phenomenon. The support of rural landowners was crucial, as there was a rapid decline of the church as a proprietor in the sixteenth century. English aid was also decisive. In February 1560 the Treaty of Edinburgh laid the foundation for a new alliance with England and in June that year the Scottish Parliament accepted the Protestant religion in the name of Queen Mary. A general Assembly was head of the new church, as it was impossible for Queen Mary, since she was a Catholic.

The treaty of Edinburgh in 1560 marked the start of an unstable period, with Episcopalians and Presbyterians competing for the lead. In 1572 the

---

[37] Larner, *Enemies of God*, 194; Larner, C., *Witchcraft and Religion. The Politics of Popular Belief* (Oxford, 1984), 35–67.

[38] Levack, *Witch-hunting in Scotland*, 19–20.

[39] Reformation Switzerland 1525/1536; Sweden 1527; Denmark 1536; Norway 1537.

church became overtly Episcopalian. In 1574 Andrew Melville returned
to Scotland after several years in Geneva where he had been influenced
by the teachings of Calvin's successor Theodore Beza. Melville thought
the church had come to rely too much on the laity and what was needed
was a church of dedicated professionals who could transform a society
rather than only reflect it. This church should have no bishops. The work
of ordinary ministers should be supervised through a structure of church
courts with presbyteries and synods above the kirk sessions. Presbyteries,
meetings of groups of ministers from designated areas, could admit new
ministers and supervise the work of existing ones. Melville's ideas were
approved by the General Assembly in 1578, but the government was less
inclined to accept them. Only in 1592 did the Parliament approve of a
Presbyterian system. A compromise was achieved. King James managed
between 1597 and 1612 to have bishops reinstated while retaining presbyteries. The church of Scotland was more monolithic and cohesive than
in England and other Protestant countries partly due to the control over
society exerted by kirk sessions and presbyteries.

The early reformers were more concerned with establishing a church
at parish level than with developing a sophisticated body of theological doctrine. The institutions which were established at parish level by
the reformers in the decades after 1560; the new ministry, the systems of
education and poor relief, and especially the kirk sessions, proved to be
enduring and resilient in the face of the religious and political upheavals
of the seventeenth century. Superficially the kirk underwent a series of
major changes during this period; the confirmation of episcopacy in 1584,
the acceptance of Presbyterianism in 1592, a return to episcopacy in 1610,
the reintroduction of a Presbyterian system under the Covenanters in
1638, the restoration of episcopacy in 1661 and finally William of Orange's
acceptance of a Presbyterian structure in 1690. The parish and its kirk session began to replace the barony and its court as the unit of local administration. In the late sixteenth and seventeenth centuries in most parts of
the Lowlands, the parishes had an average population of about 1,000. The
church took over many of the functions of kinship and lordship, notably
poor relief. The success of the discipline imposed by the church was partly
due to the support it received from the civil authorities. The state continued to support the church by making a number of moral offences crimes;
witchcraft and adultery in 1563, fornication in 1567, Sabbath breaking in
1579, and drunkenness in 1617. Anyone excommunicated by the church
was also outlawed by the state. From 1572 excommunicated people were

not allowed to hold any office or act as witnesses. From 1609 they were banned from receiving the income of lands and rents. Civil penalties for excommunication were abolished 1690.

There was little progress for the reformers during the first years after 1560 due to difficulties regarding its legal position and a lack of finances. Still the aims, set out in a programme known as the First Book of Discipline, were clear. 'Their vision did not stop with the creation of a protestant church but embraced a "godly Commonwealth", a society which, by submission to divine will would come to be a mirror of the Kingdom of God, a partnership in which the state governed in accordance with the church and where the church had the backing of secular authorities in imposing moral discipline.'[40] Its concern was the preaching of the word, the proper administration of the Sacraments, prayers in the vernacular and education in religion for everyone. Ministers were expected to work their way through the Bible systematically in their preaching. In the early years after the Reformation, the church was short of trained ministers and had to use readers, persons who read the scripture, but were not allowed to perform the full work of a minister. The masters of households were required to ensure that their families and servants had sufficient religious knowledge to survive an annual examination by the minister. Education was an important part of the programme with the aim of having a schoolmaster in every parish and education, free if necessary, for even the poorest. Reform of universities was also necessary, if they were to produce a trained graduate ministry. Despite financial difficulties, partly due to inflation, the new ministers were better off than their pre-Reformation counterparts. The Reformation created the clergy as a new and wealthy elite. Lay participation in the church was centred on the kirk sessions, comprising the minister of a parish and a dozen or more lay elders, initially elected annually from among the most worthy local men. The later sixteenth and early seventeenth centuries saw an important shift in power in society away from feudal magnates and nobles towards these middling groups. In a sense the kirk session elders came to represent the society of seventeenth-century Scotland more realistically than the magnates.

An important feature of the Scottish Reformation was its relative peacefulness and lack of violence. However, the changes went slowly. Throughout the Lowlands the new church did not get a firm grip of

---

[40] Whyte, *Scotland before the Industrial Revolution*, 99.

the minds until 1620s. In the Highlands the structure of the old church was dismantled, but slow to be replaced. In these areas the contents of Catholicism survived long after the actual faith had decayed. There was a shortage of Gaelic-speaking ministers, which lasted until the nineteenth century.

Map 2: Scotland divided into its Shires by H. Moll, imprint London 1745, NLS, Map Library.

CHAPTER THREE

MAINLAND SCOTLAND—WHAT FIGURES CAN TELL

In this chapter, I would first like to present an updated survey of Scottish witchcraft research. The Scottish sources used in this study will then be described. Quantitative analyses of Scottish witchcraft trials are an important part of my study. Facts drawn from the sources will show interesting connections between the factors in my analytical framework, and will provide a solid background for the close-readings of sources that follow in later chapters.

Earlier Research on Scottish Witchcraft Trials

The field of witchcraft research has increased enormously during the last thirty years. Only selected studies can be mentioned more than cursory. Christina Larner's first work on Scottish witchcraft, published together with Christopher Hyde Lee and H. McLachlan, was *A Source-Book of Scottish Witchcraft* (1977).[1] This book shows the scope and variety of Scottish witchcraft source material, and is in that respect important for later research. Larner's next book, *Enemies of God: the witch-hunt in Scotland* (1981) is the first study to make the Scottish witch-hunt known internationally. This book is a pioneer study of Scottish witchcraft trials. It emphasizes the role of religion: 'This book is about the women and men (in a ratio of about four to one) who, during this period, were identified by their neighbours, their ministers and elders, their landlords, and the officials of their government, as enemies of God'.[2] Larner saw the European witch in this light—as an enemy of God and the godly society. She has also published a collection of essays titled *Witchcraft and Religion*.[3] Brian P. Levack has written articles and books about the witchcraft trials in Scotland, including *Witch-hunting in Scotland. Law, Politics and Religion* (2008).[4] Levack's work

---

[1] C. Larner, C. H. Lee, and H. McLachlan (eds.), *A Source-Book of Scottish Witchcraft* (Glasgow, 1977).
[2] Larner, *Enemies of God*, 5.
[3] Larner, *Witchcraft and religion* (Oxford, 1984).
[4] *Witch-hunting in Scotland. Law, politics and religion* (New York, 2008). Among articles to be mentioned are 'Themes of Recent Witchcraft Research' in *Arv, Nordic Yearbook of Folklore*, vol. lxii (2006), 7–32, 'The Great Scottish Witch Hunt of 1661–1662', *Journal of*

provides important knowledge particularly with regard to legal aspects of witch trials. P. G. Maxwell-Stuart has written several books on Scottish witchcraft, focusing on regional studies as well as magic and witchcraft.[5]

The team behind the Survey of Scottish Witchcraft has published several books on the topic.[6] The first, *The Scottish witch-hunt in context* (2002), contains eleven articles, covering among other witch hunting and the state, regional studies of Aberdeen, Fife and Renfrewshire, the Devil and the domestic sphere, folk healing aspects, and the decline of the witch-hunt.[7] The second book from the SSW team, *Witchcraft and Belief in Early Modern Scotland* (2008), is a collection of ten chapters spanning from witchcraft panics to the folkloric beliefs behind witchcraft prosecutions.[8] The most recent book is *Scottish witches and with-hunters*.[9] In addition, Julian Goodare has written on folkloric aspects.[10]

Several doctoral theses have been written on the topic of Scottish witchcraft, particularly related to folk belief; Lizanne Henderson has written about traditional Scottish fairy belief, Joyce Miller has written about witchcraft and healing, and Alaric Hall has written about fairy belief.[11] My own thesis is a comparative study of Scottish and North Norwegian witchcraft trials.

A number of scientific and popular articles provide additional knowledge to the field. The gender perspective of the Scottish witch-hunt has been dealt with in articles by Christina Larner and Julian Goodare.[12]

British Studies, xx (1980), 90–108 and 'Judicial Torture in Scotland during the Age of Mackenzie', *Miscellany* IV, SS, il (2002), 185–98.

[5] Maxwell-Stuart, P. G., *Satan's Conspiracy: Magic and Witchcraft in Sixteenth-Century Scotland* (East Linton, 2001).

[6] The SSW team consisted of Julian Goodare, Lauren Martin, Joyce Miller and Louise Yeoman.

[7] Edited by J. Goodare.

[8] Edited by J. Goodare, L. Martin and J. Miller (Hampshire, 2008).

[9] J. Goodare (ed.), *Scottish witches and witch-hunters* (Basingstoke, 2013, forthcoming).

[10] Goodare, J., 'The cult of the seely wights in Scotland', *Folklore*, 123 (2012); Goodare, J., 'Flying witches in Scotland', in Goodare (ed.), *Scottish witches and witch-hunters*.

[11] Henderson, L., *Supernatural Traditions and Folk Beliefs in an Age of Transition: Witchcraft and Charming in Scotland, c. 1670–1740* (University of Strathclyde, Ph.D. thesis, 2004); Miller, J., *Cantrips and Carlins: Magic, Medicine and Sociey in the Presbyteries of Haddington and Stirling, 1600–1688* (University of Stirling, Ph.D. thesis, 1999); Hall, A., *The Meaning of Elf, and Elves, in Medieval England* (University of Glasgow, Ph.D. thesis, 2005).

[12] Goodare, J., 'Women and the witch-hunt in Scotland', *Social History*, xxiii (1998), 288–307; Goodare, J., 'Men and the witch-hunt in Scotland', in Alison Rowlands (ed.), *Witchcraft and Masculinities in Early Modern Europe* (Basingstoke, 2009), 148–70; Larner, C., 'Was witch-hunting woman-hunting?', *New Society*, (8. Oct. 1981), 11–13.

Studies from separate parts of Scotland have contributed to knowledge of the witch-hunt. Stuart Macdonald and Julian Goodare have studied the witches of Fife and Aberdeen respectively, and P. G. Maxwell-Stuart the North Berwick witches.[13] Maxwell-Stuart and Levack have both studied the witch-hunt of 1661–62.[14] Anna Cordey's thesis about the witch-hunt in Dalkeith is a valuable contribution to studies of a local witch-hunt.[15] The literature mentioned above provide a variety of interpretations and bring interesting perspectives into the research field.

Sources

My analyses of Scottish cases are mainly based on primary witchcraft documents kept in the National Archives of Scotland, Edinburgh. Most of the Scottish sources consist of court records from central, mixed central-local and local trials, in addition to kirk session and presbytery minutes. The sources from the Scottish witchcraft trials vary greatly in length and quality. Relatively few complete trial records have survived. However, dittays (endictments) are often found. These notes record the confessions by suspects and statements by neighbours before the formal trial took place, often as a result of interrogation before a kirk session or presbytery.

The Witchcraft Trials: Frequency, Gender, Panics

The information presented in this chapter is based on findings in my doctoral thesis, where quantitative methods were used to analyse central issues related to witchcraft trials in Scotland. The analyses are performed on three levels. Firstly, frequencies are analyzed. Secondly, bivariant combinations of variables have been tested. Thirdly, cause and effect relations have been discussed.

The categories analyzed statistically are gender, ethnicity, frequency of witchcraft cases, panic versus non-panic periods, types of trial, verdicts and sentences, torture, the demonological element, neighbourhood

---

[13] Macdonald, S., *The witches of Fife. Witch-hunting in a Scottish Shire, 1560–1710* (East Linton, 2002); Maxwell-Stuart, *Satan's Conspiracy*; Goodare, J., 'The Scottish witchcraft panic of 1597', in Goodare, *The Scottish witch-hunt in context*, 51–72.

[14] Maxwell-Stuart, P. G., *An abundance of witches. The Great Scottish Witch-hunt* (Gloucestershire, 2005).

[15] Cordey, A. L., *Witch-hunting in the Presbytery of Dalkeith, 1649 to 1662* (University of Edinburgh, M. Sc., 2003).

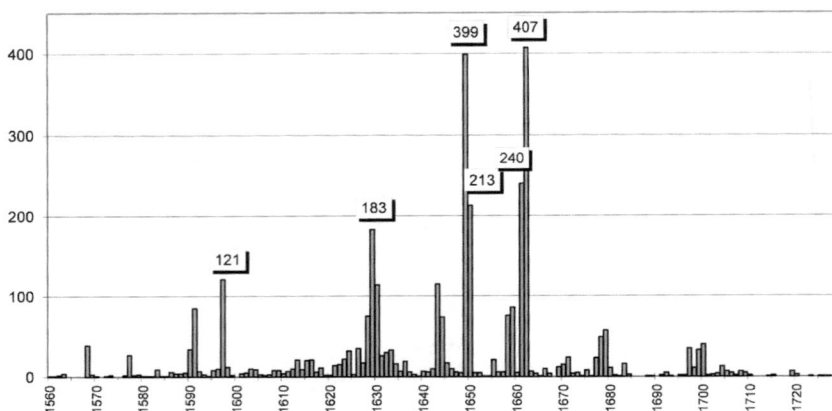

Chart 1: Witchcraft trials by year Mainland Scotland 1561–1727 (SSW).

disputes and fairy belief.[16] Gender is an aspect of the witchcraft trials which is highlighted throughout the study. Information about ethnic conditions will relate to cultural encounters and belief systems. The frequency of witchcraft cases relates to the implementation of trials by the judiciary apparatus, including variations seen in the course of panic years as well as non-panic years. Various analyses are related to types of trial—whether the case is brought before a first or a second instance court, and the consequences of this. Analyses of verdict, sentence and torture will give information about the severity of the hunt. The demonological element will be seen as an ideological factor underlying denunciations and explosive panic periods. Neighbourhood disputes were often the first steps on the road to a witchcraft accusation and should be considered among the causes influencing the hunts. Folk belief, particularly the belief in fairies, might contribute—by means of content or on structural grounds—to the reception and sustenance of demonological ideas in a community. In total the factual findings in this chapter will complement the qualitative analyses carried out in later chapters and give important information to be used during the comparison.

The number of persons accused of witchcraft in relation to the population makes Scotland to stand out as an area of Europe which suffered severe witchcraft persecution. Frequency of cases for the period 1561–1727

---

[16] Willumsen, *Seventeenth-Century Witchcraft Trials*, 34–90.

is shown in the chart above. In Scotland, a total of 3219 persons were accused of witchcraft during the period 1561–1727.[17] Of these, Mainland Scotland had 3120 cases, Orkney had 68 cases, and Shetland 31 cases.

Since gender is a central aspect of several questions posed in relation to witchcraft trials, I find it appropriate to let gender be a recurrent theme for discussion throughout the thesis. I will first present some facts about distribution of gender in Scottish witchcraft trials, and relate the findings to the European average. Women as well as men were accused of being witches during the European witch-hunt. Women were clearly in majority among the accused in most European countries, as pointed out by several scholars.[18] There seems to be consensus among scholars that between 75% and 85% of persons accused of witchcraft were women.[19] Particularly high percentages of women tend to coincide with intensive witch-hunt in a region, a fact that is underlined by the broad range of articles covering European witchcraft in Golden's *Encyclopaedia of Witchcraft*. However, it is also important to point out, perhaps surprisingly for many, that also men were accused of witchcraft.[20] They were accused on the same grounds as women. In some regions, less than 50% of those accused of witchcraft were women. Interest in male witches has risen in recent years and studies related to this theme have appeared.[21] For Mainland Scotland, 83.9% women, 14.5% men, and 1.4% with unknown gender were prosecuted.[22]

A characteristic feature of European witchcraft trials is the considerable fluctuations in the annual rate of prosecutions. A substantial number of witchcraft trials in Scotland occurred in concentrated periods. Christina Larner says: 'There were lulls in which there were almost no cases, there were periods in which there was a regular small supply, and there were

---

[17] SSW, www.arts.ed.ac.uk/witches (archived January 2003, accessed February 2007).
[18] Wiesner-Hanks, M., 'Gender' in Golden, *Encyclopedia*, 4 vols., ii, 407; Golden, R. M., 'Satan in Europe: The Geography of Witch Hunts', in B. P. Levack (ed.), *New Perspectives on Witchcraft, Magic and Demonology*, 6 vols., ii: *Witchcraft in Continental Europe* (New York, 2001), 21.
[19] Wiesner-Hanks, 'Gender', 407; Levack, *The Witch-Hunt in Early Modern Europe*, 141.
[20] Levack, *The Witch-Hunt in Early Modern Europe*, 141.
[21] Estonia, Russia, Normandy and Iceland were such areas. Ref. Levack, *The Witch-Hunt in Early Modern Europe*, 142; Rafnsson, M., *The Witch-hunts in Iceland* (Hólmavik, 2003). Apps, L. and Gow, A., *Male Witches in Early Modern Europe* (Manchester, 2003); A. Rowlands, (ed.), *Witchcraft and Masculinities in Early Modern Europe*; Schulte, *Man as Witch*.
[22] Willumsen, *Seventeenth-Century Witchcraft Trials*, 37.

five peaks of intensive prosecution'.[23] The word 'panic' has, within scholarly witchcraft research, been used to denote intensive witch-hunting in
defined periods. Even if the word in ordinary usage often has connotations
to a state of mind, it is appropriate to use about a concentrated number
of linked witchcraft trials. Hence I follow Larner's usage and understand
the term 'panic' as accused persons 'tried in groups during epidemics of
witch-hunting'.[24]

There has been broad consensus, but not total agreement, among
scholars about which periods in the Scottish material should be defined
as panic periods. J. K. Swales and Hugh V. McLachlan make a distinction between panic periods and non-panic periods.[25] They conclude with
1628–30, 1649–50, 1658–59, and 1661–62 as 'panic' periods. Larner operates
with five peaks of intensive prosecution: 1590–91, 1597, 1629–30, 1649, and
1661–62.[26] Julian Goodare mentions five great witchcraft panics.[27] Stuart
MacDonald operates with six peaks; in addition to those mentioned by
Larner he adds 1658–9.[28] The SSW 'Introduction' operates with the same
years as Larner, with an addition of 1628. For the Scottish material, I define
a panic as more than 70 cases per year. As obviously a panic also reflects
a certain state of mental alertness, I include years with less than 70 cases
per year with a high frequency of cases if they immediately precede or
follow the undisputed panic year.[29] According to this definition, there are
seven peaks.[30] The large witchcraft panics, as defined by me, took place in
1590–91, 1597, 1628–30, 1643–44, 1649–50, 1658–59, and 1661–62. The panic
1643–44 is not included in earlier studies.

In this section, the panics will be analyzed with respect to gender,
and to execution. The present study expands the study of Swales and
McLachlan in two directions. Firstly, by researching the combination of
gender, execution and panics. Secondly by using the more complete SSW
database, compared with *The Source-Book of Scottish Witchcraft*, which

---

[23] Larner, *Enemies of God*, 60.
[24] Larner, *Enemies of God*, 17.
[25] Swales, J. F. and McLachlan, H. V., 'Witchcraft and the status of women: a comment',
British Journal of Sociology, vol. xxx, no. 3 (1979) 349–58.
[26] Larner, *Enemies of God*, 60.
[27] Goodare, 'Witch-hunting and the Scottish state', 122.
[28] Macdonald, *The Witches of Fife*, 19.
[29] This has relevance for the year 1590.
[30] See e.g. SSW 'Introduction to Scottish Witchcraft'; Martin, L., 'Scottish Witchcraft
Panics', in Goodare et al. (eds.), *Witchcraft and Belief*, 119.

Swales and McLachlan used. I would like to pose the following questions: Are peak periods (panics) just a scaled-up version of the normal occurrence of witchcraft trials of the period? This means, do the peak periods have the same percentage of variables studied as the periods in between the peaks, for instance the percentage of men, the percentage of executions, the same relative distribution of elements. In short: Is there anything qualitatively different in panic periods compared to non-panic periods? The bulk of Scottish witchcraft trials took place in panic years, which in total covered only 14 years. 66% of the accused were tried during panic periods, while 34% of the accused were tried during non-panic periods.[31] In panic periods there were on average 151 cases annually, against about seven cases annually in non-panic years. The majority of witchcraft trials took place during a few years where panics occurred. This is a marked feature of the witch-hunt.

Did panics affect the gender composition? The relative frequency of women in panic years is 85.8% and in non-panic years 80.6%.[32] These figures show that there was a slight weighting towards women in panic years. A more detailed test indicates that there is a significant difference of frequency between panic and non-panic periods for female accused. Women were more exposed to witchcraft accusations than men in panic years.[33]

We also have to consider the consequences of being tried. Was the frequency of executions higher in panic years versus non-panic years? The analyses show that the sentences during non-panic periods were more lenient than those passed during panic years.[34] The frequency of executions was generally higher in panic years versus non-panic years, so that panic periods were more dangerous than non-panic periods for all those accused of witchcraft. It must be emphasized that in the Scottish source material the known figures for verdicts and sentences are low compared to the number of individuals accused of witchcraft.[35] A detailed test confirms a relative over-frequency of execution in panic years compared to non-panic years.[36]

---

[31] Willumsen, *Seventeenth-Century Witchcraft Trials*, 41.
[32] Willumsen, *Seventeenth-Century Witchcraft Trials*, 41.
[33] Chi-square 11.076.
[34] Willumsen, *Seventeenth-Century Witchcraft Trials*, 41.
[35] Martin and Miller, 'Some Findings from the Survey of Scottish Witchcraft', in Goodare et al., *Witchcraft and Belief*, 51–70, at p. 53.
[36] Chi-square 37.078.

I will next look at gender and panics and focus on the frequency of sentences of execution in panic years for women versus men. My hypothesis is that women were more exposed than men to execution during panic years due to confessions based on demonology, which were considered very seriously by the judiciary. When examining the group of women executed in panic versus non-panic periods, this assumption is confirmed. Women who were brought to trial were more frequently executed in panic years than in non-panic years, and the result is highly significant.[37] For men, the analyses show that they were slightly more exposed to execution in panic years than in non-panic years.

It has been possible to reveal the gender bias and the vulnerability of women during panics. My results show that there was a significantly higher frequency of women accused during panic years than during non-panic years.[38] The proportion of accused individuals in witchcraft trials who were sentenced to execution was much higher in panic years than in non-panic years.[39] As for the gender difference related to executions during panic versus non-panic years, my findings are that in panic years the relative proportion of women being sentenced to execution was much higher than in non-panic years. For men, the proportion of those sentenced to execution was slightly higher than expected in panic years compared to non-panic years. If someone was accused of witchcraft during a panic period, the chance was high that this person was a woman and the risk of being burned was also very high. This question has not been examined previously.

Ethnicity

The question of ethnicity related to Scottish witchcraft trials has to do with the two ethnic groups living together in the country, the Lowlanders and the Highlanders. There are different opinions among witchcraft researchers whether the Highlands has been exposed to severe witch-hunt, like the Lowlands. Scholars like Christina Larner, Robin Briggs and Ronald Hutton maintain that there were either none or very few witchcraft trials in the

---

[37] Chi-square 33.309.
[38] These findings support Swales and McLachlan's conclusion. Ref. Swales and McLachlan, 'Witchcraft and the status of women', 353.
[39] This is the same as Swales and McLachlan's findings. Ref. Swales and McLachlan, 'Witchcraft and the status of women', 352.

Highlands.[40] On the contrary, Stuart Macdonald, Lizanne Henderson and Laureen Martin argue that there in fact was witchcraft persecution also in the Highlands.[41] I would here like to look at the question of ethnicity on the basis of the registrations made in SSW.

First some comments on the region called the Highlands: Defining the borders of the Highlands is not easy. The Highlands is a historic region of Scotland. It was culturally distinguishable from the Lowlands from the later Middle Ages into the modern period, when Lowland Scots replaced Scottish Gaelic throughout most of the Lowlands. The Highlands has been used as a term to define the areas where Gaelic language and clan system survived into the early modern period. In geographical terms the Highlands has been used for the area north and west of the Highland Boundary Fault, although exact boundaries are not defined. The Highland Boundary Fault is a geological fault that traverses Scotland from Aran and Helensburgh on the west coast to Stonehaven in the east. It separates two distinctly different physiographic regions, the Highlands and the Lowlands.

The SSW has only 13 registrations of cases wherein persons with Gaelic ethnic origin were accused of witchcraft. These 13 cases refer to 10 persons. In this group there were seven women, two men and one person of unknown sex. Four persons have age reported; one man 40 years old, one woman 65 years old, and one woman 100 years old. The only cases of this group of Gaelic origin registered as having taken place in the Highlands are one case from Ross in 1630 and one case from Argyll in 1680. The rest were living in Edinburgh, Aberdeen, Haddington, Kinross, Perth, and Renfrew, which means in the eastern parts of the Lowlands. The trials took place from 1591 until 1697. The first one, Marion Ersche, a weaver's wife, was involved in the North Berwick trials of 1591. It was claimed that she participated in trying to sink the royal ships. Her case started in 1591 and ended in 1608. She was found guilty and executed. Then there were two women of Gaelic origin involved in the Aberdeen trials of 1597, Marioun Wod and Elspett Moines. Wod was referred to as the 'Catnes norische'; a nurse coming from Caithness. The Highland case in 1630 was against Dod Moir, living in Ross, There were three persons of Gaelic origin accused

---

[40] Larner, *Enemies of God*, 81; Briggs, *Witches and Neighbours*, p. xi; Hutton, R., 'Witch-Hunting in Celtic Societies', *Past and Present*, no. 212, (1012), 43–71, at pp. 43–50.

[41] Macdonald, *The Witches of Fife*, 22–23; Henderson, L., 'Witch Hunting and Witch Belief in the Gàidhealtachd', in Goodare et al. (eds.), *Witchcraft and Belief*, 95–118; Martin, L., 'Scottish Witchcraft Panics Re-Examined', in Goodare et al., (eds.), *Witchcraft and Belief*, 119–143, at pp. 127–129.

in 1643, which was a panic year in mainland Scotland.[42] These were two women, MacNiven and Neane MacClerik,[43] and one man, John McIlvorie, living in the regions of Kinross and Perth, north of the Firth of Forth. Neane MacClerik confessed to practizing healing humans and animals. She was a widow, a sister daughter to Nik Neveing, known as the famous witch of Monaie. The last two Highland cases against persons of Gaelic origin were one in Argyll in 1680, against Issobel McClartich, and one in Renfrew in 1697, against Angus Forrester, called the 'Heiland body'.

We see that most of these trials are before 1650. There is one sentence of execution among these persons, Marion Ersche mentioned above, tried in Haddington in 1608. The trials against persons of Gaelic origin are not characterized as demonic in SSW, nor is any Devil worship registered. In one case, practising healing humans and animals was mentioned. This documentation shows that persons of Gaelic origin were tried in witchcraft cases, early as well as late during the period of witch-hunt. Most of them were living outside the borders of the Highlands. They did not confess to demonological witchcraft, and only in one case to benevolent magic, which means they were accused of malefice. There is no midwifery registered.

However, there probably is an under-registration of persons of Gaelic origin in the SSW.[44] Therefore one has to look for other indications to find the number of Highlanders accused during the witch-hunt, for instance place of residence. Several persons accused of witchcraft were living in areas defined as the Highlands, even if they are not registered to be of Gaelic origin. As pointed out by Stuart Macdonald, there were in fact trials in the Highlands. Even if these were not numerous, the same was the case for many Lowland counties.[45] Lauren Martin maintains that the percentage of cases per head of population in fact was higher in what she called the Highland region than elsewhere.[46] In the opposite direction, Hutton argues that the Scottish Gales were reluctant to try witches in the north and west, and concludes that almost 'a third of Scotland being the

---

[42] Willumsen, *Seventeenth-Century Witchcraft Trials*, 39.

[43] Original spelling surnames: NikNeveir and Vcclerick.

[44] For instance are persons accused in Bute and clearly reported to be speaking Gaelic, not entered in SSW as persons of Gaelic origin.

[45] Macdonald, S., *The Witches of Fife*, 22–23.

[46] The Highland Region is defined by Martin according to the SSW as Cromarty, Inverness, Nairn, Ross, and Sutherland. Ref. Martin, 'Scottish Witchcraft Panics Re-Examined', 125.

core of its Gaelic region, barely participated in witch-hunting during a period in which it was severe in Scotland as a whole'.[47] A different approach is taken by Lizanne Henderson. She argues for a cultural rather than a regional definition of the Highlands. This, she maintains, 'allows for the incorporation of evidence of Highland witch belief turning up in non-Highland contexts'.[48] My findings absolutely support this argument, as many of those persons referred to as of Gaelic origin had moved to the Lowlands. Some of the persons of Gaelic origin were tried during panic years, where the atmosphere over large areas was heated and therefore many persons came in the searchlight for witchcraft.[49]

The viewpoints above are interesting, not only because they interpret the cultural encounter between the Scots and the Highlanders in basic different ways. The participants in this discussion also place the geographical region of the Highlands within various frames, hence making it possible to operate with many or few regions hit by the witch-hunt. As my analyses are based on information from the SSW, my conclusion with regard to occurrence of persons with Gaelic ethnic origin accused in witchcraft trials, is this: The SSW gives enough information about persons of Gaelic origin and Highlanders accused of witchcraft to maintain that in fact such a persecution took place. The extent of this persecution is difficult to state, mainly because documentation is missing. However, the bulk of Scottish witchcraft persecution clearly took part in the southwest; the Lothian, Fife and East Border region. The subsequent questions, namely whether or why these regions of Scotland were reluctant to try witches, will be discussed in the final comparative chapter, related to the discussion of folk belief.

Types of Witchcraft Trials

This section will focus on the connection between type of court and the result of a witchcraft trial. The SSW contains very good information about the type of court wherein witchcraft trials were held. Quantitative analyses will illuminate the issues of gender and relative frequency of type

---

[47] Thus Hutton gives support to Larner and Briggs. Ref. Hutton, 'Witch-Hunting in Celtic Societies', 49.
[48] Henderson, 'Witch Hunting and Witch Belief in the Gàidhealtachd', 97.
[49] This point is also made by Henderson. Ref. Henderson, 'Witch Hunting and Witch Belief in the Gàidhealtachd', 105.

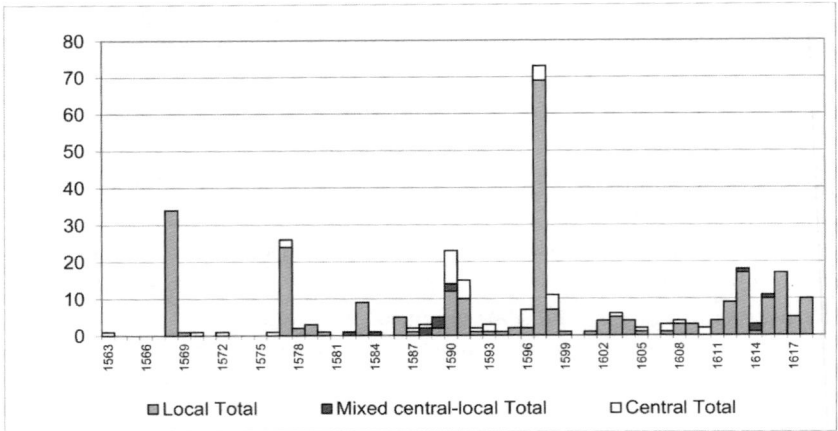

Chart 2: Accused persons and types of trial, Scotland, 1563–1619 (SSW).

of trials over time. Three types of trial existed: central, local and mixed central-local trials. Mixed central-local trials comprise circuit courts and local trials with central representatives.[50] Circuit courts, which the authorities had attempted to use occasionally in the sixteenth and seventeenth centuries, began to function in a more regular fashion after 1671 and resulted in far more acquittals than those in which local commissioners acted as judges.[51] For the witchcraft persecution as a whole, an absolute majority of the trials, 80.4%, were held in local courts.

The next point to be examined is the total distribution of women and men in the material as a whole seen in relation to the total distribution between the three types of trial. The distribution between women and men in the three types of trial is not what one could expect. During the entire period of Scottish witch-hunt, women are over-represented in local trials. Men are over-represented in central and mixed central-local trials.[52] The difference between these three types of trial is significant for gender. A woman had a higher probability of being tried in a local court than a man. Types of trial affect gender composition.

To capture the observation that the relative frequency of types of trial changes over time, the period of witch-hunting is divided into three

---

[50] Willumsen, *Seventeenth-Century Witchcraft Trials*, 45.
[51] Levack, *Witch-hunting in Scotland*, 137.
[52] Willumsen, *Seventeenth-Century Witchcraft Trials*, 46.

periods of about equal length. Each period is represented below in a separate chart. Note that the scales on the vertical axis of the charts are different for the three periods.

For the period 1563–1619, both central, local and mixed central-local trials are represented. Local trials clearly dominate this period. There were a few mixed central-local trials in 1582, 1584, 1588, 1589 and 1590. These may have to do with attempts made by the government to revive the old Scottish system of justice ayres, that is, judges periodically travelling through the country to try persons accused of various crimes. This system, where judges from central court were active in the local districts, was used, for example, in an early witch-hunt in 1568–69.[53] A serious attempt to revive this system was made by James VI in 1587.[54] However, the central criminal court could not handle the burden of both a substantial number of cases in Edinburgh and a circuit of the shires: 'The old system of justice ayres gave way, therefore, to the occasional appointment of justice deputes to particular areas and the granting of conciliar commissions to local magistrates from either the privy council or parliament, during whose sessions the privy council did not sit'.[55] This is the reason why local trials, held by judicial commissions issued to local magistrates and other elite figures were the prevailing type of trial throughout the period of Scottish witch-hunt until 1662, with some exceptions for the years 1655–1661, as will be seen below. Requests from local authorities to have witches tried were responded to by the central government. In most cases local authorities got permission to try the suspected witches in their own local court by a commission of justiciary appointed by the Privy Council, a fact clearly demonstrated in Chart 2.[56] During the period 1563–1610 there were a few central trials, most of them in 1590–91. The North Berwick witches of 1590–91 were tried in the Justiciary Court in Edinburgh, which accounts for the central trials these years.[57] However, Chart 2 does not catch all cases during the panic years of 1590–91 because trial type to a large extent is unknown for those years.[58]

[53] Goodare, 'Witch-hunting and the Scottish state', 126.
[54] Levack, *Witch-hunting in Scotland*, 27.
[55] Levack, *Witch-hunting in Scotland*, 28.
[56] Levack, *Witch-hunting in Scotland*, 135.
[57] Goodare, 'The framework for Scottish witch-hunting', 240–41.
[58] According to SSW.

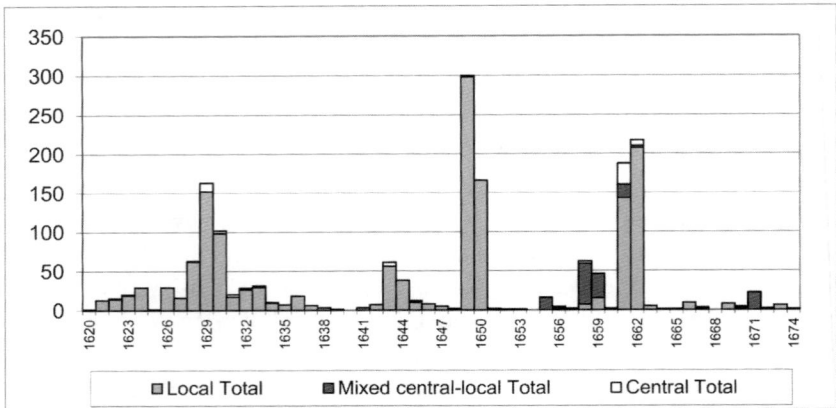

Chart 3: Accused persons and types of trial, Scotland, 1620–1674 (SSW).

Chart 3 above documents types of trial from 1620 until 1662, the middle period of the Scottish witch-hunt. Also for this period the majority of trials were local trials. Most of these trials were authorised by commissions of justiciary: 'During the 1620s and the 1630s the Privy Council had authorised more than 85 percent of all witchcraft prosecutions by granting commissions to local authorities to conduct the trials by themselves'.[59] Appointments of commissions to try witches in local courts were dependant upon a well-functioning Privy Council. Political events during the years around 1640 led to a situation in Scotland in which the Privy Council was weakened.[60] The revolutionary legislation of 1641 deprived the king and the Privy Council of much of their power and transferred it to the Scottish parliament. Due to this there was a strong reduction in the percentage of witchcraft trials by commissions of justiciary during the 1640s. However, in 1643–44 and 1649–50 the Privy Council and parliament supported the prosecution of a number of moral crimes, including adultery and witchcraft, in such a way that local pressure was intensified. It is to be noted that parliament itself, which emerged in 1649–50, and again in 1661, issued

---

[59] Levack, *Witch-hunting in Scotland*, 59.

[60] These events were the Bishops' Wars of 1639 and 1640, the first civil war, 1640, and the parliaments summoned in 1640. Also the signing of the Solemn League and Covenant, 1643, the capture of the king, 1646, the second civil war, 1648, the execution of the king, abolition of the monarchy and establishment of a republic in 1649 contributed to weaken the vigour of the central Scottish authorities.

many commissions for trying witches.[61] The Privy Council continued to operate, at least nominally, from the 1630s until 1651, but from 1638 onwards there were several periods in which its functions were largely taken over by the committee of estates or parliament. The Cromwellian occupation abolished the Privy Council in 1652. It was restored with the monarchy in 1660, and abolished again in 1708. However, The Privy Council's practice of granting commissions of justiciary to try witches did not manage to meet the demand from local authorities in the 1640s. This can be seen in a request for a standing commission to try witches in East Lothian, sent to the Privy Council in 1649.[62] However, this request was not assented to.

The period illustrated in Chart 3 above includes the panics of 1628–30, 1643–44, 1649–50, 1658–59 and 1661–62, i.e. the bulk of witchcraft trials in Scotland. Several of these panics coincided with dramatic political events, mentioned in chapter 2, by Levack called 'critical junctions'; the panic starting in 1649, the year when Charles I was executed; the panic of 1658–59, the last years of the protectorate, and the last panic, 1661–62, took place shortly after the Restoration of 1660 had ended.[63]

The witch-hunt entered a different phase after 1650, as illustrated in Chart 3 above. There was a sudden reduction of total trials and an increased use of mixed central-local trials. Mixed central-local trials took place in 1655, 1658, 1659 and 1671, with the numbers 16, 52, 31 and 22 respectively for these years, also seen from Chart 3. It had been difficult to make the system of circuit courts function effectively, but during the Cromwellian occupation of the 1650s these courts operated as intended, an increase clearly noted from Chart 3 above. In addition, it should be noted that in 1671 indeed all trials were mixed central-local. An explanation for this particular year might be that a system for holding regular circuit courts was established after 1671.[64] In contrast to the local trials, which dominate the former part of the period 1620–74, the mixed central-local trials towards the end of this period are not characterized by denunciation of other suspects.[65] The cumulative concept of witchcraft, where confessions naming other accomplices were frequent, had reduced influence after 1662. Thus

---

[61] Hughes, P., 'Witch-Hunting in Scotland', ch. 5 in Goodare (ed.), *Scottish Witches and Witch-Hunters*; Goodare, 'Witch-hunting and the Scottish state', 135.
[62] Levack, *Witch-hunting in Scotland*, 60.
[63] Levack, *Witch-hunting in Scotland*, 135.
[64] Levack, *Witch-hunting in Scotland*, 137.
[65] For instance in 1671 only one accused, Geilles Burnett, Aberdeen, was named by another. Ref. Willumsen, *Seventeenth-Century Witchcraft Trials*, 49.

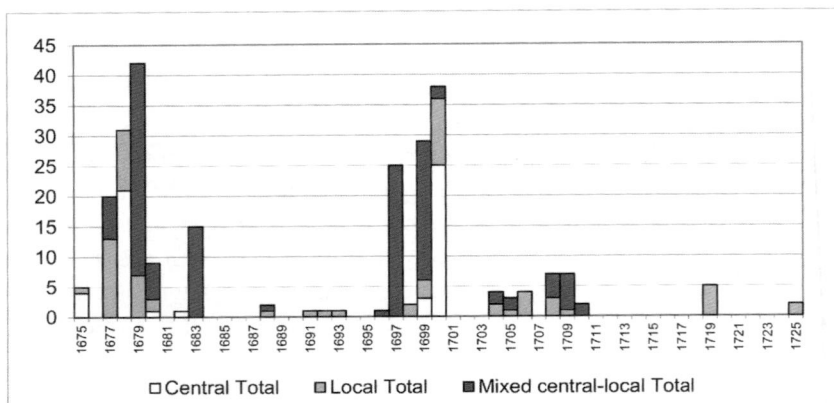

Chart 4: Accused persons and types of trial, Scotland, 1675–1725 (SSW).

the numbers of accused were kept at a low level towards the end of the period in question and we do not see any more of the sudden increase in trials characterizing panics.

Central trials were few in number during the period 1620–1674, as Chart 3 illustrates. There was a shift away from central jurisdiction, elucidated by the decline in the number of cases during the mid-century decades held in the Court of Justiciary in Edinburgh. Only 47 cases out of more than 500 dealing with preliminary investigations for witchcraft reached this court during the period 1641–50.[66] The acquittal percentage in the central court was probably higher than in local courts. We know that eight of the 47 tried were executed; the fate of the rest we do not know.[67]

Chart 4, representing the period 1675–1725, presents a sharp change in proportion of the three types of trial compared to previous years. A broader effort by the Scottish government to keep up standards of judicial proof, to reduce judicial torture and to supervise trials, led to a reduction in trials as well as a reduction in convictions and executions. According to Privy Council's order of April 1662 all trials, especially those of witchcraft,

---

[66] Levack, *Witch-hunting in Scotland*, 59.
[67] Most of the accused came from the Lothians. Even if the judiciary court had jurisdiction over the whole of Scotland, the cost of bringing accused and witnesses to Edinburgh for trial had as its result that the accused persons living in the areas around Edinburgh, Lothians, were most likely to be brought before the central criminal court, see Martin, 'Scottish Witchcraft Panics', 124–5; Levack, *Witch-hunting in Scotland*, 59.

should be conducted by properly constituted authority.[68] What happened in 1662 was that the Lord Advocate and the judges of the Justiciary Court managed to impose effective checks on local witch-hunting by reducing the number of commissions of justiciary issued and instead funnelling local cases into the central court. The same ruling elite that activated the witchcraft machinery, ended it in the spring of 1662 'by acquitting a number of suspects, curtailing powers of arrest and torture, imprisoning two witch-prickers, and simply declining to authorise further trials'.[69] As a result of these steps taken by the central authorities to take control of the witch-hunt, there was a marked decrease in number of witchcraft trials.

Closer supervision by the central authorities from 1662 onwards is seen by an increase in central trials and mixed central-local trials.[70] The successful implementation of the circuit court system continued during this last phase of the Scottish witch-hunt. The number of acquittals in these courts was high and the number of executions very low, resulting in only two individuals executed by circuit courts during the period 1671–1709.[71] The Privy Council also took a tighter grip on the trials conducted by commissions of justiciary by claiming that a justice depute from Edinburgh should be included among the commissioners. Thus a central representative was present during the trial and ensured that strict legal standards were followed.

As Chart 4 shows, local trials were not totally absent during the period 1675–1725, but they constituted a minority for most years, with the exception of 1677, where there were thirteen local trials and seven mixed central-local trials. For most years, the number of local trials was fewer than ten. After 1700 the number of local trials was not more than five per year.

To summarize the analyses of types of trial: The proportion between the different types of trial changed over time. There was a clear tendency in direction of local trials, which strongly dominated the first two-thirds of the period of Scottish witch-hunt, to be replaced by central and mixed central-local trials in the last about fifty years. After 1655, and in particular after 1670, there was an increase in mixed central-local trials which was undoubtedly related to successful re-implementation of the circuit court system.[72] The change in the relative proportion of types of trial over

[68] Levack, *Witch-hunting in Scotland*, 137.
[69] Goodare, 'Witch-hunting and the Scottish state', 142.
[70] Willumsen, *Seventeenth-Century Witchcraft Trials*, 68.
[71] Levack, *Witch-hunting in Scotland*, 137.
[72] Levack, *Witch-hunting in Scotland*, 137.

time indicates that stronger control from central judicial authorities contributed to the decline and subsequent end of witchcraft persecution in
Scotland.

Questions related to women and panics might throw light on why
women were in majority among the accused and the executed in witchcraft trials. As already established above, accused women tended to
receive a harsher treatment in panic years versus non-panic years. Does a
certain type of trial dominate when women are accused in panic periods?
A comparison of accusations and sentences of women in panic years versus non-panic years demonstrates that women were tried more frequently
in local trials than in central trials in panic years. In central and mixed
central-local trials we see that there were more women tried in non-panic
years than in panic years. Of central trials, 58 out of 139 were in panic
years, which is 42%. Of mixed central-local trials, 98 out of 240 were in
panic years, which is 41%.[73] In local trials, however, we see that 71% were
tried in panic years. The correlation between local trials and panic years
for women is significant.[74] This means that there was a higher likelihood
of a woman accused of witchcraft being tried in a local trial during panic
years than during non-panic years.

For men accused in central trials, relative frequencies are approximately
the same for panic versus non-panic periods. So here we see a different
treatment of men compared to women. With regard to mixed central-
local trials, for men there are ten trials out of 52 in panic periods, which
is one-fifth.[75] The tendency is the same for men as for women related to
mixed central-local trials; most were in non-panic periods. However, the
tendency is stronger for men than for women. When looking at local trials, the tendency is the same for men as for women.[76]

To sum up the findings of the analyses of gender and type of trial
throughout the period of witch-hunt: the over-representation of women
in local trials in panic years is significant. Men are also over-represented
in local trials in panic years.[77] But the clearest result is that for men there
are very few occurrences of mixed central-local trials in panic years. It

---

[73] Willumsen, *Seventeenth-Century Witchcraft Trials*, 52.
[74] Chi-square 118.340. Ref. Willumsen, *Seventeenth-Century Witchcraft Trials*, 53.
[75] Willumsen, *Seventeenth-Century Witchcraft Trials*, 52.
[76] In local trials there are 158 men in panic periods and 92 men in non-panic periods,
about 63% and 27% respectively. Ref. Willumsen, *Seventeenth-Century Witchcraft Trials*, 52.
[77] Chi-square 34.507. Ref. Willumsen, *Seventeenth-Century Witchcraft Trials*, 53.

should be noted, however, that few men are included in this category. Generalizations may therefore be interpreted with care.[78]

The gender analyses show that panics seem to have had a strong influence on the distribution of trial types. Women and men were treated equally in that for both groups we find a greater number in local trials than expected in panic years. There is relatively little difference between women and men with regard to types of trial in non-panic periods.

The analyses of relative frequency of trial types warrants several interesting conclusions. Firstly, a change in the relative proportion of central, mixed central-local and local trials throughout the witch-hunt over time, is established beyond doubt. Secondly, the changing role of the state most likely explains that the changes in the relative proportions of trial types were linked to amendments in national jurisdiction and politics. Thirdly, panic periods lead to a sudden upsurge of trials in local courts. The analyses relate indirectly to the demonological element by showing the connection between panic periods and local trials. I will argue that witchcraft panics were connected with the demonological element due to the multiplying mechanism inherent in the collective aspect of this doctrine—i.e. pressure from the interrogators during the accused person's confession to obtain the names of accomplices who had taken part in witches' meetings or collective witchcraft operations. Such a denunciation resulted in many new suspects, who were interrogated in turn. Fourthly, the analyses show that women were treated differently from men in panic years.

I will return to the influence of the demonological element during various periods throughout the witch-hunt and argue that this element contributes to explaining the severity of witchcraft trials in panic periods, measured in number of death sentences out of the total number of accused. Hence the following sections will deal with the execution rate and demonological confessions.

Verdict and Sentence: The European Context

The chance of being accused in witchcraft trials were very unevenly distributed throughout Europe during the period of witchcraft persecution.[79]

---

[78] Willumsen, *Seventeenth-Century Witchcraft Trials*, 53.

[79] Levack, Brian P., *Witchcraft in Continental Europe: Local and Regional Studies* (New York, 1992), ix–x, in *Witchcraft, Magic and Demonology*, B. P. Levack (ed.), vol. 5; Levack, *The Witch-Hunt in Early Modern Europe*, 204.

A glance at the European background is useful when evaluating the witch-hunts in Scotland and Finnmark. Throughout Europe, the witchcraft persecution had certain characteristic features. There was a marked difference between the number of people living in Europe and the number of people accused in witchcraft trials. The scope of accused witches is not overwhelming compared to the population of Europe at the time. However, it is necessary to look more closely at the intensity and severity of the witch-hunt. It becomes clear that for those accused of practising witchcraft in early modern period, this was extremely dangerous.

Exactly how many people were accused and how many were executed during the European witchcraft trials is very difficult to answer. With regard to the geographical scope of the witch-hunt, Richard M. Golden says: 'The English south-east, the German south-west and the northern duchy of Mecklenburg, the lowlands of Scotland, the Basque region in Spain, Switzerland, Lorraine, Franche-Comté, the outlying provinces of France, Dalarna in Sweden, western and central Poland, and the western coast of Finland endured intensive witch hunting'.[80] Here the Scottish Lowlands are included among European areas which suffered severe witchcraft persecution. Some of the figures in Golden's article must be updated due to recent research.[81] Still the main tendency of his estimates is valid.

Golden's estimate is between 40 and 53 thousand executed during the European witchcraft trials.[82] His four-volume *Encyclopedia* reconfirms earlier estimates.[83] Robin Briggs's estimate is that the number of people executed for witchcraft in Europe was somewhere between 40,000 and 50,000, 'figures which allow for a reasonable level of lost documentation'—an estimate very close to Golden's.[84] Marko Nennonen's estimation is fewer than 40,000; Wolfgang Behringer's estimate is 50,000; Rita Voltmer estimates between 50,000 and 60,000, Raisa Maria Toivo between 40,000 and 60,000, and Brian P. Levack approximately 45,000.[85]

[80] Golden, 'Satan in Europe,' 22.

[81] For instance in Golden's article the figure 1337 executed for Scotland relating to a population of 0.8 million, has to be replaced by calculations based on data from SSW. I use 1 million as the population estimate.

[82] Probably research from Eastern Europe will be better known as for instance Golden's encyclopedia has articles on several eastern European countries.

[83] Golden, *Encyclopedia of Witchcraft*.

[84] Briggs, *Witches and Neighbours*, 225.

[85] Nennonen, "Witch Hunts," 165; Behringer, W., *Witches and Witch-Hunts* (Cambridge, 2004), 156; Voltmer, R., "Vom Getrübten Blick auf Frühneuzeitlichen Hexenverfolgungen—

Related to Golden's estimated population for 24 European countries around year 1600, which was between 92 and 95 millions, his total number of executed persons represents about 0.5 per thousand of the population. Information about total accused is missing.[86]

The severity of the European witch-hunt comes clearly to the fore both in Golden's survey mentioned above and in a survey presented by Levack, including 13 different European regions. Levack's list gives the number of people tried, the number of executions for these areas and the percentages of those executed relative to accused in each area, showing a range from 21% executed in Geneva to 90% executed in the Pays de Vaud.[87] Of the 13 regions, five have a percentage of more than 50% executed, three have between 40 and 50% executed and two regions have between 30 and 40% executed among those tried for witchcraft. Among other countries, Scotland and Norway are listed in this survey; Scotland with 307 persons tried and 206 executions and Norway with 730 persons tried, whereof 280 were executed.[88] For Scotland, it is possible to make plausible estimates that suggest higher numbers. For Norway, it must be mentioned that for the Finnmark region, the execution rate is higher than for Norway as a whole, with 67% executed out of 135 tried individuals. The severe witchcraft trials in northern Norway have only recently attracted attention among witchcraft historians internationally due to publications in English.[89] The witch-hunts in Scotland and Finnmark were extreme in a European context both when measured by intensity, number of accused related to the population and by severity, number of persons executed among the accused.

Versuch einer Klärung," *Gnostika. Zeitschrift für Wissenscahft und Esoretik*, no. 11 (2006), 66; Toivo, *Witchcraft and Gender*; Levack, *The Witch-Hunt in Early Modern Europe*, 23.

[86] See 'Geography of the Witch Hunts,' in Golden, *Encyclopedia*, II, 413.

[87] Levack, *The Witch-Hunt in Early Modern Europe*, 23.

[88] Levack, *The Witch-Hunt in Early Modern Europe*, 23; Martin and Miller, 'Some Findings from the Survey of Scottish Witchcraft', 51–70, 56. In this survey, Norway has 38% executed out of 730 persons tried (fates known). In studies of Norwegian witchcraft trials, Hans Eyvind Næss, *Trolldomsprosessene i Norge på 1500–1600-tallet*, has calculated that 280 were executed out of 863 accused, which results in 32%. Rune Hagen, *Dei europeiske hekseprosessane* (Oslo, 2007) has calculated that 301 were executed of 768 accused, which results in 39%.

[89] Næss, H. E., 'Norway' in Golden, *Encyclopedia*, 4 vols., iii, 838; Levack, 'Themes of Recent Witchcraft Research', 7–32; Willumsen, L. H., 'Witch in the North', *Scandinavian Journal of History*, vol. xxii, no. 3 (1997), 199–221 and 'Witches in Scotland and Northern Norway: Two Case Studies', in A. Kruse and P. Graves (eds.), *Images and Imaginations: perspectives on Britain and Scandinavia* (Edinburgh, 2007), 35–66.

Verdicts and Executions in Scotland

In this section, I will present analyses of the verdicts in relation to trial types, then I will present an estimate of executions in Scotland and, finally, I will present an analysis of non-capital sentences passed. The verdict is defined in SSW as 'the final ruling on whether or not the accused witch was guilty of the crime of witchcraft (as opposed to the individual indictments made against her or him)'.[90] Only 299 verdicts have been registered. The relatively small figure indicates, as in the case of sentences and executions, that considerable information from the trials is missing. In the 299 cases for which the verdict is known, 236 were judged guilty, 45 not guilty, 11 not proven and 7 half guilty. 78 verdicts were given in mixed central-local courts. These verdicts can be split further into verdicts given in circuit courts and those given in non-circuit courts. In mixed central-local non-circuit courts the ratio of 'guilty' and 'not guilty' verdicts is 3:1. In the circuit courts the ratio of 'guilty' versus 'not guilty' is about 2:1. If we consider all the trials, there are 212 'guilty' verdicts in non-circuit trials and 34 verdicts of 'not guilty'. The ratio of guilty to not guilty is then about 6:1. It is obvious that there is less occurrence of the 'guilty' verdict in circuit court trials than in non-circuit courts. From the sample of known verdicts, the chance of being judged 'guilty' in a non-circuit court was about three times as high as in a circuit court, a fact which will be discussed in greater detail below.

The following questions will be discussed in the following: What were the execution rates in Scottish trials, i.e. how can we extrapolate from the few known sentences in order to find out how many witches were executed in Scotland? Having established a valid estimate of executions in Scotland, how does that number relate to the population of Scotland? And finally: How does the 'execution per capita of population' relate to the overall European average, or to other specific European countries?

The intensity and severity of witchcraft trials in Scotland will be illuminated by analyses in relation to types of trial and in relation to panic years. There already exist several estimates for those executed in Scotland. Christina Larner suggests 1,337 executions. Out of 2,208 accused persons, the estimated proportion of those executed is 60.6%.[91] The 'Introduction

---

[90] DDD, SSW, 41.

[91] Larner operates with a possible error of 300 either way. She gives no indication how this error margin is calculated. Ref. Larner, *Enemies of God*, 63; Larner, *SBSW*, Tables 1 and 2, 237.

to Scottish Witchcraft', SSW, operates with 67% executed among the accused. The same do Lauren Martin and Joyce Miller in an article.[92] However, there are 2,903 trials with unknown sentences in SSW.

My first method for estimating the execution rate is based on extrapolation of known sentences. We know of 307 detailed sentences. Out of these, SSW has in total registered 206 executions. By extrapolating from these figures, the result is an estimate of 67% executed among those who received a sentence. It seems clear that one should be cautious with regard to estimate of sentences based on a small sample. Still, it is possible to explore the SSW data more thoroughly, to find new and more accurate estimates of executed persons in the Scottish witchcraft trials.

I will use the information that the sentences were given with different frequencies in different types of trials, and I will use the relative frequency of trials for extrapolation to the total population. In addition, I will use the fact that the frequency of executions varied over time. From the relative frequency in different periods I will extrapolate to the total number of trials. Results from these new and different methods are surprisingly close to each other, as will be shown, and indicate a higher execution rate than what has been assumed previously.

My second method exploits the variation in execution frequency over time. By using this detailed information, I am in a better position to estimate the total number of executions. The rate of executions when the sentence is known, about 67% for the total period of Scottish witchcraft trials, is markedly highest in the period when the majority of trials take place. I make the assumption that the frequency of executions for those with unknown sentences within each subgroup is identical to the frequency for the persons with known sentences. The total estimate of executions will then be 80.2%. This new and improved estimated rate of execution is significantly higher than previous estimates of executions in Scottish witchcraft trials.

My third method for estimation of execution rate utilizes information in SSW about types of trial for the three distinct periods. When three distinct time periods are combined with the three trial types, in effect, there will be 9 combinations of time period and type of trial. Each combination will provide full information about the sentences given. One advantage with such a method is a more refined description of all sentences. A

---

[92] 'Introduction', SSW; Martin and Miller, 'Some Findings from the Survey of Scottish Witchcraft', 56.

further advantage will be that more exact relative proportions can be cal-culated, and errors due to extrapolation of broad averages will be avoided. This new and final prognosis of total executions shows the estimated rela-tive frequency of execution for accused persons where trial type and time period is known. Thus, for the 2405 accused, the execution rate is 79.9%.

I have now presented three calculations to estimate the frequency of exe-cutions in Scottish witchcraft trials. The first one, based on extrapolation of known sentences has an estimate of 67%. The next two methods both resulted in an estimated execution rate of about 80%. It is interesting that this result is achieved by exploiting the more detailed information that is actually included in the SSW, but which has not previously been used with the intention of estimating the rate of execution.

Golden's estimated average execution rate for witchcraft trials in Europe is 0.5 per thousand of the population. More recent research estimates the total number of those executed in Europe within the same range as Golden.[93] When it comes to Scotland, this country has five times the European average.[94] About 2,500 estimated executed out of a population of 1 million are 2.5 per thousand. Germany had, out of a population of 16 million, 1.6 executed witches per thousand—a bit more than half that of Scotland. Switzerland had, out of a population of 1 million, 3.5 executed witches per thousand.[95] A few places with small populations in central Europe endured severe witchcraft persecution as well. The Electorate of Trier had, out of a population of 75,000, 10.6 executed witches per thousand.[96] In the territory of Imperial Abbey of St Maximin, situated just outside the city walls of Trier, witchcraft persecution probably ranked among the worst in the Holy Roman Empire.[97] Also the district of Finn-mark in Northern Norway experienced severe witchcraft trials. Out of a population of 3000 in c. 1600, 91 persons were executed. The intensity of witch-hunting in Finnmark was 60 times the European average. If the authorities in Finnmark had executed an average number of witches, they

---

[93] Behringer, *Witches and Witch-Hunts*, 149.
[94] Golden, 'Satan in Europe,' 20.
[95] Monter, W., 'Geography of the witch hunts,' in Golden, *Encyclopedia*, ii, 413.
[96] Dillinger, J., 'Trier, Electorate of', in Golden, *Encyclopedia*, iv, 1135–36.
[97] Voltmer, 'Vom getrübten Blick auf frühneuzeitlichen Hexenverfolgungen'; Voltmer, R., 'St Maximin, Prince-Abbey of', in Golden, *Encyclopedia*, iv, 1082–83. The article speci-fies that the figures are approximate; about 500 persons were executed out of about 2200 persons living in St Maximin, which is 22.7% of the population.

would have executed 1 or 2.[98] St Maximin and Finnmark are both areas with small populations, not countries. With regard to commensurability with areas on different administrative levels, it should be remembered that when some administrative units within, for instance, national boundaries have registrations above average, other administrative units will necessarily have registrations below average.

To conclude: Total executions in European witchcraft trials have been subject to highly variable estimates. The more extreme estimates that have been published have apparently been based primarily on guessing and less on systematic studies of primary sources. Incomplete archival registration of primary witchcraft sources is the main obstacle to overcome in the process of arriving at accurate and reliable estimates. In recent years of accumulated scholarly witchcraft research, the intensity of witchcraft persecution has been measured by the number of executed persons in relation to estimated population in an area. In this study, a similar way of measuring the intensity has been performed. In addition, the severity of witchcraft trials has been estimated by examining the number of executed in relation to the accused persons. Thus a measure of probability of being executed once imprisoned and brought to trial has been found. The witch-hunt in Scotland was extremely severe in a European context.

The Scottish witchcraft trials lasted for a period of 150 years, but with great variations in frequency. Local trials were the most frequent trial type by far, amounting to 80% of the total documented trials. Executions were more frequent in local trials than in central and mixed central-local trials. New methods for estimation of total execution rate indicate estimated execution rates close to 80%.

Distribution over time of types of trial shows stronger central control towards the end of the witch-hunt due to actions taken centrally to reintroduce circuit courts.[99] There is a clear tendency in Scottish witchcraft sources that local trials resulted more frequently in executions than all other trials. Over the total period of the witch-hunt the composition of trials changed. During the last third of the period the relative frequency of

---

[98] Goodare, J., 'The Finnmark Witches in European Context', in R. L. Andreassen and L. H. Willumsen (eds.), *Steilneset Memorial. Art, Architecture, History* (Stamsund, 2013, forthcoming); Willumsen, *Seventeenth-Century Witchcraft Trials*, 53; Willumsen, *Witchcraft Trials in Finnmark, Northern Norway*, 9; Willumsen, L. H., *Steilneset. Memorial to the Witches of the Finnmark Witchcraft Trials* (Oslo, 2011), 5.

[99] Levack, *Witch-hunting in Scotland*, 137.

local trials decreased and mixed central-local trials increased. This coincided with a decrease in executions. It is my view that the reduction of local trials also caused the decline in executions. The change in composition of type of trials most likely had to do with stronger central control of the judicial process in local courts.

The analyses of executions point towards the local courts as the main arena for the witch-hunt. Witchcraft panics were clearly related to local courts. Execution sentences were passed mostly in local courts. The use of torture is documented mainly in local courts, and must be seen as an influential factor in driving forth the trials. In a European context the execution rate in Scottish witchcraft trials is found to be very high.

Non-capital Sentences

The Scottish witchcraft act of 1563 did not allow for non-capital sentences, according to Levack: 'Convicted Scottish witches were supposed to be executed, even though some did in fact have their sentences commuted to banishment or other forms of non-capital punishment'.[100] Still, a steady trickle of non-capital sentences was passed. Banishment was a sentence seldom used. The few occurrences of this type of sentence were distributed throughout the whole period of witch-hunt.[101] The regular occurrence of banishment indicates that it was used as a sentence during both panic years and non-panic years, but most frequently during panic years. In addition, 9 people in 1678 and 2 people in 1679 were declared fugitives, meaning that the authorities had not succeeded in arresting these suspects. Of miscellaneous sentences, 1 person was publicly humiliated in 1595 and 2 persons were put to the horn in 1633.

The bulk of released persons came after the most intensive period of persecution: 1 in 1579, 1 in 1670, 4 in 1677, 1 in 1678, 9 in 1679, 1 in 1680, 1 in 1683, 7 in 1697, 25 in 1700, 1 in 1708 and 1 in 1709. These numbers indicate that the option of releasing accused persons was activated after the most intense witchcraft trials had stopped, thus showing the correspondence

---

[100] Levack, *Witch-Hunting in Scotland*, 3.
[101] 1 banishment per year in 1563, 1586, 1596, 1612, 1615, 1628, 1650, 1658, 1661, 1670, 1679, 1700, 1706, 2 banishments per year in 1709, 3 ditto per year in 1598 and 1662, 6 ditto per year in 1597. The calculation is made from the number of 307 trials with verdict and sentence known.

between the decline of witch-hunting and types of sentences passed with regard to harshness.[102]

Torture

Extensive use of torture during witchcraft trials in Scotland is an indication of the severity of the witch-hunt. The use of torture was of the highest importance for the process and outcome of a witchcraft trial. I will argue that the use of torture in Scotland as well as in Finnmark was one of the main reasons for the abrupt increase in witchcraft trials defined as panic periods, and for the intensity of the witch-hunt as such in the two regions. Torture was used during the interrogation of those suspected of being witches mainly to extract demonological confessions and to get hold of the names of accomplices who had attended witches' meetings or taken part in collective witchcraft operations. Scholars agree that severe torture took place during witchcraft trials in Scotland.[103]

For definition of the term 'torture' I follow Langbein, 'the use of physical coercion by officers of the state in order to gather evidence for judicial proceedings'.[104] The question what kind of torture methods are included in the term torture has been debated. Here different scholars give different answers. There seems to be a consensus that the use of physical methods like the rack, the boots and the thumbscrews are to be reckoned as torture. SSW includes the use of stocks as torture, and I follow this in my analyses. It may be argued that use of stocks not necessarily implied physical coercion. Still there might be situations during imprisonment of witches when the use of stocks functioned in the same way as torture, so in my opinion it might be argued that stocks could be considered as torture. Opinions also differ whether waking and witch-pricking should be considered as torture. Some scholars argue that the two methods should be included as torture.[105] Larner, however, argues that sleep deprivation and pricking for marks are distinct from direct torture.[106] Stuart Macdonald argues for a broad definition of torture including six elements: judicial

---

[102] Levack, *Witch-hunting in Scotland*, 131–144.

[103] This view is in accordance with studies of the Scottish witch-hunt by Larner, Levack, Macfarlane and Thomas.

[104] Langbein, *Torture and the Law of Proof* (Chicago, 2006), 3.

[105] Levack, 'Torture', in Golden, *Encyclopedia*, 4 vols., iv, 1129; Levack, *Witch-Hunting in Scotland*, 23.

[106] Larner, *Enemies of God*, 114–15.

torture, witch-pricking, sleep deprivation, harsh jail conditions, mob violence and the method of execution. In my view the last three points are
too general to be included in the term torture as defined above by Langbein. When it comes to pricking of a witch, this has been categorized
differently among witchcraft researchers. Anna Cordey includes witch
pricking as torture, arguing that the accused persons confessed just after
such pricking.[107] Witch-pricking had to do with finding an insensitive spot
on the suspected person's body which did not bleed. In Scotland professional witch-prickers, of whom John Kincaid was the most famous, trav-
elled from place to place to prick witches.[108] The use of pricking in order
to obtain a 'proof' that the accused had entered a pact with the Devil
is a good example of circumstantial evidence necessitated by the peculiar type of crime witchcraft was. In SSW waking is included in torture,
but not witch-pricking. As the SSW data will be the basis for my statistical treatment, my calculations will not include witch-pricking as torture,
while sleep deprivation is included.

To what extent was torture used in Scottish witchcraft trials? Due to
scarcity of documentation of torture in the sources, this is a difficult question to answer. The scarcity of documentation occurs for two main reasons.
Firstly, in the majority of cases torture was used illegally during Scottish
witchcraft trials and therefore was not entered to its full extent in the
records. Secondly, lack of documentation is linked to the general situation
regarding witchcraft trials in Scotland, where the bulk of primary sources
is missing, especially those from local courts. Nevertheless, the sample
of documented torture incidents that remains, gives an indication of the
types of torture used, the types of trial in which it was used, and whether
it was used during interrogation before the actual beginning of the trial.[109]
The relationship between torture and the number of accused in Scotland
is emphasized by several scholars. Levack maintains that torture was fre-

---

[107] Cordey, *Witch-hunting in Scotland*, 60.
[108] Goodare, J., 'Pricking of suspected witches', in Golden, *Encyclopedia*, 4 vols., iii, 930–
2; Larner, *Enemies of God*, 76. Witch-pricking has been discussed also by McDonald, based
on secondary sources. Ref. McDonald, 'The Devil's Mark', 510.
[109] Documentation of torture in Scottish witchcraft trials is found in primary sources
as well as in secondary sources. Ref. Melville, R. D., 'The Use and Forms of Judicial Torture
in England and Scotland', SHR, 2 (1905), 225–48; Larner, *Enemies of God*, 107–109; Levack,
'Judicial Torture', 185–98; Levack, *Witch-hunting in Scotland*, 22–23; Macdonald, S., 'Torture and the Scottish Witch-hunt: A Re-examination', *Scottish Tradition*, 28 (2002), 95–114;
Maxwell-Stuart, *Satan's Conspiracy*, 74–75.

quently used in Scottish criminal cases, contributing to an identification of Scottish criminal justice with that of continental European countries. In Scotland, torture was evident in the prosecution of two types of crime, witchcraft and treason. Levack gives several examples of extensive judicial torture during the 1650s and early 1660s.[110] The Privy Council had to intervene to stop judicial torture in witchcraft cases. During the 1660s the Privy Council found it necessary to prohibit local magistrates from torturing witches and to take action against those who violated that prohibition.

When torture was used during witchcraft prosecutions in Scotland, this was in contrast to England. The official use of torture in the Scottish courts was very restricted, as it was only legal interrogation procedure in criminal trials if a special warrant from the Privy Council had been granted. In addition, warrants could come from the Scottish parliament, because the Privy Council was inactive when the parliament had sessions. The Privy Council issued such warrants 'when they considered information from the accused to be vital to the state'.[111] These might be crimes of a political nature, such as 'treason, rebellion, sedition, attacks on prominent statesmen, and religious subversion'.[112] In addition to the crimes mentioned above, witchcraft was considered a crime of similar seriousness. However, it is clear that the necessary warrant from the Privy Council to use torture was not granted in the majority of witchcraft cases.[113]

As comes to the fore in SSW, torture is only mentioned sporadically in the sources, something which probably reflects the fact that the use of torture during witchcraft trials was illegal unless warrants issued. It should be remembered that the preserved witchcraft sources are fragmented compared with complete source coverage. What is documented in SSW must be regarded as incidences of reported torture; the actual figure was much higher. However, the lack of complete documentation of torture in the sources makes it difficult to perform statistical calculations. Close-reading of sources shows that torture might be implicated as more 'hidden' formulations in the documents. This is one of the issues dealt with in my qualitative analyses which follow.

---

[110] Levack, *Witch-hunting in Scotland*, 22.
[111] Levack, *Witch-hunting in Scotland*, 22.
[112] Levack, *Witch-hunting in Scotland*, 22.
[113] Levack points to the astonishing fact that during the whole period of the witch-hunt in Scotland only two warrants to use torture in witchcraft cases were granted, one in 1591 and the other in 1610. Ref. Levack, *Witch-hunting in Scotland*, 22.

Macdonald is reserved with regard to the extent of torture, maintaining that in his study from Fife the data show no clear evidence of direct torture or judicial torture. However, he points out that witch-pricking and sleep deprivation 'were adequate to drive the witch-hunt'.[114] If one includes waking among torture methods, torture was in use in Fife. If we also include witch-pricking, torture was frequently in use. In SSW the occurrences of witch-pricking in Fife are in fact registered as torture.

I find in SSW 110 occurrences of registered torture mentioned in 52 trials. It is thus documented that 52 individuals were reported tortured. As there are more documented cases of torture than individuals being tortured, some people were tortured in several ways. The documented cases of torture have been linked to types of trial, confessions, panic years and gender. Which types of trial dominated when torture was used? The data give evidence that torture took place in all types of trial, and that women as well as men were tortured.[115] Women were affected by 100 out of the 110 cases of torture. Most of the torture occurred in local trials.[116] 14.5% of torture cases took place in mixed central-local trials.[117] In central trials five torture cases were registered.[118] The likelihood of an accused man being tortured was less than the likelihood of an accused woman being tortured.[119] Men were tortured once, while women were tortured repeatedly.[120] The general pattern is that men were tortured less than women in relation to what we know about the proportion of men in Scottish witchcraft cases in general. In Scotland men comprised 15% of the accused in witchcraft trials. However, men comprise 4.5% of the reported torture cases. The number of torture cases linked to men is remarkably low.

It can be noted that torture was documented as being in use from the first witchcraft cases of the 1590s onwards. There is documentation of

---

[114] Macdonald, 'Torture', 96, 101.
[115] Willumsen, *Seventeenth-Century Witchcraft Trials*, 82.
[116] Of these, 83 cases affected women, 1 affected a man and 5 affected individuals of unknown gender. Of the women exposed to torture, 67% were tortured in local trials, 26% in mixed central-local courts, and the rest in the central courts. Willumsen, *Seventeenth-Century Witchcraft Trials*, 82.
[117] 14 cases affected women and 2 affected men. Willumsen, *Seventeenth-Century Witchcraft Trials*, 83.
[118] 3 cases related to women and 2 related to men. Willumsen, *Seventeenth-Century Witchcraft Trials*, 83.
[119] Of the 52 individuals who are documented as having been tortured, 88% were women, 10% were men, and 2% are unknown. Willumsen, *Seventeenth-Century Witchcraft Trials*, 83.
[120] Willumsen, *Seventeenth-Century Witchcraft Trials*, 83.

intermittent use in the decades after 1620 and frequent use during the panics of 1661–62. It is interesting to note that torture was registered as being used in the 1670s and the 1680s, not long before it was abolished.

Torture methods in Scotland resemble those used in Europe as a whole. Among Scottish torture methods are 'the rack, the thumbscrew, the pilniewinkis or pinniwinks, the boot, the cashilawis or caspitaws or caspicaws, the "long irons", the "waking", the "Turkas", needles, scourging, breaking on the wheel, burning, strangulation, mutilation, dismemberment, flaying, and many other ingenious minor varieties, such as, for example, wreching ("thrawing") the head with ropes, specially resorted to in dealing with cases of witchcraft'.[121] 'Thrawing' is mentioned in connection with several early cases.[122] The most common types seem to have been sleep deprivation, burning feet, bound with ropes, hanging by thumbs, whip and stocks. Irons is mentioned in three cases, and bow strings, cashielaws, haircloth, tied to a pole and wedges on the shins are mentioned in one case each. One person could be tortured with up to five different torture methods.

There is clear evidence that use of torture had the wanted effect, which can be seen by comparing the chronology of the date of torture and the date of accusation. Torture was mostly used to extract confessions in order to apply to the Privy Council for a commission for trying witches. Thus one would expect torture dates to precede case dates, as torture was necessary to make suspected individuals confess before the official trial started. Judging from the sample of torture cases in SSW, this was the case.[123] Of those persons who were reported tortured, 18 were tortured before the case dates, one was tortured after the case date,[124] and for four individuals we do not know, due to lack of information about the accurate torture date. What we do know, is that they were tortured in the same year and in the same month as the trial.[125] This illustrates clearly that suspected people were tortured as part of the interrogation before the trial was a fact. Their confessions were necessary to the local judges when they applied for a commission to try witches in local communities. This is

---

[121] Melville, 'Judicial Torture in England and Scotland', 236.

[122] Both Fean and Angus Sampson are reported to have been 'thrawn' according to *Newes of Scotland*. Ref. Willumsen, *Seventeenth-Century Witchcraft Trials*, 83.

[123] Date of torture is registered in SSW by month and year, while case date is registered by date, month and year. Ref. Willumsen, *Seventeenth-Century Witchcraft Trials*, 84.

[124] Kathrine Remy, 1658. Ref. Willumsen, *Seventeenth-Century Witchcraft Trials*, 84.

[125] Alesoun Balfour, 1594; Agneis Kirkland, 1650; Kathrine Remy, 1658 (tortured several times); David Stewart, 1650. Ref. Willumsen, *Seventeenth-Century Witchcraft Trials*, 84.

a good indication that pressure to try witches in the first place came from local communities.

The findings show that torture is documented to have played a part during the witch-hunt. Torture as part of the interrogation before the trial started, was frequent. Severe methods of torture were used to extract confessions. There is a connection between the use of torture and panic years.[126] Torture affected mostly women and took place mostly in local trials. The use of torture decreased drastically after 1662. Related to the analyses above of panic years, execution rates, the demonological element, types of trial and gender, the results support an interpretation of the witch-hunt as influenced by several factors, with the use of torture playing an important part in pressing forth confessions. This will be analyzed in further detail in the qualitative analyses.

The Demonological Element

The introduction of demonological ideology played a prominent role in the historical witch-hunt. This doctrine made its way into literature, into the laws, into the preaching of the church and into the mentality sphere of the peasants, which will be demonstrated in my qualitative analyses. The spread of demonological ideas among the learned elite through books and among the peasants by means of orally transmitted narratives, and the preaching of the church, prepared the ground for the many Devil's pact confessions we meet during the witchcraft trials.

The demonological witchcraft confessions are rooted in an understanding of the Devil as a figure with the power of temptation, individuals as easily tempted to enter a pact with him, and the pact as an individual relationship. Both the state and the church worked to make these ideas understandable and convincing to the common people. Nathan Johnstone has pointed out that the concept of the Devil underwent a process of cultural change in the hands of the Protestant reforming clergy in England, a change in which emphasis on the Devil's ability 'to enter directly into the mind and plant thoughts within it that led people to sin'.[127] The weight of this image of the Devil in post-Reformation preaching, combined with the

---

[126] 32 of the 52 tortured persons are registered in panic years. Ref. Willumsen, *Seventeenth-Century Witchcraft Trials*, 84.

[127] Johnstone, N., *The Devil and Demonism in Early Modern England* (Cambridge, 2006), 1.

conviction of, and anxiety of, this powerful Devil among the learned elite, are important factors that influenced witchcraft persecution.

The influence from learned demonology comes to the fore during witchcraft trials, both in the form of direct influence from the interrogators and in the form of knowledge about demonology among the accused. In the following I will concentrate on highlighting demonological features in the confessions, the naming of others suspects, and finally the gender bias of demonological confessions. According to the cumulative concept of witchcraft, a pact with the Devil, the Sabbath, night flights and metamorphosis are central ideas. These notions were vital drives behind the witchcraft trials, and an important reason for the high frequency of cases during the panics. Demonic pact confessions in the Scottish material have been studied by, among others, Stuart Macdonald and Lauren Martin. Macdonald's study from Fife concludes that the Scottish populace did not readily accept demonological notions. Lauren Martin maintains that the demonic pact was brought to common people by ministers, magistrates and prosecutors, and thus rapidly got foothold among ordinary people. This will be illuminated in following chapters in close-readings of accused person's confessions.[128]

The registered demonic pact confessions in SSW covers several of the concepts known from learned demonology, first and foremost a covenant between the accused person and the Devil. This pact was sometimes sealed by a ritual, in which the individual entering the pact held a certain posture and promised to be the servant of the Devil from the top of her head to the sole of her foot; from this ritual came the SSW labels 'Body and Soul' and 'Head and Foot'. The frequently used expression 'from the crown of the head to the soles of the feet' is borrowed from the medieval ban of excommunication. During the pact ritual, the Christian baptism was renounced and the person was given a new name by the Devil. In some cases the person entering the pact kissed the Devil's bottom as a sign of obedience. Sometimes the pact was accompanied by the Devil putting his mark on the person's body. Sex with the Devil was often confessed in relation to entering the pact, often in connection with witches' meetings. Often the Devil promised that the person entering the pact with him should 'Want nothing', which means that everything this person needed,

---

[128] Macdonald, 'In search of the Devil in Fife', in Goodare, *The Scottish with-hunt in context*, 47. Presumably Macdonald's result is due to the range of sources he has used, as confessions from local courts are not included in his study; Martin, 'The Devil', 75.

would be provided. Renouncing Christian baptism and getting a new
name, thus becoming the child of the Evil One, is mentioned by more
than two-thirds of those whose confessions are recorded.[129]

Also witches' meetings were narrated in great detail, most often meetings with the Devil present. In addition, dancing and singing as well as
food and drink were confessed to have been elements of witches' meetings.
There is often an aspect of merriment related to the witches' meetings, as
well as some areas of 'illegal' activities, like 'Communal sex'. Both women
and men confessed to participation at witches meetings, women eight
times as often as men.[130] An accused person often named other people
who took part in the meeting and thereby gave the names of accomplices
and further suspects to be interrogated. On this hinge—the sudden emergence of many names—rests the possibility of a panic spreading rapidly.
There is a strong statistical correlation between periods when accused
individuals were implicated by another person and the panic periods. This
means that in panic years there was a greater chance of being implicated
as a person suspected of witchcraft than in non-panic years.[131]

The decrease in demonological confessions towards the end of the
witch-hunt is related to the more restricted use of torture after 1662, when
it was proclaimed illegal by the Privy Council.[132] An aspect of this relative
decrease—the relation between reduction in denunciations and reduction in trials—may be illuminated from one angle by looking at the frequency of naming others in different types of trial during the last period
of the Scottish witch-hunt. After 1677 relatively fewer were implicated by
others.[133] Central trials occurred particularly in 1678 and 1700 during the

---

[129] Willumsen, *Seventeenth-Century Witchcraft Trials*, 73.

[130] The contents of witches' meetings as elements of confessions is registered by SSW
for 213 women and 28 men. Ref. Willumsen, *Seventeenth-Century Witchcraft Trials*, 73.

[131] Chi-square 101.762. In panic years, the ratio between those who were implicated
by another witch and those who were not implicated, is 2:1. In a non-panic year, the proportion is close to 5:1. Ref. Willumsen, *Seventeenth-Century Witchcraft Trials*, 75; Goodare,
'Witch-hunting and the Scottish state', 137.

[132] Larner, *Enemies of God*, 108–109; Levack, *Witch-hunting in Scotland*, 138–41.

[133] In 1679, 2 individuals out of 7 in local trials were implicated by others. In 1700, there
were 11 local trials, 1 in Dumfries and 10 in Ross. None of the accused persons was implicated by others. After 1700, the number of local trials did not reach more than 5 per year.
In 1709 there was 1 local trial in Dumfries, with no-one implicated by another person, and
in 1719 there were 6 local trials, all in Caithness, in which no person was implicated by
others.

late period of the witch-hunt.[134] After 1700 there were no central trials. The tendency with regard to central trials and the naming of other suspected witches is clear; it decreases towards the end of the century.

During the period 1675–1725, there were few suspected in mixed central-local trials.[135] In 1699 there were 23 people tried in mixed central-local trials. Of these, only two were implicated by others. For mixed central-local trials the pattern seems to be that very few accused people were implicated by others during the late period of the witch-hunt.[136] The exceptional year 1697, a very special case took place. A laird's eleven-year-old daughter in Renfrew accused a number of her father's servants, tenants and tenants' children of bewitching her. Seven out of 20 people accused were executed. Cases originating from this initial case came up as late as 1699.[137]

Summing up: When the frequency of denunciations is examined, the link between denunciations and demonology is strengthened. For local trials the pattern seems to be that naming other suspected individuals occurs until 1700, but the number of suspected witches never explodes, as we saw to be the case in previous panic years. This indicates that denunciation of others, which is closely connected to demonological confessions of witches' meetings, decreases towards the end of the witch-hunt.

Compared to the relative gender distribution in the Scottish witchcraft material, the proportion of women confessing to the demonic pact is higher than expected. But it is also important to be aware that men confessed to the demonic pact, so there is no exclusive connection in the Scottish material between demonic pact and women. An argument in this book is that demonological trials were very dangerous because of the implicit potential for panic outbursts. There is a relation between the demonological element and panic periods. Almost twice as many females confessed to the demonic pact in panic years compared with non-panic years. This

---

[134] In 1678, 13 people out of 22 tried in central trials were implicated by others. In 1700, 6 out of 25 people tried in central cases were implicated by others.

[135] In 1677, none of the accused in mixed central-local trials was implicated by others. In 1679, only 1 out of 35 persons tried in mixed central-local trials was implicated by someone else, namely Jannet Hunter, Haddington. Ref. Willumsen, *Seventeenth-Century Witchcraft Trials*, 76.

[136] In 1683, none of the 15 people tried in mixed central-local trials was implicated by others. In 1697, where 27 people in total were tried in mixed central-local trials, 21 are registered as having been implicated by others. These trials were in Renfrew. The trials in 1699 were in Renfrew and Lanark. Those implicated by others were Issobel Henryson and Elspeth Wilson. Ref. Willumsen, *Seventeenth-Century Witchcraft Trials*, 76.

[137] Larner, *Enemies of God*, 77.

finding is very much in parallel with the total number of women in panic versus non-panic years. Men are under-represented in panic years with regard to demonic pact confessions.

The frequency of demonic pact confessions follows the upsurge of panics.[138] These findings draw the attention to the presence of the demonological element throughout the seventeenth century, inclusive after the last panic year. My interpretation is that demonological ideas continued to live strongly as part of the mentality sphere of the common people after interest in witchcraft persecution had decreased among legal officials. This indicates that the oral transmission of demonological notions and their potential to remain in the oral arena for a long period of time, are issues to be aware of when the complex factors influencing witchcraft trials are analyzed.

Neighbourhood Disputes

The local community is an important arena to look into to find explanations for the witch-hunt, especially as regards the start of witchcraft accusations and the role of neighbours' testimonies during the trials.[139] As for gender, most of the registrations of neighbourhood disputes in SSW point to the importance of women. We are largely within the circles of women when it comes to disputes of this kind caught by the legal system during witchcraft trials. This fact points to networks of women as important for local witchcraft accusations. Neighbourhood quarrels are mentioned in all trial types and can be seen throughout the whole period of the witch-hunt.[140] There is no indication that neighbourhood disputes were increasing during panic periods.[141] The finding supports an assumption that in the local communities, scolding for witchcraft was a constant phenomenon during the entire period of the witch-hunt. This indicates that peasants knew the severity of this type of accusation and that scolding for witchcraft was rooted in conflicts in daily life situations.

---

[138] 1590–91 with 5 demonic pact confessions, 1597 with 9 confessions, 1628–30 with 26 confessions, 1643–44 with 9 confessions, 1649–50 with 61 confessions, 1658–59 with 36 confessions, 1661–62 with 77 confessions. In addition, in 1678 there are 16 confessions and in 1697 there are 19 confessions. Ref. Willumsen, *Seventeenth-Century Witchcraft Trials*, 78.

[139] Briggs, Larner, Martin, Goodare and Cordey have all emphasised the social context in their studies.

[140] Willumsen, *Seventeenth-Century Witchcraft Trials*, 85, 295.

[141] Chi-square 0.563. Ref. Willumsen, *Seventeenth-Century Witchcraft Trials*, 296.

Looking at the relation between neighbourhood disputes and execution, analyses show that among those persons for whom we know the sentence, and who were involved in neighbourhood disputes, a high number were executed.[142] This underlines the seriousness of the first step in the local community, no matter if everyday conflicts springing out of jealousy or anger were the modest beginnings of the conflict. No doubt neighbourhood disputes were treated seriously when brought to court, and this emphasizes that the whole atmosphere in local communities must have been poisoned by fear of scolding or being named as a witch. A few angry words in everyday life might have huge consequences, demonstrating the strong fear of witches at all levels of society. When angry words about witchcraft were uttered, there were ears willing to listen to this and bring the rumours within the reach of the kirk or the judicial apparatus. However, I think it is important to underline that these conflicts only became dangerous when they were taken to court. And frequently they grew to the huge dimensions they assumed in the courtroom after demonological notions had been added to the original accusations. It should also be born in mind that a lot of angry words and accusations about witchcraft never resulted in trials. Neighbourhood conflicts will be explored in greater detail as part of the close-reading of trial documents in following chapters.

Folk Belief

Folk belief is a broad concept for the seventeenth century, and covers a wide range of beliefs. Probably the mentality horizon of a seventeenth-century man or woman was quite different from what we are able to imagine today.[143] The demonizing of folk belief is an important feaure of the witchcraft trials, as common people accused of witchcraft often experienced that their folkloric beliefs were used by the legal authorities as a starting point for more serious demonological notions to be added.[144] Several witchcraft scholars have studied folk belief, and related to the

---

[142] Out of 52 accused persons for whom we know the sentence, and who were involved in neighbourhoos disputes, 38 were executed and 9 released. Ref. Willumsen, *Seventeenth-Century Witchcraft Trials*, 86, 296.

[143] Goodare, 'Scottish Witchcraft in its European Context', 30–38; Larner, *Enemies of God*, 7–14.

[144] Henderson and Cowan, *Scottish Fairy Belief*, 106–141; 209–214.

Scottish witchcraft trials the belief in fairies has been focused on, as this
might provide a link to a common notion of the other world.[145] Particularly
Lizanne Henderson and Edward J. Cowan have shown that fairy belief
was demonized, and that it was the first step in introducing the demonic
into witch testimony. Even King James in his *Demonology* presented the
accused persons' confessions containing fairy belief as an attempt to
explain that their activities would be attributable to the fairies. In that
way the accused hoped to escape the inevitable. However, Henderson and
Cowan maintain that only a 'thin diabolical crust' covered the voices of
the accused witches, as fairy belief endured the obstacles of the witch-
hunt.[146] The notion of another world has also been linked to a specific
feature, presumed to exist among the Highlanders, namely the second
sight, an ability to foresee the future and experience places not possible
to see for ordinary people.[147] This belief would fit in easily with the notion
of witches' metamorphoses and flights to remote Sabbath places.[148] In the
following, I will discuss fairy belief as it is represented in SSW.

Fairy belief is the element of folk belief which has been most clearly
focused on in relation to witchcraft trials in Scotland, because belief in
fairies is supposed to be a particular Scottish folklore element. In SSW, 150
different aspects of fairy and elf belief are registered.[149] These aspects of
confessions are distributed fairly evenly throughout the whole period of the
witch-hunt. This indicates that there is no particular upheaval of confessions containing fairy belief during panic years. Fairy belief existed among
the peasants like an undercurrent during the whole period of witch-hunt,
like it did before and after this period. There is no evidence that intense
witchcraft persecutions during panic years increased the proportion of
confessions containing aspects of fairy belief. With regard to gender, we
find about the same proportion of women and men who mentioned fairies in their confessions.[150] Clearly the material from Scotland documents

---

[145] Joyce Miller, Alaric Hall, Lizanne Henderson, Edward J. Cowan, Julian Goodare and
Ronald Hutton have contributed to this field of research.

[146] Henderson and Cowan, *Scottish Fairy Belief*, 138.

[147] Campbell, J. G., *Witchcraft and the Second Sight in the Highlands and Islands of
Scotland* (Glasgow, 1902); Macgregor, A., *Highland Superstitions* (Stirling, 1922); Hunter,
'The Discovery of Second Sight in late 17th-Century Scotland', *History today* (June, 2001),
48–53.

[148] Black, R., Introduction to Campbell, *The Gaelic Otherworld* (Edinburgh, 2005).

[149] Willumsen, *Seventeenth-Century Witchcraft Trials*, 87.

[150] Willumsen, *Seventeenth-Century Witchcraft Trials*, 87.

a belief in fairies among the peasants. In the courtroom, the knowledge of fairies was exploited in the direction of demonology, to obtain the type of confession which the interrogators desired.

Healing

Several aspects of the activity of healing is registered in SSW; among them whether the accused person was a recognised healer, whether the accused healed humans, and whether the accused healed animals. In total, 195 accused persons are mentioned in connection with healing. The proportion of healing in panic years shows that both healings of humans and animals are slightly more frequent in panic years than in non-panic years.[151] However, there is no statistical valid proof that healing was a special panic year phenomenon. This indicates that healing was an activity performed regularly before, during and after the period of the witch-hunt, and was not affected by the mechanisms that initiated panics. The relative proportion of healing of humans for accused men and women is equal to the proportion of men and women in total. Men are over-represented in the activity of healing animals. SSW gives evidence that some persons accused of witchcraft were mentioned as healers with reputation as such—either performing healing of humans or animals.

Conclusion

The quantitative analyses of Scottish witchcraft trials have shed new light on a number of interesting issues. The Scottish witchcraft trials lasted for a period of 150 years, but with great variations as for frequency. Sources document that about 3200 individuals were tried. About 84% of these were women. As for gender composition, in Scotland the percentage of women is slightly higher than the European average.

The occurrence of panics instigating witchcraft trials is well documented in the Scottish sources. In the few panic years there is an average of about 150 annual cases, while in non-panic years, the majority of the period, the annual average of cases is 7. Not only the number of trials distinguishes panic years from non-panic years, also a gender bias exists.

---

[151] Willumsen, *Seventeenth-Century Witchcraft Trials*, 88.

Women are more prone to be accused in panic years than in non-panic years, and they also get more severe sentences in panic years than in non-panic years.

Local trials are the most frequent trial type by far, with 80% of the total documented types of trial. Women are over-represented in local trials, whereas men are over-represented in central trials. This may contribute to explain that relatively different sentences were given to men and women.

Detailed information on verdict and sentence is known in only about 10% of all Scottish cases. Based on these cases I have estimated the execution rate for all cases where name is known, about 3200 cases. I have estimated total executions by three methods. The first method indicates that about 67% of the accused were executed—a number very close to earlier estimates made for Scottish witchcraft trials. By using two more elaborate methods, higher estimated execution rates appear. By combining information about trial type and change in composition of trial type over time, I have estimated that probably as many as 80% of the accused were executed. I consider the estimate of executions to be a novel finding reached by using more detailed data and more advanced estimation methods than have previously been applied to the problem.

A wide range of demonological aspects are documented in Scottish witchcraft trials: renouncing of Christian baptism, entering a pact with the Devil, the Devil's mark, being the Devil's servant, acceptance of the Devil's offer of 'Want nothing', and sex with the Devil, to mention a few. These aspects are frequently mentioned in the confessions. In addition, participation at witches' meetings is often confessed to. This contributes to panics arising by the mentioning of accomplices participating at the same witches' gathering.

The use of torture is not frequently documented in Scottish witchcraft sources. This stands in contrast to the consensus among scholars that severe torture was extensively used during these trials. The solution to this paradox is probably that torture was used illegally during the witch-hunt in Scotland. Legal restrictions existed on the use, as a warrant from the Privy Council had to be issued before torture was permitted. However, very few such warrants have been documented issued during the period of Scottish witchcraft trials. To the extent that torture was used without the required permission, the practice existed without being recorded. From the documentation of torture found in SSW, we can nevertheless conclude that females were clearly more frequently tortured than men.

Torture primarily was applied to obtain a confession at an early stage of the witchcraft trial. This confession was needed in order to have an application sent to the Privy Council to get allowance to try suspected persons for witchcraft in local courts. Hence torture was used as a method to press forth a confession urgently needed.

CHAPTER FOUR

MAINLAND SCOTLAND—CLOSE-READINGS

While the analyses presented in the previous chapter are based on statistical data, thus showing tendencies in the source material as a whole, the following analyses will—by close-readings of separate court records— be based on discourse-focused interpretation. The two ways of analyzing the primary sources complete each other and are inter-related in that statistical analyses of specific topics create a back-drop against which it is possible to draw when it comes to analyzing the texts. The quantitative analyses prepare the ground for analyses of courtroom discourse.

The different voices of individuals participating in the trial will throw light on important issues: justification of the case; definition of the type of witchcraft to be dealt with; reliability of the witnesses' testimonies; the interrogators' questioning of the accused; the accused person's confession; delivery of the verdict, and passing of the sentence. As will be seen, different accents characterize the discourse. By keeping the voices of the scribe, the representatives of the law, the witnesses and the accused person apart when analyzing the text, attention is drawn towards the functioning of the discourse.

Margaret Wallace, 1622

The first case to be analyzed is the trial of Margaret Wallace, which took place in 1622.[1] The choice of this trial rests on several points. The surviving witchcraft document is detailed, with sufficient coherence to be suitable for a narratological analysis. The trial of Margaret Wallace may serve as an example of a relatively early case mirroring this stage of development in legal witchcraft discourse. The trial was held at the Justiciary Court in Edinburgh and will represent a type of trial in which the professional judicial officials discuss central elements related to the crime of witchcraft, thus displaying attitudes with regard to the legal interpretation of this crime. As will be seen from analyses of later local trials, the legal

---

[1] I would like to thank Diane Baptie for the transcription of the document.

rhetorical discourse in the central trial of Margaret Wallace appears to be more embellished than trials held in local courts, where the officials had less judicial training and perhaps less enjoyment in practising legal rhetoric. The trial may illustrate witchcraft trials with malefice as the main accusation, not demonology. The case is a very good example of a type of after-rationalisation which often occurs in witchcraft trials, based on the linearity of events. Witnesses' testimonies, given after an alleged accident, are used to establish cause and effect relations between an unexpected accident and some words muttered by a person reputed for witchcraft before the accident. The case brings up not only the performance of sorcery, but also consultation with reputed witches.

Margaret Wallace was a woman from Glasgow, married to the craftsman John Dyning. She was arrested without a warrant and accused of *maleficium*, healing and consulting a known witch.[2] According to a note from the Privy Council of Scotland dated 19 February 1622, she was due to be tried in the Justiciary Court in Edinburgh on 20 March 1622. Several men from Glasgow would prosecute her case. She had been denounced for witchcraft 'five or six years since' and had been called up in front of the Kirk session of Glasgow for 'railing' followed by disease.[3] She was then accused of killing a minister. This must most likely have been in 1613, as the minister died in 1614.[4] During the 1622 trial, ten articles were presented, each containing accusations either about malefice, healing or the consultation of two known witches, Christiane Graham and Katherine Blair. A long series of witnesses testified against her. A verdict of guilty was passed, and she was executed at the Castle Hill, Edinburgh.[5]

The Voice of the Law

The voice of the law is in this study understood as the letters of the law as well as the voices of the representatives of the law. Margaret Wallace was 'Dilaitit of dy[ver]s poyntis of sorcerie incanta[tio]n and witchcraft at lenth spe[cife]it in hir dittay'.[6] After the ten arguments against her had been presented, a long discussion between the lawyers over points of law followed. The voice of the law is characterized by very elaborate defence

---

[2] NAS, Books of Adjournal, JC2/6, fo. 75r.
[3] 'railing' is here to be understood as reproaching, insulting, abusing.
[4] SSW, sub Margaret Wallace.
[5] Fasti, iii, 378; ECA, Edinburgh Town Treasurer's Accounts, iv, (1612–1623), 1136–37.
[6] NAS, Books of Adjournal, JC2/6, fo. 59v.

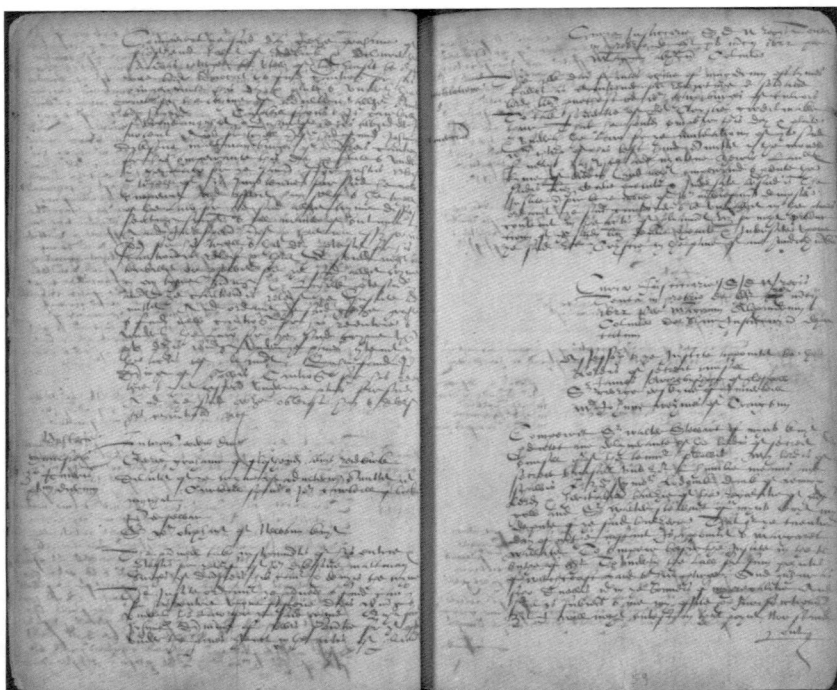

Figure 1: Court records Margaret Wallace, 1622. NAS, Books of Adjournal, JC2/6, fo. 59v.

pleadings, in which the prosecution and defence cite different passages.[7] The assessors to the judge were James, Archbishop of Glasgow, Sir George Erskyn of Innerteyle and Mr John Weymes of Craigtoun. The jury consisted of 15 individuals, all burgesses of Glasgow, five of them merchants.

The style used in the legal discourse is heavy, with long sentence constructions, something which puts its stamp on the document as a whole. References to divine and secular laws are detailed, for instance the references to the fifth book of the Old Testament:

> the devyne Law of almy[gh]tie God set doun in his sacred woird speciallie in the 20 chap of Leviticus and 18 chap of Deuteronomie Agains the usearis and *practizeris of witchcraft sorcerie charmeing and soothesaying and against the seikeris of help and responssis of thame* thraitni[n]g & denu[n]ceing to

---

[7] NAS, Books of Adjournal, JC2/6, fo. 60v.

the co[m]mitteris of sic *devillisch practizes* the puneishme[n]t of daith [*My italics*].[8]

As we see here, not only those who practised traditional sorcery but also those who received help from sorcerers were included among those who should be punished for witchcraft. This is an important point because one of the serious charges against Margaret Wallace was that of receiving help from a 'notorious' witch, Christiane Graham, who had already been burnt.

The interplay between phrases used in divine and secular law might be of importance for interpretation of legal argumentation. As some key terms related to demonology, for instance the demonic pact, is lacking in the 1563 Witchcraft Act, an interesting question is to what extent specific Bible verses could help to clarify, and possibly expand, formulations in this act. The Margaret Wallace case might throw some light on this relation. During the case, there is reference to divine as well as secular law; to the Bible and to the Witchcraft Act. The first biblical reference is to Deuteronomy 18:10–11. Julian Goodare has pointed out that these verses from Deuteronomy may have influenced the 1563 Witchcraft Act.[9] With regard to the biblical influence on this act, there is an interesting difference between the Geneva Bible of 1560 and the Authorised version of 1611, which might have held significance for the kirk's official understanding of witchcraft. The Geneva Bible says in verses 10–11: 'Let none be found among you that maketh his sonne or his daughter to go through the fire, or that vseth witchcraft, or a regarder of times, or a marker of the flying of soules or a sorcerer // Or a charmer, or that counselleth with spirits or a sothesayer, or that asketh councel at the dead'.[10] The same verses in the 1611 edition say: 'There shall not be found among you any one that maketh his sonne, or his daughter to pass throw the fire, or that useth diuination or an observer of times, or an inchanter, or a witch // or a charmer, or a consulter with familiar spirits, or a wizard, or a necromancer'.[11] The difference between the 1560 and the 1611 editions is that the word 'diuination' has replaced 'witchcraft' in the expression 'that vseth diuination or an observer of times', which might suggest that malefice has been taken into account and understood as part of witchcraft. It is also interesting that the

---

[8] NAS, Books of Adjournal, JC2/6, fos. 75r–75v.

[9] Goodare, J., 'The Scottish Witchcraft Act', *Church History*, lxxiv, no. 1 (2005), 39.

[10] Geneva Bible (1560).

[11] *The Holy Bible* (London, 1611), authorised version.

words 'charming and sothesayer' are mentioned in the court records of
Margaret Wallace's trial, corresponding to the 1560 Bible wording, while in
the 1611 edition we do not find the word 'soothsaying'. Instead the words
'inchanter', 'witch', 'charmer', and 'wizard' are used. Hence a richer spectre of words covering witchcraft and sorcery is used in the 1611 edition
than in the 1560 Bible. However, in the court records of the Wallace case
formulations used are closest to the older Bible. It should be noted that
'witchcraft' in the 1560 edition is replaced by 'a witch' in the 1611 edition,
a concept individualized and personified. The use of singular in the 1611
edition, might refer to the personalized relation between the witch and
the Devil which is seen through entering into the Devil's pact. It is to be
noted that the term 'consulter with familiar spirits' has entered this new
authorised 1611 Bible. A familiar, most often a cat or a domestic animal,
often related to English witches, was believed to assist them in their evil
deeds. These imps were given as gifts from Satan to his faithful followers.
It was also believed that witches took the forms of their familiars when
travelling to witches' gatherings.[12]

In the Witchcraft Act the word 'necromancy', understood as the sum-
moning of evil spirits for magical purposes, is used. This word is not used
in the 1560 Bible, Deuteronomy 18:10–11. Still, this biblical text might have
influenced the Witchcraft Act via the words charming and soothsaying,
which might parallel the expression 'necromancy'. Even if the demonic
pact is not directly mentioned in the Witchcraft Act, there might be an
allusion to it by the use of the word 'necromancy'. If this is so, then the
absence of this word in Deuteronomy is relevant for its use in connection
with the seventeenth-century witch-hunt.[13] The Deuteronomy verses may
additionally have influenced the Witchcraft Act by mentioning 'witchcraft'
as well as 'sorcerer', a completion that continued to live in the formulation
of the act.

The second biblical reference in the Margaret Wallace court records
is to Levicitus 20:27, which in the Geneva edition says: 'And if a man or
a woman haue a spirit of diuination or sothesaying in them they shal
dye the death: they shal stone them to death, their blood shalbe vpon
them'.[14] The same verse in the 1611 edition says: 'A man also or a woman
that hath a familiar spirit, or that is a wizard shall surely be put to death:

---

12 Williams, M., 'The Witch's Familiar, Past and Present', *New Age*, May 1 (2000).
13 Goodare, 'Scottish Witchcraft Act', 62.
14 Geneva Bible (1560).

they shall stone them with stones: their blood shalbe upon them'.¹⁵ In the same way as in Deuteronomy, we see that 'familiar spirit' and 'wizard' have entered into the 1611 edition of the Bible. The former of these terms may indicate that ideas about this evil animal, the familiar, have entered into the biblical formulations, hence demonological ideas are included in the divine law.

The word 'devillische' is frequently mentioned in the court records. This word is not mentioned in either of the Bible editions, or, as will be seen below, is the Witchcraft Act. Particularly since this case deals with accusations against a maleficent rather than a demonological witch, the mention suggests that by 1622 the link had been implicitly made between malefice and devilish witchcraft. Frequent repetitions of 'devil' and 'devilish' will be seen in the court records throughout the period of the witch-hunt. When references to the Bible are used in these court records side by side with reference to laws, it suggests that the legal interpretation of witchcraft was that it was a violation of God's laws as well as the clerical laws.

In the Wallace case, the reference to secular law is 'the 73 act':¹⁶

> As also be dy[ver]is actis of p[ar]liament and municipall Lawis of this kingdom alsweill publeist and sett furth be his maiestie in his awin tyme As in the dayis of his maist noble progenitoris Namelie be the 73 act of the parliament haldin be his hienes darrest mother Quene marie of worthie memorie It is expreslie provydit *statute & ordanit that na maner of persone or persones of q[uha]tsome[v]er estait degrie or conditioun thay be of Presume nor tak upone hand to use ony maner of witchcraft sorcerie or negromancie nor gif tham selfis furth to haif ony sic craft* or knawlege thairby abouseing his hienes people & subjectis And that *na persone seik ony help respons or consultatioun at ony sic usearis or abusearis foirsaidis under the pane of death alsweill to be execute upone the usear & abusear as the seiker of the respons or consultatioun* As in the saidis Lawis and actis of p[ar]liament at mair lenth is contenit [*My italics*].¹⁷

The sentences in italics above are almost word for word from the Witchcraft Act.¹⁸ What has changed is the use of 'witchcraft' in the singular in the records, while the act has the plural, 'Witchcraftis', and the wording 'thairthrow abusand the pepill' in The Witchcraft Act, is here 'abouesing his hienes people & subjectis'. The latter amendment does not change the

¹⁵ Authorised Bible, 1611.
¹⁶ Goodare, 'Scottish Witchcraft Act', 39.
¹⁷ NAS, Books of Adjournal, JC2/6, fo. 75v.
¹⁸ E. Henryson (ed.), *Actis and Constitutionis of the Realme of Scotland* (Edinburgh, 1566). Ref. Goodare, 'Scottish Witchcraft Act', 39.

meaning much, although his highness and his subjects are underlined. The use of the singular for witchcraft might refer to the demonological understanding of witchcraft as a power given from the Devil to one person through the pact.

The term malefice was not found in the Witchcraft Act. Therefore the accusation against Margaret Wallace had to be covered by the words witchcraft, sorcery and necromancy. Necromancy might in this case be the most obvious link between Wallace's performance of malefice and the criminalisation of her sorcery. As several key words later taken into use in witchcraft persecution were not mentioned in the Witchcraft Act, this might have to do with the intention of it being a device against Catholicism, as suggested by Clark and Goodare.[19] Clark has pointed to demonology as working within the confessions of both Catholicism and Protestantism.[20] Interesting in this respect is a vernacular catechism as early as 1552, published by the Archbishop of St Andrews to evangelize the laity.[21] In fact, it seems that the wording used in the 1552 catechism could be an early draft of the Witchcraft Act, using all the words 'wytche, sorcerar, cownqerar, or siclike disserveris' and 'Wytches, Nigromanceris and siclikes, *workis be operation of the devil under a paction*'.[22] [*My italics.*] What is notably omitted in these words in the Witchcraft Act is the demonic pact, which may be ascribed to the difficulties of getting the act passed in contemporary circumstances. It was known that Queen Mary and her counsellors would object to specific words used. Nevertheless, the idea of the demonic pact was a reality in pre-Reformation times in Scotland. Obviously sermons and religious literature were important in educating people in the Protestant faith. However, legislation was also important in this respect, as is seen from the court records of Margaret Wallace.

Margaret Wallace's practice of sorcery, as well as her consultation of a known witch, is emphasised in the records. As seen from the discussion above, the term *maleficium* was not used in the Witchcraft Act, and it was not used in legal discourse, although there was no doubt that Wallace was a maleficent witch. She was a person with power to perform sorcery

---

[19]   Goodare, 'Scottish Witchcraft Act', 59; Clark, *Thinking with Demons*, ch. 35.

[20]   Clark, S., 'Protestant Demonology: Sin, Superstition, and Society (*c.* 1520–*c.* 1630)', in Ankarloo and Henningsen, *Early Modern European Witchcraft. Centres and Peripheries* (Oxford, 1993), 47.

[21]   Larner, *Enemies of God*, 163.

[22]   Larner, *Enemies of God*, 163.

from knowledge or inherent talents in addition to the use of charms and objects, rather than power obtained by a pact with the Devil.

After the assize was made known, the accused made objections to four of the persons. The objection against the first was that he had contracted an evil will against her husband. The Justice admitted him. The objection against the second was that he was brother-in-law to one of her alleged victims. He was to stand down and another was called. The objection against the third was that he was brother-in-law to one of the informers. He was admitted because he was not a pursuer. The objection against the fourth was that he 'should not be admitted as she had sold him drugs which he had not paid for, she had then taken him to court and an enmity had arisen between them. He was nonetheless admitted'.[23] These objections show that this witchcraft trial followed standard legal procedure, where the accused person was heard and had somebody to speak for her. There was considerable legal argument between the pursuers and defenders and members of the assize during the case.[24] After the final reading of the accusations against Margaret Wallace, 'The justice nochtw[ ]thstanding of dy[ver]is allegeances maid be hir & hir procu[ra]toris agains the relevance th[air]of *Quhilkis war all repellit in respect of the dittay* and my lord advocattis answris maid in fortificatioun th[air]of'. [*My italics.*][25] The italicized phrase shows that Wallace and her procurators were allowed to have their protests heard, even if these were rejected.

During the final parts of the trial, the charges against Margaret Wallace and the dual reference to the laws were repeated, 'be sorcerie witchcraft charmeing and incantatioun and uth[er]is Devillish and unlaw[fu]ll means expreslie prohibetit and forbidden be the Lawis of almytie god and municipall Lawis of this kingdome'.[26] It was also stressed that the verdict in this actual case should have an effect upon the people in general: 'The said margaret wallace hes contravenit the tenno[u]r of the saidis Lawis & actis of p[ar]liament and incurrit the panes & puneishme[n]t of daith set doun th[air]intill q[uhi]lk aucht & sould be execute upone hir w[i]th all rigour to the terro[u]r & example of utheris heireftir'.[27] The actions taken before the verdict was delivered are described in detail:

---

[23] NAS, Books of Adjournal, JC2/6, fo. 67r.
[24] NAS, Books of Adjournal, JC2/6, fos. 71v–75r.
[25] NAS, Books of Adjournal, JC2/6, fo. 78r.
[26] NAS, Books of Adjournal, JC2/6, fo. 77v.
[27] NAS, Books of Adjournal, JC2/6, fo. 78r.

The saidis persones of assyse removet altogidder furth of court to the assyse
hous q[uhai]r thay be pluralitie of voittis electit & choset the said Johnne
Lawsoun in chanceller Ressonit & voittit upone the poyntis of the said dittay
And being ryple & at lenth advyset th[ai]rw[i]th togidder w[i[]th the depositiones of the witnessis ressavit sworne & admittit in th[ai]r p[resen]s and
audience & uth[e]r depositiones producet in proces to that effect reenterit
agane in court quhair thay be the repoirt and judiciall declaratioun of the
said chanceller ffand pronu[n]cet & declairit *for the maist p[air]t the said
margaret wallace to be fylet culpable & convict of the foure severall poyntis
& articles of dittay abone writtin and of the generall poynt abone spec[ife]it
subscryvet th[air]to* [My italics].[28]

The expression italicized above shows firstly that the assize was divided,
with a minority voting to acquit, and secondly that she was found guilty
of witchcraft. Like most of the Scottish witches sentenced to death, Margaret Wallace was taken to the place of execution 'And th[air] to be wirreit
at ane staik to the deid and hir body th[air]eftir to be brunt in ashes And
all hir moveabill guidis to be escheit & inbrocht to o[u]r sov[er]ane lordis
use and uth[e]ris haifand ryt th[air]to as culpable & convict of the saidis
crymes'.[29] The voice of the law during the closure of the trial is a steady
and determined one. There are no extenuating features to be traced.

The Voice of the Accused Person

Margaret Wallace's voice is rendered either by the witnesses or in the
legal discourse. The first time we hear her own uttered words is in article 8
of the dittay, where her quarrel with William Mure, flesher, is rendered,
a dispute which had arisen because he had called Cristiane Graham a
rank witch. Margaret allegedly said to him, 'Goe thy wayis hame bludie
boutcher that thow art thow sall nevir sie the calsay againe bot sall sud-
danlie schute to deid in thy awin chyre'.[30] The next day he died in his
own chair. Another episode was her quarrel with Cuthbert Greg. Cristiane
Graham was involved also here. Graham had desired a dog from him. This
he refused, 'Answring to hir agane I rather ye and my hussie baith (mean-
ding be margaret wallace) war brunt or ye get my dog'.[31] When Margaret Wallace got knowledge of this, she said to him, 'fals land ploupper
loun that thow art sayes thow that cristiane grahame and I sall be brunt

---

28 NAS, Books of Adjournal, JC2/6, fo. 78r.
29 NAS, Books of Adjournal, JC2/6, fo. 78v.
30 'Chyre' means 'chair'. NAS, Books of Adjournal, JC2/6, fo. 62r.
31 NAS, Books of Adjournal, JC2/6, fo. 68r.

for witches I vow to god I sall do to ye ane evill turne'.[32] 'Foure or five dayis' afterwards Cuthbert Greg fell sick. However, he recovered. He was asked before the court whether he had heard her utter the words that 'he sould mak hir (sic) w[i]thin few dayis nocht of habilitie to wyn ane caik of breid denyis that he hard sic woirdis bot only scho sould do him ane evill turne'.[33] His sickness was one of 'sweitting and brotheing' and he 'was nocht able to gang'. Related to another accusation of sickness, Jon Robertson testified 'that the said margaret wallace avowit to be avenget upone his flesche and that schortlie th[air]eftir conforme to the dittay the s[ai]d seiknes was laid upone him'.[34] Two events happened consecutively, one being the uttering of threatening words by Margaret Wallace, the other being sudden sickness that affected the threatened person. In addition to the addressee of the uttered words, the time factor connects these two events. Behind this logic lies a conviction that words uttered by witches are endangering.

An episode involving Christiane Grahame was told by one of the witnesses, Marion Mitchell. She said that during a visit at Alexander Vallange's, Margaret Wallace suddenly became sick and 'was sa extreme-lie handillit that scho was liklie to ryve hir selff'.[35] Two persons had to hold her. She asked for Christiane Grahame to come to help her, and she did. 'Sayis th[ai]reftir that Cristiane grahame tuik margaret wallace be the schaikill bane [*the wrist*] and kist hir and in hir airmes cayreit hir doun the stair saying to hir nothing sould aill hir'.[36] Afterwards the sickness was transferred to Margaret Montgomery's child. The morning after this, Margaret Wallace came to see the child and asked the child's mother 'to send for Cristiane grahame making all that tyme ane grit mone for the bairnes seiknes To quhome m[ar]garet montgomerie answrit I haif nothing ado w[i]th Cristiane grahame and will nocht send for hir for gif God hes laid on that seiknes on my bairne he will at his awin plessour tak it af againe'.[37] Still Margaret Wallace wanted to send for her, 'Gif ye knew Cristiane grahame skeill and q[uha]t scho can do ye wald nocht refuis to send for hir for scho can do als mekill as god in the heavin'.[38] In addition Margaret Wallace 'maist blasphemouslie and devillischlie answrit agane

---

32 NAS, Books of Adjournal, JC2/6, fo. 68r.
33 NAS, Books of Adjournal, JC2/6, fo. 68r.
34 NAS, Books of Adjournal, JC2/6, fo. 68v.
35 'ryve' means 'destroy'. NAS, Books of Adjournal, JC2/6, fo. 69r.
36 NAS, Books of Adjournal, JC2/6, fo. 69r.
37 NAS, Books of Adjournal, JC2/6, fo. 69v.
38 NAS, Books of Adjournal, JC2/6, fo. 69v.

that the said Cristiane grahame culd do als mekill in that eirand in cureing of that diseas as gif God him selff wald cum out of hevin & cure hir'.[39] These stories were told with pride by Margaret Wallace. The admiration and respect Margaret Wallace had for Christiane Grahame and her knowledge was based on devotion. There are no signals in the document denoting fear on the part of Margaret Wallace. On the contrary, she seemed to trust Christiane Grahame and her mastery of the craft.

There also seems to be a considerable interest in rituals performed by the alleged witches, judging by the description in the records. Margaret Wallace's removal of Cuthbert's sickness is described thus: 'At quhais cu[m]ing scho to manifest hir skill for his help tuik him be the schaikill bane w[i]th the ane hand And laid hir uther hand upone his breist and w[i]thout ony word speiking saif only to moveing of hir lipis past fra him at that instant'.[40] A ritual performed by Christiane Grahame and Margaret Wallace together to cure the child mentioned above is described thus:

> the said m[ar]garet liftit up the bairnes heid and the said Cristiane tuik hir be the shaikill bane and brocht the bairne furth of hir bed q[uhai]r scho was lying bedfast in grit payne of befoir and th[ai]reftir setting hir doun upone ane stuile w[i]th sum croces & signes maid upone hir And be uttering of dy[ver]is woirdis (nocht knawin quhat thay war) restoiret hir to hir helth[41]

It seems that the two women were working together trying to cure sickness, 'the said m[ar]garet wallace w[i]th the said Cristiane grahame past that same nyt betwix ellevin and twelf ho[u]ris under silence & clud of nyt to the yaird of James fynlay burges of glesgow quhair thay remanit the space of ane hour togidder practizeing sorcerie & witchcraft for cureing of the said bairne'.[42] Both of them obviously liked to use their craft, for instance Margaret Wallace 'geving out hir selff to haif skill in the cure of the said seiknes'.[43] Margaret Wallace referred to the deceased Christiane Grahame to a surprising degree, both in terms of quotations and in terms of descriptions of Graham's sorcery rituals. Even if Christiane Graham was not in court in person, she still played a role through stories about her being retold. Two knowledgeable women tried to cure sick persons, but they were also aware of their reputation and wanted to get paid for their 'jobs'. It seems they were laying on hands and taking off sickness. Joyce

[39] NAS, Books of Adjournal, JC2/6, fo. 76v.
[40] NAS, Books of Adjournal, JC2/6, fo. 76r.
[41] NAS, Books of Adjournal, JC2/6, fo. 76v.
[42] NAS, Books of Adjournal, JC2/6, fo. 77r.
[43] NAS, Books of Adjournal, JC2/6, fo. 77r.

Miller maintains that charming, or folk healing, 'provided society with means to counter the threat of malicious witchcraft'.[44] But in the case of Wallace, as well as many other accused women's cases, the voice of the law forced healing activities to be interpreted within a demonic frame.

The Voices of the Witnesses

Four witnesses were brought before the court. Their testimonies contain renderings of what they heard Margaret Wallace utter in different situations. They also describe in detail having seen the sick Cuthbert. Thus they confirm the connection between words uttered and harmful consequences of these words. In addition, a witness document, a warrant written by the archbishop of Glasgow relating to the trial of Christiane Grahame, was read out in court to prove Margaret Wallace's relation with the executed person. The same document was read to Christiane Grahame before her execution.[45]

The Voice of the Scribe

The scribe's voice is subdued. He makes no effort to intervene or intrude, and seems to agree with the dominant legal code in the text. A sensitivity to variations in language can be noted; When rendering the discourse of the legal officials, heavy rhetoric based on the written laws dominates; when rendering the accused person or the witnesses, the oral field of language dominates, and is particularly detailed during the rendering of the charms and incantations.

Even if this was not a trial characterized by demonology, the word 'devillisch' was used to denote the type of sorcery Margaret Wallace was accused of having committed, which would be punished by death. Words originating from 'devil' are mentioned nine times in the records, in phrases like 'hir devilische meanis', 'hir divilrie & witchcraft', 'hir devillische charmes', 'the said margaret wallace maist blasphemouslie and devillischlie answrit agane', 'hir devillische airt alsweill for cureing of hir selff', 'hir devillrie sorcerie & witchcraft', 'hir devillissche practizes' and 'witches & sorceraris instrumentis of the devill'. These words are connected to Margaret Wallace's way of performing sorcery as well as the practice of those whom she had consulted. An interesting sentence in

---

[44] Miller, 'Devices and directions', 105.
[45] NAS, Books of Adjournal, JC2/6, fo. 76v.

which the word 'devil' is used was uttered by Margaret Montgomery, one of the witnesses. She was the mother of the child Margaret Wallace had allegedly cast sickness upon. Wallace wanted to send for Christiane Graham to have the sickness taken away: 'And the said margaret mont-gomerie haifing (*a word after 'haifing' crossed out*) absolutelie refuisit sa to do saying to hir *scho wald co[m]mit hir bairne to God and nocht mell w[i]th the devill or ony of his instrumentis*' [*My italics*].[46] This remark suggests that by this time there was a common understanding in the community that curing sickness by using charms was the work of the Devil. However, this is the only place in the document where 'devil' is used by one of the witnesses; in all other instances the word is used in legal discourse to denote Margaret Wallace's practice or the practice of one of the other reputed witches she had consulted.

Conclusion

Margaret Wallace's case shows that several terms not mentioned in the Witchcraft Act had found their way to the courtroom and were used in legal argumentation by 1622. Even if the Witchcraft Act was cited, the scope of arguments for Wallace's crime by far extended the expressions written down in the act. In the court records of Wallace's case it becomes clear that malefice was considered a serious crime. The Devil was frequently mentioned in relation to malefice. Practising healing and charming was interpreted by the law as ungodly and devilish. The references to the Bible as well as to the Witchcraft Act show that this type of crime was considered to be a violation against divine as well as clerical laws. Hence the case serves as a good example of support for an interpretation of the witch-hunt's purpose as cleaning the country from ungodliness. At the same time it seems clear that demonological ideas centred round the Devil had penetrated the discourse of the judges and were used repeatedly in argumentation, while the case was not the same for the peasants or the accused. This suggests an interpretational practice in the court in which the restrictions implied in the Witchcraft Act were actively exceeded by pressing the boundaries of *maleficium* to equal demonological ideas, thus signalling a harsher climate in the legal treatment of sorcery.

---

[46] NAS, Books of Adjournal, JC2/6, fo. 76v.

Margaret Duchill, 1658

I have chosen this case for analysis because it allows close-reading aimed at exploring the demonological contents of accused persons' confessions. Both Margaret Duchill's own confession and the confessions of four other women accused at the same time as her, shed light on particular ideas of demonological origin, coming to the fore in the women's voices heard during interrogation. Apparently the women knew these notions before they were imprisoned, hence the following analysis is a contribution to show how demonological ideas spread and became assimilated into popular mentality. It is important to remember the spoken word with regard to the spread of demonological ideas among the common people, as these stories were spread due to oral transmission.[47]

The document first to be studied is a confession given by Margaret Duchill before the Presbytery of Alloa on 11 May 1658.[48] As she died before her confession was heard at the Presbytery session on 23 June, her confession before the presbytery was read aloud during a court meeting at which justices of peace were present: 'The said brethren and justices of peace present having receavit and at lenth heard & considerit ane paper under the hand of Mr James Meldrum Session clerk of alloway bearing the confessioun of Margaret Duchill (who is now dead) of witchcraft and dilating others the tennor of w[hi]ch paper is heirby appoyntit to be insert and is accordinglie done as followes'.[49] So in fact here we have a document taken down into script from an oral confession and passed on orally to an audience that would use the contents in order to get evidence to try other alleged witches. Speech is the transmitter of information.

Two primary documents exist connected to the trial of Margaret Duchill. There are the minutes from Stirling Presbytery mentioned above, which give the confession of Margaret Duchill from 1658. In addition, there are the records from Stirling Court from 1659, which give the confession of four witches later imprisoned and tried because of Duchill's denunciation, and also include a pre-trial dossier.[50] Duchill is also mentioned in a letter from Major James Holburne accompanying the pre-trial document, 'For the right honourable the commissioners for administration of justice

---

[47] Fox, A., *Oral and Literate Culture in England, 1500–1700* (Oxford, 2000) 194, 196.
[48] I would like to thank Diane Baptie for the transcription of the document.
[49] NAS, Stirling Presbytery records, CH2/722/6, p. 90.
[50] The court records from Stirling Court have reference BL, Egerton MS 2879. I would like to thank Julian Goodare for letting me read his transcription of this document.

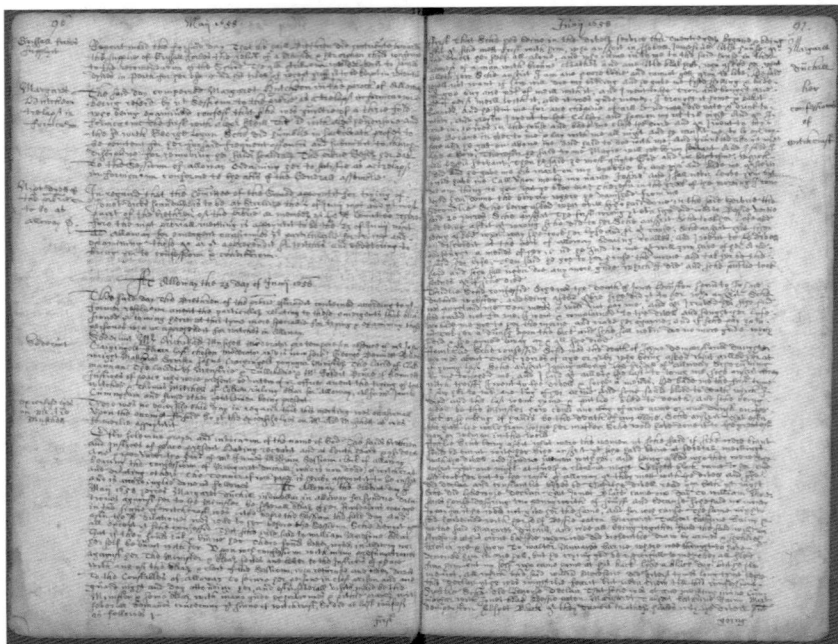

Figure 2: Case against Margaret Duchill, 1658. NAS, Stirling Presbytery records, CH2/722/6, p. 90.

in criminal causses to the people of Scotland', sent on 8 July 1658.[51] This letter also mentions that five women had been apprehended lately upon suspicion of witchcraft. 'One of them who was first under restraint confessed the renunciation of her baptisme, and that she did enter into Covenant with the Devill and committed many murders and other mischiefs; but she died in the place of her restraint.'[52] The one who died in prison, mentioned here, is apparently Margaret Duchill. In the Egerton court records Duchill is repeatedly mentioned in the confessions by the women later accused. She is also mentioned in the testimonies of the witnesses, and thus information about her comes up retrospectively.[53] The presbytery minutes and the Egerton document complement each other with regard to the Margaret Duchill case, as will be seen below. They give in addition valuable information about the linked trials of Alloa in 1658–59.

[51] BL, Egerton MS 2879, fo. 1r.
[52] BL, Egerton MS 2879, fo. 1r.
[53] BL, Egerton MS 2879, fos. 3r–16r.

A secondary source about the witches of Alloa is an article from 1908, which gives a summary of the main points of Duchill's confession.[54] These trials, including a study of Margaret Duchill, have also been discussed by P. G. Maxwell-Stuart.[55]

According to Stirling Presbytery Minutes, on 19 May 1658 Mr George Bennett and Mr Matthias Sympson were appointed to go to Alloa to 'conferr with' the persons who were imprisoned for witchcraft.[56] The next presbytery session was appointed for 23 June at Alloa 'for emergent occasiounes th[ai]r particularlie for trying and examining those q[uh]o ar th[ai]r apprehendit for witches and endevoring to bring th[e]m to confession & convictioun'.[57] In other words, there was a situation to be dealt with immediately.

Those present at the presbytery session in Alloa on 23 June were the moderator Mr Archibald Muschett, and the younger ministers George Bennett, Robert Wright, Matthias Symson, John Craigengelt, the Laird of Clakmannan, the Lairds of Menstrie & Tullibodie and Mr Robert Bruce of Kennet, Justice of the Peace, were also present 'be virtew of th[ai]r offices anent the trying of the witches'.[58] Two of the younger ministers were the ones who had arrived from Stirling to 'confer' with the imprisoned witches.

The accused persons had been imprisoned for more than a month when the presbytery meeting of 23 June took place. Margaret Duchill had been interrogated before 11 May, when she 'confessid that sche haid said to william Moresone eldar that if they sould tak & burne her there sould better wyves in alloway nor herself be burnt with her'.[59] A letter was then sent to the justices of the peace, delivered by one of the elders and the clerk of the session, and they returned an order, 'direct to the Constables of alloway to secure her persone in closs prison and ane guard night and day attending her, and eftir severall visits maid be the Minister & some eldaris with many gude exhorta[tio]unes & pithie prayeris with severall demands concerning th[a]t sinne of witchcraft, so did at last confess'.[60] Sleep deprivation was the most common torture method used in Scotland, with a guard constantly watching the imprisoned person, in order for

---

54 Fergusson, R. M., 'The Witches of Alloa', *Scottish Historical Review*, iv (1908), 40–48.
55 Maxwell-Stuart, P. G., *An Abundance of Witches* (Gloucestershire, 2005), 92–106.
56 NAS, Stirling Presbytery records, CH2/722/6, p. 89.
57 NAS, Stirling Presbytery records, CH2/722/6, p. 90.
58 NAS, Stirling Presbytery records, CH2/722/6, p. 90.
59 NAS, Stirling Presbytery records, CH2/722/6, p. 90.
60 NAS, Stirling Presbytery records, CH2/722/6, p. 90.

this one not to fall asleep. Duchill must have died between 19 May, when
the two ministers at the presbytery meeting at Stirling were appointed
to go to Alloa, and 23 June. It is unclear whether she was dead before
3 June, when the four other women were interrogated. Three of these
were extrajudicially tortured and burnt with hot stones by four local men.
The witchcraft suspects were confronted with each other to get more
information, a method often used. No further action was taken.[61] The
women seem to have been ordinary women from the parish. We know
that one of them was married and had children. Margaret Duchill used
to work with spinning during daytime, noting in her confession that she
went to 'the Calsey and span on my rok till night'.[62]

The case against the four women denounced by Margaret Duchill
was finished on 24 June. In the final statement the presbytery, together
with the Justices of the Peace, had an interesting formulation related to
the gravity of the four women's guilt, in which they distinguish between
Margaret Tailyeor and the other three,

> finding that Margaret tayleor hes clairlie confest witchcraft and *express pact-*
> *ioun with the devill and some malefices* and th[a]t th[ai]r ar great presump-
> tiounes that *the other thrie ar guyltie of witchcraft* doe th[ai]rfore judge it
> expedient that a letter be writtin in name of this meiting to the judges com-
> petent in criminal causes representing the case forsaid unto th[e]m, and
> desyring that they may tak cours with the s[ai]ds women as accords of the
> Law [*My italics*].[63]

This is an interesting distinction, because it suggests that confession of the
demonic pact and malefice was looked upon and treated more seriously
than confession of 'witchcraft' in general. It seems that the other three
did not confess to the demonic pact in the first place. But in spite of the
confessions made and the confrontations which were arranged before the
session, the four women refused to confirm their previous confessions.
However, one year later, during their trials in 1659, they confessed to the
demonic pact as well as confirming their previous confessions.[64]

---

[61] The three were Kathrine Remy, Bessie Paton and Margaret Tailyeor. Ref. The Survey,
sub Margaret Tailyeor.
[62] NAS, Stirling Presbytery records, CH2/722/6, p. 91. Calsey seems to be a place name,
as it is written with capital letter, but 'the calsey' might also mean the causeway or the
street.
[63] NAS, Stirling Presbytery records, CH2/722/6, p. 96.
[64] BL, Egerton MS 2879, fos. 4r–7v.

The presbytery apparently saw a witchcraft case as an important one to handle. Still, they had other duties to carry through. A silent sigh from the brethren may be heard in the last sentence of the minutes of 24 June, after having struggled for two long days with four alleged witches who refused to confirm their previous confessions extracted during torture: 'In regaird that the day is now spent and that the brethren cannot entir this night on th[ai]r other pr[es]b[yte]riall bussiness & refer[ence]s, doe th[ai]rfore adjourne th[ai]r meitting till the morrow at 8 a cloak in the morning'.[65] Even if two of the brethren were asked 'to goe to the saides four women apairt and seriouslie & gravlie by prayer & exhorta[tio]un to deall with them towards confessioun & endevor to convince th[e]m of th[ai]r haynous offencis', report was made the next day that this expedition was in vain—'but fand no more from th[e]m nor wes formerlie confest be th[e]m'.[66]

In addition to the presbytery minutes referred to above, the Egerton manuscript throws additional light on Duchill's case through testimonies of witnesses. Hendrie Towart declared on oath that Margaret Duchill said

> that Elisabeth Blak was hir brother Thomas Duchall his death and that shoe was as great ane witch as hir self, and that shoe laid seiknes on her awne son and came to hir to tak it aff againe, quhilk the said Margaret did and laid it on the said Elisabeth hir awne horse, who died immediatly, and thairafter the said Elisabeth did exclame against hir and called hir witch for doeing thairoff.[67]

At the end of the testimonies against Elisabeth Blak a paragraph is added. 'Bessie Patoun (wha is brunt) did declare whill shoe was in prison at Alloway that Elisabeth Blak, wpone ane anger against hir awne sone James Demperstoun, did lay on ane heavie seiknes wpon him'.[68] After Elisabeth Blak had gone to Bessie Patoun and asked her to take off the sickness, and she refused, she went to Margaret Duchill and bade her do it, which she did. The testimonies from the witnesses indicate that the women accused of witchcraft knew each other and also had the reputation of being charmers and healers. As Margaret Duchill's name came up several times, she was one of these reputed persons.

---

[65] NAS, Stirling Presbytery records, CH2/722/6, p. 97.
[66] NAS, Stirling Presbytery records, CH2/722/6, p. 97.
[67] BL, Egerton MS 2879, fo. 8v.
[68] BL, Egerton MS 2879, fo. 9v.

The Interrogation

How can a reader today possibly find out what happened during the
witchcraft interrogations? One approach is to scrutinise the document
looking for indications of questions posed by the interrogators, so-called
shadow questions. Such questions have to be constructed in retrospect by
the researcher as the answers indicate what the questions were. Another
method is to look for direct indications of questions in the records. The
case of Margaret Duchill is one wherein such evidence is found. Her
itemized confession given before the presbytery consisted of six points.
Four of these contain the formulation 'being asked'. After the first point,
which contains her narrative about the pact and the rituals related to it,
the second point contains her answers to specific questions, '*sche being
asked* what evill scho haid done in the said service the said 20 yeires sche
answerit the first wrong th[a]t evir sche did wes to Bessie Vertie and
being askit q[uha]t wrong sche did to her sche answerit sche took her lyfe
and *being asked* what way sche took her lyfe and for q[uha]t cause' [*My
italics*].[69] The first questions had to do with the severity of her sorcery.
The next questions had to do with her confessing to being the cause of the
death of a twelve-year-old girl, John Demperstoune's daughter: Margaret
Duchill '*being asked* what ailled her at th[a]t young lass', and related to
the same event, '*sche being asked be the Minister* how could ane tug of ane
arme or ane dunsh on the back or shaking of hands be the death of any
bodie' [*My italics*].[70] We see that her motives for performing evil as well
as the inexplicable in her witchcraft power are themes the minister liked
to have more information about. The last questions posed to her had to
do with denunciation of other women: '*sche being askit* what were the
women th[a]t sche said if sche were burnt sould be burnt with her sche
answerit th[a]t sche haid beine at severall meittings with the divell and
syndrie women with her and *being asked* who they were' [*My italics*].[71]
The last question of course led to the naming of the other women who
were apprehended. This is a good example of how a panic could arise
from the confession of the first imprisoned person.

The purpose of all the questions posed during the presbytery interrogation was to push the confession further on specific points, namely what

---

[69] NAS, Stirling Presbytery records, CH2/722/6, p. 91.
[70] NAS, Stirling Presbytery records, CH2/722/6, p. 91.
[71] NAS, Stirling Presbytery records, CH2/722/6, p. 91.

kind of evil-doing she had performed, her motives for performing evil and the names of other persons who had participated in witches' meetings. Of special interest is the question from the minister about her power, a question which required an answer related to her receiving power from the Devil. The questions asked here circle around demonological notions. Even if there does not seem to be any questionnaire involved in the interrogation, as there often was in southern Germany,[72] the questions posed contribute to explaining the rapid growth of a witchcraft panic. All the questions were presumably answered by Margaret Duchill in a state of bewilderment due to sleep deprivation. It seems clear that the interrogators tried to take advantage of her distress and lead her confession in the direction they wanted.

The use of leading questions during interrogation is evident in the Egerton manuscript as well. At the end of the manuscript there is a declaration by J. Craigengelt, who had heard the confession of Margaret Duchill. He testified that Duchill, 'who died a confessed witche in firmance in our toune of Alloway' was asked by the minister

> if shoe would be content to be brunt and they should burne Elspit Blak with hir, shoe ansueared, with all my heart even, tomorrou if ye will, The minister said O what a great envy and malice hath shoe against this Elspit Blak, She said again, I have good reason to envy hir, hir mother was my brothers death; Well, said the minister, and ye war the death of hir daughter, who answeared, it is true and weell allowed the same.[73]

The oral tone is evident in this citation, in which the dialogue between Margaret Duchill and the minister is rendered, and the minister's attitude towards her witchcraft is clear. When the minister visited her before she was burnt, this was 'not as a witch bot as a dying woman'.[74]

In other words, he was preparing her for death. She was asked by him

> if nou shoe would forgive all them who had wronged hir, shee said, shoe would, and being asked more particularly be the said minister, if shoe would forgive Elspit Blak, shoe ansueared shoe would never forgive hir,

---

[72] Voltmer, R., 'Netzwerk, Denkollektiv oder Dschungel?', *Zeitschrift für historische Forschung*, 34:3 (2007), 486–87; Voltmer, R., 'Hexenjagd im Territorium der Reichsabtei St Maximin vor Trier', in W. Reichert, G. Minn, and R. Voltmer, *Quellen zur Geschichte des Rhein- Maas- Raumes* (Trier, 2006), 249–50; Behringer, W., *Hexen und Hexenprozesse* (München, 1995), 279–81.

[73] BL, Egerton MS 2879, fo. 15r.

[74] BL, Egerton MS 2879, fo. 15r.

the minister said how shall then God forgive you, if ye will not forgive your neightbour shoe ansueared, I did nevir such offence to God as shoe did to me, I will nevir forgive hir.[75]

She also confessed, after being asked, that she had been a witch for twenty-two years and that Elisbeth Blak learned from her, 'and agane being asked hou long has Elspit Blak beene a witch then, shoe ansueared nyne years'.[76] The final sentence about Margaret Duchill is even more interesting: 'Then all admired the lying and envy of the said Margaret Duchell aganst [sic] the said Elspit Blak, and thought good to testifie the same, lest the said Elspit Black should come ondir hazard of hir lyf by the malice and envy of the said defunct Margaret Duchell confessed witch'.[77] The attempt to hinder a trial for Elisabeth Black was successful this year, but she was arrested and tried again in 1662. The outcome of that trial is not known.

Demonological Elements

The presbytery minutes document a wide range of demonological ideas based on oral narratives confessed by the five women involved. The richness of detail and the unity of elements we hear repeated in the confessions by one accused person after another suggest that these narratives were part of an oral tradition well known in the community. This can be no coincidence. Individuals probably told these stories to each other and when pressed during their interrogation, they retold these stories as answers to leading questions—just in the way the interrogators wanted to hear it.

The pact with the Devil is the first point in Margaret Duchill's confession and the most important one, as all the other points are subordinate to this. She had been in the Devil's service for 20 years and met him first

in Issobell Jamesones litle house q[uhai]r sche dwelt her self all alone, and who came in to me to the said house in the likeness of a man with broune cloathes and ane litle blak hatt, who asked her, what ailleth yow sche answerit I am ane poore bodie and cannot gett q[uhai]ron to live, he said ye sall *not want* if yow will doe my bidding and he gave me fyve shilling & bade me goe buy ane pek of meill with it, and I went to the tron and bought ane pek of peis meill with it, and *it wes gude money*. I brought it home &

[75] BL, Egerton MS 2879, fo. 15r.
[76] BL, Egerton MS 2879, fo. 16r.
[77] BL, Egerton MS 2879, fo. 16r.

bakit bannoks, and he sent me for ane chopine of aill and *wee did eate &*
drink together.[78] [*My italics.*]

This confession resembles many other witchcraft confessions in Scotland,
not only as far as the main content is concerned, but also with regard to
specific phrases, such as the Devil's offer that she should not want, she
would be secure. This points to some important hinges for transference
of oral narratives, namely short and pointed expressions, which makes the
narrative easy to remember and easy to retell. The phrase 'gude money'
indicates that it did not turn into leaves or dung, as the Devil's money
sometimes did.[79] In addition, the meal with the Devil as part of the ritual
is frequently found in demonological witchcraft cases; one could take in
the power of the Devil's witchcraft through food and drink, bringing into
the picture the inverted communion, in this case eating and drinking to
become the child of the Evil Master.

Sexual intercourse as part of the ritual is found in some countries, in
others not. The Scottish confessions have this element present, but it
differs from, for instance, Germany, in terms of the extent of the sexual
orgies. It also differs from Finnmark, where the confessions do not contain
this element as part of the pact or meeting. So Scotland is in a middle
position here. In the case of Margaret Duchill, this element is described
thus: 'And q[uhe]n I came in, he wes in the house and bade me close the
doore and q[uhe]n I went to my bed he came in over to me & lay with
me all night and he causit me to ly on my face and he gatt on abone me
and haid to doe with me, and grunkled [*grunted*] abone me lyke a kow'.[80]
In the image portrayed here, the woman plays the subordinate part in
more than one sense. But there is no sign of resistance to the intercourse
on the woman's part. Whether or not she was easily tempted by the Devil,
the text does not say, so the argument set forth by some demonologists,
that women were easily tempted, cannot be supported from this text.[81]
Instead the text appears to support an interpretation that she seemed to

---

[78] NAS, Stirling Presbytery records, CH2/722/6, p. 91.
[79] This we find echoed in German as well as in Norwegian witchcraft sources. For German cases, the same idea is found, ref. Landeshauptarchiv Koblenz, 211/No. 2222, fo. 7; In a Norwegian case, a woman said that she was promised all she wanted by the Devil, but he kept this promise like the dog he was, ref. The Archives of Finnmark District Magistrate, no. 10, Court Records 1654–1663, fo. 267v.
[80] NAS, Stirling Presbytery records, CH2/722/6, p. 91.
[81] This is one of the points characterizing women in *Malleus Maleficarum*.

be tempted more by the prospect of 'not wanting' and a good meal, rather than the prospect of sexual intercourse.

Renouncing baptism, a new name, the Devil's mark and a loyalty for ever are ingredients that belong to the demonic pact. In Scotland particularly, it was common to have a new name.[82] So also here, 'Thereftir he said to me Magie will yee be my servant And I said I wold be his servant, then he said ye most quyte God and yo[u]r baptisme, which I did and he gave me his mark on my eyebrie by ane nip and bade me q[uhe]nsoevir ye wold have me call upon me by my name Johne and I sall nevir leave yow but doe any thing to yow that yow bide me'.[83] All these elements are found in demonological confessions from other places as well, even the notion that the eyebrow is important. In the material from Finnmark, one of the accused women confessed that the executioner, who tortured her, cut off her eyebrows because the Devil was supposed to be inside.[84]

What kind of evil was performed and why the accused performed it also comes to the fore during the confessions. This is a point of interest with regard to a socio-economic explanation of witchcraft because the accused person frequently gave such reasons as a dispute at work or neighbourhood disputes which required revenge. So also here,

> sche [*her friend*] answerit that *sche & I discordit at the pow of alloway bearing coalles*, and I went to the divell and sought a mends of her, and he said to me q[uha]t will yow have of her And I said her lyfe, then said he goe to her house the morne and *tak her be the hand and sche sal nevir doe any more gude* which I did and sche p[rese]ntlie took seiknes q[uhai]rof sche died [*My italics*].[85]

Disagreement and quarrelling with neighbours, as expressed in confessions, were related to everyday situations. Money was part of this. The next motive Margaret Duchill gave had to do with money: Jonet Houston would not pay her the money she owed her, 'and q[uhe]n I craved her sche said sche cared not for me, I went & complained to the divell and sought her lyfe who bade me goe to her the morne and crave her agayne, and if sche pay yow not tak her a dunsh upon the back and sche sall nevir doe no more gude which I did & sche pyned away ay & q[uhi]ll sche died'.[86] With reference to oral discourse, there is a double negative—

---

[82] SSW has a search option for 'New name'.
[83] NAS, Stirling Presbytery records, CH2/722/6, p. 91.
[84] Marrite Thamisdatter, 1634, SATØ, AF, no. 2543.
[85] NAS, Stirling Presbytery records, CH2/722/6, p. 91.
[86] NAS, Stirling Presbytery records, CH2/722/6, p. 91.

a type of repetition—'sche sall nevir doe no more gude', which suggests that these narratives contained expressions easy to remember.

In the confession we also hear the discourse of one of her victims, rendered in the episode in which she fell into a dispute with the twelve-year-old Johne [*Joan*] Demperstoune, daughter of Elisabeth Blak. Margaret Duchill said that the reason for doing her harm was this:

> I going allong the bridge of alloway *sche run[n]ing by me touched me*, and I said q[uha]t ailleth the lass to touch me, *sche answerit away witch theiff*, I went to the divell & socht a mends, he bade me the first tyme I saw her to tak ane tug of her arme and sche sould blood to death which I died (*sic*) and the lass went home & p[rese]ntlie bled to death. [*My italics.*][87]

The girl apparently knew Margaret Duchill's reputation for sorcery and called her a witch. In those days it might be dangerous to be called a witch, since the legal reaction was so strong. The minister was interested in her ability to perform witchcraft, and in her own words her strength was unlimited, 'scho answerit that eftir sche gatt the word from Johne her master sche wold have done it to the greatest man or woman in the world'.[88]

Shape-shifting was often related to witches' meetings and collective witchcraft operations. In Margaret Duchill's confession she gives the background for such a collective operation, in which the element of shape-shifting is easily placed. Another woman, Jonet Black, had been refused snuff from William Moreson because she had no money to pay for it,

> and for w[hi]ch cause the same night sche conveined with her self Bessie paton margaret Talzeor kathrine Rainy & me the said Margaret duchill, and wee all being togither fand the said william Moresone at his owne backsyde whom wee did violentlie draw by armes & shoulderis throuch yce & snow to Walter Murrayes barne where wee thought to have drowned him in ane holl, but he crying god be mercifull to me, they all fled from him but my self who came home at his back lyke a black dog *but he saw me not*, all which the said willia[m] Moresone did divers tymes long tyme before this declair th[a]t he wes mightilie fearit *but nevir knew till this confessioun* [*My italics*].[89]

Whether or not William Morrison was attacked by dogs we do not know, but he confirmed in front of the presbytery that he was scared by the women. Through the telling of this event several names of other witches were revealed, which made it possible to call in other women.

---

[87] NAS, Stirling Presbytery records, CH2/722/6, p. 91.
[88] NAS, Stirling Presbytery records, CH2/722/6, p. 91.
[89] NAS, Stirling Presbytery records, CH2/722/6, p. 91.

The Egerton manuscript gives additional information about Duchill's alleged shape-shifting. Barbara Erskine confessed on 14 March 1659 that 'about thrie yeirs since or thairby Margaret Talyor, Jonet Blak, Bessie Paton and Margaret Duchell did goe to the Blak Grainge and perished a boat thair with fyve persones thairin, but shoe and Margaret Duchell stayed in the Cambus till they had done: And they wer in the lyknes of corbies'.[90] The same Barbara was confronted with another accused person, James Kirk, on 14 March 1659 and 'did most boldly affirme that the said James was at twa severall meitings with them in the cuning yaird and plaed on his whisle to them and they all danced but shoe and Margaret Duchell for they wer but twa waly dragles'.[91] Thus in Barbara Erskine's confession attention is drawn towards Margaret Duchill's participation in witches' meetings, and metamorphosis was mentioned. In addition, several witnesses, James Lindsay, Jone Kirk and Andro Thomson, declared on oath on 15 November 1658,

> that Margaret Duchall did declare, and did constantly byd be it till the houre of hir death (wha died in prison), that the said Elisabeth Blak was at all meitings with them, at destroying of bairnes, horses and kyne, and that ane night the said Elisabeth Blak came to hir at midningt and took hir out of hir awne house to the crofts of Alloway, quhair the Devill came to them, and as shoe said, rede them both.[92]

Witches' meetings often contained elements of joy and merriment, which might be seen as elements of disorder.[93] When the alleged witches in Alloa gathered, they 'dancit in otheris hands with the divell p[rese]nt going up and doune among them some of them singing & some of th[e]m dancing and Bessie paton leading the ring'.[94] But there is a sudden change in the confession from a state of innocence to turpitude, which undermines the idyllic aspect. The last point of her confession shows, like several other witchcraft confession, a tendency to escalation based on the dissolving of the language structure. The coherence of the text disappears and the syntax dissolves into fragmented sentence clauses. Also the meaning gets completely out of control and coherence from one sentence to the next disappears. As part of witches' meetings they kill one person after the other,

---

[90] BL, Egerton MS 2879, fo. 3v.
[91] BL, Egerton MS 2879, fo. 6r.
[92] BL, Egerton MS 2879, fo. 8v.
[93] Larner, *Enemies of God*, 153.
[94] NAS, Stirling Presbytery records, CH2/722/6, pp. 91–92.

sche confest ane meiting in the Cuningar of all the sevine with the divell in the likeness of catts who went to the gran(ge)?—[*letters obscured*] and destroyed ane kow to Edward turnour, Ane other meitting ane night and they went to Tullibodie & killed ane bairne Anoth[e]r meiting & went to the bow house & killed ane hors & ane kow to willia[m] Menteith an other meitting & they went to Clakmannan and killed ane chyld to thomas bruce, anoth[e]r meiting and they went to Coldones & wes the death of tuo bairnes of his.[95]

In my opinion this is a sign of distress, possibly resulting from torture, and an example of how the language in itself, through the way of speaking, may convey knowledge about what happened during witchcraft interrogation. The last point of the confession is chaotic on all levels, syntactic as well as semantic, and we see an intensifying additive structure in which elements are piled together. All of this contributes to underline Margaret's misery.

This confession of Margaret Duchill's was cited at the session on 11 May, 'and eftir the dilatiounes wes read to her before the Sessioun sche denyit th[e]m all'.[96] This denial was probably fatal to her. After a confession like the one she had delivered, she was trapped. If she confirmed, she would be burnt. If she denied, she would be tortured worse than before. This illustrates the dilemma of the accused person's situation and points to the complex of psychological mechanisms that took effect during a long period in prison. There was no other direction for such a person to look than towards her own death. For many of the accused, this pressure finally led to a confession, knowing well that in doing so they sealed their way to the stake.

Conclusion

The case of Margaret Duchill is typical for the height of the Scottish witch-hunt. Duchill was reputed as a witch. Neighbour disputes related to every-day situations as well as economic matters were mentioned by witnesses as motives for suspecting her of witchcraft. Once imprisoned, the chances of acquittal were small. She was tortured and pressed to confess. Her confession contains classic demonological elements. She was asked leading questions, all stressing demonology. But even if she was led to certain points that should be answered, the knowledge of demonology apparently was her own. She must have known demonological elements before she

---

[95] NAS, Stirling Presbytery records, CH2/722/6, p. 92.
[96] NAS, Stirling Presbytery records, CH2/722/6, p. 90.

was imprisoned, as part of the orally passed stories among the peasants. Her answers are given in a state of mental distress, and she gives comprehensive answers to brief and open questions. Torture led to the disintegration of the language and contents of her confession. She refused to confirm her confession. The minister was there to prepare her before her death. As gravity of guilt was equated to the demonic pact, the outcome of her case was clear at an early stage.

Janet Morrison, 1662

Janet Morrison lived in Bute, which is situated in the Highlands. People in this area, the Highlanders, spoke Gaelic. The case of Janet Morrison is chosen for close-reading because it contributes to the understanding of witchcraft persecution in a district wherein the Highlanders were living. Hence ethnicity enters the picture, as ethnic groups were supposed to master the art of sorcery to a greater extent than the rest of the nation.

General

In *Highland Papers* we find a verbatim transcription of records connected to charges of witchcraft in the parish of Rothesay, Bute, in 1662.[97] This witchcraft paper documents six women who were accused of witchcraft and questioned during the period January-February 1662 as part of the nationwide panic. The Bute document as a whole is a web of smaller stories, each focusing on one woman. It is a document most likely addressed to members of the Privy Council in order for them to appoint a commission for trying the accused women.[98]

Janet Morrison was the first of the six women questioned. Her questioning took place from 15 January until 29 January 1662, eight times altogether, and on four of these occasions both in the morning and in the afternoon. Apparently she was first questioned in her home on 15 January, where she gave a declaration. Then she was taken to the tolbooth on 18 January and questioned morning and afternoon. On 19 January she is

---

[97] MacPhail, J. R. N. (ed.), 'Papers related to Witchcraft 1662–1677', *HP*, iii, SHS, 2nd series, 3 (1920), 2–30. The document was placed at the disposal of the Scottish History Society by His Grace the Duke of Argyll.

[98] Goodare, 'Framework for Scottish Witch-Hunting', 240–1; Wasser, M., 'The privy council and the witches: the curtailment of witchcraft prosecutions in Scotland, 1597–1628', *SHR*, 82 (2003), 22.

again said to have been questioned at home, but the place is probably a mistake, because she had already been imprisoned. In connection with her questioning, which always took place before a group of men, the minister, John Stewart, is mentioned seven times; once he is the sole questioner. Twice it is recorded that she herself sent for the minister 'to speik with her'.[99] The provost of Rothesay, John Glas, questioned her six times. The other persons mentioned as participating in the questioning were several burgesses of Rothesay, and the bailiff. On 21 January Janet Morrison gave a declaration before eleven men, on 22 January she sent for the minister and was questioned both morning and afternoon, on 23 January she was questioned twice, before the minister and the provost, and on 29 January she was questioned by the minister.

The Voice of the Scribe

The scribe's voice has a register of different accents; one of these is the accent of a clerk, briefly reporting dates, names and places, a second is the short but pointed rendering of the witnesses' declarations, a third is the slightly coloured accent when rendering the women's confessions, including short portrayals of the women's states of emotion during the confessions, a fourth is the accent of the scribe as the person handling a case in progress. With regard to the voice of the accused person, there are no signs of scepticism in the text, no distancing devices used by the scribe when Janet Morrison's declarations and confessions are rendered.

The scribe gives precise information about the names of the witnesses and their family relations. Details concerning the time aspect are taken care of, telling how long has passed since an event happened. This holds true for both the witnesses' declarations and the declarations of the accused, for instance 'about twa years sine',[100] 'about a forthnight afore halountayd last', 'about three nights before Hallowday last',[101] 'one frayday thereafter being the liventh of January 1662',[102] or 'in summer last being gathering herbs'.[103] Place is also taken care of by mentioning place names, for instance: 'Shee declared that on a tyme heirefter being cuming from

---

[99] *HP*, iii, 20.
[100] *HP*, iii, 3.
[101] *HP*, iii, 24.
[102] *HP*, iii, 21.
[103] *HP*, iii, 22.

Kilmorie in the evening'.[104] In fact, the document contains several textual elements that are found in orally transmitted narratives.

Sometimes the scribe inserted explanatory comments within brackets, like: 'Shee declared (*after being challenged at the Session*)' and 'she declared *over againe*'. [*My italics.*] Thus he commented on Janet Morrison's situation, giving information extra to her declaration, telling the reader what had gone before her declaration or that this was yet another declaration in a long series. The use of 'etc.' is also an interesting comment from the writer, 'quairin she promised to be his servant *etc.*'[105] [*My italics.*] My interpretation of 'etc.' here is that the scribe, and also, as he assumes, the reader of the document, knows well enough what does come after 'his servant', namely the implied services the woman was supposed to render to the Devil as part of the pact. In other words, there is a sign that the elements and content of the declarations the accused are supposed to deliver when questioned are well-known among ordinary people and it is therefore unnecessary to write more. It might also have been used because the document was written to the Privy Council in order for them to decide if they were going to appoint a commission, and the members were supposed to know a formulaic confession.

For the Bute document as a whole, the aspect of ethnicity comes to the fore. The scribe chose to render some phrases of the charms in Gaelic, quotations from the confessions of the accused women. Even if these quotations are not directly related to Janet Morrison, they add some interesting perspectives on the Highlanders as a group on the part of the scribe. The quotations in Gaelic might have been used to underline the obscurity of the text, denoting that the business of healers and charmers—such as the accused women allegedly were—was dangerous and mystical, and so was their language. There might also have been an assumption that the power of the words would be stronger when uttered in Gaelic. By rendering some oral expressions in Gaelic, the Highlanders are in a way established as 'the others' in the text, compared to the rest of the Scots.

It is likely that the accused persons probably gave their confessions in Gaelic, as this was the language spoken in that area.[106] In a contemporary

---

[104] *HP*, iii, 21.

[105] *HP*, iii, 22.

[106] Withers, C. W. J., 'Gaelic in Scotland before 1609' in *Gaelic in Scotland 1698–1981. The geographical History of a Language* (Edinburgh, 1984), 16–41; Withers, C. W. J., *Gaelic Scotland. The Transformation of a Culture Region* (London, 1988), 34–7; P. McNeill and R. Nicholson (eds.), *An Historical Atlas of Scotland c. 400–c. 1600* (St Andrews, 1975), 178.

geographical context, Bute was mentioned as belonging to the Highlands, because it was said about one of the imprisoned women that she escaped from the tolbooth of Rothesay and fled to the Lowlands.[107] In addition there was the minister sent for by Morrison herself. He had a thorough knowledge of Gaelic, because he had translated the scriptures into Gaelic.[108] It is likely that she sent for him because he was able to understand her. She had 'sent for Mr John Stewart to speik with her at her own house the 19 January 1662 before John Glas proveist of Rothesay, Mr John Stewart minister there and Johne Gray burgess in the said Burgh'.[109] We have then three persons meeting her, 'and *being enqueired be us* if she knew (...)'.[110] [*My italics.*] The use of 'us' here indicates that one of the questioners was the scribe. This fact points to John Stewart, who was able to question her in Gaelic and simultaneously could record in Scots. It should also be noted that Morrison's name of the Devil, 'Klarenough', is an English phrase, which may suggest that she deliberately used English in contrast to Gaelic to emphasize certain aspects of her confession.

The questioning of a person suspected of witchcraft often lasted for several days, thus increasing the accused's exhaustion. In the Bute document, we see that the writer forms a kind of compressed expression of what had happened earlier, when he states: 'Quhilk day she repeitted severall particulars of her former declarations viz. her meiting with the devil severall tymes and her trysting with him, her covenant with him (...)'.[111] The use of an abbreviation like 'viz.' shows that the writer had authority enough on his own behalf to make a short summary of the main points in Janet Morrison's declaration thus far, focusing on her meetings with the Devil and the demonic pact.

A more formal sign on the part of the scribe is the use of numbers in front of each paragraph in Janet Morrison's confession.[112] Probably the numbers indicated itemizing. Many Scottish dittays have 'Imprimis' or 'Item' to indicate a new point, not numbers—but serving a similar function.

---

[107] J. Cameron and J. Imrie (eds.), *The Justiciary Records of Argyll and the Isles 1664–1705*, 2 vols. (SS, 1949–69), 1, 20.
[108] Fasti, biography John Stewart.
[109] *HP*, iii, 20.
[110] *HP*, iii, 20
[111] *HP*, iii, 23.
[112] Question list were not in use in Scotland, in contrast to the use of numbered catalogues, which for instance is known from witchcraft persecutions in Germany. Ref. Behringer, *Hexen*, 279–81; Voltmer, 'Netzwerk', 486–87; Voltmer, 'Hexenjagd', 249–50.

The Voices of the Witnesses

Those who witnessed against Janet Morrison were two neighbours. The first time Morrison is mentioned is in a declaration given by her neighbour Robert Stewart. His declaration is the story of a quarrel between his wife and Janet Morrison, told with the comments of Stewart's wife rendered in indirect discourse and Janet Morrison's comments in direct discourse. They are vividly portrayed, like actors on the stage, thus showing the oral brilliance of a good story-teller, who knows how to put small dramatic episodes into his narrative. Apparently the two women used strong and spicy words. Janet exclaimed when she did not get what she deserved from the other woman: 'I garne to have it and I will garr yow rue it or it be longer'.[113] The accusation against Morrison was made by Robert Stewart on behalf of his wife. Stewart said that his wife 'was going in the byre felt something strik her there, the whole house darkened which continued a long space with her'.[114] Stewart's wife had afterwards complained that Janet Morrison was to blame for this. Apparently, despite such a vague accusation, this seems to have been enough to initiate the case and imprison Morrison. There are no signals that imply that the scribe doubted Stewart's declaration. When Robert Stewart refers to what his wife said, 'she still complains that', his statement loses authority. He was not a witness himself; under ordinary legal prosecution this tends to weaken and diminish the range of the declaration. Still, such an accusation was considered to be sufficient for further inquiry. It is worth noting that a woman's testimony was not usually accepted in criminal trials, but after 1591 an exception was made for witchcraft.[115] Ministers were used to interrogate women in the kirk sessions.

The basic structures of a narrative are revealed in Robert Stewart's short statement, including the order of events; one event is placed after another on a linear time-line. Stewart starts his declaration in this way: 'Declares that about *twa years sine* (...) *Quhen* his wife said to her (...) the said Jonet said (...) and *within a quarter of ane yeir ther after* the said Glens wife *as she was going in the byre* felt something strik her there (...) she *still* compleins that it was Jonet Morison that did it'.[116] [*My italics.*] It

---

[113] Means: I am going to have it or I will make you regret it.
[114] *HP*, iii, 3.
[115] Wasser, 'Privy council and the witches', 42; Goodare, 'Witch-hunting and the Scottish state', 130.
[116] *HP*, iii, 3.

seems to have been important for Stewart to strengthen the sequence of events, and at the same time important for the scribe to have this written down. The correspondence between the order of events as they are placed in the story and the chronological order of the same events also points to another dimension of Stewart's narrative, namely that there is a cause-effect connection between the events, imposed after the sickness of Glen's wife commenced. First the two women quarrelled, then as a consequence something struck Glen's wife. The end of Stewart's declaration, that his wife is still accusing Morrison of this, is nothing more than an assertion. Nothing is proved, but certainly Stewart appears to have thought that emphasizing the connection between the events strengthened his wife's accusation. The more the basic narrative structures come to the fore in the manner of telling, the more obvious it is that the content of what is told seems to be the opinion of both witness and schribe. An interpretation might be that the special type of logic that may be read into Stewart's story, points to the conclusion that Janet Morrison is guilty of what she is accused of.

Even more surprising is the other accusation, a declaration by Nans (Agnes) Mitchell. She neither met Morrison nor quarrelled with her, she just saw her in a dream, and shortly afterwards her child fell ill and died. A dream is a product of the imagination and refers to what is happening in the minds of persons. When dreams or other states of consciousness are rendered in fiction, it is a literary device used intentionally to express the character's state of mind.[117] The same stylistic device is used here in a legal context to support an accusation. In addition, we see here how narrative structures like linearity, sequential ordering of events and cause-effect relations create the textual glue of Mitchell's declaration, how adverbial phrases are used to specify certain events and how words pointing backwards in the text[118] are frequently used, often pronouns referring to persons. These stylistic devices structure the text in a recognizable way, thereby increasing the reliability of the statement:

> Nan. Mitchell declares that *about two years syne* she took a dreaming of Jonet Morisone *in her bed in the night*, and was afrighted *therewith*, and *within half ane hour after wakning*, her young child took a trembling a very unnaturall lyke disease *quhair* of he died and Jonet Morisone being desired to heal *the said child* said it was *twice shot* and could not be healed[119] [*My italics.*]

---

[117] Cohn, *Transparent Minds*.
[118] Such words are called deictic expressions.
[119] *HP*, iii, 3.

Both the above-mentioned declarations have to do with malefice; the sickness of an adult and the death of a child as a result of alleged sorcery. Mention of the child being 'twice shot' might refer to elf-shot or fairy arrows or elf arrows. Traditionally, elf-shot has been understood as prehistoric arrowheads believed to have been made by the fairies or elves to harm livestock.[120] This definition has been used to categorize the phenomenon when mentioned in witchcraft cases in the SSW, resulting in numerous findings. We find the same understanding of elf-shot in John Gregorson Campbell's book *The Gaelic Otherworld*.[121] Alaric Hall argues that two systems for aetiology of illness—fairies and witches—must have co-existed for centuries and did so throughout the period of witchcraft trials.[122] With regard to the Bute document, it is important to bear in mind that the words 'shot' and 'elf errow stone' have to be interpreted in the traditional meaning of the words, because the connection between 'elf', 'stone' and 'errow' is indisputable in the context. It should also be noted that when the Devil enters the stage, the whole picture becomes more complex. Morrison claimed that a child had been shot. Her confession did not mention fairies, but contained a reference to the case of Margrat NcWilliam, one of the other questioned women, who mentioned an 'elf errow stone'. She got the stone from the Devil, and she used it to kill her own son because she was in poverty and looked forward to a reward from the Devil. So what we have in the Bute document is a notion that the shot is connected to *maleficium* and the Devil, and thus could be part of a demonological confession. In that respect it is correct to say that a magic object originally related to fairy-belief during the historical witchcraft persecutions was incorporated into demonological ideas.

In addition, the document shows that it was common to 'shoot' a new person in order to free a person shot before, as it was suggested by the Devil that Janet Morrison should shoot Niniane Ker baylie and put him in Adam Ker's stead in order to bring home Adam Ker. She was even asked by the Devil 'to tak the lyfe of John Glas proveists dun[123] horse by shooting him and put him for William Stephen who was lying sick sore payned',[124] but she refused to do this. The Devil also told her that he intended 'to

---

[120] Miller, *Magic and Witchcraft*, 58.
[121] Originally published 1900–1902, new edition 2005, edited with commentaries by Ronald Black.
[122] Hall, *Meaning of Elf*, 33.
[123] 'dun' means dull brown.
[124] *HP*, iii, 23.

tak John Glas his barne'.[125] She also refused 'to tak Walter Stewart, bayly, his lyfe by shooteing him to put him for ane neighbour of his that dwelt in the highlands'.[126] This shows the belief that it was possible to 'shoot' a person and replace him with another person. As can be seen, the intended victims of these desired shootings were mostly officials, bailies and the provost, while those who stood to gain their life and health were poor people and common people. So a social perspective is certainly present in Janet Morrison's evil-doings.

Both accusations against Morrison seem to have been loosely founded. What becomes clear is the fear and anxiety ruling this community, making it natural for people to draw connections between mischance and certain persons known to be cunning in sorcery. There seems to have been a widespread understanding in this community, where witchcraft and unnatural death were rampant, that sickness as a cause of death simply was not accepted as real, and witchcraft was regarded as both culprit and solution.

The Voice of the Accused Person

A world of fantastic and realistic elements mingled together is conveyed in Morrison's confession, some probably from traditional folk beliefs, others from the demonological field. To draw a line between these spheres of notions is not possible, as new notions quickly disseminate and become part of the mentality of the peasants. However, some folkloric motifs, like fairies and elves, are reckoned to be particular Scottish. In Morrison's confession, elf-shot is mentioned. An important question is whether these features are considered to be good or evil. Laurence Normand and Gareth Roberts argue that folkloric features, which originally were regarded as good by the peasants, after learned demonological influence came to be regarded as evil. Normand and Roberts say that by 1590 'any relationship between human and spirit, whether fairy or elf, could be seen only as evil'.[127] They claim that there is a great difference between 1576, the Bessie Dunlop trial, and 1590, the first North Berwick trial, due to fifteen years of theological indoctrination by protestant ministers and the experience of other trials: 'By 1590 interrogators, and perhaps uneducated people too,

---

[125] *HP*, iii, 23.
[126] *HP*, iii, 23.
[127] L. Normand, and G. Roberts (eds.), *Witchcraft in Early Modern Scotland* (Exeter, 2000), 80.

were familiar with the rudiments of protestant demonology. When the
accused were questioned they had some idea of what was being asked of
them'.[128] In the case of Morrison, this argument holds true. When elf-shot
is mentioned in her confession, it is used for harming. The relationship
between her and the elves has evil-doing as its consequences. Fairy belief
became dangerous in the same moment fairies were related to evil and
in that way could be connected to the demonic. Therefore, in my view,
demonological ideas were the real danger.

Morrison's confession contains elements of demonology as well as folk
belief. A dead man called Adam Ker is mentioned several times in her
declaration. Apparently he was killed by means of sorcery and figures as
a spirit who can be brought back to life, which is what Janet Morrison
wants. First, she one evening meets 'a black rough fierce man who cam
to her and desired her till go with him' and in return he promised her
to 'give the a Kayre[129] and make the a Lady'.[130] She agreed to meet the
man and he repeated his promise, 'I'll make the a Lady and put the in
a brave castall quhair thou shalt want nothing and I will free the of all
the poverties and troubles thou art in and learn the a way how to bring
home Adam Ker'.[131] The second time she met with the Devil, she made a
covenant with him, in which he promised to give her anything she desired
and to teach her how to bring home Adam Ker, 'quhairin she promised to
be his servant etc.'[132] This is a narrative of temptation, which follows the
pattern of most demonic pact confessions. First the woman is reluctant to
enter the pact, but after a while she is persuaded, especially when wealth
is in sight.

On a direct question, 'if she knew what man he was', she answered that
'she knew him to be the divill and at the first she grew eyry'.[133] The name
'Klarenough' and the appearance of the Devil are noted in the records, and
were probably seen as important. The Devil is portrayed as 'a black rough
fierce man', 'a mane naked with a great black head'. The somewhat special name of the Devil reflects a double meaning, even somewhat humorous, because the Devil might have answered that it was clear enough who
he was, and then she took this as his name. Use of humour is an aspect

---

[128] Normand and Roberts, *Witchcraft*, 80–81.
[129] Cart, a wagon pulled by horses. Ref. Mr R. Black, e-mail 11.03.2006.
[130] *HP*, iii, 20.
[131] *HP*, iii, 21.
[132] *HP*, iii, 22.
[133] Means affected by fear or dread. Ref. Mr Ronald Black, e-mail 11.03.2006.

known from traditional tales about the Devil. At her first meetings with the Devil, he was alone, but one time she met him together with 'a great number of men that she asked at him quhat were these that went by who answered they are my company and quhen she speared where they were going he answered that they were going to seek a prey'.[134] An image like this is frightening, a signal that people felt haunted and followed by evil spirits, witches and others, roaming about, and that they all might be the next casual victim. What is portrayed seems to be the Wild Hunt or Furious Horde. This is a folk myth prevalent across Europe; a phantasmal, spectral group of huntsmen in mad pursuit across the skies or along the ground. The hunters may be the dead or the fairies.[135] Essential components of this are found in Scottish cases, even if no case records such a hunt in full.[136]

Elements of Christianity are found in Morrison's declaration. After she had made the covenant, she was baptized by the Devil. Her new baptism, which is a well-known element from other witchcraft confessions, is clearly a mockery of religious baptism: 'he asked quhat was her name and she answered Jonet Morisoun, the name that God gave me, and he said believe not in Christ bot believe in me. I baptize the Margarat'.[137]

Morrison had a reputation as a healer and was used by people in the community to heal sick persons. She is mentioned several times in the Rothesay Kirk Session Book in connection with healing, as well as when the term 'witch' is directly connected to her.[138] It seems to have been a short step between having a reputation as a healer and having a reputation as a witch. Those who were mentioned several times in the kirk sessions in connection with healing might easily come into focus as a suspected witch. It seems clear that people sought Morrison to cure diseases and mental illness. Therefore she was vulnerable to accusations of witchcraft.

The interaction between individual and communal suspicion, which is treated by Robin Briggs, may be exemplified in the case of Morrison.[139] She is mentioned in April 1660 in the Rothesay Kirk Session Book in connection with treating a young girl, who after being sick of the pox, could neither speak nor see. Morrison, being wanted by the girl's father, 'came

---

[134] *HP*, iii, 23.
[135] The hunter may also be an unidentified lost soul, a deity or spirit of either gender, or a historical or legendary figure.
[136] Goodare, 'Scottish Witchcraft in its European Context', 32.
[137] *HP*, iii, 22.
[138] NAS, Rothesay Kirk Session Book, CH2/890/1, pp. 80, 100, 102.
[139] Briggs, *Witches and Neighbours*, 138.

to her house and bound up her head and gave her a piece salvets rub to her breast'.[140] This means that people came to her to ask for cures for sick people. She also made use of various remedies, probably some herbal medicines, to cure the sick. At the next session, Morrison declared that she did nothing more than bind up the girl's head, and she was supported by two witnesses' testimonies.

Morrison was mentioned again, in May 1661, this time suspected of charming. She turns up at the kirk session, 'being challenged for certain speeches whilk she spoke to Elspeth Spence anent the said Elspeth her daughter that was lying sick'.[141] Even if Morrison denied it, it seems clear that she was fetched to cure sick people. At the next session, 6 June, she was warned after two people witnessed against her: 'the session did discharge the said Jonet Morisone in time coming to use the giving of any Physick or herbs to any body under the certification that she shall be esteemed a witch if she do so'.[142] This is the first time the word 'witch' is used about her; this was only seven months before a more serious prosecution of her begins.

The element of healing is recorded in the Bute document as part of Morrison's confession: 'She declared that in Summer last being gathering hearbs to heall Patrick Glas daughter who was laying seick of a very unnatural disease'.[143] She was later asked 'anent her heiling of Mcfersoun in Keretoule his dochter who lay sick of a very unnaturall disease without power of hand or foot both speechless and kenured [?]'[144] A question mark is written in the transcribed document behind the word 'kenured', stating that the scribe did not know the meaning or was unsure of the meaning. The meaning of this word is not known today either.[145] In addition to the healing noted, another healing performed by Morrison is mentioned, 'her heiling of Alester Bannatyne who was sick of the lyk disease answred that he was blasted with the fairyes and that she heiled him thereof with herbs'.[146] There might have been a connection between the poke and the

---

[140] NAS, Rothesay Kirk Session Book, CH2/890/1/80.
[141] NAS, Rothesay Kirk Session Book, CH2/890/1/100.
[142] NAS, Rothesay Kirk Session Book, CH2/890/1/102.
[143] *HP*, iii, 22.
[144] *HP*, iii, 22.
[145] It has not been possible for me to find any certain interpretation of this word by consulting dictionaries and experts, but it is likely that it refers to one of the senses, as it is juxtaposed with 'speechless'.
[146] *HP*, iii, 22.

blast.[147] The use of herbal healing seems to have been combined with the use of charms, a well-known combination in traditional healing practice. As for the herbs that were used, they 'seem to have been quite typical of herbal medicine in general'.[148]

Among the questioners there is an interest in blasting and shooting. It seems that the interrogators' understanding of 'shooting' in the Bute document was a type of shooting that was intentionally harmful and could cause death. In addition, blasting as well as arrow stone are clearly connected to elves and fairies in the documents' formulations. This seems to strengthen the assumption that magic objects like elf arrow stones were originally associated with fairies among the peasants. But there also seems to have been an idea that these remedies had been and still were used in connection with *maleficium*. Whether the fairies had been contacted for healing operations, remains unknown. In one of her declarations Morrison said that 'John Glas his bairne quhilk he hade in fostering was shot at the window'.[149] As for blasting contrasted to shooting, Janet Morrison 'again being inquired' what was the difference, she answered for the shooting that 'quhen they are shott ther is no recoverie for it and if the shott be in the heart they died presently bot if it be not at the heart they will die in a while with it yet will at last die with it'.[150] Blasting, she explains, 'is a whirlwinde that the fairies raises about that persone quhich they intend to wrong and that tho ther were tuentie present yet it will harme none bot him quhom they were set for'.[151] Blasting can be healed either by herbs or by charming. It seems clear that it was important for the questioners to obtain knowledge they did not possess, and the inquiry about blasting and shooting was undoubtedly seriously meant. Apparently Morrison was asked this question several times, as an opportunity for outsiders to learn the secrets of a knowledgeable person.

Denunciation of other witches was constantly one of the questions on the witch-hunters' agenda. One way for the witch-hunters to get additional names on their list was to ask the accused about participation in witches' meetings. This was also the case with Morrison. First she said that she had seen 'the devil and a company with him comeing downe

---

[147] E-mail Mr Ronald Black, 11.03.2006. Cf. *The Gaelic Otherworld*, p. xl.
[148] Miller, *Magic and Witchcraft*, 29.
[149] *HP*, iii, 28.
[150] *HP*, iii, 27.
[151] *HP*, iii, 27; Black, *Gaelic Otherworld*, p. xl; Mr R. Black, e-mail 11.03.2006.

the hill side underneath Brod chepell'.[152] In this instance she mentioned eight people who were in company with the Devil, declaring that all these were witches.

The other way for witch-hunters to get names of new suspects was to press forth names of persons practising witchcraft. Morrison related in detail how persons had performed *maleficium* leading to the death of William Stephen, Adam Kerr and Alester McNiven. In addition they took the lives of cows, threw spells on horses and took the milk of cows. Their method was mostly a pock of 'witchrie', which they put somewhere inside or outside the house or in the barn. This 'poke' or 'wee bag' was a little four-cornered bag packed with diverse exterminating diseases in the familiar likenesses of hair, grease, nail parings, shoe-tackets, salt and powder.[153] Probably these small bags existed, so that a witchcraft object was a reality. The people mentioned by Morrison were (among others) McLevin, Margaret NcWilliam, and two daughters of Margaret NcWilliam, Katharine and Elspeth. An interesting account is given of how they took Adam Kerr's life by using harmful sorcery, and Margrat NcWilliam fled from the place so that she should not be suspected. Before this, they had taken the power 'of his side from him by making two onsets [*attacks*] on him for he was a man little worth and he hade little ill in him so he had also little good that therfor they got overtane of him'.[154] This sentence might imply that attacks with elf-shot were effective on people who were either very good or very bad, but not so effective on people of 'little worth' one way or the other.[155] A more straightforward reading would be that they could harm him because he had 'little good', meaning that his faith was not strong enough. Questions about the pock of witchcraft seemed to be important. For instance, Morrison said that 'Nclevin did put a pock of Witchcraft in the east roof of Finley Mcconochie in Ballicailes stable above the horse on the north side of the house'.

There was often a tight web of denunciations during a witchcraft panic. Janet Morrison referred to a remark made by Jonet NcNicoll, 'that day quhich she was challenged at the Sessione, that Jenet NcNicoll came to her in Patrick Rowans house and said Jenat, Look that the fyle none bot

152 *HP*, iii, 24.
153 Stewart, W. G., *Popular Superstitions and Festive Amusements of the Highlanders* (Edinburgh, 1970), 202.
154 *HP*, iii, 25.
155 Mr Ronald Black, e-mail 11.03.2006.

yourself'.[156] How closely sorcery seems to have had a root in the daily disagreements of life, from the point of view of the accused herself, we may see from the following example. Morrison declared that NcWilliam and her daughters took Alester McNiven's life by using witchcraft: 'the quarrel was that because he craved sorely some malt silver that Katrine Moore [*one of NcWilliam's daughters*] was owing him'.[157] Getting hold of Morrison's knowledge of sorcery and getting hold of her knowledge of the network of operating witches are two major themes during her questioning. To the very end, the task of getting additional names of suspicious persons written down was continued, as we can see from the short notes finishing her hearing.

The Final Fate

The Bute questioning had consequences, as expected. A commission was appointed by the Privy Council on 7 May 1662 for four of the women mentioned in the Bute paper on witchcraft, among them Janet Morrison.[158] The Bute document does not contain any records from the trial, which must have taken place after the warrant reached Bute. There is no information about the final fate of the accused women in the Bute document. But a later source throws light on their destiny, namely the Justiciary Records of Argyll and the Isles.[159] It states that one of the women mentioned in the Bute document, but not in the commission, Jonet NcNicoll, was tried later, in 1673. She managed to flee to Kilmarnock in 1662:

> she being apprehended anno 1662 foresaid and imprisoned within the tolbuith of Rothesay and *fearing to be putt to death with the rest who suffered at that time,* It is true and of veritie that she brake ward and escaped out of the said tolbuith and fled to the Lowlands quher she remained in Kilmernock and other places ther about these twelf yeers'.[160] [*My italics.*]

Thus she escaped the trial, but was rearrested in 1673, tried in a local trial and executed. However, 'the rest who suffered at that time' must refer to the other women mentioned in the Bute document. Therefore the final fate of Janet Morrison was execution.

---

[156] *HP*, iii, 27.
[157] *HP*, iii, 25.
[158] *RPC*, 208.
[159] J. Cameron and J. Imrie (eds.), *Justiciary Records of Argyll and the Isles* (SS, 1949), 1.
[160] J. Cameron and J. Imrie (eds.), *Justiciary Records*, 1, 20.

Conclusion

A narratological analysis contributes to the understanding of witchcraft in Bute in 1662 in several ways. Because the different voices heard in the document are allowed to speak separately, information given by the scribe and information given by the accused individuals and the witnesses may be kept separate. The narrator's voice brings to the fore an instability, created most of all out of the tension between the scribe's wish to order the text and the magical content of the confessions. It is possible to trace a specific accent of the scribe's voice through evaluating judgements, emotive words and particularly coloured ways of portraying individuals. In particular, the scribe's voice might have been biased when it came to rendering the accused persons' discourse. He describes a woman respected on the one hand for her skills in healing, but on the other hand considered as a threatening individual due to the same skills.

The scribe's voice also gives accurate information of great value for searching other sources. As for factual information he functions as a neutral recorder, who leads the researcher to other historical documents illuminating the case.

Bessie Weir, Annabell and John Stewart, 1677

The last witchcraft trials from mainland Scotland to be studied in detail are from Paisley, in 1677.[161] I have chosen to focus on the voice of the law because it displays legal attitudes in a late phase of the witch-hunt.

General

In January and February 1677, a group of five women and one man in Paisley were charged with an attempt to murder the landlord Sir George Maxwell of Pollock. They were accused of having cast an illness on him by roasting his wax image.[162] The trials were mixed central-local, that is, local trials with central representatives. The accused in the alleged plot against the landlord were Jonet Mathie, Annabell Stewart, John Stewart, Bessie Weir, Marjorie Craige and Margaret Jackson. They were all 'apprehendit and imprisoned as suspect guiltie of witchcraft by entering unto paction

---

[161] I would like to thank Diane Baptie for the transcription of the document.

[162] These cases have been dealt with by Sinclair in *Satans Invisible World Discovered* and by R. L. Harris in 'Janet Douglas and the Witches of Pollock' in S. R. McKenna (ed.), *Selected Essays in Scottish Language and Literature* (Lewington, 1992), 97–124.

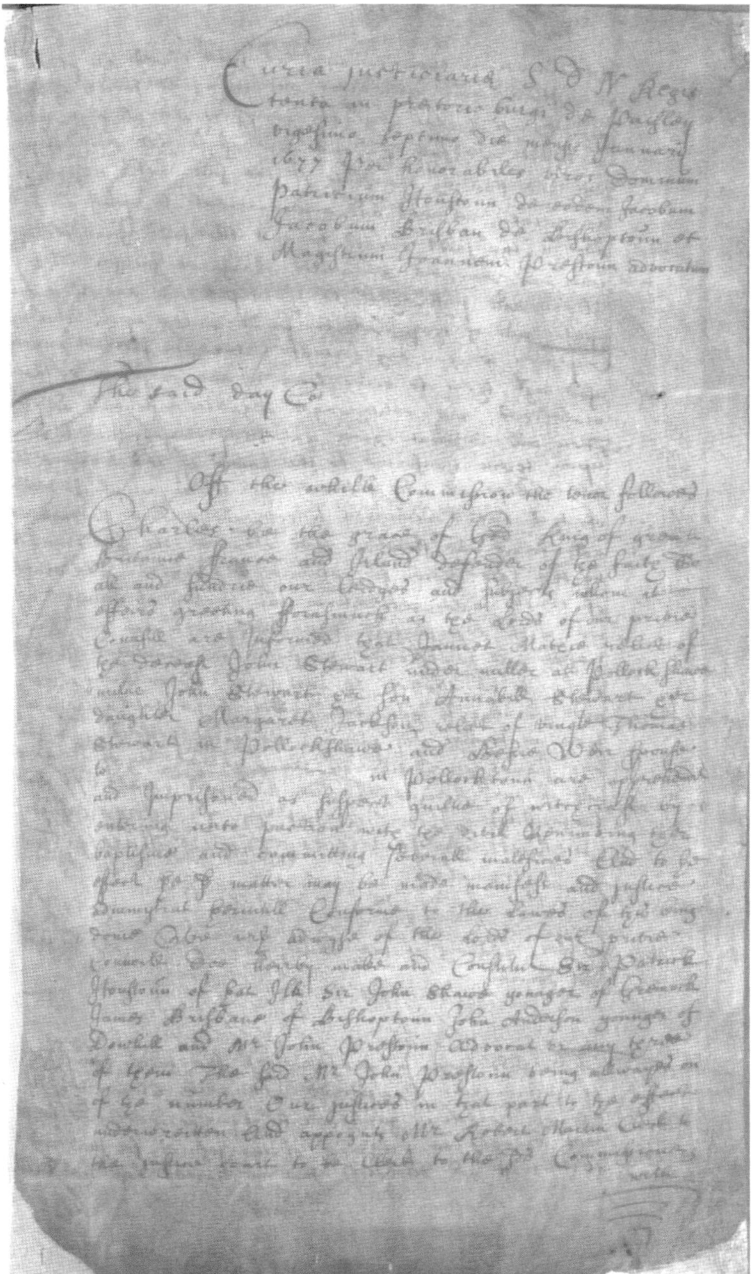

Figure 3: Trials against Bessie Weir, Annabell and John Stewart, 1677. NAS, Circuit Court Books, JC10/4, fo. 1r.

with the divill Renuncing ther baptisme and committing severall malefices'.[163] The commission appointed by the Privy Council to put them to trial stated explicitly, 'if they shall be found guiltie upon voluntar Confession without any sort of torture or indirect meanes used ag[ains]t them to bring them to ane confession or that malefices are otherwayes legallie instructed and proven'.[164] When it was found necessary to underline that torture should not be used, it suggests that torture frequently was used, and—as we shall see—it was used also in this case.

Jonet Mathie was the 50-year-old mother of Annabell Stewart and John Stewart. She was the wife of an undermiller and of middling socio-economic status. Annabell Stewart was 14 years old. John Stewart was 16 and lived in a house of his own. For this reason he must have been regarded as self sufficient. Margaret Jackson had been widowed for 20 years. She was in-law to three other persons accused in the group. Marjorie Craige was Irish and had a son in Ireland. She had been married in Ireland and was separated from her husband. Bessie Weir was married in Paisley, the wife of John Patton, weaver. She escaped from prison and fled to the parish of Carmanack[165] where she pretended to be Bessie Aikin, married to a man named Chrystie in Glasgow. Bessie Weir was supposed to be the 'officer', the leader to the meetings, according to confessions by Annabell Stewart and Jonet Mathie.

Seven witnesses gave their testimonies, two of whom were servitors to the Laird of Pollock and one servitor to John Maxwell younger of Pollock. The finding of some images of wax and clay, representing Sir George Maxwell of Pollock, seems to have been important to prove through the testimonies of the witnesses. One wax image was found in Janet Mathie's house, 'in a litle holl of the wall at the back of the fyre'.[166] Another witness, Lodovick Stewart of Auchinhead, went to 'the house of John Stewart warlock in Pollockshawe and ther he found a picture of clay in the (word crossed out) bedstrae of John Stewart depons that ther were three pins in the s[ai]d picture of clay and that ther wes on[e] in each syd and on[e] in the breast'.[167] The pins were removed, something which had an immediately beneficial effect on Sir George Maxwell's health. The third image, a model of earth, 'wes found in the prison of Paisley under the cod or

---

[163] NAS, Circuit Court Books, JC10/4, fo. 1r.
[164] NAS, Circuit Court Books, JC10/4, fo. 1r.
[165] SSW suggests this means Kilmarnock.
[166] NAS, Circuit Court Books, JC10/4, fo. 7r.
[167] NAS, Circuit Court Books, JC10/4, fo. 7v.

bolster of Jannet Mathie the pannalls bed'.[168] All the witnesses testified
that they had either been present at one of the findings of the effigies
or that they had seen Sir George Maxwell's sickness increase around the
fourteenth or fifteenth of October, when the alleged witches' meeting in
John Stewart's house had taken place, and the same sickness decrease
around the eleventh or twelfth of December, when the effigies were found
and the pins removed.

Torture was used during the trial. One of the witnesses, Robert Kirlie,
officer in Paisley, testified to a strange happening when Janet Mathie
managed to get loose from the stocks, 'being by ordor of the justices putt
in the stoks within the prison of Paisley and ther being in a cod distant
from the stocks the breadth of the house the deponent found her sitting
upon the cod the nixt morning tho no person hade hade access to her all
the whill that she hade bein in the stocks befor that time'.[169] The emphasis
here is on the inexplicable, namely Janet Mathie's ability to break physical laws. Thus the mentioning of torture, that she had been in the stocks,
appears rather haphazardly in the document. It is good example of the use
of torture being 'concealed' in the witchcraft documents, and only coming
to the fore if one of the witnesses mentions it by accident, as here, or if
the accused person withdraws her or his confession and says it was given
due to use of torture.

The alleged meetings at which the effigy of Sir George Maxwell was
roasted took place from October 1676 onwards, the last meeting being held
on 3 January 1677, as reconstructed by the confessions of the accused. The
trial started on 27 January 1677, but the interrogation had started earlier.[170]
The trial continued on 15 February, at which date the verdict and sentence
was given. The Privy Council commission for trying Annabell Stewart and
'diverse other persons' was given on 18 January 1677.[171] The Commission
for trying Marjory Craige was given on 1 February 1677.[172] This means that
the last commission was appointed after the trial had started. The date of
execution was set for 20 February at Gallow Green, but the execution of
Annabell Stewart was delayed.

---

[168] NAS, Circuit Court Books, JC10/4, fo. 9v.
[169] NAS, Circuit Court Books, JC10/4, fo. 9v.
[170] NAS, Circuit Court Books, JC10/4, fo. 1r.
[171] *RPC*, 3rd series, v, xxxv–xxxvi, 95, 104–5, 148.
[172] *RPC*, 3rd series, v, 5, 104.

The accused persons' confessions and the sworn testimonies of the witnesses are recorded as third-person narratives, while the discourse of the legal officials is recorded as a monologue.

The Voice of the Law

Mention of the divine as well as the secular law is here similar to the study of Margaret Wallace's case above. As has been argued by Larner, by the 1670s indictments were 'purely common form', as the legal phraseology seems to have been well standardized.[173]

> Ye are indyted and accused that wher notwithstanding be the divine Lawe of almightie God sett doun in the Sacred word especiallie in the *20 chap: of Leviticus and 18 chap: of Deutronomie* and be the lawe and practiq[ue] of all nations and be the Lawe & practiq[ue] of this kingdome and namlie be *73 act 9 par: Q M* It is expresslie provydit statut and ordained that an maner of person of whatsomever degree quality or condition they be of presume or take upon hand to practise or use any maner of witchcraft sorcerie or necromancie therthrow to abuse the leidges under the paine of death.[174] [*My italics.*]

The argumentation in this paragraph is overwhelming and echoes a frequently used legal rhetoric from decades back. When these expressions are used as late as 1677 without any modification, this is a signal that legal witchcraft discourse had become formulaic. This was 60 years before the repeal of the witchcraft statute in Scotland, and the massive arguing we hear in this document shows no sign of doubt related to the fundamentals of the witch-hunt.[175]

The same 'double' argumentation related to the clerical and secular sphere comes to the fore when the charge against Weir is expressed. In participating in the meeting with the Devil 'ye the fors[ai]ds witches having shacken off all fear of Gods dew reverence & regaird to his divin ordinance & Lawes and to the acts of parlia[men]t of his kingdome and having wickedlie & unjustly conceaved a cruell malice ag[ains]t Sir George Maxwell of Pollock'.[176] This is an insistent style, in which adjectives and adverbs with the same meaning are heaped up.

---

[173] Larner, *Enemies of God*, 130.
[174] NAS, Circuit Court Books, JC10/4, fo. 1r.
[175] Goodare, J., 'Introduction', in Goodare, *The Scottish witch-hunt in context*, 14.
[176] NAS, Circuit Court Books, JC10/4, fo. 6r.

The information that Bessie Weir was the 'officer' of the meetings was repeated by several of the accused. The legal officials addressed her as 'ye in the qualitie of the divills officer'.[177] This expression is repeated once more in Bessie Weir's confession. The notion of a man being an officer of a witchcraft group is frequently found in Scotland.[178] Here a woman has the same function, as is also seen in witchcraft cases in Dunfermline in Fife.[179] This might indicate that a masculine pattern is taken over by women when they confess the organisation of their witchcraft activity.

> Neverthelesse it is of veritie that ye the s[ai]d Bessie Weir are guiltie of and hes committed the cryme of witchcraft in suae fare as in harvest i^{m}vi^c & sevintie six you came to the house of Jannet Mathie in Pollockshawe milne your fellow witch and you with the s[ai]d Jannet did intyse Annabill Stewart her daughter to resigne her self to the divill which she did by putting her on[e] hand to the crown of her head and the other to the sole of her foot[180]

In the voice of the law we hear a very detailed rendering of the sorcery that has been performed, based on previous confessions. This suggests that the legal officials feel a need to being extremely accurate in order to be convincing. We often see in witchcraft documents this urge for accuracy with regard to placing events in a linear sequence and underlining the cause and effect between sorcery actions and their disastrous results. In the paragraph below, a description of Sir George Maxwell's misery in falling sick for the second time, this connection is marked:

> And *upon the making of the s[ai]d effigies & placing the pins* as affores[ai]d the s[ai]d Sir George *did relapse into his former sicknes* and his paines and torments did greatlie increase And the effigies by the goodnes of almightie God being discovered and found in the bed of the s[ai]d John Stewart within his house in Pollockshawe upon the eighth of January last and *the pins taken out* of the s[ai]d effigies the s[ai]d Sir George did *most sensiblie & remark-ablie recover* in a great measure his health'.[181] [*My italics.*]

The argumentation is based on the view that magic works and that a magical object like the effigy really could mean a matter of life and death. The analysis above shows that the legal officials believed that this type

---

[177] NAS, Circuit Court Books, JC10/4, fo. 6v.
[178] Goodare, 'Men and the witch-hunt in Scotland', in Rowlands, *Witchcraft and Masculinities in Early Modern Europe.*
[179] Macdonald, 'In search of the Devil in Fife witchcraft cases' in Goodare, *Scottish witchhunt in context*, 41.
[180] NAS, Circuit Court Books, JC10/4, fo. 6v.
[181] NAS, Circuit Court Books, JC10/4, fo. 6v.

of sorcery and witchcraft worked and that the accused had the power to effect witchcraft. Taking into consideration that this was at a late stage of the witch-hunt, and that witchcraft as a crime by this time started to be questioned, it is likely that the discovery of physical objects made the question of guilt more convincing for the judicial authorities.

Conclusion

The case of Bessie Weir, Annabell and John Stewart shows some features typical of a late witchcraft case. The use of forms with open blanks to fill in a set of information shows that by 1677 the legal procedure was common to witchcraft cases. At this stage of the witch-hunt it was even more important than before to have details about the alleged witchcraft to 'prove' that the crime had been committed. Likewise the interest in the wax effigies on the part of the interrogators supports the interpretation that physical objects were considered to be solid proofs of performed witchcraft. Torture was used in this case, as was witch pricking. The argument for postponing Annabell Stewart's sentence was that she had only recently been ensnared by the Devil and therefore was to be considered less hardened than an elderly person. This underlines that when considering whether a person was a witch or not, reputation over time and the length of the person's alleged cohabitation with the Devil were important points for the legal officials to consider. It might be a sign of a late case that the linguistic creativeness may be slightly paler here than in witchcraft cases some decades earlier.

PART TWO

ORKNEY AND SHETLAND

Map 3: Orkney Shire by H. Moll, NLS, Map Library.

CHAPTER FIVE

THE NORTHERN ISLES—HISTORICAL BACKGROUND

Historical Background

Compared to mainland Scotland, the reduced number of witchcraft trials in Orkney and Shetland seems to be a conspicuous feature, with 68 and 31 persons accused respectively. However, the number of trials has to be considered in relation to the population of the northern islands, which for Orkney has been estimated at around 18,700 in the seventeenth century.[1] The population of Shetland has been estimated at 9,750–12,000 in 1600 and 12,000 in 1632.[2] In that respect Orkney suffered from the witch-hunt to a greater extent than mainland Scotland, while witchcraft persecution in Shetland was more lenient.[3] The trials in Orkney and Shetland took on a different character from those in mainland Scotland. As for Orkney, the majority of trials took place during the early period of the witch-hunt, before 1650. As for Shetland, even if the total number was not more than 31 cases, two-thirds took place before 1650. The national witch-hunts of mainland Scotland did not reach the northern isles, which may have its explanation in the contents of the trials and the accused persons' confessions. For Orkney as well as Shetland it holds true that the demonological element did not get the same foothold as on the mainland. Demonological features are scarce, particularly in Shetland, and consequently large-scale panics did not arise, even if small panics occured. Probably the geographical distance from mainland Scotland tended to weaken the intensity of the witch-hunt, especially because the organisation and functioning of official institutions on the northern islands differed from mainland Scotland.

In this and the following chapters I would like to explore whether Orkney and Shetland had certain characteristics as geographical regions

---

[1] J. G. Kyd (ed.), *Scottish Popular Statistics including Webster's analysis of population 1755* (Edinburgh, 1952), 82. In 1755 the population was 23,382 with 20% reduction. In 1831 the population had increased to 28,047, according to *The New Statistical Account of Scotland*, vol. xv (Edinburgh, 1845), 213.

[2] D. J. Withrington (ed.), *Shetland and the outside world 1469–1969* (Oxford, 1983), 151.

[3] Mainland Scotland had 0.32% accused in relation to population, Orkney 0.36% accused and Shetland 0.26% accused.

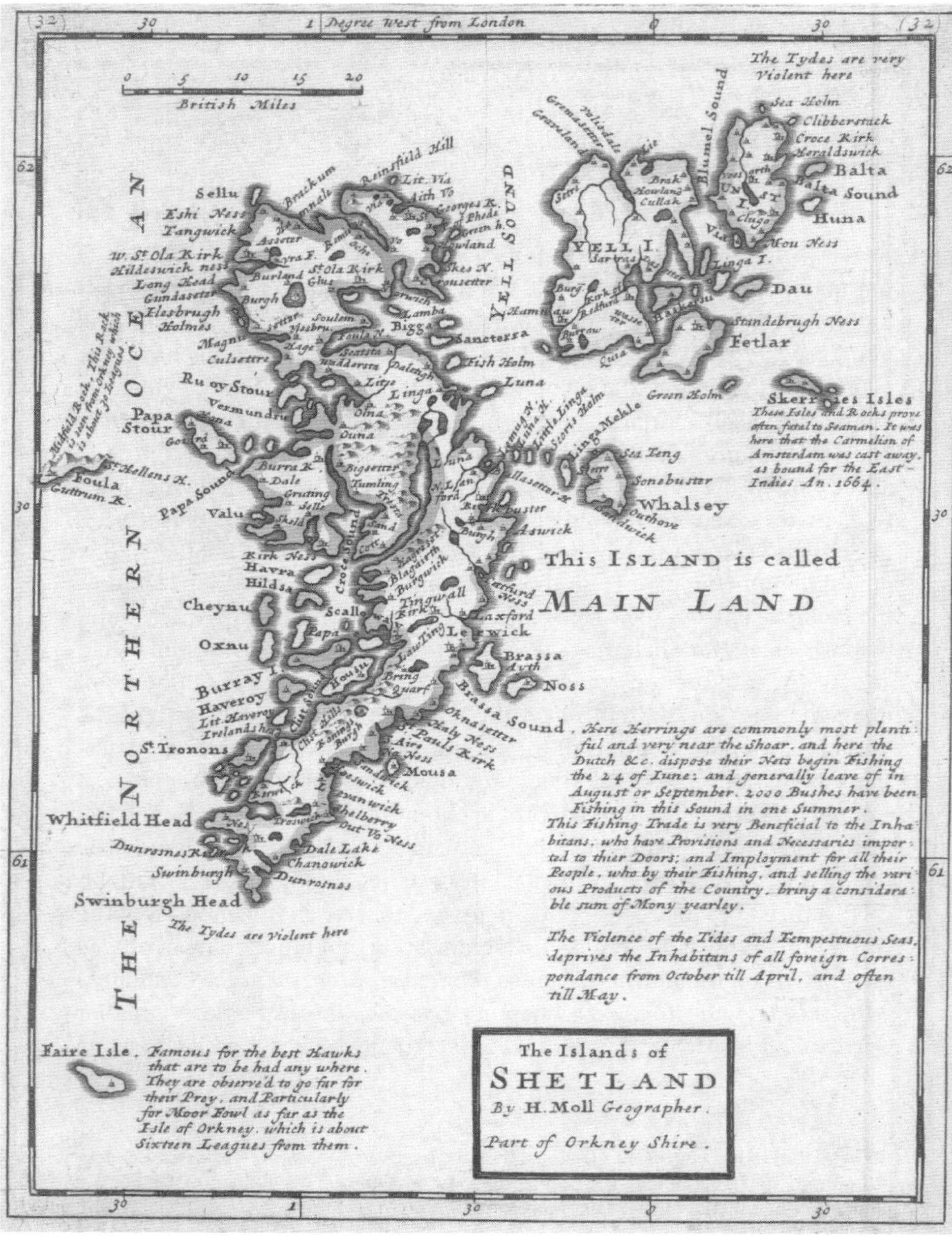

Map 4: The Islands of Shetland by H. Moll, NLS, Map Library.

which might have influenced the witch-hunt, features that will best be shown by treating the northern islands as entities of their own. Historically there were tight relations between the northern islands and Norway, particularly as far as Shetland was concerned. In 1195 Shetland was detached from the earldom; from now on it became ruled by governors appointed directly from Norway, and lands in Shetland were owned by Norwegians.[4] Thus Shetland was for a long period mainly Norse with regard to administrative officials. Then there was a formal change in the fifteenth century, as Orkney in 1468 and Shetland in 1469 were transferred from Norway to Scotland.[5] During the sixteenth and early seventeenth centuries the northern isles were ruled by Robert Stewart (1533–1593), Earl of Orkney, Lord of Shetland, and his son Patrick Stewart, Earl of Orkney, Lord of Shetland (c.1565–1615).[6] After political tumults in 1614, Patrick Stewart was executed in 1615. This meant the end of the rule of the Stewart earls on the northern islands.[7] As will be seen in the following, the continuing influence of Norwegian culture and law after the transactions of 1468–69, when the kingdom of Scotland reached its final frontiers in the north, may be traced for a considerable time after the transactions took place. In addition, the organisation and functioning of political, legal and clerical institutions in the early modern period may have influenced the witchcraft persecution in Orkney and Shetland. Included here is the setting up of new institutions after the downfall of Patrick in 1614.

The most important Norse influence may have been in the legal arena. The acquisition of the earldom by James III in 1470 was followed by a change in jurisdiction from the Archbishop of Nidaros to that of St Andrews.[8] Nevertheless, this change did not abolish Norse laws on Orkney and Shetland. In fact, Norse laws were in use on the northern islands for several centuries after this year, officially authorised by a decision of Parliament from 1567, stating that the islands ought to be subject to their own law.[9] This decision of Parliament—stating that the northern islands were exempt from Scottish law—made itself felt during the two

---

[4] Donaldson G., 'The Scots Settlement in Shetland', in *Shetland and the Outside World*, 9.

[5] Donaldson, 'The Scots', 8.

[6] The date of Patrick Stewart's birth is not known, as the records of his infancy are inaccurate. P. D. Anderson suggests that he was born in 1565, *Black Patie* (Edinburgh, 1992), 149.

[7] Anderson, *Black Patie*, 139.

[8] Thomson, W. P. L., *History of Orkney* (Edinburgh, 1987), 125.

[9] Thomson, *History*, 174.

generations of Stewart earls, who more or less took the law into their own hands. This is seen in one of the treason charges against Patrick in 1610; that he had caused a number of people to be tried before 'pretended deputes and judges'.[10] Thus the northern islands were legally self-contained.

Looking at the old Norwegian laws, these might be of relevance for the witch-hunt in Orkney and Shetland, as they show that sorcery was seriously treated already in the eleventh century. We find the oldest known Norwegian prohibition of sorcery in *Landskapslovene*, which were regional laws.[11] In an article on sorcery, 'On Divination and Magic Chants' in the Gulathing Law—a written code of customary law for the Gulathing area—Christianity challenges heathendom for the very first time in Norwegian legislation. This law decreed that a man convicted of having practised soothsaying or of having told fortunes 'shall be an outlaw and shorn of all personal rights; and all his chattels to the last penny shall go one half to the king and one half to the bishop'.[12] The severity of being sentences as an outlaw was equal to a death sentence. However, a certain procedure had to be followed. In the section on Christianity, it is stated that six witnesses must decide whether a woman suspected of sorcery is guilty. The suspected person could refute the charge by taking a sixfold oath. Knut Robberstad argues that it was the Gulathing version of Magnus Lawmender's Lawbook, accepted in 1274, which came to be introduced in Shetland and Orkney, not the new legal code for Iceland from 1280, called the *Jonsbok*.[13] In the Court Book of Shetland for 1602–1604 we see the sixfold oath still being imposed in serious cases of witchcraft, at least in the first instance. The Orkney rentals for roughly the same period show several portions of land 'escheat for witchcraft'.[14] The penalty for sorcery is death. A person may repudiate suspicions of sorcery with an oath confirmed by twelve people of his own social standing. Spreading rumours of witchcraft about another person is tantamount to defamation, and action may be taken against a person who calls a freeman serf, demon or sorcerer.[15]

---

[10] Thomson, *History*, 173.

[11] The old Gulating Law was written down during the eleventh century, and the articles concerning witchcraft were re-edited in the middle of the following century.

[12] OLA, MC, D31/4/4, 10.

[13] Robberstad, K., 'Udal Law', in D. J. Withrington (ed.), *Shetland and the Outside World 1469–1969* (Oxford, 1983), 51.

[14] OLA, Marwick, D31/4/4, 10.

[15] Willumsen, *Trollkvinne i nord*, 56.

With King Magnus Lawmender's[16] national (1274) and city (1276) codes, all parts of Norway were subject to uniform legislation. Sorcery is mentioned in connection with serious crimes; for murder and consorting with spirits, for every kind of divination, for out-sitting—the practice of leaving one's body—to raise demons, and thereby the advancement of heathen practices.[17] Whoever is guilty of sorcery or commensurate crimes has forfeited his livestock, peace, all real property, and all his belongings. No significant changes were made to Magnus Lawmender's national code until Norway entered into a union with Denmark in 1387. During the period of union 1387–1537, Danish Law gained a foothold in Norway despite the union treatise stipulation that each country should be governed in accordance with its own legislation. Notable legal concepts in the period preceding the Reformation include church jurisdiction and Canon law.[18] Remnants of church jurisdiction were maintained after the Reformation in Denmark in 1536 and in Norway in 1537 in cases which were exempted from civil prosecution and subject to specially instituted ecclesiastical courts.[19] The approach to witchcraft as a *crimen exceptum* was confirmed by Danish Law as early as in 1521/1522, in King Christian III's Ecclesiastical Law. Torture was now permitted in witchcraft trials. However, the enactment is somewhat withdrawn in Christian III's Københavnske Reces in 1558, but repeated in Koldingske Reces of 1588.[20] On the northern islands Norse law could also have made itself felt by King Christian IV's Norwegian Code of Laws from 1604. In this code of laws, sorcery practised with lethal consequences is placed in the same category as serious crimes and 'such people shall be shown no mercy, whether they are killed by the king's representative or by others whom they have transgressed against'.[21] Otherwise, sorcerers were banished. On the Northern Isles, the old Norse laws were not abolished until 1611, by an act of the Scottish Privy Council, and

---

[16] In Norwegian *Magnus Lagabøte*.

[17] In Norwegian the word used for sorcery is *trolldom*. Ref. Magnus Lagabøte's National Law Code, Mannhelgebolken, chapter 4; Willumsen, *Trollkvinne i nord*, 56.

[18] Canon law: 'a set of legal instruments that were established by the Catholic church', (Gulbrandsen 1980:101); 'Canon Law is the body of laws and regulations made by or adopted by ecclesiastical authority, for the government of the Christian organizations and its members' (*Catholic encyclopedia*).

[19] This applied to trials of church and school officials and in litigation between the clergy and parishioners.

[20] Cf. Ankarloo (1971:65) who refers to *Samling af gl. da. Love IV*, p. 224 and Den Koldingske Reces 1558, p. 262.

[21] From Jacobsen, J. C.: *Danske Domme i Trolddomssager i Øverste Instans* (Cph. 1966:146).

superseded by the laws of Scotland.[22] Parliament's decision of 1567 was
reversed: from now on all 'foreign laws' in Orkney and Shetland were abolished.[23] The magistrates of the islands were instructed 'to use the proper
lawis of this kingdome to his majesties subjectis in all thair actions and
caussis'.[24] Donaldson mentions that one reason for the act of 1611 might
have been that in Norway King Magnus Lawmender's Law Book, dating
from 1274, had been revised by Christian IV, James VI's brother-in-law,
in 1604, and it would hardly have been appropriate for the northern isles
as part of the Scottish king's dominions to adopt laws freshly devised in
a foreign country.[25] The systematic application of Scots law in Shetland
after 1611 took place explicitly to avoid the possibility of Christian IV's Norwegian law of 1604 being invoked.[26] If old Norse laws had an effect on
witchcraft persecution on Orkney and Shetland, it is likely that Magnus
Lawmender's national code contributed to the focus on *maleficium*, not
demonological witchcraft. These laws would have contributed to calming
the witch-hunt during the important first decades of the seventeenth century on the northern islands, as the demonological element was not fully
legally formalised in Denmark-Norway until a decree dating from 1617.[27]

Clerical and Political Conditions

The abolition of old Norse law in Orkney and Shetland was partly due
to King James's re-introduction of episcopacy and the restoration of the
bishops, a process which lasted from 1606 till 1610, when the consecrated
episcopate was restored. James Law was appointed bishop to Orkney,
and he came to play an important part within the church as well as in
the legal area of the northern islands. In 1612 Orkney was permanently
annexed to the crown, with the exception of the kirk estates.[28] In 1614 the
widely scattered kirk estates were acquired by the king. As compensation,
the bishop was granted a more compact and united territory by crown
charter.[29] After the excambion of 1614 the bishopric territory comprised,

---

[22] *RPC*, 3rd series, ix, 181.
[23] Thomson, *History*, 173–4.
[24] G. Donaldson (ed.), *Court Book of Shetland 1615–1629* (Lerwick, 1991), xii.
[25] Donaldson, *Court*, xii.
[26] Robberstad, 'Udal', 49–68.
[27] Willumsen, *Trollkvinne i nord* (1994), 56–59.
[28] *APS*, iv, 481, c. 15.
[29] *RMS*, 1609–20, 1119.

in the main, the Orkney parishes of Sandwick, Stromness, Orphir, St Ola, Holm, Shapinsay, Hoy and Walls. In these areas Bishop Law assumed the function of sheriff, by virtue of his charter.[30] The northern part of Orkney, outside the bishopric, with the whole of Shetland, constituted the principal sheriffdom, with Sir James Stewart of Killeith acting as sheriff.[31] The magistrate went on circuit throughout the islands in June and July each year; afterwards he held a central court, the Lawthing of Shetland, in July or August.

Prolonged Norse influence after the transaction of 1468–69 was stronger in Shetland than in Orkney. Scottish influence had already made itself felt in Orkney over a long period. Donaldson maintains that Shetland in 1469 was essentially Norse, in race, in language and in institutions, whereas in 1468 Orkney was already very largely Scotticised'.[32] There was a considerable immigration of Scotsmen to Orkney before 1469.[33] Donaldson argues that the reason for the distinction between the two groups of islands is to be found in their earlier political history. The earls of Orkney had been half-Scottish by birth since before 1200, and by the fifteenth century the administration of Orkney was in the hands of Scotsmen, while from 1195 onwards Shetland's governors were appointed directly from Norway.[34] There was one channel, however, through which Scots could find their way into Shetland as well as Orkney, and that was the church. There was a difference between laymen and churchmen, as Scots found their way into the kirk in Shetland as well as in Orkney. The diocese of Orkney always included Shetland. There were Scottish bishops in Orkney from the late fourteenth century, and Scottish bishops in Orkney were likely to mean Scottish clergy in Shetland.[35] The archdeaconry of Orkney, as well as Shetland, was held by Scots long before 1469. So the role played by Scottish laymen and Scottish churchmen differed when it came to official positions in Orkney and Shetland. Governmental influence from central Scottish authorities through administrative officials was stronger in Orkney than in Shetland.

---

[30] *RMS*, 1609–20, 119. The Court Book of the Bishopric relates to proceedings within this territory.
[31] The Court Books of Orkney and Shetland record proceedings from these regions.
[32] Donaldson, 'The Scots', 8.
[33] Donaldson, 'The Scots', 9.
[34] Clouston, J. S., *History of Orkney* (Kirkwall, 1932), 229, 236–7, 240–9.
[35] Donaldson, 'The Scots', 9.

The most striking illustration of the sharp contrast between Orkney and Shetland, according to Donaldson, is to be found in the linguistic arena. The Norse tongue was on its way to being superseded in Orkney before the transaction of 1468, in contrast to the situation in Shetland. In the 1430s the lawman in Orkney was using Lowland Scots, while in Shetland there are a number of documents in Norse dating from the sixteenth century, with the last as late as 1607. This suggests that there was a time-lag of something like a hundred and fifty years between the point at which the Scots tongue prevailed in Orkney and the point at which it prevailed in Shetland. During the sixteenth century, Scottish influence over Orkney grew and gradually the Norse way of life and language slipped away. By the late seventeenth century the Orkney variant of the Norse language, Norn, was spoken only by the inhabitants of one or two remote parishes.

The political unrest around 1614 was the result of previous events. Profound changes occurred in the political history of these islands around 1600, preparing the ground for a self-contained economy and society. By a charter dated at Stirling in 1565, Lord Robert Stewart, a natural son of King James V, received from Mary, queen of Scots, his half-sister, a feu charter in respect of the old earldom and crown lands in Orkney and Shetland, together with the office of the sheriffship.[36] In return for an annual duty of 3.000 merks to be paid to the crown, Lord Robert was free to acquire what he could in rent and dues, and from the fines gathered by his court.[37] The rule of the Stewarts on the northern islands has been described by Robert S. Barclay as an era of tyranny.[38] Robert Stewart, illegitimate son of King James V, named 'Bad Earl Robert' by Peter D. Anderson, is portrayed with few virtues; his 'reputation has been uninterruptedly odious from his early manhood to the present day'.[39] His son, Patrick Stewart, is portrayed by Anderson as a complex and interesting character with an extravagant temperament, 'and the arrogance and groundless optimism which went with it'.[40] His various feuds and extravagant use of money contributed to bring the Stewart interlude in the history of the northern islands to a close.

---

[36] *RMS*, v, 2078.
[37] Barclay, R. S., 'Introduction', in R. S. Barclay (ed.), *Court Books of Orkney and Shetland 1614–1615*, v. 3, (Edinburgh, 1967), xviii.
[38] Barclay, 'Introduction', xxvii.
[39] Anderson, P. D., *Robert Stewart. Earl of Orkney, Lord of Shetland* (Edinburgh, 1982), 143.
[40] Anderson, *Black Patie*, 146.

Patrick Stewart had been accused of exploiting the old laws for his own advantage. In 1614, while Patrick Stewart was still in prison, his deputies on both Orkney and Shetland were discharged of their judicial offices and orders were issued that the castles of Kirkwall and Scalloway were to be surrendered.[41] The relationship between Patrick and James Law was bound to be difficult, particularly because of property-related rental incomes. As Patrick was deep in debt, negotiations between his creditors turned out to Law's satisfaction. In 1608 Patrick was forced to hand over his palace to Law, who in the same year wrote a letter of complaint to the king about Patrick's oppression of his poor subjects on the islands. As a result, Patrick was summoned to appear before the Privy Council in 1609, which he failed to do. He was then denounced as a rebel, the beginning of a six-year long alternation between confinement and the relaxation of his imprisonment which lasted until his death. During this period he appointed his only son, Robert Stewart (–1615), depute on Orkney. In November 1611 Robert and his followers were denounced as rebels, and by spring 1612 there were rumours of a rising in Orkney and Shetland. However, James Law succeeded in having Robert Stewart surrender his father's houses. Patrick was pressed by the council to resign all his rights in the earldom of Orkney, which he at last did.[42] In 1614 a new attempt at an uprising was made by Robert Stewart, but after first to have had success in Orkney, he was besieged in Kirkwall Castle and obliged to surrender.[43] He was condemned to death and executed in Edinburgh on 1 January 1615. Patrick hoped to obtain a royal pardon, but the fact of an open rebellion had put Patrick beyond King James's mercy and he was executed on 6 February 1615.[44]

Against this background of political drama the first decades of witchcraft persecution in Orkney took place. As for jurisdiction, Bishop Law, after having outmanoeuvred Patrick, held sheriff courts first in Orkney, in the cathedral of St Magnus, and afterwards in Shetland, at Scalloway castle. In Kirkwall he appointed bailies and councillors, ordering them to assist in the kirk's work, naming the mercat day, and curbing drunkenness. During these courts he passed a number of acts to deal with lesser crimes.[45] Thomson comments that it is difficult to see how these acts differed from

---

[41] *RPC*, ix, 181, 182.
[42] Anderson, *Black Patie*, 98, 99, 103–4.
[43] Barclay, 'Introduction', xx.
[44] Thomson, *History*, 178.
[45] Anderson, *Black Patie*, 99.

the laws which Patrick was accused of having treasonably made.[46] Law also received a blank commission to remove anybody from Orkney on a ten day's notice, just as Patrick was accused of doing. Probably the judicial changes of Bishop Law around 1614 did not bring better justice to the northern islands. In my view the changes in law and court procedure that took place in Orkney and Shetland in the early seventeenth century were important for the witch-hunt. However, these changes would not have taken place without the church reform that restored the bishops. Scottish political intervention made its impact as well, but the setting up of new courts with Bishop Law was probably most relevant.

Sources

The court books are the most important source material documenting witchcraft trials on the northern isles. The Court Books of Orkney and Shetland 1612–13 and 1614–15 give interesting information about the administration of the legal apparatus during the early years of Scottish law in these islands, when a change from the Stewart earls and Norse laws to the law of Scotland took place, administered in turn by the bishop and the king's sheriff. The books show the constitution of the courts after the establishment of separate sheriffdoms, the system of court procedure under new officials, and how the law continued to be upheld. Also important are the country acts of Shetland and Orkney, dated respectively Scalloway 3 August 1615 and Kirkwall 7 November 1615. A similar, shorter series was passed at Scalloway in 1612.[47] The purpose of the country acts was to meet local needs, and to temper Scottish law to former usages.

The Court Book of 1612–13 begins with the proceedings of a court held in the cathedral church of Saint Magnus in Kirkwall, in July 1612. The presiding official was James Law, bishop of Orkney, the king's commissioner, sheriff and justice in Orkney and Shetland. Bailies and counsellors were elected and acts were passed. Bishop Law next appeared with his court in Shetland before he returned to Orkney in September 1612, and the period until May 1613 is concerned with proceedings in Kirkwall under the jurisdiction of Mr Henry Aitkin, sheriff depute. Authority was vested in the bishop. As Robert S. Barclay puts it: 'The ancient code of laws had been

---

[46] Thomson, *History*, 175.
[47] R. S. Barclay (ed.), *The Court Book of Orkney and Shetland 1612–1613* (Kirkwall, 1962), 19–24.

revoked, and court procedure and terminology approximated to that of a Scottish sheriff court'.[48]

The first sitting of sheriff James Stewart's court took place on 5 May 1615 in Kirkwall. The presiding officials were Henry Stewart and William Livingston, sheriff deputes. The procurator fiscal was Robert Coltart, who also held that office in the bishopric. The clerk to the court was Henry Aitkin, sheriff depute in the bishopric. Ten days later the court was on circuit on the islands of Rousay, Stronsay and South Ronaldsay; afterwards it returned to Kirkwall, where several sittings were held in June, among them the trials of Janet Drever and Katherine Bigland for witchcraft. Both sheriff deputes were usually present.

Of previous works within the field of Orkney witchcraft, the books by Ernest Walker Marwick (1915–77), a scholarly expert on Orkney folklore and tradition, must be mentioned. He studied oral as well as written sources. Marwick's private archive material was donated to the Orkney Archives.[49]

The names of persons accused of witchcraft in Orkney are mainly documented in court records and presbytery minutes. Several trials have been published in transcription in *The Court Book of Orkney and Shetland 1612–1613* and the *Court Books of Orkney 1614–1615*. In addition, there are manuscript sheriff court records until 1630 entitled *Sheriff Court Book Orkney and Zetland 1612–1630*, comprising the Court Book of Orkney and Shetland 1612–13. Several records have been published by historical associations.[50] In addition, trials have been published in folklore editions, and early travel books contain extracts from trials and references to trials.[51]

Even more than the witchcraft sources from Orkney, the witchcraft sources from Shetland contribute to strengthen the argument that

[48] Barclay, 'Introduction', xxvii.

[49] Among with other material, a list of Orkney witches is found related to an unpublished manuscript for an article. Ref. Marwick, E. M., 'Northern Witches. With Some Account of the Orkney Witchcraft Trials', OLA, MC, D31/4/4. This list contains the names of 65 witches for the period 1594–1880. 23 of these are not in SSW.

[50] *RPC* contains some names of accused persons in connection with appointment of commissions. Several witchcraft documents are published in the Maitland Club Miscellany, Edinburgh, 1840, no. 51, vol. 2, part 1. Records of six trials and one kirk session examination have been printed in the Miscellany of the Abbotsford Club, Edinburgh, 1837, vol. 1.

[51] N. W. Thomas (ed.), *County Folk-Lore. Examples of printed folk-lore concerning the Orkney & Shetland Islands*, collected by Black, G. F., vol. 3 (London, 1903); Low, G., *Tour through Orkney and Shetland* (Kirkwall, 1789), Dalyell, G., *The Darker Superstitions of Scotland* (Edinburgh, 1834). MC also contains reference to Rogers, C., *Social Life in Scotland. From Early to Recent Times*, vol. iii (Edinburgh, 1886), 265–333.

geographical distance from the Scottish mainland tended to weaken the
intensity of the historical witchcraft trials. In Shetland the witchcraft trials
were few in number. The demonological element was present for a short
period, but it did not get a foothold. Therefore we do not see any large
panics.

If one compares the court proceedings from Shetland from 1602–4 with
those from 1612 and 1615–29, a huge difference is evident, demonstrating
that judicial practice as well as way of recording had changed. Brian Smith
maintains that Shetland's seventeenth century began, abruptly, in 1611,
when the 'foreign laws' were abolished, four years before Patrick Stewart
was guillotined in Edinburgh. 'By these actions they effectively handed
administrative power in Shetland to the Sinclairs, the Mouats, the Chey-
nes and the Bruces, the "Scottish lairds" as we call them in Shetland'.[52] As
for language, the Norse tongue continued to be in general use for a long
time in Shetland after 1469.[53]

---

[52] Smith, B., '"Lairds" and "Improvement" in the 17th and 18th century Shetland', in
T. M. Devine (ed.), *Lairds and improvement in the Scotland of the enlightenment* (Stratchclyde, 1978), 11.
[53] Donaldson, 'The Scots', 9.

CHAPTER SIX

ORKNEY AND SHETLAND—WHAT FIGURES CAN TELL

Orkney

Frequency

Orkney witchcraft covers approximately the same period as on the Scottish mainland, starting in the 1590s and continuing until 1708. The SSW registrations from this period will be the basis of the statistical treatment.[1] Annual frequency is shown in the chart below.[2] The periods

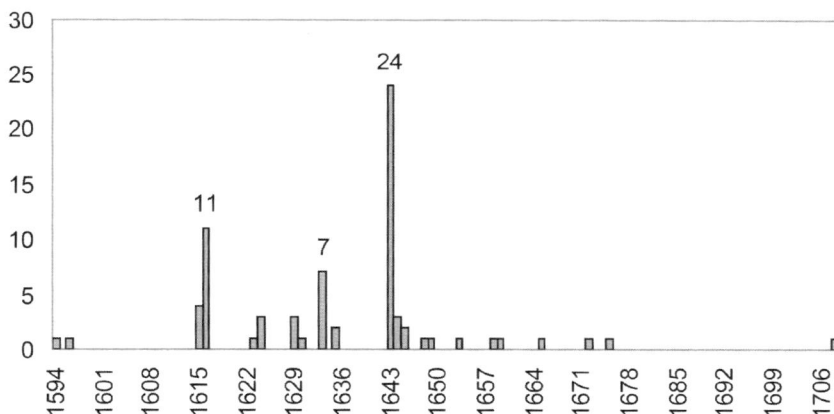

Chart 5: Witchcraft trials by year, Orkney, 1594–1708 (SSW).

---

[1] In SSW, 72 cases are registered. One person was brought before the presbytery twice, in 1643 and 1648, Marjorie (Marion) Paplay. SSW has Marjorie Paplay and Marion Paplay registered as two different persons, but it is the same person. As for names, SSW has three double registrations, Katherine Craige, 1643, is also registered as Unknown Elsinquoy. Helen Wallis and Helen a Wallis, 1616, denote the same person, tried 13/6/1616, ref. MC D31/4/3. Janet Drever and Jonet Drever is the same person. She is documented in 1615, but the reference to 1675 must be wrong. SSW has referred to Larner's sourcebook here, but Larner has only Janet Drever 1615. So the number of individuals accused is 68.

[2] As for Jonet Drever, both Marwick and Larner's Sourcebook (no. 3067) have 1615. Larner's reference is *The Court Book of Orkney and Shetland*, date 7.06.1615. The person registered in the Survey as Unknown Unknown is Janet Rigga, case date 11.11.1629, ref. OLA, MC, DC11/791. The year of the trial of Scota Bess is c.1630, ref. OLA, MC, D31/4/4.

1594–1614 and 1646–1708 are characterized by isolated cases, few in number. The first two cases, Alesoun Balfour in 1594 and John Stewart in 1596, are famous. Balfour was tried in a local trial, accused of being hired by John Stewart to poison his brother, Patrick, Earl of Orkney. Extensive use of torture is documented, for instance the use of stocks and cashie-laws. Alesoun's husband and children were tortured before her eyes. She was executed on Hedding Hill in Kirkwall. John Stewart was tried in a central trial in 1596, accused of murdering his brother. The verdict was not guilty.

During the years 1615–45 there were three linked trials; the first from 1615–16 totalling 15 cases, the second in 1633 totalling 7 cases and the third in 1643–45 totalling 29 cases. It is notable that the most severe years of witchcraft persecution Orkney do not coincide with any of the five largest panics on the Scottish mainland. Although 1643 was a panic year on the mainland, it was overshadowed by the larger panics. However, a similar pattern of local panics, not necessarily coinciding with the national ones, can be found in numerous Scottish counties.

Political and religious unrest in the years before an outbreak of a witchcraft panic has attracted attention among scholars.[3] If we look to Orkney to find triggering factors related to political or religious unrest in the years before the first panic, 1615–16, we see that dramatic events took place due to the 1614 uprising and its suppression. The abrogation of Norse law was also an important factor because the legal focus of malefice then decreased and made possible a greater focus on demonology. The 1615–16 panic may have been a 'new regime' witch-hunt following the establishment of the sheriff court. Robert S. Barclay points out that the king's sheriff seemed to have certain rights within the bishopric, shown by the sheriff's protest in 1614.[4] For the year 1614 the sittings of the local court were few; in 1615 there were four sittings, all in Kirkwall and presided over by Mr Henry Aitkin, sheriff depute, who had served James Law in that capacity in previous years.[5]

There must have been an atmosphere of anxiety and fear in Orkney due to political unrest around 1614. But it is also important to bear in mind that the change to Scottish jurisdiction might have led to an increasing interest in witchcraft cases. By this time Scotland had experienced several witchcraft panics, while in Norway only witchcraft persecution on

[3] Among others Swales, J. K. and McLachlan, H. V., 'Witchcraft and the status of women: a comment', *British Journal of Sociology*, xxx, no. 3 (1979), 349–57.
[4] Barclay, 'Introduction', xxviii–xxviv.
[5] Barclay, *The Court Book of Orkney and Shetland 1612–1613*.

a minor scale had taken place.[6] Studying more closely the persons accused of witchcraft in 1615, four individuals were tried before the sheriff court in Kirkwall in June 1615; Katherine Bigland, Janet Drever, Marioun Lening and Marioun Tailzeour.[7] Three of them came from the north, Bigland and Drever from Westray and Lening from Papa Westray. Bigland was sentenced to execution, Drever was banished, Lening's and Tailzeour's sentences are not known. In 1616 eleven cases are registered in SSW, referring to nine individuals. All trials were held before the sheriff court. Three of these were tried in March, the rest in June. Sentence is known only for Elspeth Reoch, who was executed.

Between 1617 and 1632 there was one case in 1623, three in 1624, three in 1629 and one in 1630. Two sentences of execution are known, Marable Couper and Anie Tailzeour, both tried in 1624 and burned on Lonhead in Kirkwall. Couper had been tried earlier for witchcraft and was banished, but refused to leave. Sentences are not known in the rest of the cases.

In the period 1633–42, seven cases are registered for 1633 and two for 1635. Three death sentences were passed, for Maryon Layland, Bessie Skebister, and Issobell Sinclair. In addition, one sentence of branding, for Katherine Grieve, was passed in 1633.

A distinctive increase in trials occurs for the year 1643, with 24 cases. 17 individuals were brought before the presbytery suspected of witchcraft. In the minutes we can read that from 5 April till 2 June, 12 people were 'considered of points of witchcraft'; two individuals were accused of using charms and one person for embracing charms.[8] Several of these came from the islands in the north, Westray, Stronsay and North Ronaldsay.[9] It was sheriff depute Henry Aitken who brought accusations for witchcraft against three persons living in North Ronaldsay.[10] Nine people were implicated by another accused person.[11] Two death sentences are known, for Jonet Reid and Katherine Cragie. These two received their sentences on the same day and had a wide range of sorcery accusations levelled against

---

[6] Cf. Næss, *Trolldomsprosessene i Norge*; Knutsen, G., *Trolldomsprosessene på Østlandet. En kulturhistorisk undersøkelse* (Oslo, 1998); Botheim, R., *Trolldomsprosessene i Bergenhus len, 1566–1700* (University of Bergen, Master's thesis, 1999), 136, 215–227; Stave, T., *Da Lucifer kom til Vardøhus* (University of Tromsø, Master's thesis, 2012), 82.

[7] According to SSW Bigland, Drever and Lening were tried on 6 June, for Tailzeour only June is given. The court was sitting in Kirkwall 6–8 and 10 June 1615, cf. Barclay, 'Introduction', xxiv.

[8] OLA, OPR, CH2/1082/1, pp. 227–32.

[9] OLA, OPR, CH2/1082/1, pp. 223–35.

[10] Barbara Yorston, Janet Pekok and Helen Tailzour.

[11] This is a high proportion of the 14 people in total in the Orkney material who were implicated by others. Ref. WDB_ImplicatedByAnother, SSW.

them; in addition to Reid's confession that she kept company with the Devil, they both had reputations for *maleficium*, healing and white magic. For most of the cases in 1643 we do not know the verdict and sentence.

The panic of 1643 may have been related to political and religious unrest in Scotland. In the three-kingdom situation after 1603, faced by James VI and I and Charles I, the problems were multiple, especially in matters concerning the church. The triumphs of the Covenanters' revolution in 1638 and the Solemn League and Covenant of 1643 may have put their stamps on the witch-hunt in Orkney, as Charles I pawned the lands to finance the royalist cause in the Civil War.[12] The Orkney earldom estates were leased by the king to a series of tax collectors, culminating with the seventh earl of Morton. By charter under the great Seal dated 15 June 1643 a document of the earldom and lordship to the earl of Morton was confirmed by the crown.

With regard to the trials taking place in the 1640s, it should be borne in mind that the Privy Council and parliament supported the prosecution of a number of moral crimes, including witchcraft, so that local pressure increased. In the period after 1643 fourteen witchcraft trials took place in total, three in 1644, and two in 1645; the rest were scattered one per year, and after 1675 there was a final one in 1708. The sources are mainly presbytery records. For the later cases information comes from secondary sources, and is scarce. For Elspeth Culsetter, in 1644, there is a post-trial note in presbytery records that she was burnt for witchcraft. Effie Rosie was banished in 1658, but for the rest of the cases the verdict and sentence are not known. By 1665, Kathareen Manson had been questioned repeatedly by the kirk session over the course of 15 years for charming and witchcraft.

To sum up: The Orkney witchcraft persecution increased in the period 1615–45. This is documented as peaks in the material, mostly in single years. After 1645 there was an even, but very low, flow of single witchcraft cases. After 1675 there is only a sole latecomer in 1708. This pattern does not coincide with mainland Scotland, where intense witchcraft persecution took place until 1662 and where panics occurred at intervals.

Gender and Status

Of the registered cases in Orkney, around nine-tenths were women and one-tenth men, a higher part of females than the mainland.[13] There were no

---

[12] Donald, P., *An Uncounselled King. Charles I and the Scottish Troubles* (Cambridge, 1990), 318–19.

[13] Willumsen, *Seventeenth-Century Witchcraft Trials*, 161.

men accused of witchcraft in Orkney after 1643. Information about marital status is scarce. We know that five women and one man were married. One woman was widowed. Family relations seem to have played a part during the witchcraft trials. Katherine Bigland and Marioun Tailzeour, mother and daughter, were involved in the 1615 panic. In some cases, like the one of Elizabeth Rennie in 1643, husbands were involved. However, information about gender, family relations and marital status is not sufficient to allow generalization to the total of cases.

Information about socio-economic status is also scarce.[14] We know that four women came from the lower socio-economic layer and three very poor women are registered. There are a few female vagabonds in the material. However, this is not enough evidence to maintain that poor women were particularly exposed to witchcraft persecution in Orkney.

The Demonological Element

There is some evidence around 1630–40 that demonological features were activated, either in the form of leading questions from the interrogators or in the accused persons' confessions, as will be seen exemplified in the analysis of Barbara Bowndie's case below. Jonet Rendall, 1629, confessed to the demonic pact. Her demon was called Walliman. He had white clothes and a white head and a grey beard. In the 1630s several demononic cases came up. In 1633 Marion Layland confessed to witches' meetings, and Katherine Miller confessed to the same, also in 1633. Helen Isbuster confessed to having entered the demonic pact with a black man in 1635. In 1633, John Sinclair carried his distinguished 'sister' around at the direction of the Devil. Katherine Grieve confessed to witches' meetings and relations with a black man, again in 1633. Jonet Reid confessed in 1643 to having kept company with the Devil. When a confession of participation in witches' meetings was given, denunciation of others was also a feature.

Panics versus Non-Panics

In the Orkney material, a panic is defined by me as seven or more linked trials per year. Chart 6 illustrates panic versus non-panic periods and gender in Orkney. The predominance of women in panics is clear. However, of the few men in the material, all, with one exception, are accused in panic years. This shows that men were not accused in isolated cases, but were

14 Willumsen, *Seventeenth-Century Witchcraft Trials*, 162.

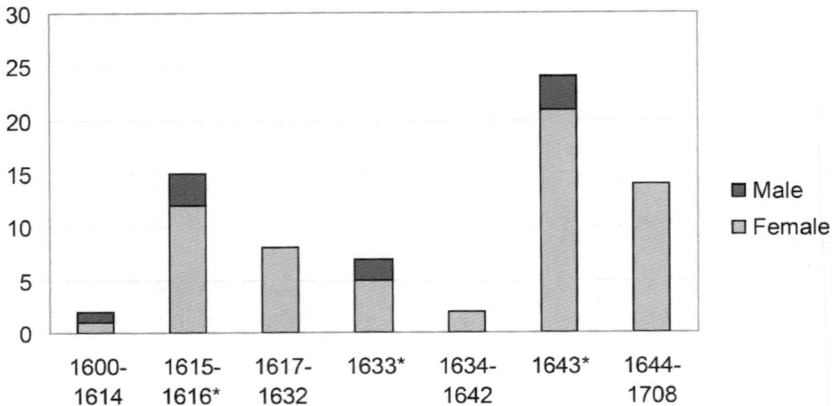

Chart 6: Panics versus non-panics, Orkney.
Asterisk denotes the three panic periods.

involved in linked trials. For instance, William Gude and Magnus Lindsay were tried on 13 June 1616, the same date as Helen Wallis, Agnes Tulloch, Geillis Schlaitter and Agnes Scottie. Lindsay was accused of *maleficium*.

Maleficium, Healing and Fairy Belief

For an area with relatively little evidence of demonology during witchcraft trials, other aspects of sorcery represented in the material will come clearer to the fore. I have chosen to focus on three aspects of traditional sorcery represented in the material: *maleficium*, healing and fairy belief. Witchcraft persecution in Orkney is very much tied up with *maleficium*, mentioned in accusations as well as in confessions. This is the most frequent form of sorcery mentioned in the sources, notably in most instances mentioned also in cases with demonological features. Healing is mentioned almost to the same extent as malefice, while the belief in fairies is documented, though not as a dominant feature.

Malefice is registered in SSW with spells causing human and animal illness and death: 13 cases of human illness, 5 cases of human death, 11 cases of animal illness and 8 cases of animal death. The overall picture for Orkney is an emphasis on spells causing human and animal illness and death. This is traditional sorcery, well known in the centuries before witchcraft trials started. Thus there is evidence in the material that people rumoured to know and practise sorcery were vulnerable to witchcraft accusations.

Healing humans is registered in 13 cases for women and 2 cases for men. Healing animals is registered in 7 cases for women and 1 case for men. No midwife is registered in the Orkney sources. Thus healing is at the same level as malefice and must be said to have put a stamp on the Orkney trials. In the later cases, divination comes in as an accusation, for instance in the case of Margaret Greeg in 1649.

The belief in fairies is represented in Orkney witch cases, but not to a large extent.[15] Issobel Sinclair confessed in 1633 to fairy belief and second sight. The same year James Knarstoun confessed to fairy belief. Fairies were mentioned in 1643 by Mareon Cumlacoy. In 1644, Elspeth Culsetter mentioned fairy belief along with substantial knowledge of malefice and healing. In 1644 Barbara Bowndie mentioned fairies, as will be seen in the analysis below.

Neighbourhood Disputes

Neighbourhood disputes, quarrelling and cursing, seem to have played minor roles as motives for witchcraft accusations in Orkney. As prominent features of cases, SSW has registered 4 cases of neighbourhood disputes, as less marked features of cases similarly 4 cases are registered.[16] Quarrelling is registered in the cases of 8 women and 1 man. Cursing is registered in the cases of 6 women and 2 men. Refused charity as a prominent feature is registered in 2 cases, and as a less marked feature in 6 cases.

These numbers suggest that disagreements in local communities did play a part in the witchcraft trials as motives, but they can not be said to have played major roles. However, it has to be born in mind that the focus of witchcraft persecution was the practice of different types of sorcery and witchcraft, not the motives for performing. The interrogation concentrated on practice of witchcraft. Much of the surviving sources come from the kirk and the presbytery. These contexts certainly had to do with witchcraft as part of an ungodly society, rather than the origin of accusations within the neighbourhood sphere of local communities.

---

[15] As a primary characterisation, a prominent feature, fairy belief is mentioned in 2 cases. As a secondary characterisation, a less important feature, it is registered in the cases of 6 women and 1 man.

[16] In SSW called primary and secondary characterisation.

Types of Trial, Verdict and Sentence

Most of the trials, in Orkney 82%, were local.[17] Of the local trials, 88%
women and 12% men were tried. The Sheriff Court, which passed the sentences, was a circuit court trying individuals suspected of witchcraft in all
parts of the islands. In several of the early cases, like those in 1615–16, the
accused persons were brought before the Court of the Bishopric as well as
the Sheriff Court.

Of the cases for which the verdict is known, is the case of John Stewart
mentioned above, who was accused in a central trial and found not guilty.
In local courts 15 women were found guilty, while only one woman was
found not guilty. No men in Orkney were found guilty in local trials. The
figures indicate that once a woman was brought before a local court in a
witchcraft case, her chances of acquittal were small.

As for sentences, it is known that 12 women were executed, two banished and one branded, all in local courts.[18] This shows that out of the
15 women found guilty in local courts, four-fifths were executed.

Shetland

Frequency

Shetland witchcraft trials are documented from 1602 until 1725. The total
number is 31.[19] Of the accused persons 8 were men and 23 women. This
means 26% of the accused were men, a higher percentage than for Scotland in general, and also for Orkney. Five of the men were accused up to

---

[17] Willumsen, *Seventeenth-Century Witchcraft Trials*, 165.

[18] Willumsen, *Seventeenth-Century Witchcraft Trials*, 165.

[19] SSW documents 29 accused persons from Shetland when accused is linked to Case_
date. However, one person is mentioned twice, as Jonka Kyneis is the same person as Jonet
Dynneis. To these 28 persons three persons must be added. The first is Helen Stewart's
mother, ref. Sinclair, G., *Satans Invisible World* (Edinburgh, 1685), 231 and Larner, C., Lee,
C. H. and Maclachlan, H. V., *A Sourcebook of Scottish Witchcraft* (Glasgow, 1977) 221, where
two unnamed persons from Shetland are listed (nos. 2901, 2902). Larner has used the year
1675 for these two cases. The reference is Sinclair's book mentioned above, which was published 1685. Sinclair says: 'In Shetland a few years ago (...)'. So the year seems to be a bit
uncertain according to the Sinclair reference, and Larner does not give any other source.
So it is uncertain from where she got the year 1675 for Helen Stewart's trial. The second is
Magnus Laurenson, 1674, whose trial records are in possession of John and Wendy Scott,
Gardie House, Bressay, Shetland. The last person is Jonat Archibald, 1602, ref. Donald-
son, *Court*, 29. She is also mentioned in Thomas, *County*, 160. She is neither mentioned in
Larner's Source Book nor in SSW. This adds up to 31 persons. Ref. *Willumsen, Seventeenth-
Century Witchcraft Trials*, 175.

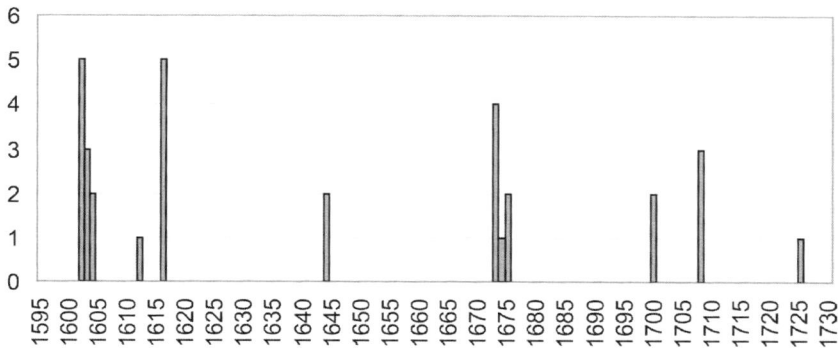

Chart 7: Witchcraft trials by year, Shetland, 1602–1725 (SSW).

1612, 1 in 1616, and 2 were accused relatively late, in 1674 and 1708. Three-quarters of the cases were before 1675.

The frequency of Shetland witchcraft trials is shown in Chart 7 above. Ten witchcraft trials took place before 1610: five in 1602, three in 1603 and two in 1604.[20] These early cases are characterized by brief entries in the court records, stating only the accused person's name, the type of crime they were accused of, and the sentence.[21] The cases deal mainly with accusations related to stealing milk and butter from neighbours, a traditional form of sorcery now for the first time criminalized and brought before the courts as witchcraft. The accused individuals were fined when they failed to quit themselves with the 'sixter aithe'—making six persons swear an oath that they were innocent—or with the 'larych aithe'—making two persons swear an oath of innocence.

---

[20] G. Donaldsen (ed.), *The Court Book of Shetland 1602–1604* (Edinburgh, 1954). The names from 1602 are Mareon Geilsdochter, pp. 22, 57, Poile Watson, pp. 22, 57, Wife of Poile Watson, pp. 22, 57, Nicole Culsetter, pp. 30, 61, from 1603 Mareon in Houle, pp. 90–91. In the SSW she is listed as Mareon Unknown.

[21] Those from 1603 and 1604 are documented partly in J. G. Dalyell's *The darker superstitions of Scotland*, and partly in *The Court Book of Shetland 1602–04*. The names from Donaldson, *The Court*, (1954) are: Catherine Thomasdochter, pp. 72, 92, 97; Nicole Swannesoun, pp. 72, 92. In SSW he is listed as Nicole Unknown, with unknown gender. Nicole is a man, married to Catherine Tomasdochter, ref. Donaldson, *The Court*, (1954), 72, 92. Larner has Nicole as a female. From 1604 Mareoun Cromertie is mentioned pp. 122, 136, 145. Andrew Duncane 1604 mentioned in Dalyell, *The Darker*, 521, ref. to court records 15 July 1604, and in Donaldson, *The Court* (1954), 128, court records 16 July 1604.

In the period 1611–20 six trials took place, one in 1612 and five in 1616.[22] In particular, three of the cases in 1616, Barbara Scord/Tomasdochter, Katherine Jonesdochter and Jonet Dynneis, are of interest, as this is the first time demonological trials appear in the Shetland sources. The records are detailed and give information about a new type of witchcraft trial of a much more severe kind than before—focusing on the Devil and what relations with the Devil could lead to. The accusations range from rather innocent stealing of milk and butter from neighbours to causing human sickness and death. Specific objects as well as charms are used for performing sorcery.

In the period 1621–40 there were no cases. In the period 1641–50 two trials took place, both in 1644, Juenit Fraser and Marion Pardoun.[23] The Pardoun case will be studied in detail below. Fraser is mentioned in Pardoun's confession as dead. Fraser had been convicted as a witch, 'whom you desyrit the devil to move her to assist you doth prove, qlk she both before and after her conviction did testiffie'.[24] Thus the cases of Fraser as well as Pardoun seem to have demonological features, which for the Pardoun case will be seen in the close-reading of the document below.

In the period 1651–70 there were no witchcraft trials. In the 1670s there were seven trials. Four of these took place in 1673.[25] These trials were held on the same day and were linked through family relations. However, information about the cases is scarce. There were no trials during the 1680s and 1690s, but after the turn of the century five trials took place in the period 1700–10. Of these, two trials took place in 1700.[26] Three trials

---

[22] Dalyell, *The Darker Superstitions*, 235; Donaldson, *Court*, (1991), 25–26. Dalyell has probably got the reference to Faw's trial wrong, as he is referring to 12 August 1612, 'Rec. Ork, f. 9, 10', instead of Donaldson's ref. fos. 4v–5r. There is no doubt that it is the same case. The five trials in 1616 are documented in Dalyell and in *The Sheriff Court Book of Shetland 1615–1629*. Donaldson, *Court*, Barbara Scord/Tomasdochter, Katherine Jonesdochter and Jonet Dynneis, 38–43; SSW has Jonet Dynneis registered twice, also as Jonka Kyneis; Dalyell, *The Darker*, 378, documents Patrick Peterson and Marjorie Ritchie.

[23] Proceedings against Marion Pardoun, 1644, in possession of John and Wendy Scott, Gardie House, Bressay, Shetland; Thomas, *County*, 88–99. Marioun Pardoun's surname is also written Peblis. SSW has Peebles as her surname.

[24] Thomas, *County*, 96.

[25] Four of them are documented in *RPC*, 3rd series, iv, p. 5. In addition, Helen Stewart's mother is documented in Sinclair, G., *Satans Invisible World*, 231, see Larner's *Source-Book*, 221.

[26] These cases are documented by *The New Statistical Account of Scotland*, Edinburgh, 1845. The book is divided into parts according to geographical area, and for each new part the pagination starts at 1. These persons are mentioned in the Shetland part of the book, p. 60.

took place in 1708, when three siblings, Andrew, Kathren and Elizabeth Ratter, were accused of witchcraft.[27] These members of the Ratter family were examined before the presbytery on 9–11 June 1708 at Sandness and Walls. The presbytery asked Reverend Mr George Duncan 'whither or not he had "caused cite" the persons suspect of witchcraft sorcery & deluding the people'.[28] He answered that he had commanded this family to be summoned and produced a list of witnesses. The heads of the families were called in and decided that the family should be dealt with further. The Ratter family were vagabonds, roaming from farm to farm asking for food, wool or a place to stay overnight. The charges against them were that they caused human and animal sickness and death and destruction of crops, always as a consequence of them being refused charity. The last witchcraft trial in Shetland took place in 1725, the case of Margaret Watson.[29] The case will be studied in further detail below.

The sources vary considerably in length and quality. According to John H. Ballantyne and Brian Smith, Shetland has not been fortunate in the survival of its historical records, especially those that were in private hands.[30] But the preserved archival documents have been taken care of and several of the court books published. Even if the entries from the first years are very brief, the court books give valuable insights into court procedure as well as accusations and verdicts. However, the confessions are not possible to distinguish in these earliest witchcraft records.

When we come to 1616, the records are richer and give access to court procedures, accusations, testimonies and the contents of confessions. With regard to printed literature, G. Sinclair's book *Satans Invisible World* is interesting because it was a seventeenth-century edition, published in 1685. It falls into the same category as the *New Statistical Account of Scotland* and J. G. Dalyell's *The darker superstitions of Scotland*, published in 1834, when it comes to the documentation of witchcraft. They all mention the cases briefly, but do not have the quality of the court records.[31]

---

[27] SMA, SPR, CH2/1071/1, fos. 152–9.
[28] SMA, SPR, CH2/1071/1, fo. 152.
[29] SMA, SPR, CH2/1071/2 fos. 300, 304, 309, 312, 315.
[30] Ballantyne, J. H. and Smith, B. (eds.), *Shetland documents 1580–1611*, (Lerwick, 1994), xix.
[31] It must be mentioned that Dalyell contains footnotes with exact references to the dates and places of the trials, even if Orkney is often miswritten for Shetland.

Types of Trial, Verdict and Sentence

The trials were local trials, held in the Sheriff Court. The early cases, 1602–04, were characterized by *maleficium* and the sentences were lenient. Most often the accused person was 'dempt' to quit herself or himself with the 'saxter aithe', where six persons had to give an oath that the suspect was innocent, or with the 'laryct aithe', where two persons had to give an oath of the suspect's innocence.[32] The application of these oaths probably remained from the old Norse laws, in which the same procedure was often used. In most cases the accused failed to quit themselves with oaths and had to pay fines, often 'ii merkis'[33] of silver or more. Patrick Stewart acted as judge during the case of Mareon Cromertie in 1604. The first demonological trials in Shetland, the trials of Jonet Dynneis, Katherine Jonesdochter and Barbara Scord in 1616, were presided over by William Levingstoun, sheriff and justice depute.

Sentences of execution are known for Jonet Dynneis, Barbara Scord and Katherine Jonesdochter in 1616, Juenit Fraser and Marion Pardoun in 1644 and Helen Stewart in 1675. This indicates that the most severe sentences in Shetland were connected to demonological cases and that all those who are documented as having been burnt, were women. In Shetland those sentenced in witchcraft cases were strangled and burnt at the gallows. The old gallows were often situated on hills near villages. One of the execution places where witches were burnt is located on the Berrie Hill near Scalloway, known from oral tradition.[34] The gallows hills of Shetland are very old, dating from before 1300, and very local. Brian Smith points to the centralisation of legal justice in Shetland, a change from a medieval system 'where decisions about life and death were taken in local districts and by potentates throughout the islands, to a seventeenth century one, where sentences were handed out in Scalloway'.[35]

---

[32] For instance Nicole Culsetter, 1602, and Poile Watson and his wife, 1602, failed to quit themselves with the 'saxter aithe'. Mareoun Geilsdochter, 1602, and Mareoun in Houle, 1603, failed to quit themselves with the 'larycht aithe'.

[33] Plural of 'mark' or 'merk', a unit of weight used especially for gold and silver, equivalent to 8 oz. In Orkney and Shetland 'mark' was also used as a weight of victual, butter, oil and tallow or of an amount of butcher-flesh, equalling one twentyfourth of a lispund, ref. *DOST*.

[34] William Moore, Scalloway, showed me on 21 April 2007 the place where witches were burnt on Berrie Hill, information orally transferred to him from earlier generations.

[35] Smith, B., 'Gibbets and gallows. Local rough justice in Shetland, 800–1700', paper presented at the conference 'Recent developments in North Atlantic Studies', arranged by Northern Studies and Aberdeen University, Aberdeen 13–15 April 2007.

The Demonological Element

The word 'witchcraft' was mentioned from the earliest cases onwards in Shetland, seemingly to denote a serious crime. In the case of Poile Watson, 1602, he was given the option to quit himself with a 'saxter aithe because the action is wechtie'.[36] He failed to quit himself with the oath and had to pay 'vi merkis silver and to underly the law thairfoir as witchcraft'.[37] However, neither the Devil nor the demonic pact is mentioned in the earliest witchcraft cases in Shetland.

There was a change in the contents of Shetland witchcraft trials by 1616. During a triple trial on 2 October 1616 in Scalloway the confessions of three accused women brought to the fore a range of demonological ideas, all known from cases on the Scottish mainland: the demonic pact, the Devil's mark, the Devil's child, a promise from the Devil, and sex with the Devil. Metamorphosis was not confessed. Almost the same expressions that are known from the Scottish mainland were used in these cases, which suggests that demonological ideas had been brought to the islands and woven into the oral narratives of the common people. Such an assimilation can be traced in the lengthy confessions as being part of the knowledge these three women had before they entered the courtroom. As will be shown in the analysis of the Barbara Bowndie case from Orkney below, leading questions during interrogation were used to bring onto the agenda certain topics. However, the detailed confession indicates that demonological knowledge around 1616 was part of common people's mentality sphere.

The confession of Katherine Jonesdochter documents the demonic pact, sex with the Devil, who is called the 'bowman of Hildiswick and Eschenes', the Devil's mark, power from the Devil to cause human death and to transfer sickness and death from one person to another, and a promise from the Devil that 'she sould be hable to do ony thing she desired'.[38] She also confessed to having seen 'trowis ryse out of the kirkyeard of Hildiswick and Holiecross Kirk of Eschenes and thet she saw them on the hill callit greinfaill at monie sindrie tymes and that they come to ony hous quhair thair wes feasting or great mirrines, and speciallie at Yule'.[39] This is the nearest one comes to a witches' meeting in the confessions this year. The bunch of 'trowis' from the churchyard to a certain extent

[36] Donaldson, *The Court* (1954), 22.
[37] Donaldson, *The Court* (1954), 22.
[38] Donaldson, *Court* (1991), 38.
[39] Donaldson, *Court* (1991), 39.

resembles a notion closely related to ghosts, the 'Wild Hunt' or 'Furious Horde', mentioned for instance by Goodare, 'spirits of people who had died prematurely and were compelled to wander until their allotted time was up'.[40] This notion of a horde of dead people arising from the church-yard is known also from Norway.[41]

The confession of Barbara Scord documents the demonic pact, keep-ing company with the Devil, who is called 'the bowman', mention of 'the bowmanes bairne' among her own children, getting power from the Devil to cast sickness upon human beings, and taking power from the 'private member' of a man who had promised to marry her, but quit.[42] In the confession of Jonet Dynneis the Devil's pact is not mentioned, but 'Dev-ilrie' is mentioned as an accusation. She is accused of having caused the drowning of two men. The three confessions from 1616 complement each other with regard to a range of demonological notions and give evidence for knowledge of demonological ideas among the peasants of Shetland during the second decade of the seventeenth century. Even if the witches' meeting is hardly mentioned and metamorphosis is not mentioned, there is ample evidence of demonological notions.

The non-continuation of demonological trials in Shetland is the oppo-site of the occurrence of demonology in Finnmark, where a remote region far from the capital of Denmark-Norway experienced an intense witch-hunt with a strong demonological impact over more than five decades. However, what we see in Shetland, is a development of witchcraft perse-cution similar to what we see on the west coast of Norway, particularly in the Bergen area, which was not far from Shetland. In the town of Ber-gen, there were four accused persons who confessed to diabolism in the period 1584–1590, but the demonological ideas never developed further so that panics arose in Bergen. However, in the district around Bergen, called Bergenhus, there were scattered demonological confessions in the period 1650–1680, but not more than three cases per year. Therefore, if the Bergen area had influenced Shetland trials, it must have to do with the late sixteenth-century demonic trials from Bergen town.[43] The period of witchcraft trials in Shetland characterized by demonology was dominated by female accused. This means that the men in the material from Shetland

---

[40] Goodare, 'Scottish Witchcraft in its European Context', 32.
[41] 'Gongferd, feigd og spøykjeri. Framsynte folk', *Bøfferding* (1981), 54–57.
[42] Donaldson, *Court* (1991), 40–41.
[43] See Botheim, *Trolldomsprosessene i Bergenhus len, 1566–1700*, 136, 215–227; Stave, *Da Lucifer kom til Vardøhus*, 82.

were not particularly focused on during the decades when demonological features are found in the sources. In several of the most serious cases, two or three female trials were linked together by denunciation. This is an indication of collective practice of witchcraft, or cooperation between witches, something which connects the trials to the cumulative concept of witchcraft.

Maleficium, Healing and Fairy Belief

The early cases were characterized by accusations such as the stealing of milk, and the sieve and shears.[44] Human illness and death or animal illness and death are mentioned in most of these cases. Malefice is also mentioned in the demonological cases from 1616, suggesting that the undercurrent of traditional sorcery continued to stay alive side by side with demonological notions. Katherine Jonesdochter confessed to malefice, taking profit from bewitched milk. Barbara Scord confessed to using a thread and the bone of a dead man's finger when she performed sorcery. She caused human sickness, made a man marry her daughter and was involved in suspicious kirning of milk. Jonet Dynneis confessed to malefice, stealing of butter. She used cursing and called evil upon people, which in turn came true. For the later part of the period of the Shetland witch-hunt, malefice is again the reason for accusations. For most of the cases where information is given, malefice seems to be mentioned. The use of objects for performing sorcery and the use of charms and cursing are all well-known procedures from traditional sorcery and folk belief. John Faw, 1612, was said to have learned his art from the 'Egyptians' (gypsies).

Healing is mentioned in the Shetland witchcraft material, but to a very modest degree. Healing humans is mentioned in connection with four women, while healing animals is mentioned in connection with one woman. Midwifery is not mentioned in the Shetland cases. As a whole, there is no evidence that these aspects had a notable impact on the witchcraft trials in Shetland.

Fairies are mentioned in SSW related to one Shetland case. This is the above-mentioned case of Katherine Jonesdochter, 1616, where 'trowis' are

---

[44] A method of divination by observation of the motion of a sieve suspended from the points of an open pair of shears.

mentioned.[45] The word 'trowis' is interpreted as 'fairies' by SSW. However, the word trows in Shetland folklore, heard about from the seventeenth century onwards, has a bit different meaning than fairies. The trows 'were small men and women, often dressed in grey, who lurked outside the township boundaries. They roamed the hills, and lived inside hills— some called them "hill-folk", and at home and furt they usually moved around in swarms.'[46] The trows enjoyed eating and drinking, and could be generous to their neighbours when they were in a good mood. But if they did not get what they wanted, be that music, cows, children, human nursing mothers, they could be vindictive and punish human beings. The trows are also different from the Norwegian *trolls*, giant creatures known already in the saga literature. What comes closest to the Scottish fairies in Norwegian folk belief is an *alv*. These figures are small and friendly and live in the hills and mountains.[47]

Social Status and Neighbourhood Disputes

The material gives little information about marital status. At least seven women were married and one was widowed; the rest are unknown. Couples seem to have been accused in the early as well as in the late periods. Mother-daughter relationships played a part in some linked trials in the 1670s, and siblings were accused in 1708.

For the Shetland material there is not enough information to say anything about socio-economic conditions for the majority of cases. An

---

[45] In SSW this is registered as secondary characterisation of case, which means it is not a prominent feature of the confession.

[46] The Shetland Folklore Development Group (ed.), *Da Book on Trows* (Lerwick, 2007), vii. This book also contains a collection of stories about trows.

[47] *Trolls* as giants are mentioned in Fljotsdale Saga. See 'Introduction' in *Da Book on Trows*. For Norwegian folklore, see the collected traditional fairy tales of Peter Christian Asbjørnsen and Jørgen Moe, published in the 1830s, 1840s and 1850s. *Trolls* are known from Norwegian folklore, being small or big supernatural creatures living in the mountains, the forest or in the sea. They represent another world, a world we cannot see, thus resembling the fairies. But they are often evil and not connected with magic to the same extent as fairies. *Trolls* are most frequently presented in traditional Norwegian tales as dangerous for humans to have contact with, as they may *fortrolle* people so that they remain for ever in the world of *trolls*. *Trolls* play a dominant role in the tales collected by the folklorists Asbjørnsen and Moe, see for instance *Norske Folkeeventyr* (Christiania, 1852). Another interesting figure is Norwegian folklore, also inhabiting the otherworld, is the *hulder*, a siren, beautiful in appearance, who inhabits the hills and mountains. She tempts men and might be revealed when you see a long, cow-like tail. Ref. Asbjørnsen, P. C., *Norske Huldre-Eventyr og Folkesagn*, (Christiania, 1845–48). The fairies are not prominent in the range of figures inhabiting the Norwegian 'otherworld'.

interesting motif for transferring sickness from one person to another, which might have had its root in economic relations, is mentioned by Katherine Jonesdochter. She transferred sickness from her husband to a merchant 'because he was ane stranger, rather nor ony contreyman'.[48] Refused charity is also mentioned in the sources (although not to a great extent), as some of the accused in the later cases were vagabonds.

Neighbourhood disputes are in 5 cases mentioned in SSW as characterization of the Shetland witchcraft trials. This indicates that disputes between neighbours occasionally were mentioned during the trials. The early cases are characterized by stealing milk and butter from neighbours. Most cases in which traditional sorcery is involved, also involve neighbours or acquaintances. So quarrelling and cursing might have been the first step of a witchcraft case. Having a reputation as a witch was of great importance as well. Neighbourhood disputes had an impact on the Shetland cases in relation to the initial accusations of witchcraft in the local community. However, the severity of such quarrels and angry words only got consequences when the accusations were brought before the court and resulted in a formal trial.

---

[48] Donaldson, *Court*, (1991), 38.

CHAPTER SEVEN

ORKNEY AND SHETLAND—CLOSE-READINGS

Orkney

Barbara Bowndie, 1644

The first part of this chapter will deal with the case of Barbara Bowndie, living in Kirkwall in Orkney, accused of witchcraft and interrogated before the presbytery in 1643. She was accused in a linked trial, being denounced for witchcraft by another woman. Bowndie's case is chosen for analysis because it is a rich text which interestingly might throw light on some central questions within witchcraft research. Firstly, the context of her case offers information about the functioning of the courts in Orkney and the relation between the presbytery and the Sheriff Court with regard to prosecution of witchcraft. Secondly, the case offers insight in pre-trial questioning as well as interrogation before the presbytery. The discourse is rendered in an accurate way, with questions as well as answers clearly marked. Therefore it is possible to analyse the interplay between the interrogator and the accused, and examine the strategies used by both parties. Thirdly, demonological notions as well as folkloric beliefs come to the fore during the interrogation of Barbara Bowndie, and distinction between these two spheres of ideas as they appear in this case, will form part of the analysis. Fourthly, oral transference of new ideas about witch-craft among peasants in the local communities is a topic which will be approached due to information implied in the sources. Fifthly, the role of the scribe will be discussed, and relate to international research on this topic. These questions in total fathom widely and will contribute to the comparison of Scotland and Finnmark as well as well as a broader scope of research.

The Context

The case of Barbara Bowndie had a pre-history, and it is necessary to go back to 1642 to see why she came in the searchlight for witchcraft. This year, a woman named Elsbeth Culsetter was tried for witchcraft and burnt. She denounced another woman, Marjorie Paplay. As the focus on

Marjorie Paplay is a recurrent theme also in the trial of Barbara Bowndie, some information about Paplay is relevant. On 3 November 1642, Mr Henry Smith, Minister of Shapinshay, tried to start a trial against Marjorie Paplay. He referred to laws and former practice, stating that no person reported to the civil judge as guilty of witchcraft, 'be any who hes been convict and execut for witchcraft should be heard to complaine that they are slandered'.[1] If they wanted to have their name cleansed of slander, they had to go to the civil judge, where the case was filed, or else stand the trial. Henry Smith called in the sheriff depute, Mr Henry Aitken, 'to declare if Elspeth Culsetter witch did delate that Marjorie Paplay mother to James Baikie of Tankernes was a witch; Answered that the said Elspeth did indeed declare that the said Marjorie was the greatest witch of them all'.[2] He required that Paplay 'might be enacted in the Shirref court bookes to underly the Law, as others who were delated be the said Elspeth Culsetter as guiltie of witchcraft, were'.[3]

However, Paplay's son protested against the slandering of his mother. He desired a summon against certain persons whom he alleged to be slanderers of his mother. The brethren could not condescend unto this, in respect of Henry Smith's protestations, and their approbation thereof. So the situation was that the minister, Henry Smith, argued that Marjorie Paplay should herself pursue her slanderers by giving in a bill of complaint, as he had argued before, and he requested the presbytery to take the same considerations. Apparently the presbytery agreed with Smith's protestation and thus refused to allow a slander case or to hand over relevant documents. In practice this means that Henry Smith on formal grounds tried to make it difficult for Marjorie Paplay to get herself cleansed of slander. Instead he pressed for her being tried for witchcraft before the presbytery. He had many accusations against Marjorie, among them the death of his mother-in-law, related to 'some hard speeches uttered be the said Marjorie to her quinto Martii 1632' as well as Marjory cursing other people.[4] Marjorie was left with a warning in 1642, but she was still in the searchlight for witchcraft. When the case against Barbara Bowndie started one year later, she was frequently asked to name Marjorie Paplay as a witch, as will be seen in the following.

---

[1] OLA, OPR, CH2/1082/1, p. 203.
[2] OLA, OPR, CH2/1082/1, p. 204.
[3] OLA, OPR, CH2/1082/1, p. 204.
[4] OLA, OPR, CH2/1082/1, p. 203.

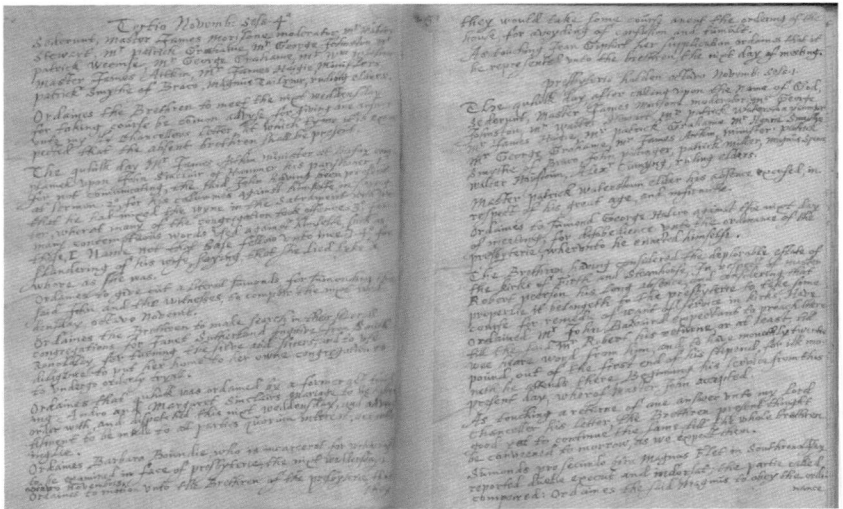

Figure 4: Case against Barbara Bowndie, 1644. OLA, Minutes of the presbytery of
Orkney, GB241/OCR/4/1, pp. 250–51.

The Trial

Barbara Bowndie was first accused in 1643, the worst year of witchcraft
accusations in Orkney, and the same year as a national panic was going
on in mainland Scotland.[5] On 3 November 1643 there is a note in the
Presbytery minutes that precautions should be taken against tumults:
'Ordaines to motion unto the Brethren of the presbytrie that they would
take some course anent the ordering of the house, for avoiding of confu-
sion and tumult'.[6] A witchcraft case was coming up, and the presbytery
might have been worried about what tumults this could lead to, caused
either by friends of the accused person, or spectators. The person accused
was Barbara Bowndie; she was 'incarcerat for witchcraft'.[7] In addition it
is made known 'that three Brethren shall be examinators of her in face of
the presbytrie and that every brother shall give information unto these
three, and if any Brother that thinks his Information not fullie acted, shall
have Libertie (having protested for Lieve) to examine her himselfe, upon

---

[5] Willumsen, *Seventeenth-Century Witchcraft Trials*, 39.
[6] OLA, OPR, CH2/1082/1, pp. 250–51.
[7] OLA, OPR, CH2/1082/1, p. 250.

the points to be laid unto her charge.[8] Master George Johnston and Master Patrick Waterstoun, younger, were ordained on 8 November to concur with the Moderator of the presbytery in the examination.[9] As it appears, any of the brethren could in addition question her in front of the presbytery, if they felt this necessary.

Next day it turns out that there shall be a 'private' questioning before the formal one.[10] Apparently, four men then went to see Barbara. The two mentioned above asked Mr David Watsone, minister, and Patrick Smythe of Braco, ruling elder, to assist them in going to Barbara Bowndie 'who was then presently in ward to deall with her *in private, by prayer, and conference* before they came in publick'. [*My italics*][11] This informal questioning of her will form the back-curtain for the public interrogation, as it is often referred to, using the expression 'concerning her saying'. As will be seen, the formal interrogation in fact took the informal questioning as its outset. This was five days after Barbara was imprisoned, and during these days she had been exposed to pressure. It comes forth retrospectively that persons have threatened her, calling her a thief and warned her against lying on others. That people came to her in prison, threatening her, must be seen in the light of common people's fear for denunciation, and that they might be named by her. On 9 November, 'After prayer and conference with the said Barbara in privat, she was presented publickly before the presbytrie and accused upon the points following.'[12] Nine points are recorded, all of them related to the Devil, use of devilish witchcraft or witches' meetings.

The Voices of the Interrogators and the Accused

The voices of the interrogators and the accused are intertwined in the rendered discourse, but in a way which makes it possible to distinguish the questions posed to her and the answers given. All the time it is referred to what she has confessed informally during the pre-trial questioning. The interrogators tried to get as much out of her about the Devil as possible,

---

[8] OLA, OPR, H2/1082/1, p. 253.

[9] The Moderator of the presbytery was Patrick Waterston, minister in Orphin 1624–42. He was probably the father of Patrick Waterston, the younger. It is not clear whether he also took part in the interrogation.

[10] I would like to thank Diane Baptie for the transcription of the document.

[11] OLA, OPR, CH2/1082/1, p. 254.

[12] OLA, OPR, CH2/1082/1, p. 254.

from point 1 onwards: '1. primo, concerning her saying, that the Devill
told her that if she should be put to death, the whole cornes should be
blowne in the ayre by him. *Answered* she sp-rt [*unclear word at end of
line*] for weaknesses of her owne flesh, and for feare of her [life?]'[13] [*My
italics.*] From the beginning, the interrogators try to make her confirm
what she has said earlier, and use everything she had said against her.
The Devil is mentioned by the interrogator, but referring to a confession
previously given by her. Thus it is clear that she knows about the Devil
and apparently has been using his mighty power as a threat, in order to
prevent a death sentence. This means that already from the beginning of
her imprisonment, she is aware of notions centred around the Devil and
also what might be the outcome of the trial. There is no denying on her
part that she has said these words about the Devil. However, she gives
reasons for her previous confessions; saying that she confessed out of fear
for her life. Thus she is retracting her former confession. The insistence
upon demonological features on the part of the interrogators is repeated
in the next point. Barbara Bowndie has been to Shetland, where she was
travelling with her small child, not yet baptised, and therefore an alleged
easy pray for evil powers. The interrogators want her to admit that she out
of need had entered into a pact with the Devil at that time. She does not
confirm this, instead she is turning the interrogation in another direction,
mentioning an event in Shetland, a period of 24 hours, when she had been
speechless and tormented. At this point, the interrogators introduce an
element of folk belief, the fairies, suggesting, based on what 'the people
said', that she had stayed with the fairies:

> 2. Secundo, *Being asked*, if she upon *occasion of necessitie* in Zetland, did
> condescend to serve the Devill. *Answered* that being travelling with ane
> unhoven[14] childe four years and being fainted by the way she became
> speechless, and so remained for the space of 24 houres, and was sore tor-
> mented, and *the people said*, that she had been with the Farie. She *answered*,
> she saw no Farie.[15] [*My italics.*]

The interrogators here move swiftly from the Devil's pact to the fairies. There seems to be an assumption that being with the fairies has a

---

[13] OLA, OPR, CH2/1082/1, p. 254.
[14] Means unchristened, to hove means to raise, i.e. here a child not raised at the font.
[15] OLA, OPR, CH2/1082/1, pp. 254–255. The case of Elspeth Reoch is discussed by
D. Purkiss in *Troublesome Things*, 90–96.

demonological aspect.[16] The representation of fairy belief in witchcraft cases is a Scottish phenomenon. The way interrogation develops in the second point, shows that the questions posed introduce the Devil's pact as well as the fairies. It is not Barbara who brings in these elements, the interrogators do that. However, Barbara Bowndie is familiar with the Devil's power as well as the world of fairies, as the questions are posed within a frame where it is expected that she knows what it is all about. Her strategy is that she avoids answering about the Devil's pact and says she did not see any fairy during the hours she was speechless. So she knows these are dangerous elements that should not be touched upon. So far the voice of the interrogator is a persistent and active voice, suggesting new elements and frequently referring to what she had confessed informally. The voice of the accused is elusive and non-cooperative, trying to turn the interrogation away from dangerous elements.

Denouncing other as witches is a central point during a demonological interrogation. The third point introduces that she herself might have been active as a discoverer of witches, and in that respect might have some names to give: '3. Tertio, Being asked concerning her giving her selfe out for a discoverer of witches. Answ: That *she denyes the same.*' [*My italics.*][17] Then additional demonological notions were brought onto the agenda: '4. Quarto, being posed *in particular,* concerning the Devill his apparitions in diverse shapes *upon the Ball-Ley,* and his having *carnall copulation* with Marjorie Paplay at that tyme, as a man hes adoe with a woman'. [*My italics.*][18] Again it appears from the discourse that the interrogator introduced a demonological element by referring to her previous confession, where she had confessed to participation at a witches' meeting. So this type of demonological knowledge Barbara Bowndie had at the time of the pre-trial questioning, which means she must have known it before the imprisonment. The question introduces the witches' meeting as well as sexual intercourse with the Devil at such a meeting. It is not about Barbara Bowndie herself having intercourse with the Devil, it is about Marjorie Paplay, which means that Marjorie's name must have been brought into the questioning. The Ball-Ley as a place for witches' meeting is interesting with regard to transference of ideas about witchcraft, something which will be returned to in the Finnmark chapters. Having sexual intercourse

---

[16] Cf. Henderson, 'Witch Hunting and Witch Belief', in Goodare, Martin and Miller, *Witchcraft and Belief in Early Modern Scotland,* 102.

[17] OLA, OPR, CH2/1082/1, p. 255.

[18] OLA, OPR, CH2/1082/1, p. 255.

with the Devil is a common element in Scottish demonological witchcraft cases. Again the answer given by Barbara Bowndie is an elusive one.
She admits that she has spoken about the witches' meeting, but she gives
as the reason that she had been brought ale, and was not sober. This is
objected by Patrick Waterston, one of the brothers which interrogated
her, resulting in a dispute about the point of time when she got the ale:

> *Answ: That Steven Anguson brought stark aill to her, which made her to speake*
> *these wordes in Mr Patrick Waterstoun, and Master Patrick Weemse their*
> *hearing.* Wherupon Mr Patrick Waterstoun replyed that she spake these
> words in presence of the Brethren, before Mr Patrick Weemse did speake
> with her and repeated it over againe before the brethren in both their audi-
> ence, *being as yet sober,* and *that it was afterwards, that a drink of small aill*
> *was brought unto her* by Steven Angusone *at her earnest requyst, to quench*
> *her thirst,* and (she—*interlined*) *did but take one drink of it,* all the quhyle
> that the said Master Patrick was with her, reserving the rest in the stoup:
> And being oftentimes in publick exhorted be Master Patrick Waterstoun,
> that she should not lie upon Marjorie Paplay, nor no honest woman, did at
> that tyme reply unto him, *God forgive you that beares over much with them*
> All which was spokene *before she got that drink of aill'.*[19] [*My italics.*]

This passage has clear features of orality. An additive sentence structure is
clear, a time-line is attempted drawn, which has importance for the main
argument about drinking ale, and direct discourse in the present tense is
inserted in the narrative. This is Barbara Bowndie's reply to Patrick Waterston, asking God to forgive him for having caused that suspicion is thrown
on honest women.

The same language features are seen in the fifth point, which repeats
the previous one on the part of the interrogator, while Barbara Bowndie
brings into the discourse a new element, saying that she was led by a
commissionaire, John Aitken, to give out wrong information about Marjorie Paplay and other women. When she is referring to Aitken's comment 'never want thy Lyfe', this is en expression usually pronounced by
the Devil offering persons to enter the Devil's pact. With this connotation
to the Devil's discourse, she is implicitly comparing Aitken with the Devil.
Also this time Barbara Bowndie's answer is exhaustive, with the comment
of Aitken rendered in direct discourse, thus making the scene lively:

> 5. Quinto, Being asked againe whither she knew it to be of veritie, that she
> had seen the Devill ly with Marjorie Paplay on the Ball-Ley? *Replyed that she*
> *knew nothing of it, but such as she was tryed upon,* And being asked what that

---

[19] OLA, OPR, CH2/1082/1, p. 255.

meant to be tryed upon? *Replyed that the young co[m]missar John Aitkin had said to her, tell mee about Marjorie Paplay what ane woman she is, and thou shall never want thy Life,* spake more then enough of the said Marjorie at that tyme, and of sundrie other honest women, such as Elspeth and Marion Paplayes, and Elspeth Baikie and the good wife of Essinquoy. *But Barabra Boundie said that she never knew no ill to these women.*[20] [*My italics.*]

Barbara Bowndie withdrew all her denunciations, as she had spoken 'more than enough' of the women, and she refused to repeat the denunciations.[21] It seems that the misery she might cause for other women, has become problematic for her. In a local society wherein the fear of witchcraft accusations is prevailing, a name given in the context of a witches' meeting, might lead to catastrophe. Barbara Bowndie is finishing her answer underlining the mentioned women's innocence, as a sigh from the heart. Also here, an oral accent comes through in Barbara's comment, marked by the use of double negotiation, 'she *never knew no* ill to these women' [*My italics*].

In the sixth point, Marjorie Paplay is mentioned again, this time for having caused the death of Thomas Lentron. The alleged witchcraft performance is one of *maleficium* this time, not demonological witchcraft:

> 6. Sexto, being asked concerning Thomas Lentron his being put to death by Marjorie Paplay her witchcraft by putting a quhyte thing lyke calk in his drink. *Answ: that what she had spoken therof was put in her mouth by Master Patrick Weemse.* Master Patrick Waterstoun replyed that that could not be, in respect he was beside and knew the contrair, and declared further, that it being inquyred be Master Patrick Weemse if she knew that Thomas Lentron had gotten any wrong, *after long entreate* made to her to declare the same, if she knew ought of that matter, *did at length declare that the said Thomas was witched be Marjorie Paplay*; and upon his demand *she told the manner of it*, by scraping in etc. Barbara Boundie *answered that she had never spoken concerning Thomas Lentron, if she had not been spired at, be the said Master Patrick Wemmse.*[22] [*My italics.*]

Barbara and the brethren argue contrary to each other when it comes to what was said about Paplay. Again Barbara Bowndie maintains that she was lead by one of the brethren to say this about Marjorie Paplay,

---

[20] OLA, OPR, CH2/1082/1, p. 255.

[21] According to SSW the named witches during Barbara Bowndie's trial were Elspeth Baikie, Elsinquoy Unknown, Elspeth Paplay, Marion Paplay, Marjorie Paplay. As mentioned above, Marion Paplay is identical with Marjorie Paplay, and Elsinquoy Unknown is identical with Katherine Craige. The case against Elspeth Paplay started on 3 November, the cases against Marion Paplay, Elspeth Baikie and Katherine Craige started on 9 November. Katherine Craige was burned on 22 July 1643.

[22] OLA, OPR, CH2/1082/1, p. 256.

while the other brother supports the first mentioned, confirming that he
was also in the room and heard what was being said. Again establishing a time-line is important to find out when the various elements were
mentioned, as it was of uttermost importance to find out who had first
mentioned Paplay's witchcraft towards Lentron. The brother argued it
was mentioned by Barbara first, and that she in detail had explained how
Paplay's witchcraft was carried out, while Barbara maintained she would
not have said anything unless this point was brought forth by the one
posing the questions. The strategy of Barbara is one of defence, she is
protesting to the interrogators' version of the pre-trial questioning. At the
same time she has to admit that she in fact said something about Paplay
causing Thomas Lentron's death. It appears that Barbara Bowndie has the
knowledge the interrogators are interested to hear about, and that it was
only 'after long entreate' she was willing to tell what she knew.

The seventh point repeats the previous one, also this time with denial
on the part of Barbara as a result: 'The said Barbara being asked now
againe, concerning the realitie of it, whither the said Marjorie had witched
the said Thomas Lentron, as she had spoken before? *Denyed the same*'.[23]
Repetition of questions, as we saw above for point 4 and 5, is used again,
it was probably a method the interrogators knew that would work, as it
created an effective pressure. The mixture of malefice and demonological elements seems to characterize the interrogators' suspicion towards
Paplay, and they were eager to know about both these elements.

The interrogators are circling about a limited number of items. In the
eighth point, demonology is again focused, as a witches' meeting comes
up. Barbara is asked 'if she was one of the fourscore and nynteen that
danced on the Links of Munes in Hoy? *At first denyed, but therafter confessed that she said it,* which being conferred with her first words in saying
that it was but six yeers, since the Devill deceived her, is found to varie
in her speeches, *for it is elleven yeers, or thereby, since the dancers in Munes
were first spoken of*'. [*My italics.*][24] Here the number of dancers in Munes,
four score and nineteen, draws attention towards evil powers. This is a
good indication that oral narratives with demonological content had been
told by peasants in the area for many years. It is stated that the story
about a witches' gathering, the dancers of Munes, had started to be told
in the area eleven years ago, not six years ago, as Barbara Bowndie said

23 OLA, OPR, CH2/1082/1, p. 256.
24 OLA, OPR, CH2/1082/1, p. 256.

was the time since the Devil deceived her. Barbara Bowndie apparently has been giving contradictory information about this event.

In the last point, focus is again on the questions posed to Barbara about Marjorie Paplay during the previous questioning. 'Being asked what questions John Aitkin spired concerning Marjorie Paplay? *Answ*: he spired about the hand of the dead man, that lay above her bed head and stired about her aill; But spired not, if the Devill lay with her upon the Ball Lay; neither yet spired he about any of her sisters, nor of Elspeth Baikie'.[25] [*My italics.*] Here Barbara Bowndie maintains that the commissionaire was more interested in the detailed practice of malefice than in demonology. A hand of a dead man, which Barbara had above her bed, used as protection for illness, or other parts of dead persons for various practice of witchcraft, is commonly related to *maleficium*.

As the formal interrogation of Barbara Bowndie was over, several witnesses gave their declarations. Much of the information thus coming up retrospectively, points to what had happened with Barbara Bowndie during the period of imprisonment. It becomes clear that Barbara Bowndie had been offered remedies to hang herself:

> Patrick Smythe of Braco declared that *Barbara Boundie had said unto persons of respect*, that they should have a care to bid the officers keep away some folk from her, In respect that offer had been made unto her by a Ledder of a tow to hang her selfe, or of a knyfe to stick her selfe, quhilk would be ane easier death for her, then to be burnt. *Denyed that either she said it, or yet that it was true.*[26] [*My italics.*]

It is difficult to judge whether Barbara Bowndie has been offered remedies to commit suicide, because it should be an easier death than being burnt. If that is so, it says much about the atmosphere during the witch-hunt, as those offering her these remedies clearly signalled what would be the outcome of the trial. Maybe she had been in great despair while imprisoned, unable to see any way out. Hence the possibility of suicide might have been an option. But also now she continues to deny everything, as she has seen this strategy as the solution in a difficult situation.

Also the investigators appointed to assist the brethren during the pretrial questioning, gave their declarations. Patrick Graham, one of the men who had examined her first, reported that Barbara Bowndie said that shortly after she was put in ward, 'John Baikie his woman came unto her,

---

25 OLA, OPR, CH2/1082/1, p. 256.
26 OLA, OPR, CH2/1082/1, p. 257.

and said false co[m]mon thief Looke that thou lie not honest women, *Denyes'*. [*My italics.*][27] Apparently, people also came to her while imprisoned, urging her not to denounce innocent women. Even if Barbara Bowndie again denies that this happened, this is an indication of the fear and anxiety in the local community. Once people knew that a woman was imprisoned, they were afraid. They knew the methods used to obtain a confession and they feared that they would be named. Apparently women were more afraid of denunciation than men. The wife of John Baikie, who came to warn Barbara, could have been Elspeth Baikie, who in fact was denounced by Barbara during the pre-trial questioning. In that case she was afraid of herself being named. But this woman could also be related to James Baikie, the son of Marjorie Paplay. In that case this would be a warning that Barbara should not denounce Paplay.

The same Patrick Graham declared that Barbara Bowndie said to him 'that the Farie appeared unto her beside the Ball-Ley coming out of Essinquoy, and told her all that she had spoken of Marjorie Paplay unto the ministers. *Denyes this also'.*[28] In this situation of unequal power display, wherein a mighty man witnessed towards a poor woman, no doubt, the man would seem the most reliable. And when this man declared that Barbara had told him she had had contact with fairies near the meeting-place for witches, he is credible. Still Barbara Bowndie denied.

The commissionaire John Aitken had been mentioned several times by Barbara Bowndie, as an insistent investigator bringing accusations against her. This apparently could not be tolerated by his brother, who gave witness:

> Master James Aitkin *for cleiring of his brother John Aitkin* said that she had spoken these speeches of Marjorie Paplay, in Fubister, *before she met with John Aitkin after her taking. Denyed it*, and said that when she was taken, she ran into the sea, to her craig, and was flyed out of her wit. And being further delt with be Master James Aitkin anent his brother, said that if he had not first lifted that purpose, she would not have lifted that purpose to him. Being asked touching Cummer Dyk, if she knew any witchcraft to her? *Denyed*[29] [*My italics.*]

Again, for the strength and reliability of an argument, it seems important to have established the order in which utterances were said. John Aitken's brother maintains that she had spoken about Paplay before she

---

[27] OLA, OPR, CH2/1082/1, p. 257.
[28] OLA, OPR, CH2/1082/1, p. 257.
[29] OLA, OPR, CH2/1082/1, p. 257.

was imprisoned and before she was questioned by John Aitken, while she denied this. She argued, like she had done before, that John Aitken was the one bringing up elements related to Marjorie Paplay, and she would not have done this on her own behalf. She also refers to her own reactions when she was imprisoned, that she ran out into the sea, and she was out of her wit. This reaction tells much about the feeling of disaster related to an imprisonment for witchcraft, and is one of the places where Barbara Bowndie's voice comes to the fore in all its distress. To the very end of the interrogation the brothers try to make her denounce other women, but she refused.

Due to all Barbara Bowndie's denials, it was decided to use torture, which required that a warrant was issued from the Privy Council. On 10 November, Mr Walter Stewart and Mr David Watsone[30] were ordained to form a supplication to 'the Secret counsell for purchasing a co[m]mission to put Barbara Boundie to tortures, upon grounds publicklie declared in the presbyterie'.[31] Master Thomas Cok and Master George Johnston were ordained to go to 'the Shirref, and desire him that Barbara Boundie now in firmance, should be still retained unto such tyme as all lawfull meanes of tryall that can be thought upon, be used towards her'.[32] They reported that the sheriff had promised to retain Barbara Boundie in prison, till the answer of his letter returned from the south, 'And that he should doe nothing thereanent but be the Brethren's advyse'.[33] This shows the cooperation between the presbytery and the sheriff in witchcraft cases. The institutions had separate areas of authority, and they had to follow the same judicial practice as in mainland Scotland. This meant that a warrant from the Privy Council was needed in order to use torture, and they had to wait until they had received this document. Still, it is stated that the brethren should advise the sheriff with regard to prolonged imprisonment. This is the last which is recorded about Barbara Bowndie in 1643.

The next spring, however, Barbara Bowndie's name was mentioned again in the presbytery minutes. Her case ended on 3 April 1644, when there was an entry that they would wait for more information about her from Shetland: 'As touching Barbara Boundie, whom the Shirref promised to retaine in firmancie, according as the presbyterie should advyse him;

---

[30] Watson was minister in Posesay and Eglisay until 1635, when he was transferred to Westray.
[31] OLA, OPR, CH2/1082/1, p. 258.
[32] OLA, OPR, CH2/1082/1, p. 258.
[33] OLA, OPR, CH2/1082/1, p. 260.

the Brethren thought good this day that she should be retained still, untill such tyme as they expected dittaes against her to come from Zetland, and the Shirref to be advertised of this be Mr George Johnston and David Heart'.[34] So it seems she has been kept in prison for half a year. But the need for information about the time she lived in Shetland lead to a delay in finishing her trial. The final fate of Barbara Boundie is not known.

The other woman frequently mentioned, Marjorie Paplay, was acquitted in 1643. But she was still under suspicion. On 1 May 1644, James Baikie, her son, declared that he wanted an extract of Barbara Bowndie's examination, which was granted him. He was still complaining about the slandering of his mother, and he continued his protests until 1645. He then referred to his earliest protests, in 1642, 'that he might have the extract of the Law, and practice of this presbyterie, wherupon the condescent of the brethren unto Master Henrie Smythe his protestation tertio novemb: 1642 Sess.2. was grounded, viz That no person delated unto the civill Judge, as guiltie of witchcraft, should be heard to complaine that they are slandered etc.'[35] James Baikie was probably an educated man, due to his style and way of arguing. Marjorie Paplay was brought before the presbytery again in 1648, and even though the outcome is unknown, her case is a good illustration of the reputation of witchcraft clinging to a person for years.

The Functioning of the Courts

The witch-hunt in Orkney shows that there was a need for trials enforced from above by the Scottish legislation and by the implementation of this legislation in all parts of the kingdom, through kirk and secular courts. This consolidation was taken care of particularly by the presbytery. The case of Barbara Bowndie gives a glimpse of judicial practice in Orkney in the 1640s, with regard to the role of presbytery as well as sheriff courts. The same holds true for the case of Marjorie Paplay, often referred to. Barbara Bowndie lived in Kirkwall and Marjorie Paplay lived in St Ola, both areas where Bishop Law had assumed the function of sheriff. It might be expected that the power of the kirk was strong also in relation to the secular field, an expectation which is supported in the Bowndie case by the strong role the brethren played as advisers for decisions to be taken by the sheriff, for instance when it came to prolonging the period of imprisonment

---

[34] OLA, OPR, CH2/1082/1, p. 278.
[35] OLA, OPR, CH2/1082/1, p. 286.

for Barbara Bowndie. It seems clear from the cases of Bowndie and Paplay that the presbytery is the active part, and the part handling the interrogation. Hence the presbytery is in position to decide what should be questioned about, and thereby define the contents of the crime. As seen in the Bowndie case, the cooperation between presbytery and sheriff took place after the interrogation of her was finished. As northern part of Orkney and Shetland were administered together by the sheriff court, the relative passive role of this court as for witchcraft persecution might be one of the answers to the question why witchcraft persecution was milder in Shetland than in Orkney. In Shetland there were only two cases in 1644, contrasted with 24 cases in Orkney. Looking at mainland Scotland, there was considerable witchcraft persecution in 1643–44, which could have been related to political and religious unrest.[36] The cases in Orkney in 1644 might possibly be seen as a prolonging of the activity of witchcraft persecution in mainland Scotland in 1642–43. Echo of these events may have reached Orkney, thus explaining the upheaval of witchcraft cases in 1643. Also the encouragement of the Privy Council and the parliament in the 1640s to search for witches in local communities might have had an effect. However, there are two points where one might find a difference in Orkney in contrast to mainland Scotland. The first point is the change in the legal system around 1610 and the setting up of new legal institutions with Bishop Law and the sheriff courts. These changes might have contributed to the occurrence of witchcraft trials in Orkney during the next three decades. The second point is difference in frequency, as the witch-hunt in Orkney was more or less over before 1650. As the largest national hunts of mainland Scotland never reached Orkney, there might be local historical reasons which could convincingly explain how the development of witchcraft trials in Orkney continued. Thomson maintains that the first half-century of Scottish rule on Orkney is characterized as a period of peace. Under Lord Henry Sinclair's management, 'a remarkable revival of family fortunes restored the essential substance of power'.[37] A self-contained economy and society in Orkney might have calmed the tendencies to witch-hunt. Similarly, remains of restrictive Norse laws related to witchcraft persecution might have influenced the period of witch-hunt. However, the Orkney sources give scarce information about

---

[36] Willumsen, *Seventeenth-Century Witchcraft Trials*, 39.
[37] Thomson, *History*, 131–32.

the handling of the totality of witchcraft this year, so caution is needed when it comes to drawing conclusions.

Different formalities tied up to the function of the presbytery and the sheriff court concern the relations between Orkney and the central authorities in Edinburgh, for instance sending a request to the Privy Council anent a warrant for torture. It could also concern the relations within Orkney, for instance where a slander case should be dealt with and filed. The debate going on for several years between the son of Marjorie Paplay and the minister of Shapinshay shows that they are arguing contrary to one another as for starting a trial; the son arguing that his mother's name be cleansed by the sheriff court, thus delaying the case, while the investigating minister is pressing for persecution. In any case, it seems clear that in the Barbara Bowndie case the presbytery took the first steps and was the driving force with regard to the development of the case, also when it came to the formalities related to obtaining a warrant to allow torture being used. The same was the case with the Marjorie Paplay trial.

The Discourse

The particular position of court records is pointed out by Elizabeth Cohen.[38] In an article on testimonies, she says:

> These testimonies and additional texts all occupy in-between positions on a spectrum between oral and written domains of expression. Sharing an intermediate textual zone that has attracted increasing scholarly attention in early modern cultural studies, these several sorts of non-literary sources invite a comparative analysis and double modes of reading.[39]

Cohen uncovers a variety of accents in the voices heard in the documents.[40] With regard to Barbara Bowndie's voice, one mode of reading shows a voice of a woman trying to defend herself from facing the worst possible outcome of the trial, namely execution. She very clearly maintains that she is tricked into giving the informal confession when questioned by the brethren, and that she would never have uttered these words unless certain issues had been brought up by the questioners. She repents the denunciations of other women she gave during the pre-trial questioning and argues that something wrong was done towards her by powerful

---

[38] Cohen, 'Back Talk'; Cohen, 'Between Oral and Written Culture', 181–201.
[39] Cohen, 'Back Talk', 95.
[40] Cohen, 'Back Talk', 95.

men, both with regard to verbal pressure and serving of beer. But she also knows that she has a strong card on her hand, namely denial. As witchcraft was a crime impossible to prove, an informal confession given by an accused person had to be confirmed formally by the accused person herself. It was not enough to have it referred to. Barbara Bowndie could not be found guilty and sentenced unless she gave this confirmation. Therefore denial was a good strategy. This accent of her voice signals a woman who has not yet surrendered to the power of persons mightier than herself. She sees all the time how her words said during the pre-trial questioning are used against her, so her strategy is to deny and say least possible. However, there are many efforts on her part to protest against the interrogators and the witnesses, particularly when it comes to arguments about the order of phrases uttered. As it comes forth, she has in fact confessed to several dangerous demonological elements, and she has denounced other women. So we hear the voice of a woman who is fighting for her life. Her strategy of denial is efficient. The interrogators do not come any way with her. Therefore the worst step, namely use of torture, is suggested. However, in the actual situation, Barbara is gaining time by denying. Therefore this could be a good example how a panic developed, torture being used as the final means of pressure when accused persons did not confess, nor denounce others.

Barbara Bowndie's strategy for answering during the interrogation has to be interpreted contextually. Her situation is serious. She is formally accused of witchcraft and the perspectives are dark. She has chosen a non-cooperative line, which means no confession. With regard to her experience and the local experience it is very dangerous to confess. In the moment an accused person confesses, she has signed her own death warrant. This is different from what research on the Salem witchcraft trials have shown. Kathleen Doty and Rista Hiltunen have studied the function of narrative patterns in these trials, and the situation is that it pays to show repentance, to confess and to cooperate with the interrogators.[41] Then the sentence will be milder and execution is avoided, in contrary to non-cooperation.[42] Barbara Bowndie's strategy seems to fit in well with

---

[41] The study focuses on representations of the historical context, the Devil, and the accused individual. Ref. K Doty and R. Hiltunen, 'I will tell, I will tell', *Journal of Historical Pragmatics*, 3: 2 (2002), 299–335, at pp. 312, 314, 315, 332.

[42] Kryk-Kastovsky, 'Historical Courtroom Discourse', 175.

many of the European witchcraft trials, for instance as it will be seen in
the chapters on Finnmark. The strategy of denial is a sensible choice in
a situation where a woman knows that confession would certainly lead
to execution. Hence the accused person's experience about how previous
witchcraft cases developed seems to be crucial as for confessional patterns. The need for a witchcraft trial which is part of a series of trials to be
studied within the frame of the whole series is therefore clear. The need
for an analysis related to the judicial practice also seems necessary, as the
legal process might differ for instance from central to local courts. The
same holds true for a geographical and historical frame, as specific factors
might contribute to certain strategies as for confession.

Another mode of reading of the Barbara Bowndie case shows the
voice of a knowledgeable woman, who must try to hide her knowledge
in several fields, be that related to traditional sorcery or demonological
witchcraft. So she has to formulate her answers in a way that does not
reveal her real knowledge, which apparently is what the interrogators are
after. She knows about witches' meetings at the Ball-Ley, the dancers of
Munes and other demonological notions, which is part of the oral sphere
in the community. She knows about remedies for keeping away disease
and lethal stuff to pour in drinks. This makes her an interesting person,
but also a dangerous person seen with the eyes of the interrogators. This
accent of her voice is subdued, but it can still be felt that she possesses
knowledge of a particular kind that she would like to keep for herself. This
accent, mainly related to traditional knowledge, which only comes forth
in glimpses, suggests that she is a habile narrator.

So far the voice of Barbara Bowndie has been discussed. But the minutes give information about the voices of the interrogators and several
witnesses as well. The voices of the interrogators are heard partly in the
frame of the presbytery questioning, partly referred to in the frame of the
pre-trial questioning. The discourse strategies used by her interrogators
display the power situation. It also reflects the gender situation. Only men
are mentioned in the minutes as persons of power and active as questioners. Only women are mentioned as those being suspected of performing
witchcraft. It is signalled already from the beginning that the task of getting a confession from Barbara might be difficult. And the methods used
for carrying this out, may be various. Therefore the two brethren who
were going to talk with her in private, a conversation including 'prayer
and conference', should have assistance of another two persons. It is also
clear that during this questioning verbal pressure as well as giving her ale,
was used. The men's voices are insistent and repetitive. When referring to

what was said and what happened during the pre-trial questioning, the brethren are covering each other and confirming the other's statement. They are the ones introducing several demonological elements, thus taking the lead during the questioning. They use imprecise references to informants, like 'the people said, that she had been with the Farie'.[43] They are referring to her consumption of ale in a deteriorating way, for instance that according to her 'earnest' request they gave her ale, and that she confessed crucial elements 'being as yet sober'. They are underlining the fact that she was a hard nail to work with, but 'after long retreate' and 'at length' she confessed. These examples are typical for showing how the interrogators exercised their power over the interrogated. However, the voices of the interrogators show the strong focus on Marjorie Paplay, probably the one they feared most, as the whole case seems to have been a vendetta circling around her. The voices of the interrogators reflect their fear of witchcraft, and their urge to press forth the type of confession they would like. Still, they have to give in at last, and give the advice that torture should be used.

The voices of the witnesses signal support to the brethren by stating that Barbara has uttered the same in other connections, even before she was imprisoned. They tend to give their informants status by using expressions like 'persons of respect'. The man, who saw it as his duty to clear his brother's name, 'dealt with' Barbara several times. Repetition on all discourse levels seem to be typical for this case, repetition of questions, repetition of elements. The voices of the witnesses seem to signal power and to expect obedience. Their voices usually have weight, and they are apparently brought there to add strength to the brethren's statements. But neither for these persons does Barbara bow.

There are clear features of orality in the discourse rendered. These features come to the fore in the voices of the accused as well as in the voices of the interrogators. Barbara Kryk-Kastovsky, who has performed a linguistic study of traces of orality in Early Modern English court records, has found that trial records have preserved many traces of orality.[44] Particularly one of the factors mentioned by Kryk-Kastovsky is prominent in the

---

[43] OLA, OPR, CH2/1082/1.

[44] The study is based on two features: turn-taking and closeness to the socio-cultural context. Turn-taking is defined as 'involving such detailed issues closely related to spoken language as responding to the interlocutor, power relations, the use of performatives and discourse markers'. Closeness to the present socio-cultural context encompasses among other meta-comments and forms of address. Ref. B. Kryk-Kastovsky, 'Representations of Orality in Early Modern English Trial Records', 209.

Barbara Bowndie's case, namely closeness related to spoken language. This
is also one of the factors mentioned by Walter Ong as an orality marker.[45]
In the case of Barbara Bowndie, several instances of insertions of direct
discourse in passages otherwise given in indirect discourse, may be seen.
This might be speech uttered by Barbara, like 'God forgive you that beares
over much with them'.[46] Or it may be speech uttered by a commissary,
like Aitken's 'Tell mee about Marjorie Paplay what ane woman she is, and
thou shall never want thy Life'.[47] This closeness to the spoken language,
which permeates the minutes, on one hand points to the context, which is
an oral one. Thus the flavour of the oral setting and the oral examination
is brought on to a reader today. On the other hand it is an indication that
the scribe had taken down the discourse as accurate as possible, and in a
very professional way.

   The field of orality interestingly comes to the fore in this case also in
another way, namely the oral transmission of ideas about witchcraft. The
passage about the dancers of Munes gives interesting information. This
story, and thereby demonological ideas, was clearly transmitted among
the populace within an oral sphere. It was well known, both as for contents and for how long it had been told in the area. This supports an understanding that narratives with demonological contents were introduced in
an area and started to be told among the populace. Probably were such
narratives of great interest, and were rapidly spread. The minutes of the
Barbara Bowndie case clearly show that the narrative about the dancers
of Munes was part of oral tradition before the imprisonment of Barbara
Bowndie. The minutes also show that the idea of witches' meetings and, as
part of these, sexual intercourse with the Devil, also was common knowledge in the area before her incarnation. Hence these notions were neither
introduced to her in prison nor during interrogation. The case of Barbara
Bowndie thus supports an understanding that demonological notions
by the 1640s were assimilated in the sphere of oral tradition and known
by the persons suspected of witchcraft before these persons were brought
to trial.

[45] Ong, W., *Orality and Literacy. The Technologizing of the Word* (London, 1988) 36.
[46] OLA, OPR, CH2/1082/1, p. 255.
[47] OLA, OPR, CH2/1082/1, p. 255.

Demonology and Fairies

The interplay between folklore, for instance belief in fairies, and demonological notions, runs as a thread through the interrogation of Barbara Bowndie. These two layers of belief, during the interrogation mingled together, seem to interest the interrogators equally. From the Bowndie case, it appears that the interrogators try to make a link between demonological notions and her presumed visit to the fairies. In that respect we see a demonising of fairy belief.[48] The interrogators mention the fairies only once, in a textual context where the Devil is first introduced, and also Barbara Bowndie's alleged relations with the Devil. The interrogators first ask whether she had agreed to serve the Devil when she was in a miserable condition in Shetland. When she denies this, they introduce the rumours that she had been with the fairies when she became speechless for 24 hours while travelling in Shetland. However, she answered she did not see any fairies. This textual closeness between the two questions creates a link between the suspected pact with the Devil and her alleged stay with the fairies, as the second question seems to follow from the first. This link is not confirmed by Barbara, as she denied it all. The second time the fairies are mentioned, it was by Patrick Graham, one of the witnesses. He makes a link between the fairies and the Ball Ley, saying that Barbara had told him that the fairies appeared to her beside the Ball-Ley. Again, there is made a contextual link between the fairies and a meeting-place for witches and the Devil. This link is made by a witness. In addition, Graham maintains that Barbara said that the fairies told her everything she had told about Marjorie Paplay to the ministers. As she denied this also, she in fact did not confirm any connection between the fairies and demonological ideas. There is nothing in Barbara Bowndie's utterances which could be interpreted in the direction that fairies are evil. She apparently was acquainted with ideas about fairies, but did not necessarily consider them evil. And, even if her knowledge about fairies was there on beforehand, the activation and demonizing of this knowledge rest upon the accusers, as the links between evil powers and fairies are made by the interrogators and a witness. Clearly, the impression that fairies are evil, is made by the prosecutors.

---

[48] See Henderson, 'Witch Hunting and Witch Belief'; Hutton, 'Witch-Hunting in Celtic Societies'.

Within a judicial context the interrogators had the urge to find the right type of witches, namely those who had a close relationship with the Devil. Ernest W. Marwick emphasises the importance of demonological elements in the seventeenth-century understanding of a real witch. Even if 'the concept of witchcraft and magic the Norsemen took with them to Orkney was one which arose out of centuries of folklore and tradition',[49] he maintains,

> if we are to understand the nature of the Orkney witch trials as legalistic exercises which were conducted according to Scottish law (itself a reflection of the prevailing climate of opinion in the sixteenth century, when it was passed by the parliament in Edinburgh) we must think of a witch as a person who has dealings with the Devil or evil spirits, and who is able by their co-operation to perform supernatural acts. In popular phraseology, the witch sold her soul to the Devil.[50]

I share Ernest Marwick's view that the relation to the Devil was the most important feature of the historical Orkney witch. In this respect Orkney witchcraft trials did not differ in principle very much from historical witchcraft trials elsewhere. This could be seen as elite versus popular as well as of Scottish versus Norse, because demonological ideas were often notions brought to the local communities by the learned elite. The prevailing view among legal officials and clergy was the same in all countries haunted by the witch-hunt. As is seen in the Barbara Bowndie case, she was asked leading questions of a demonological character. She refused to confess in public to demonological features even after verbal pressure. She denied participation. It is a good example that a person who came under the searchlight of suspicion of witchcraft at the end was decided to be tortured. Hence the use of torture as the last option to press forth a demonological confession in a witchcraft trial is supported.

The Role of the Scribe

Rendered in indirect discourse, the confession is formed as a coherent story about learning and performing witchcraft. Due to closeness to the spoken language, particularly the confessions of the accused persons might be considered as representing individualized discourse, even if it is rendered in indirect discourse. Comprehensive linguistic research has been performed on historical courtroom discourse. Barbara Kryk-Kastovsky,

---

[49] OLA, MC, D31/4/4, p. 13.
[50] OLA, MC, D31/4/4, p. 17.

who has performed a linguistic study of traces of orality in Early Modern English court records, has found that trial records have preserved many traces of orality.[51] Kryk-Kastovsky and Kathleen L. Doty maintain that courtroom records reflect the language spoken in a given historical period more faithfully than others, depending on the degree of orality.[52] Looking at the role of the scribe, features of orality are clearly found in the documents. Hence the discourse is close to the spoken language at the time, and also a source to historical knowledge. To what extent the scribe has influenced the recorded text, is not possible to say. What can be said with certainty, is that the scribe has not written down stereotype records of questions and answers. Instead, a personalized approach to the interrogation comes to the fore. The pre-trial questioning and what the interrogators knew about Barbara on beforehand, take the lead of the questioning. The discourse situation develops spontaneously, according to the answers given by Barbara Bowndie. The scribe takes down changes in tempus, like change from indirect discourse to direct discourse. Thus the liveliness of the immediately pronounced language is taken care of. In addition, orality markers like additive sentence structures, aggregative language elements, redundancy, closeness to the human life-world, and an agonistic tone, is apparent.[53] The force of repetition is strong, which is another oral feature. The scribe has not been particularly interested in making a fluent text, to ease the reading. He has made an effort to produce a text suitable for the purpose of the trial, namely a documentation what was said during the trial. He is paying equal attention to the voice of the accused and the voices of the interrogators, giving them shared space. Even if we do not know anything about the scribe, his recording is professional, and as accurate as possible. The scribe does not provide any evaluative comments to what is being told or to the persons involved. In my interpretation, the text is reliable with regard to contents.

The case of Barbara Bowndie emphasizes the melting together of traditional folkloric ideas and demonological ideas. The mentality sphere of folkloric ideas seems to be part of a Nordic context, a point made by Ernest Marwick. The influence of demonological ideas most likely reached Orkney from mainland Scotland, as this content had put its stamp on the

---

[51] Kryk-Kastovsky, 'Representations of Orality in Early Modern English Trial Records', 209.

[52] Kryk-Kastovsky, 'Historical courtroom discourse', 213–245; Kryk-Kastovsky, 'How bad is "bad data"?'; Doty, 'Telling tales', 26, 27, 39.

[53] Ong, *Orality and Literacy*, 37–45.

witchcraft persecution in mainland Scotland from the 1590s onwards.
There is no sign in the direction that there was a link between Orkney and
Norway on demonological grounds during the main period of witchcraft
persecution on the Northern isles.

Shetland

This second part of the chapter will deal with the case of Marion Pardoun
from Shetland. While the analysis of Barbara Bowndie's case focused on
a witchcraft case ending with the decision of torture, but no information
known after that, this Shetland case will show how torture is used with the
result that even the language of the accused dissolves as a consequence.
The close-reading of the document displays how details and extra-textual
comments contribute to give insight in the development of a distressful
situation, namely her steadily worse situation during the imprisonment.

Marion Pardoun alias Peblis, 1644

The Trial

Marion Pardoun was a married woman, aged 39, living in Hillswick in
North Maven. She was married to Svend Iverson. Marion Pardoun had a
servant and was apparently not a poor woman. She was well established
in the community and had a reputation of knowing sorcery and healing. She had been denounced by Jonet Fraser, a woman earlier burnt for
witchcraft.

As with many witchcraft cases from the Scottish mainland, and also
the case of Barbara Bowndie from Orkney, the first steps to this trial were
taken by the kirk. The dittay, consisting of 15 points, was first signed by
the moderator and the other brethren of the presbytery of Shetland on
15 March 1644. Then the document continues, recording the additional
interrogation and waking of Marion Pardoun. It was handed over to the
legal officials in Scalloway on 21 March. The same day, procurator fiscal James Gray desired that Marion Pardoun and Margareth Guthrumsdochter should be accused and the dittay put to the trial of an assize. The
trial document of Margareth Guthrumsdochter has been lost. The dittay
of Marion Pardoun's case contains a detailed rendering of the 15 points of
accusation, in addition to brief comments in the margin, denoting what
the accused person had confessed to. The moderator and the brethren

of the presbytery declare that they, 'having examined the doun wreattin proces, *doe find and declare the poyntis formar markit in the margine being lawfulie provin to be witchcraft*'.[54] [*My italics.*] The itemizing seems to have structured the interrogation. The comments in the margin provide important information related to the voice of the accused as well as the voices of the witnesses.

The 15 points consist of a range of accusations dealing mainly with spell-casting causing human sickness, animal sickness, and death. In one case of spell-casting causing sickness, the sick person recovers afterwards, after having drawn blood from Marion Pardoun. In total these accusations cannot be considered as very dangerous, because they do not contain accusations of human death. It is therefore of interest to notice that the interrogation continued after 15 March, in a more serious manner. Now torture in the form of waking is documented. The underlying motive for applying torture seems to have been to make Marion Pardoun confess to the overturning of a boat, resulting in the deaths of four people. In addition to the testimony of a living person, the declaration of Jonet Fraser, burnt for witchcraft, was brought forth and recited on this occasion. When the drowned people were found, Marion Pardoun and her husband Svend were called for and asked to lay hands on the dead. This they did, with the result that blood issued from the dead bodies,[55] something argued by the interrogators to be a proof of murder. Marion Pardoun's reputation as a charmer and deceiver is underlined, and in addition she was said to be 'ane covenanter, consulter and convener with the devil',[56] a figure who had been observed in several likenesses in company with her.

The presbytery found 'the pairtie guiltie, worthie of death, be the law of God and the law of the kingdome, and requyris yow judgeis to put them to the [inquest *deleted*] knowledge of ane assyse'.[57] On 21 March 1644 James Gray, procurator fiscal, desired the dittays of Marion Pardoun

---

[54] Proceedings against Marion Pardoun, 1644, in possession of John and Wendy Scott, Gardie House, Bressay, Shetland. I would like to thank Brian Smith for letting me use his transcription of the document.

[55] The ordeal-like test known as bierricht intends by corpse-touching to deter and make guilty murderers, who reveal themselves by the bleeding of the corpses of the killed persons they touched. Most important was not that corpses bled, but the reactions persons had to being asked to take the test. Ref. Gaskill, 'Reporting murder: fiction in the archives in early modern England', 10.

[56] Proceedings against Marion Pardoun, 1644, in possession of John and Wendy Scott, Gardie House, Bressay, Shetland.

[57] Ibid.

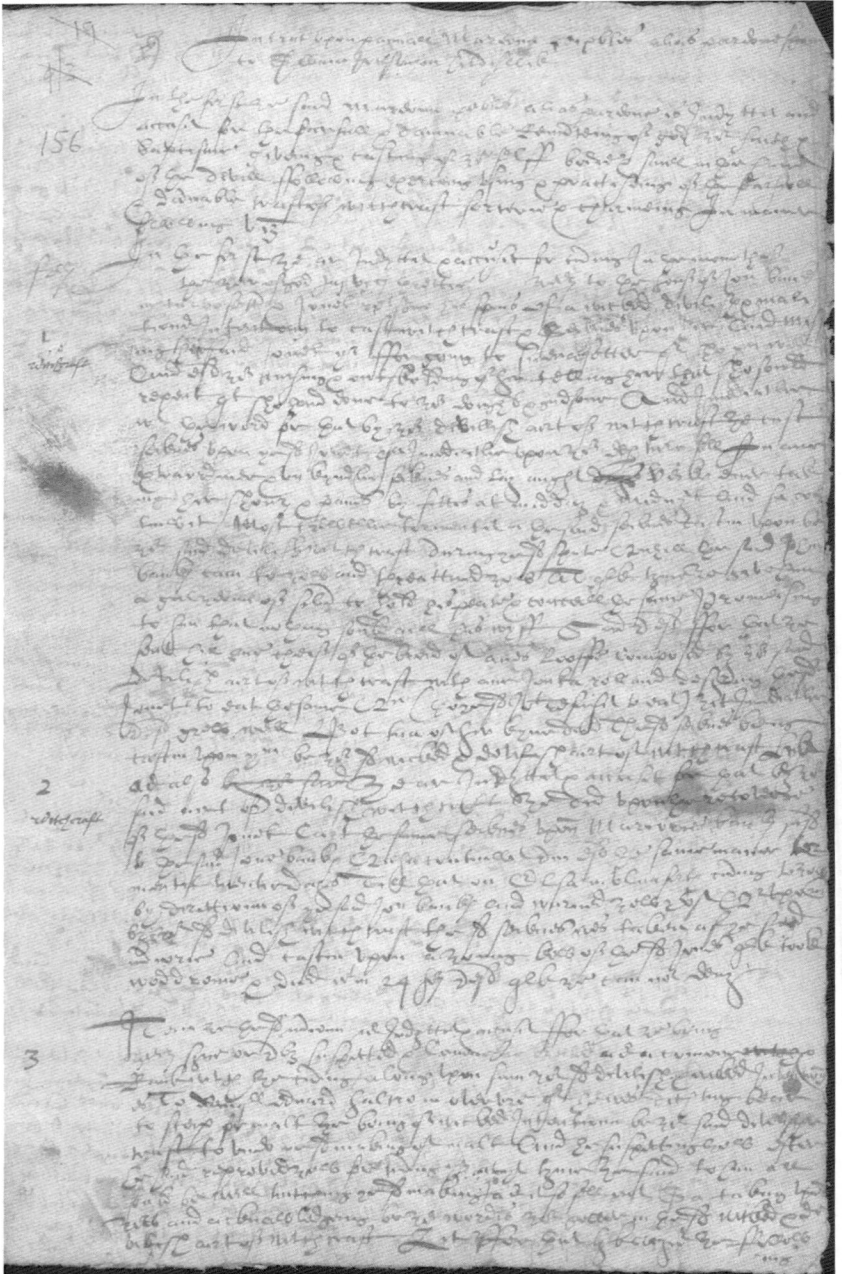

Figure 5: Proceedings against Marion Pardoun, 1644. In possession of John and Wendy Scott, Gardie House, Bressay, Shetland.

and Margareth Guthrumsdochter to be put to the trial of an assize. After having examined the dittay of Marion Pardoun, the assize found all the points of the dittay, except two, proven. The death sentence fell in Scalloway on 22 March 1644.

The Discourse

The discourse in the Marion Pardoun document is mostly a monologue on the part of the accuser. A drama performed on a stage is displayed, an 'I' talking to a 'you'—a discourse situation frequently found in Scottish witchcraft trial documents. The accused woman is spoken to in the second person: 'ye rank witch', 'which ye cannot deny'. The effect of the use of second-person address is to give the discourse an accusatory tone. This discourse situation is restricted with regard to giving access to what the accused person is really saying, as the traces of Marioun's confession are either rendered through the discourse of the interrogators or found in comments in the margin. By close-reading of the document it is, however, possible to establish parts of Marion Pardoun's confession and to put these parts together along a time-line to reconstruct a narrative.

Similarly it is possible to distinguish the voices of the witnesses from the voices of the interrogators. By a retrospective reading, the voices of the witnesses can be reconstructed, either from comments in the margin or as they are heard in the sections of the document rendering the accusations. Each of the rendered accusations represents a sliding transition from second person over to third person. The sections start with the addressing of the accused person—'ye are indyttit and accusit for'—but soon go over to third-person narration, which is required when the circumstances related to the accusation are retold. At the end of several sections we find varied repetitions of the same underlying expression, such as 'quhilk ye rank witch can not deny' or 'quhilk ye cannot deny' or 'thereby showing and proveing your said devilish practise of the art of witchcraft'.[58] Thus there is an oscillation in the mode of discourse throughout the whole document, which makes a narratological approach rewarding.

The voice of the law comes to the fore distinctly in the sections dealing with verdict and sentence, but also in the dittay, especially through the repetitive use of words and expressions denoting the devilish and malicious intention of Marion Pardoun's practice.

---

[58] Ibid.

The Voice of the Law

The voice of the law is in large parts of the document heard through fixed phrases, by which legal discourse becomes prominent. The dittay was sent to a jury for final examination, and in the final section of the document, the verdict and the sentence, pure legal discourse is heard. According to provenance, it is a legal document.

In the opening passage the voice of the law is already heard, in an accusation clearly influenced by demonological discourse. In the following section it is not difficult to hear the echo of fixed formulas used within the rhetoric of the witch-hunters:

> In the first, the said Mareoun Peblis alias Pardone is indyttit and accusit for the fearful and damnable renunceing of God, your faith and baptisme, giveing and casting of your selff, bodie and saull, in the hands of the devill, following, exerceing, using and practiseing the fearfull and damnable craft of witchcraft, sorcerie and charmeing.[59]

The last phrase is interesting. Charming was usually treated separate from witchcraft, but in the 1640s the church tried to get it included. Accusations similar to those above were frequently mentioned in witchcraft trials in connection with the ritual of the demonic pact. As will be seen, the Marion Pardoun document does not show that she confessed to the demonic pact by going through a ritual. She did not promise the Evil One her service. Nevertheless, the contradiction between being a child of God and being a child of the Devil is emphasized in the dittay, as is seen in the frequent mentioning of this theme: 'your said divilish and wicked craft of witchcraft, tormenting and abuseing thairby of poore waik christianes, Goddis people, aganes quhom ye carie evill will and malice, quhilk ye, rank witch, cannot deny'.[60] The document of Marion Pardoun displays awareness among the witch-hunters about the range of phrases that should be expressed during a witchcraft hearing, which means that the legal rhetoric in this field by 1644 was well known in Shetland.

Amidst the spectrum of words often interwoven in this text, the frequent mentioning of 'devil' and 'devillish' tops the list—a literary device of repetition used with success. When the words 'devil' and 'devillish' are mentioned about 40 times in a document of eight pages, always connected

---

59 Ibid.
60 Ibid.

to Marion Pardoun's name or her activities, one gets an overwhelming feeling that she is a person tied up with the Evil One. This repetitive method functions almost as a kind of brainwashing, because of the machine-like way in which it is presented. There is no doubt that, in the eyes of the interrogators, she is supposed to be one of the Devil's servants on earth.

Another instance of words and expressions from previous witchcraft trials apparently entering the vocabulary of the witch-hunters as well as that of the common people is a kind of 'contamination', whereby expressions used during demonic pact confessions are found used in a context other than the demonic pact. The first time it occurs is in connection with a spell Marion Pardoun allegedly threw upon James Halcro. He had a terrible sickness and was 'tormentit thairby *fra the croun of his head to the sole of his fute*, that thair wes no lyff expectit of him'.[61] [*My italics.*] The other example is related to the same accusation. Marion Pardoun had been sent for and was begged to lay her hands upon the sick James Halcro and he 'felt and fand his pane and diseas to desolve, *fra the croun of his head to the sole of his fute*'.[62] [*My italics.*] This phrase is borrowed from the medieval ban of excommunication. As we have seen previously, the phrase was frequently found in witchcraft confessions in mainland Scotland.[63] Usually in witchcraft documents this formulation was related to the demonic pact. The person entering the pact stood in a special position, symbolizing that the whole body from then onwards would be in the service of the Devil. Both the examples mentioned above show that demonological rhetoric was well known among legal officials as well as among the common people in Shetland by the 1640s. In this case the expression most likely came from those witnesses who testified about James Halcro's disease, and what we read in the dittay is a rendering of this testimony. However, it is also possible that the interrogators might have inserted this expression into the dittay. In any case, the expression here is taken out of its demonic pact context and used to describe the intensity of a sick man's pains. Thus an echo of the demonological witchcraft confessions from mainland Scotland is found in the northern isles in 1644, the expression in itself semantically unchanged, but with a different interpretation because it is used in a context other than that of a demonological confession. This means that

---

[61] Ibid.
[62] Ibid.
[63] See Chapter 3, on the discussion on demonic pact confessions, pp. 90–94.

even if demonic pact confessions were not common in Shetland, demonological ideas were well known on these islands in the mid-seventeenth
century. The expression 'fra the croun of his head to the sole of his fute'
was not used in the 1616 Scalloway witchcraft trials, even if these trials
contained demonological confessions. However, at that time the expression was frequently used in mainland Scotland. In Marion Pardoun's case
it is related to *maleficium*, which shows that phrases from demonological
thought on the Scottish mainland by the 1640s have entered the sphere of
traditional sorcery in Shetland.

The jury consisted of 15 individuals. It should be noted that in the assize
we find two of the persons who were waking Marion Pardoun; Mans Finlaysone in Burraland and Jon Erasmussone in Enisfirth. Another member
of the assize was Andro Smyth, younger, in Hildiswik. According to point
7 in the dittay, he was the person accusing Marion Pardoun of casting a
spell on his cow, so that it gave nothing but water. There is a comment
related to the mandate of the jury:

> The assyse being ressaveit, sworne and admittit, and efter reiding of the dit-
> tayis and examinatioun of the pannalls thairupoun, and heaveing ressaveit
> the depositiounes of divers famous witnesses, quha wer suorne tuitching
> the saids dittayis, proveing them, *as lykwayis in consideratioun of the confes-
> siounes and circumstances markit and set doun in and upon the saids dittayis,
> they passing out of judgement and reviseing the saids dittayis,* togidder with
> the saids depositiones of witnesses.[64] [*My italics.*]

The quotation above shows that it was considered necessary to be cautious because several of the assize have been active during the prase of
accusation. Ola Mansone of Ilisbrucht, member of the assize, was nomi-
nated as chancellor. The two women on trial, Marion Pardoun and Margareth Guthrumsdochter, were handed the same verdict. The jury found
that two of the dittay points were not proved. This indicates that the various points of accusation were discussed and decided upon. The sentence
has this wording: 'The judgis adjudges and decernis the pannalls to be
takin be the lockman to the place of executioun, to the west hill of Berrie,
and thair wyryt at ane staik and brunt in ashes, betuix 1 and 2 efter none,
quhilk Andro Chappie, dempster, gave for dome'.[65] The voice of the law
is a concise and determinative one.

---

[64] Proceedings against Marion Pardoun, 1644, in possession of John and Wendy Scott,
Gardie House, Bressay, Shetland.
[65] Ibid.

The Voices of the Witnesses

From the comments in the margin related to the 15 points of accusation it is possible to reconstruct some of the testimonies of the witnesses. One point deals with the accusation of Madda Scudda, at the time the servant of Johne, formerly the servant of Marion Pardoun. She accused Marion Pardoun of being the cause of 'a fearful madness and sickness' cast upon her, 'becaus sho wald not byd with yow',

> quhairin sho continewit most terriblie tormentit, and throw the torment of the said diseas sho wes caryit many tymes to run upon hir awin sister that keipit hir, and divers utheris, to have devorit them in hir madnes, and sa continewit a yeir and half ane yeir, till sho, *being counsallit be the nycht-bouris of Hildiswik, ran upon yow the said Marioun, and drew blood of yow, in James halcrois hous*, bytting tua of your fingers till they bled, quhairupon thairefter the said Madda Scudda recoverit of hir diseas, and cam to hir rycht sences.[66] [*My italics.*]

This is a story about how the disease hit Madda Scudda, structured along the lines of linearity and causality. Madda Scudda's testimony is a strong one, as she has experienced the spell-casting herself. In the margin this comment is written: '5 witchcraft/confessit Jhones mid[67] and that sho run on hir and thairefter wes weill/fyllis *in margin*'. This piece of information, that the maid ran on Marion and afterwards recovered from her disease, is repeated in the running text of the dittay. The testimony includes other witnesses, for instance those who stayed in James Halcro's house when Madda Scudda ran on Marion Pardoun and bit her. And it seems clear that the neighbours, who knew Marion Pardoun's reputation as a witch, were following the development of Madda Scudda's disease and gave her advice on how to get rid of the spell. People in the village must have feared Marioun Pardoun's activities. After the sudden recovery of a very sick person 'quhilk sudden recoverie, togidder with your forme and maner of charmeing and cureing of be your said tutche and charmes, being spred abroad among the nychtbours, and the same cuming to your earis (...)'.[68] Then Marion Pardoun again cast a spell on the same person, and she had to be begged to come to him to help him. Then she transferred the sickness to a cow. There is no doubt that the neighbours believed that she

---

[66] Ibid.
[67] Means 'maid'.
[68] Proceedings against Marion Pardoun, 1644, in possession of John and Wendy Scott, Gardie House, Bressay, Shetland.

was the only one who could take away a spell she herself had cast. It also
seems that even if the neighbours feared her, they were impressed by her
activities. References to the neighbours' reactions to the amazing practices of Marion Pardoun may be followed through the whole document:
either Eduard Halcro was saved from peril 'to the *admiratioun* of all the
beholderis' or a hand managed to make blood run from a dead body 'to
the greit *admiratioun* of the beholderis'. [*My italics.*]

The first point of the accusations against Marion Pardoun had to do
with Jonet Robertson's sudden sickness: 'ye cust seiknes upon the said
Jonet, quha imediatlie upon your departure fell in ane extraordiner and
unkyndlie seiknes, and lay aught [dayis *deleted*] weikis'.[69] The recovery of
Jonet Robertson was even more remarkable than that of Madda Scudda.
John Banks, Jonet's husband, came to Marion Pardoun and threatened
her, whereupon she gave him 'a gulyeoun of silver to hold his peace' and
promised him that nothing should ail his wife

> and thairefter for that ye sent hir ane cheis of the breid of anes looffe,[70] com-
> posed by your said devilish airt of witchcraft, with ane Jonka Rolland, desy-
> ring the said Jonet to eat the same, *quhen (tho the said Jonet refuisit to eat)*
> *yit imediatlie thairefter grew weill*, bot tua of hir kyne died, the said seiknes
> being castin upon them be your said wicked and devilish airt of witchcraft.[71]
> [*My italics.*]

There is no factual connection between the eating of bread and Jonet's
recovery, as she refused to eat the loaf. Nevertheless, the argumentation
continues as if there really was reason to believe that the loaf of bread
had caused Jonet Robertson's recovery, as seen by the words 'yit imediatlie *thairefter*' [*My italics.*] The recovery comes after the request to eat
the loaf of bread. This indicates that the interrogators are to a certain
extent 'deaf' when unexpected information turns up, information which
threatens to overthrow their way of arguing. They ignore the significance
of the information which does not fit in with their intention and continue
their argumentation along the same lines as usual, taking as an outset
that there is a cause-and effect connection between remedies of witchcraft used and the sickness.

---

[69] Ibid.
[70] Means a piece of bread.
[71] Proceedings against Marion Pardoun, 1644, in possession of John and Wendy Scott,
Gardie House, Bressay, Shetland.

The voices of the witnesses contribute greatly to the accuracy and logic of the text, which was necessary when a convincing argumentation about the effects of Marion Pardoun's spells should be presented. Being careful to establish a timeline, the witnesses give information about how many hours, days, weeks and years might have gone between a quarrel and the consequence of that quarrel, namely a sudden sickness or death. Thus a chain of events is created and a logical explanation made possible.

Some of the alleged spell-castings are dated in occurrence to a couple of previous years: both 1641 and 1642 are mentioned. However, some of the spells were perhaps cast a long time ago, and the year is left open, as in point 10: 'Item, ye the said Marioun is indyttit and accusit for that [*blank*] yeris syne ye being suspected to have cassin seiknes upon the said Andro Smyth elder his mother, quhairof sho lay long benume and sensles'.[72] Andro Smith, elder, pursued three of the accusations against Marion Pardoun, and it seems clear that some families in the village were much more eager to raise accusations than others.

The voices of the witnesses often reveal motives for casting spells. It seems that everyday disagreements about pasture and animals were often the starting points of an accusation of spell-casting. Sometimes a detail might be reason enough for casting a spell on a cow: 'James Halcro in Hildiswick haveing a kow *that he alledged haid pushed a kow of yours*, ye in revenge thairof, be your said divilish airt of witchcraft, maid the said James his kow milk nothing but blood, quhairas your awin kow had no harme in hir milk'.[73] [*My italics.*] That a cow milks blood after having been the object of spell-casting, is well-known knowledge related to malefice in many European countries.

The word 'devil' is mentioned only twice in the discourse of the witnesses. The word is used once by Andro Brown, who had words with Marion Pardoun's husband Svend as they were casting peat. The other place where the word 'devil' is used in the witnesses' discourse, is in quotations from the declaration of the burnt witch, Jonet Fraser. This declaration was used to testify that Marion Pardoun performed sorcery. It claims that Marion Pardoun had asked Jonet Fraser for assistance when she planned to sink a boat. So we have the situation that although Marion Pardoun does not confess to the Devil's pact, shape-shifting is mentioned in this document and used in arguing Pardoun's guilt in connection with a shipwreck.

[72] Ibid.
[73] Ibid.

Four people drowned 'rycht at the shore quhair thair wes na danger uther-wayes, nor hazard to have cassin thame away, it being sick fair wedder'.[74] One of them was Eduard Halcro, a person against whom Marion Pardoun allegedly bore 'ane deadlie and veneficall[75] malice' against. As sorcery operations were often combined with practical choices of shape, the overturning of boats was often connected with whales or seals, as here: 'be your said wicked, detestable, abhominable and divilish airt of witch-craft, being transformed in the lyknes of ane pellock quhaill (...) ye did cum under the said boat and overturne hir with thame, and drowned and devoirit thame in the sey'.[76] Marion Pardoun was asked to come to lay her hands on the drowned people, 'dayis efter the said death and away cast-ing, quhen all thair bluid wes evanished and disolveit frome any naturall course or caus to ishue and rune, the said [umquhill *underlined*] Eduard bled at the coller bane or craig[77] bane'.[78] The interrogators took the inci-dent as a sign of 'revilatioun of the judgement of the almytie' and called her a murderer, indicating that his bleeding was a sign that she was guilty in his death.[79]

The voices of the witnesses, as they come to the fore in this document, tell us a lot about the common people's beliefs, among other notions a type of sorcery which involved tying knots on a rope or a piece of cloth to get wind was mentioned. Untying the knots produced wind. This type of sorcery is also known from the Sami tradition in Northern Norway.[80] It is interesting, however, that in the Shetland tradition it is the Devil who is supposed to loosen the knot, not the sorcerer himself, as the Sami tradition denotes. It seems here to be a blurred border between the common people's retelling of the art of loosing knots to make wind and the tradi-tion as it is known in Norway. This indicates that in orally transmitted tales about the art of sorcery and the role of the Devil, variations might be traced due to transference of ideas, as the notions travel from one country to another. The same basic idea might get a new image as it appears in

---

[74] Ibid.
[75] From Latin *veneficium*, meaning poison or witchcraft.
[76] Proceedings against Marion Pardoun, 1644, in possession of John and Wendy Scott, Gardie House, Bressay, Shetland.
[77] 'craig' means neck.
[78] Proceedings against Marion Pardoun, 1644, in possession of John and Wendy Scott, Gardie House, Bressay, Shetland.
[79] See note 55 this chapter.
[80] Olaus Magnus, *Historia om de nordiska folken*, 159.

new environments, influenced by changing cultural contexts. The testimonies in the Marioun Pardon case tell us about common people's way of thinking and of reasoning. They also display the complexity of witchcraft accusations. The testimonies show that the peasants knew about the Devil and the demonic pact, as well as about wind magic. A melting together of old folkloric ideas and new demonological ideas seem to characterize the Early Modern mentality sphere of common people, which makes the document a rich source for the study of the history of mentalities.

The Voice of the Accused Person

A distinct feature of the whole document is the disruption of the coherence of the accused person's statements as the days of imprisonment pass. Following the first minutes signed by the brethren of the presbytery on 15 March, the interrogation apparently continued. Marginal comments seem to contain remnants of what she was in fact confessing: 'fyllis/witchcraft/confest ane tyme sho pat hir finger to…hir…/confest hir…in judgement and cursit him…/ Item, confest sho sent the bannok *in margin*'.[81] These marginal comments, which are no more than fragments of formulations, seem to be used as key-words for the complete text of the document. Afterwards, the whole situation is rendered in detail about Marioun's quarrelling with Andro Broun and cursing him, whereupon he fell sick; about her laying hands on Andro Broun, putting her finger on his leg; about her sending her husband with a bannock to Andro Brown with the result that the sickness left him and was cast upon a cow. An escalating tendency can be traced: the greater the pressure put on Marion Pardoun, the less coherent the text. This apparently has to do with the waking of Marion Pardoun and her distress. At the end, she is clearly out of her mind, saying that her husband lay under her head: 'Provin also be Mans Finlasone and [*torn*] Erasmussone quhen they wer waking hir sho speirit quhair the husband wes quha ansering hir speking concerning hir husbound sho answrit he lay under hir heid and wald not suffer hir to confess *in margin*'.[82]

---

[81] The forst word of the quotation, fyllis, comes from the verb fyle, meaning to find guilty, to convict. Ref. DOST; Proceedings against Marion Pardoun, 1644, in possession of John and Wendy Scott, Gardie House, Bressay, Shetland.
[82] Ibid.

In addition to the parts of her confession rendered as fragments of sentences in the margin of the document, the voice of the accused person is rendered as indirect speech in the discourse of the witnesses. There is no doubt that Marion Pardoun had cursed other persons. When rumours about the recovery of Andro Broun within 14 days were spread among the neighbours as the result of her charming and curing him, she got angry: 'ye said to the nychtbouris unhoall[83] on them that haid bewitched yow'.[84] This suggests that Marion Pardoun was afraid of rumours spread about her use of charms, and the result was that immediately he again fell in the said sickness, worse than before.[85] The threat of rumours about the reputation of sorcery seems to have been consistent in Shetland around the mid-seventeenth century.

The case of Marion Pardoun is in an intermediate position between a demonological confession and a confession rooted in traditional sorcery. Most often confessions containing the element of shape-shifting are related to witches' meetings or collective sorcery operations. Even if the case of Marion Pardoun does not contain a clear demonological confession, the element of shape-shifting is documented. Her case illustrates the pragmatic side of shape-shifting, 'being transformed in the lyknes of ane pellock quhaill'.[86] The choice of shape, as here the transformation into a whale, was appropriate to the actual situation in which the witchcraft operation was to be performed; a witchcraft operation at sea required the evil-doer to be in the shape of a whale or a bird, making it possible to master the surroundings. This shows a practical attitude to life and points to the connection between the contents of the women's confessions and their own experiences, culture and environment. Even if the narrative conveyed in the confession is fantastic, the setting of the story is realistic. The imagery is related to the maritime society, as could be expected in a fishing village on an island.

Relations to other women, as they come forth in this document, seem to go in both positive and negative directions. Other women might be a threat because of their potential to denounce a person for witchcraft. But there is also an indication that loyalty to other women is at work, for instance when Marion Pardoun gave her motive for taking away sickness

---

[83] 'unhoall' means bad luck.
[84] Proceedings against Marion Pardoun, 1644, in possession of John and Wendy Scott, Gardie House, Bressay, Shetland.
[85] Ibid.
[86] Ibid.

from a man, 'answerit that it wes not for his gud bot for Helen Clousta his spous good that he wes saved'.[87] He was saved because of Marion's sympathy for his wife.

The Voice of the Scribe

The scribe gives some 'hidden' pieces of information, both in the marginal comments mentioned above and in comments in brackets. The information that Marion Pardoun was tortured, kept awake by two men, Mans Finlaysone in Burraland[88] and Jon Erasmussone in Enisfirth, is such a comment, inserted in the document after the signing of the dittay by the moderator Nicol Whyte and the clerk M. Robert Murray. Both Mans Finlaysone and Jon Erasmussone were in the jury when Marion Pardoun and Margaret Guthrumsdochter were given their sentences.

The voice of the scribe is heard particularly through the text's repetitive demonological phrases. An understanding of Marion Pardoun's sorcery activity in relation to the Devil, thus leaving her God and Christian faith, is superimposed on her by male questioners, and this becomes distinct in the document. The whole rhetorical apparatus of condemning a fallen woman because she is an enemy of God and has given herself to the Devil is used repeatedly, almost like an exorcism. The arguments for condemning her come from the witch-hunters. They interpret her deeds in the same way as if she had confessed to the demonic pact—and judge accordingly. This demonic aspect of the text is taken good care of by the scribe, hammering and hammering on the same expressions, an indication that the text itself reveals important ideological attitudes on the part of the interrogators.

Another important feature of this text is the logic imposed on the document by the use of linearity and cause-effect relations. An efficient use of these textual elements, carefully written down by the scribe, makes it possible to establish the story structure of a document in which the discourse situation is originally like a drama, where most of the text is a monologue directed at the accused person. The cause-effect relation is established, for instance, to 'prove' the effect of spell-casting. Linearity is established by placing events one after another along a timeline, being

---

[87] Ibid.

[88] According to Ballantyne, J. H. and Smith, B., *Shetland*, p. 68, Burraland was a large farm, listed in 1589 with 12 marks land. Burrowland in 1610 is listed with 6½ marks land, 8 pennies in the mark, p. 247.

very careful with information about what came first and what came last. The professional way in which the scribe mastered the cause-effect relation as well as linearity in his writing are exemplified in the following sentence, which describes what happened after Marion Pardoun had cured a woman: 'quhairupoun by your said divilish witchcraft the said seiknes wes taken af the said Marjorie, and castin upon a young kow of the said Jones, quhilk took woddrome[89] and died within 24 hours thairefter, quhilk ye can not deny'.[90] In the quoted sentence the cause-effect relation is emphasized through the logical explanation of how the sickness was taken from Marjorie and cast upon Jones's cow, which consequently died. Likewise linearity is underlined by the mentioning of the exact number of hours it took from the cow became sick till it died. By making use of these literary devices, the scribe strengthens the argument that Marion Pardoun was to blame for the cow's death.

The range of the scribe's accents is wide. Sometimes it is possible to hear the voice of the scribe through inserted comments, such as the following: when Marion had put Eduard Halcro's life in danger by loosening some stones on his path, he was 'yit saved to the admiratioun of all the beholderis'.[91] This comment is almost a humorous one. Another accent that is rather unexpected is a poetic one, as seen in the image 'cloithing your spirit with in the said quhaill'. Such images used in the witchcraft documents show that, in spite of all expectations, witchcraft documents echo expressions used in preaching from the Old Testament, and may contain beauty and poetry.

Margaret Watson, 1725

The 1670s was a decade with seven cases in Shetland; four in 1673, one in 1674, and two in 1675. Among these was a sorcerer, Magnus Laurenson in Gonfirth, brought before the court in 1674. He had been suspected as a sorcerer for a long time. The end of his case is not known. The last cases

---

[89] 'Wod(e)nes' means madness, insanity, ref. *DOST*, 12 vols., xii, 280, 'wodrome' and 'woddram' are variants of the same word. Another explanation might be 'vomm', explained by Jakobsen as 'injury inflicted upon a person by hypnotizing influence or magic power; to kast a v. ower ane; more common forms "vam" and "vamm".'

[90] Proceedings against Marion Pardoun, 1644, in possession of John and Wendy Scott, Gardie House, Bressay, Shetland.

[91] Ibid.

in Shetland took place in 1708 and 1725; the cases of the Ratter family in 1708 and the case of Margaret Watson in 1724–25.[92]

Margaret Watson was first brought before the presbytery in Sandness in 1708 together with the Ratter family. Her name was recorded again at Southerhous in Delting on 30 September 1724 and at Olnafirth on 3 March, 26 May, 30 June and 29 September 1725. Like the Ratter family she was a vagabond, and apparently came into conflict with people and cursed them when she was refused lodgings or food. She was first brought before the court 'suspected of witchcraft & deluding the people being se[ver]all tymes before the Session of Sandness and convicted of gross & continuall cursing & impreca[tio]ns Being interrogat by the Session anent the report passed on her of being a witch'.[93] She answered them 'how could she be a witch and not know of it and affirmed as is clear by the Session process and by the Testimony of all the Inhabitants of Sandness th[a]t she did and would curse when she was prejudged or wronged by any'.[94] The only testimony against her was an episode of cursing after a refusal of lodging. The night after 'the goodwife of the house was almost out of her witts w[i]th fearfull dream & visions'.[95] Margaret Watson denied continually that she was a witch, but admitted she did curse. The way the word witch is used in this case is not related to demonology, but to scolding and cursing. The end of the case in the year 1708 was that the presbytery 'thought fitt to call the heads of families to enquire par[ticu]larly at them anent this womans life & conversa[tio]n who all declared she was a great curser'.[96]

The kirk session of Southerhouse at Delting in 1724 has a reference from Sandness about Margaret Watson. She is said to be a resident in Sandness and mentioned as an 'alledg'd witch'.[97] Her case should be laid before the Civil Magistrate by Mr Geo. Duncan, Minister of Sandness.[98] When her case came up again four times in 1725 at Olnafirth, she was mentioned as 'alledged guilty of witchcraft', 'alleadged a witch', 'alleadged witch' and 'alleadged witch'. But in spite of several reports from the kirk, the legal authorities were passive. On 30 June 1725 the minister reported

---

[92] I would like to thank Diane Baptie for the transcription of the document.
[93] SMA, SPR, CH2/1071/1, p. 155.
[94] SMA, SPR, CH2/1071/1, p. 155.
[95] SMA, SPR, CH2/1071/1, p. 156.
[96] SMA, SPR, CH2/1071/1, p. 156.
[97] SMA, SPR, CH2/1071/2, p. 300.
[98] SMA, SPR, CH2/1071/2, p. 300.

that he laid the process before Mr Stewart but got no answer.[99] And on 29 September 'the Stewart reports that he had consider'd the Sessions Reference and found nothing therein that could infer that Crime against her, But that she is a Deluder of the people and that he intended to proceed against her as such'.[100] The term 'a Deluder of the people' must refer to her cursing, as she did not confess to witchcraft. The quotation could be interpreted as indicating that Margaret Watson misled people by trying to make them believe that cursing had an effect. However, this could not be considered a serious witchcraft crime.

This last case in Shetland shows clearly the change in climate since the mid-seventeenth century. Judicial scepticism was a fact earlier than scepticism on the part of the kirk. The fear of 'devillish' witchcraft on the part of the witch-hunters has disappeared. The words 'witch' and 'witchcraft' are still used by the kirk, but these words do not elicit any response from the accused, from the heads of the families assembled, or from Mr Stewart. They all maintained that Margaret Watson was not a witch. The Devil was no longer mentioned and whatever threat Margaret Watson might have been to the communities in which she stayed due to her cursing, in 1725 this threat was not regarded as dangerous by the legal authorities. The repeated attempts by the kirk to revive her case might be a sign of irritation with this continually cursing individual, but this is not a sign of fear of an evil-doer of great calibre. Fear, which is a very strong feeling, could not be raised on the part of the legal officials towards this rather harmless woman. In this respect, the voice of the law had the last word.

Conclusion

In Shetland, the witchcraft trials by and large follow the same pattern that we know from several other regions, for instance Orkney. The early cases were characterized by accusations such as the stealing of milk and the sieve and shears—a recognized method of divining, for instance the whereabouts of stolen or lost goods.[101] There seems to have been a harsher climate as regards the persecution of witches in 1616, when five cases occurred. The pattern of two cases in 1644, four cases in 1673, one case in 1674 and two cases in 1675 gives evidence for an interpretation that

---

[99] SMA, SPR, CH2/1071/2, p. 312.
[100] SMA, SPR, CH2/1071/2, p. 315.
[101] See Donaldson, *The Court*, (1954), 128. Also discussed in Thomas, *County*, 160–65.

fear of witches existed and that witchcraft was criminalized on a modest scale throughout the century. The end of witchcraft persecution in Shetland was dominated by traditional sorcery. Even though witchcraft trials continued to 1725, the cases in the late period were few and far between. It is interesting to note the change in court procedure from the earliest cases to 1616, a development showing that influence from Norse law, exemplified in the early cases by 'sixter aithe' and 'larych aithe' gave way to a court procedure similar to that of mainland Scotland. Probably the abolition of Norse laws in 1611 influenced the witchcraft trials in the years to follow. In the 1616 trials formulations in the court records clearly give evidence that the Witchcraft Act was used. This holds true for the opening phrases of the trials, for 'certain points of witchcraft, sorcery and deceiving the people' as well as for the sentence, in which the same formulation as is known from elsewhere can be read, where the sentenced persons were to be 'tane by the lockmane to the place of execution abone Berrie useit and wount efter none and thair to be wirryet at ane staik quhill they be dead and thairefter to be brunt in ashes'.[102] On linguistic grounds this argument also holds true for the frequent repetition of words related to 'devil' in the court records from 1616 onwards.

It is interesting to note that demonological ideas seem to enter the mentality sphere of Orkney and Shetland in a similar fashion. The three trials from 1616 show a new climate in witchcraft belief in Shetland. The confessions of Katherine Jonesdochter and Barbara Scord in particular reveal both new ideas about the demonic pact and old folk belief, in spirits dangerous for humans to see. The covenant with the Devil and the witches' mark, side by side with the idea of transferring disease and spirits rising from the churchyard, illustrate a weaving together of old and new ideas of sorcery and witchcraft, which seems to have taken place in Shetland around 1600.[103] If learned ideas of demonology were introduced to the northern islands by Scottish legal officials, this seems to correspond with such ideas having been activated on the Scottish mainland during the witchcraft panics of the 1590s. If the kirk was active in spreading demonological ideas, the restoration of the bishopric may have been influential. It seems clear that the presbytery played an important part

---

[102] Donaldson, *Court*, (1991), 38, 43.
[103] The notion of spirits arising from churchyards resemble Norwegian folk belief, 'gangferd', a crowd of dead persons flying from the churchyard. Ref. 'Gongferd, feigdd og spøykjeri. Framsynte folk', 54–57.

in the interrogation of Marion Pardoun, 1644, where detailed documents have survived to document the procedure of the case.

The politically unstable situation in Orkney related to the deaths of two generations of Stewarts might have had an influence in Shetland as well, and might have contributed to the 1616 cases. However, as these turbulent historical events were geographically most closely related to Orkney, it is likely that the consequences there were more marked than in Shetland. It should also be noted that fewer sheriff courts were held in Shetland than in Orkney. The sederunts[104] documented for Orkney and Shetland for the period 1614–15 show that the court had nine sessions altogether in Shetland in June, August, September and October 1615, while during 1614–15 it had thirteen sessions in Orkney.[105] This shows that in Shetland, witchcraft accusations were not always dealt with immediately before the legal apparatus, but had to wait until the time came for the courts to be held, thus possibly contributing to calming the pressure for trials and lessening the occurrence of trials. Political unrest related to the 1643 events, which had consequences for the northern islands as discussed in the Orkney chapter, might have had some influence in Shetland, as the 1644 trials were of a severe kind.

Hostile relations within the local community at the very outset of the witchcraft trials seem to play a role whenever the sources are detailed enough to reveal this type of evidence. As regards witchcraft suspicions and accusations, the importance of disagreements within social networks in the local communities is illustrated in the brief entries of the early cases as well as in the more detailed cases from 1616 and 1644. Whether a person was reputed to be a witch was used as a point during the passing of the verdict and sentence, as can be seen in the triple trial from 1616, in which it was recorded that 'the said Jonka and Barbaray are "bruitit" as common witches'.[106] However, as was seen also from the Scottish mainland and from Orkney, the seriousness of the cases treated by the legal authorities suddenly increased enormously once the demonological confessions had been obtained. Accused persons might have reputation for knowing sorcery, but for witchcraft as a crime the decisive point with regard to the severity of a case was the demonological element.

---

[104] From Latin, meaning they were sitting; in minutes of various courts, used in its Latin sense, to introduce the list of members of the court present.
[105] Barclay, 'Introduction', xxiii.
[106] Donaldsen, *Court*, (1991), 42.

On the whole it seems that the witchcraft trials in Shetland followed a well-known pattern as regards changes in the legal, clerical and mentality spheres. Traditional sorcery was criminalized from 1600 onwards, although with lenient sentences. Demonological notions were introduced into Shetland, and became known among common people, but they did not gain a very strong foothold, as these ideas did not result in panics. Towards the end of the witch-hunt, the kirk was active in accusing those who used cursing and thus represented a factor of social disorder in communities. However, at the beginning of the eighteenth century the legal apparatus was not particularly interested in following up these cases.

If influence from Norway existed during the Shetland witchcraft trials, it might have come from the western part of Norway, where a few confessions of diabolism occurred in the Bergen district during the 1580s.[107] However, the trials in Bergen did not develop into panics.[108] The distance between Shetland and Bergen is short, and the connection between the lawman of Shetland and the lawman of Bergen and Gulathing was close.[109] Judgements from the Shetland lawthing could be brought before the king's court in Bergen for confirmation, and may be traced as late as 1538.[110] Thus a degree of influence from the west of Norway on communications related to law decisions in general in Shetland might be possible in the sixteenth century. However, Scots law formally took over shortly after the time the Shetland witchcraft trials started.

We see that there are similarities between Shetland and Norway both with regard to laws and mentalities. An argument has been brought forth that Orkney and Shetland with regard to witch-hunting should be included in a Highland and Celtic context. I think it is much more likely that the northern isles, particularly Shetland, with regard to legal influence as well as folk beliefs, should be seen in a Scandinavian context. Within the

---

[107] Botheim, *Trolldomsprosessene i Bergenhus len*, 136, 215–227; Stave, *Da Lucifer kom*, 82.

[108] In the main Finnmark panics, which involved 60–70 women, 45 women were sentenced to death.

[109] It is interesting to note that two days after a sentence was passed in Oslo by the viceroy and the Norwegian council on 22 November 1507, the viceroy, Christian II, "published his confirmation of all the laws of King Håkon V, and decreed that they were to be observed 'in the whole kingdom of Norway and lands under the crown of Norway, even Iceland, Shetland and Faroe as in other places here in Norway'." Ref. Robberstad, *Shetland*, 55. Robberstad maintains that Christian II, by publishing this decree, must have thought that 'a new king of Norway should have the power of confirming these old laws even in respect of the mortgaged land, an idea that was by no means revolutionary.' Ref. Robberstad, *Shetland*, 57.

[110] Robberstad, *Shetland*, 54.

judiciary there were connections between Norway and Shetland up to the period of witchcraft trials, and as for mentalities, the exchange over the sea might easily be accounted for. However, these links seem to be strongest in the period before the witchcraft trials started and during the very first years of witchcraft persecution, when *maleficium* dominated the picture. The appearance of demonological ideas in witchcraft cases in Shetland were probably influenced from mainland Scotland. As the same was the case with Orkney, the northern isles cannot be seen to furnish a link between Scotland and Norway so far as ideas about witchcraft are concerned. As will be seen, the connection between Scotland and Finnmark in Northern Norway is based on a direct transference of demonological ideas, a process wherein a Scotsman played a central role.

PART THREE

FINNMARK, NORTHERN NORWAY

Map 5: Map of Scandinavia. Made by Inger-Bjerg Poulsen.

CHAPTER EIGHT

FINNMARK—HISTORICAL BACKGROUND

This chapter will present a brief historical background for the seventeenth-century Finnmark witchcraft trials. A short description will be given of the demographic, political, judicial and clerical conditions in early modern Finnmark, the period 1500–1700. A survey of the Norwegian witchcraft trials as a whole will set the Finnmark trials in a national perspective.

Demography and Socio-Economic Conditions

Finnmark is both the northernmost and easternmost county in Norway. Its area is 48,649 square kilometres, in size comparable to Denmark. It is thinly populated, with a present population of 73,417 inhabitants. Finnmark is the county in Norway with the lowest population. The eastern part of Finnmark is the only part of Norway that has an arctic climate. Two ethnic groups, Norwegians and Samis, lived in Finnmark in the seventeenth century. Also today, the majority of the present ethnic Sami population of Norway inhabits Finnmark. In the seventeenth century, Sami people had Sami as their mother tongue, the Norwegians had Norwegian. Today, the majority of the present Sami population speaks Norwegian, for some as their second language. The Sami language is now recognized as an official language in Norway.

The population of Norway increased in the period from 1500 till 1650 from 100,000 to 440,000.[1] The district of Finnmark was thinly populated. The population in Finnmark was about 3,000–3,200 persons in the middle of the seventeenth century, possibly declining at the end.[2] However, during the previous century there had been a marked increase in the

---

[1] Næss, 'Norway: The Criminological Context', in Ankarloo and Henningsen, *Early Modern European Witchcraft*, 377.

[2] According to Adelaer's taxation list from 1690, there were 519 Norwegian men. If a family size of four is used for stipulation, this would be around 2073 Norwegians. With a family size of five, it would be 2595 Norwegians. Ref. Nielssen, A. R., 'Fra storvær til småbruk. Den geografiske ekspansjonen i den norske bosetting i Finnmark ca. 1570–1700' [From fishing village to small-holdings. The geographical expansion in the Norwegian settlements in Finnmark c. 1570–1700], *Heimen* no. 2 (1986), 88; Næss, *Trolldomsprosessene i Norge*, 32; Hagen, R. B., *Dei europeiske trolldomsprosessane* (Oslo, 2007), 91.

population, mostly due to people moving north along the coast of Norway in search of jobs, settling in Finnmark.[3] As labour was available and in demand in fisheries, efforts were made to induce individuals seek jobs up north.[4]

The ethnic situation with Norwegians and Samis living side by side, characterizes Finnmark. At the time of the witch trials, most Norwegians lived in fishing villages along the coast, and their income came from combining coastal fishing and small scale subsistence agriculture. Alternative to sea fishing the people got subsistence livelihood from agriculture and hunting; fresh water fishing, keeping cattle, forest hunting, seal hunting, collecting wood and goods along the shore. The most important fishing villages in Finnmark were found in the north-east: Vardø, with the fortress Vardøhus, and Vadsø, Kiberg and Ekkerøy. In addition there were small fishing villages all along the Finnmark coast. In the seventeenth century, the Sami population was not integrated with the ethnic Norwegian population. A minority of the Sami lived a nomadic life in the interior of Finnmark and migrated with their reindeer seasonally to the coast of Finnmark or to other parts of northern Scandinavia. At the time of the trials several Sami people also lived in permanent settlements along the fjords in Finnmark and some other northern parts of Norway.

The socio-economic situation in Finnmark from the sixteenth till the seventeenth centuries has been described as one from expansion to stagnation.[5] The trade in fish products between Finnmark and Bergen on the west coast of Norway was a particular feature of seventeenth-century Finnmark. Earlier, from the twelfth century onwards, a collective enterprise was common, and an important source of income for the whole northern part of Norway, which in the winter season had very rich near-shore fisheries.[6] Fishermen from Finnmark and the neighbouring district of Nordland sailed with small cargo boats to Bergen to sell stock fish in exchange

---

[3] Using taxation records, Einar Niemi has figured out the size of the population, using a family size of five persons. He finds that the population in East and West Finnmark in 1520 was 2190, and that it respectively in 1597 was 4590. Ref. *Vadsøs historie*, 94–95. A family size of four, which often is used for stipulations of population in the seventeenth century, would reduce these numbers accordingly. According to the Adelaer commission's investigation from 1690, the size of the Norwegian population declined during the seventeenth century. Ref. Nielssen, 'Fra storvær til småbruk', 88.

[4] Niemi, *Vadsøs historie*, 255.

[5] Balsvik, *Vardø*, 20–33; Niemi, *Vadsøs historie*, 69–230; Niemi, E., 'Hekseprosesser og økonomi [Witchcraft trials and economy]', *Ottar*, no. 5 (2012), 19–25.

[6] Kiil, *Når bøndene seilte*, 8–10, 35.

Hjelmsøy · Tunes · North Cape · Gamvik · Gåsnes · Honningsvåg · Kjelvik · Omgang · Hellenes · Sinkelvik · Brenngam · Båtsfjorden · Makkaur · Mefjord · Hellefjord · Syltevik · Hamningberg · Bussesund · Hammerfest · Klubben · Domen · Vardø · Hasvåg · Kvalsund · Laksefjord · Kiberg · Langnes · Porsanger · Skallneset · Rognsund · Lerresfjord · Andersby · Vadsø · Lille Ekkerøy · Komagfjord · Store Ekkerøy · Altafjorden · Årøya · Varanger · Alta

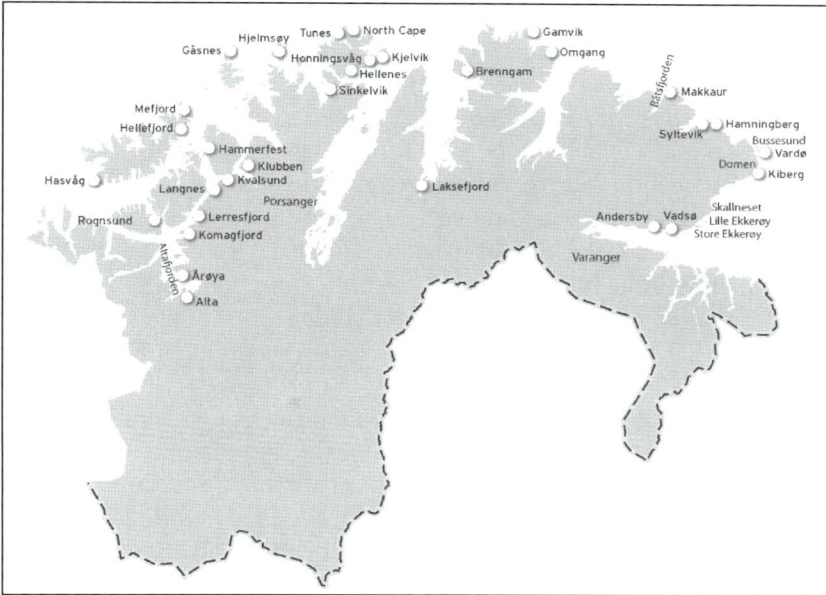

Map 6: Map of Finnmark. Made by National Tourist Routes/ Blæst Design.

for flour and other types of food. A whole fishing village could go together to provide such a boat.[7] From the middle of the fourteenth century, there was a change. The Hanseatic League had established an office in Bergen, establishing a trade based on the triangle between the Bergen merchant, the local peasant fisherman and the outfitters in Finnmark. In the local communities there was an arrangement by which outfitters supplied, by means of granting credit, the fishermen with equipment for fishing.[8] The situation created a permanent debt dependency; the local fishermen were indebted to the local outfitters, who again were indebted to Bergen merchants. The Bergen merchants gained full financial control over the local fishermen and also a royal monopoly of the Finnmark trade from 1681 onwards, a situation which lasted until 1715.[9] The trade along the coast had a strong international impact on the Finnmark communities, and

---

[7] These cargo boats were called *jekter*. Ref. Kiil, A., *Når bøndene seilte* [When the peasants sailed] (Oslo, 1993), 18–34; Niemi, *Vadsøs historie*, 88.

[8] In Norwegian the outfitters were called *utredere*.

[9] The last decision related to this monopoly situation was made in 1702, valid from 1703 until 1715. Ref. Niemi, *Vadsøs historie*, 280.

influenced the conditions in the villages during the period of the witch-craft trials. By the seventeenth century, the population in Finnmark was increasingly becoming mixed with people from Scotland, Germany, the Netherlands, the Faroese Islands and Sweden, who had settled there; a variety of nations which can be seen from persons' names.[10]

The seventeenth century was characterized by periods of less than nor-mal fish reaching the coast and several severe shipwrecks, due to which Bergen merchants living in Vadsø suffered financial losses. Common peo-ple frequently brought complaints before the local courts related to bad fisheries and poverty, as they could not manage to pay their taxes.[11] At the end of the century an official commission was sent to Finnmark to investigate the situation.[12] The latter half of the seventeenth century was also difficult for Bergen merchants due to falling fish export and increased competition internationally. At the end of the seventeenth century the Bergen merchants concluded that the Finnmark trade was unprofitable.[13] Food supplies were at this time available for the inhabitants of Finnmark not only from Bergen ships, but also from Russian and Dutch ships, so that the local fishermen got the opportunity to buy necessities also from these ships.

In addition to the Bergen trade along the coast, increasing commercial activities from abroad started to influence seventeenth-century Finnmark. The sea route to the north of Finnmark towards Russia attracted attention, and the ships passing Finnmark had to pay a tax.[14] These ships came par-ticularly from the Netherlands, but also from other European countries. There was also a dream about finding the northern passage to China and India by sailing north of Finnmark, as such a north-east passage would be shorter than the normal sailing route south of Africa.

Around one-quarter of the population in Finnmark at the beginning of the seventeenth century were Samis.[15] At the end of the century the

---

[10] The influence from other European countries may be seen in taxation lists. Ref. Niemi, *Vadsøs historie*, 90. See also register of persons' names occuring in seventeenth-century Finnmark court records, in Sandvik and Winge, *Tingbok for Finnmark 1620–33*, 344–378.

[11] Willumsen, *Trollkvinne i nord*, (1984), 86.

[12] The Adelaer commission of 1690. Ref. Niemi, *Vadsøs historie*, 280; Nielssen, 'Fra stor-vær til småbruk', 88.

[13] Niemi, *Vadsøs historie*, 289.

[14] In Norwegian this tax, which was entered into the district accounts for Vardøhus, was called *Kvitehavstollen*. Ref. Niemi, *Vadsøs historie*, 86.

[15] In 1597 there were 561 Norwegian families and 154 Sami families in Finnmark. With a family size of five, mentioned above, the number of Norwegians would be 2805 and the

relative number had increased.[16] Coastal Sami families outnumber nomadic Sami families in the beginning of the eighteenth century in a ratio of about 5:1.[17] The Samis living inland and Samis living along the coast had different ways of subsistence. Those who lived in the interior of Finnmark had much contact with Samis in the neighbouring countries Sweden and Russia. Finland did not exist as a country at this time.[18] For the inland Samis the most important trade was related to different types of fur. This trade was very prosperous in the sixteenth century, and had connection with networks of merchants in Sweden and Russia. Influence from the Russian side was strong, as trade made itself felt through travelling merchants coming from the area round the White Sea, and also from the activity of Russian-Orthodox monasteries. Due to lack of fixed borders, the Samis in these inland areas had to pay tax in three different countries; Norway, Sweden and Russia.[19] In the seventeenth century, negotiations related to taxation, jurisdiction and trade were carried through on the part of each of these countries. The Swedish king as well as the Danish-Norwegian king made initiatives to explore the possibilities for taxation in Finnmark as well as defining borders towards the neighbouring states. The Danish-Norwegian King Christian IV went in 1599 all the way to the Kola Peninsula in this errand. The Swedish crown wanted to a greater extent to get control over the Sami trade with fur, which was an important trade merchandise. Instead of individual merchants travelling round in the Sami settlements and special bailiffs installed in the Sami areas, the crown now tried to establish annual markets for buying and selling goods, and several prohibitive decrees were issued to prevent the activity

number of Samis 770 in the seventeenth century. With a family size of four, which is also used for stipulations of Finnmark population at this time, the number of Norwegians would be nearly 2100, and the number of Samis would be 660. Ref. Båkte, V. A., 'Den samiske befolkning i Nord-Norge'. Artikler fra Statistisk Sentralbyrå nr. 107 (Oslo, 1978), 14.

[16] The number of coastal Sami families were 341 and the number of nomadic inland Samis were 69 at the beginning of the eighteenth century, Hansen and Olsen, *Samenes historie fram til 1750*, 258.

[17] According to Lars Ivar Hansen and Bjørnar Olsen (2004), with reference to Ørnulf Vorren (1978), again with reference to the missionary Thomas von Westen's registrations, the number of coastal Sami families were five times the number of Sami families at the beginning of the eighteenth century. Ref. Hansen and Olsen, *Samenes historie fram til 1750*, 258; Vorren, Ø., 'Bosetning og ressursutnytting under veidekulturen og dens differensiering. *Finnmarksvidda natur—kultur*, NOU, 18 A. (Oslo, 1978).

[18] The area which today is Finland was part of the kingdom of Sweden from the thirteenth century to 1809, when it was ceded to the Russian Empire, becoming the Grand Duchy of Finland.

[19] Hansen and Olsen, *Samenes historie fram til 1750*, 239, 263.

of individual merchants.[20] Due to changes in the trade boundaries during the first half of the seventeenth century, an economical crisis occurred in the Sami settlements.[21] After 1650 the decision of annual inland markets were approved by the Swedish king, while the coastal markets were approved by the Danish-Norwegian king.

Stronger control by state authorities gradually removed the autonomous structures of Sami society, and the neighbouring states in the north divided the Sami areas between them. A tighter judicial control was established, and several new churches were built. The original Sami settlements were often not taken into consideration during the stronger grip of jurisdiction. The Sami inland settlements gradually changed from a traditional egalitarian village structure to household units.[22] The coastal Samis were living in small, steadfast settlements in fiords. While inland Sami settlements primarily lived from reindeer herding, the coastal Samis lived from fishing and small holdings. These two groups developed different trade profiles. While the inland Samis mostly paid their taxes with fur, the coastal Samis paid their taxes with money and imported merchandise from abroad, for instance silver and woollen cloth.[23] Hence it is clear that they belonged to different trade networks. Particular attention was paid to the coastal Sami settlement, as the Danish-Norwegian as well as the Swedish crown wanted to gain the right of taxation. This fight among the Scandinavia kings in order to gain supremacy over the territories in the north, had, among other, a focus on ethnic conditions. There was a constant pressure of economic character on the population during the period of the witchcraft trials, particularly related to questions of taxation.

Political Conditions

From the late fourteenth century, Norway and Denmark were joined in a union.[24] The two countries had their king in common, but otherwise their

---

[20] The merchants were in Scandinavia called *bikarler*. The Sami bailiffs were in Norwegian called *lappefogder*. Ref. Hansen and Olsen, *Samenes historie fram til 1750*, 160, 162–65, 243, 245.

[21] Institutionalized markets overtook the role of a connecting link to international trade. Ref. Hansen and Olsen, *Samenes historie fram til 1750*, 247.

[22] A traditional settlement with a village structure was called a *siida*. Ref. Hansen and Olsen, *Samenes historie fram til 1750*, 66, 93.

[23] Hansen and Olsen, *Samenes historie fram til 1750*, 242.

[24] Denmark-Norway is the historiographical name for the entity consisting of the kingdoms of Denmark and Norway, including the originally Norwegian dependencies of

political and legal administrations were kept apart. This was changed in 1536, after a civil war, when the Danish Prince Christian, heir to the throne, fought against the Hanseatic, the principal nobles of Denmark and much of the Danish peasantry.[25] This war had discredited the noblemen and prelates of the Norwegian council, who supported the losing cause. From now on, all political power was vested in the king's person and in a council without Norwegian representation. In the same way as Jytland, Sjælland and Fyn, Norway was now a province of the Danish kingdom. In 1660 absolutism was introduced. The union between Denmark and Norway lasted until 1814. Due to this union the king's council ruling in Norway after 1536 consisted mostly of Danish noblemen. The district governors were noblemen appointed by the king, also these Danish. The local bailiffs were recruited from Denmark, having often started their careers as servants in the households of the governors.[26] These bailiffs were responsible for the administration of local affairs, while their superiors frequently went away to their manors in Denmark. At this time, the two northernmost districts in Norway were Finnmark and Nordland.[27] Also in Finnmark the situation was that most of the officials, the men with authority in the regional centres and fishing villages, came from Denmark. At the top of the hierarchy in Finnmark was the Royal Commander of Vardøhus Castle. He was titled district governor until 1660, after which his title was regional governor.[28]

Most important in seventeenth-century Finnmark was the king's man residing at Vardøhus Castle. His jobs were multiple, controlling the border

---

Iceland, Greenland and the Faroe islands. Following the strife surrounding the break-up of the Kalmar Union, the two kingdoms entered into a personal union in 1536, which lasted until 1814.

[25] This war, called the Count's Feud, in Danish *Grevens fejde* lasted from 1534 until 1536. Norway lost its independent status, it should be subordinated Denmark, *som et ledemod af Danmarks rige*. It brought about the Reformation in Denmark. The feud takes its name from Count Christopher of Oldenburg, who unsuccessfully led the forces of Lübeck, the principal nobles of Denmark and much of the Danish peasantry against Prince Christian, the Lutheran heir to the thrown, son of the deceased King Fredrick I (reigned 1523–33). Christian's forces, supported by the naval power of Sweden, destroyed a Hanseatic fleet and thus ende Lübeck's power in the Baltic.

[26] The bailiffs were in Norwegian called *fogder*. Ref. Næss, H. E., 'Norway: The Criminological Context', in Ankarloo and Henningsen, *Early Modern European Witchcraft*, 367.

[27] In Norwegian seventeenth-century documents called *Nordlandene og Finmarken*. The district which today is Troms county, did not exist in the seventeenth century.

[28] In Norwegian respectively called *lensherre* and *amtmann*, due to a change of official terms for the district from *len* to *amt*. Ref. Willumsen, L. H., *Steilneset. Memorial to the Victims of the Finnmark Witchcraft Trials*, 4.

areas in the north, collecting taxes from the population, and customs from ships sailing east-bound north of Finnmark, in addition to operating the judiciary system, to mention some activities. Copenhagen was far away, it took several weeks to reach there by ship. Thus he could not rely on advice from Copenhagen, but had to take decisions on his own. The climate in Finnmark was harsh, and housing facilities at Vardøhus Castle was in such a bad condition that the governors at the end of the century refused to stay there, and moved to Vadsø.[29] The bailiffs in Finnmark mostly came from the south, whereas the deputy bailiffs often came from the local area, as did the bailiffs placed among the Samis, who knew the Sami language. Hence the appointed officials in Finnmark, due to geographical conditions, had to act with self-reliance and cope with challenging tasks with regard to the ethnic situation and unsettled borders, the collecting of taxes, the Bergen trade, the questions related to international trade and the sea route north of Finnmark to the east. The political situation was highly marked by the competition between the neighbouring countries as for the right to demand taxes from the Samis as well as the regulation of trade on an international basis. These tensions led to the Kalmar War between Sweden and Denmark-Norway, which lasted from 1611 until 1613, where Denmark-Norway was the winning part. After the Kalmar War, the coastal Samis living in Finnmark were decided to be citizens of Denmark-Norway.[30]

Judicial Conditions

The Nordic countries had written codes of law in the vernacular dating from the Middle Ages.[31] From the end of the Middle Ages until the mid-1660s the Norwegian system of justice was tripartite; firstly the lower courts, which were local courts; secondly the intermediary courts, and thirdly the High Court of Justice.[32] The lowest level of the judiciary,

---

[29] Niemi, *Vadsøs historie*, 86.

[30] Hansen and Olsen, *Samenes historie fram til 1750*, 267.

[31] Österberg, E. and Sandmo, E., 'Introduction', in E. Österberg and S. Sogner (eds.), *People Meet the Law. Control and conflict-handling in the courts. The Nordic countries in the post-Reformation and pre-industrial period* (Oslo, 2000), 12.

[32] The local courts are in Norwegian called called *lokal rett* or *bygdeting*. The intermediary court is called *lagting*. The High Court of Justice was called *Herredagen* or *Kongens Retterting*, from 1660 *Høyesterett*. Ref. Tamm, D., Johansen, J. C. V., Næss, H. E., 'The Law and the Judicial System', in Österberg and Sogner, *People Meet the Law*, 27–56, at p. 44.

the local courts, was the first instance court and decided on verdict and sentence in almost all criminal cases. However, the competence of this court could be variable.[33] The intermediary court became from 1590 the Court of Appeal for the local courts.[34] The Court of Appeal was supposed to hear second instance cases. However, there are several examples from Finnmark that this court also acted as first instance court.[35] From the introduction of absolutism in 1660 until 1797 there were four instances in the countryside and five in most towns.[36] In 1797 the system again became tripartite.

Even if Norway was in union with Denmark during the seventeenth century, Norwegian laws continued to be enforced throughout the period of union. Still, judicial officials in Finnmark were often educated in Copenhagen and might be influenced by Danish laws.[37] Governmental officials in Norway consisted after 1536 mostly of Danish noblemen. Hence the legal apparatus in seventeenth-century Finnmark was very much influenced by Danes, even if bailiffs and magistrates as time went by became integrated with the Norwegians.[38] The local court held sessions all along the coast of Finnmark. It happened that the district governor himself took part in the local court sessions, but usually the bailiff appeared there as the representative of the district governor and the crown.[39] In local courts, there was a jury of trustworthy, locally elected men, deciding on verdict. The Court of Appeal held sessions in Finnmark every third year. Then the Court of Appeal Judge, who resided in Nordland, came travelling north and held court sessions at all local court places along the coast, from east to west.[40] This practice clearly caused delay for cases brought to this court from the local courts.

---

[33] Næss, *Trolldomsprosessene i Norge*, 281.

[34] From 1607 the *lagting* became the Court of Appeal for both the district court and the council's court, called *byrådets domstol*. Ref. Tamm, Johansen, Næss, 'The Law and the Judicial System', 45.

[35] Willumsen, L. H., *Witchcraft Trials in Finnmark, Northern Norway* (Bergen, 2010), 12.

[36] The town court (*byting*) was established in 1662, and the Norwegian Court of Appeal in Christiania in 1666. Ref. Tamm, Johansen, Næss, 'The Law and the Judicial System', 45.

[37] See P. J. Jørgensen's *Dansk strafferet fra Reformationen til Danske Lov* (København, 2007); Andersen, B., '*Danske Lov' 1683* (København, 2003).

[38] Næss, H. E. (ed.), *For rett og rettferdighet i 400 år. Sorenskriverne i Norge 1591–1991*, 23–43 (Oslo, 1991), 11.

[39] Næss, *Trolldomsprosessene i Norge*, 150.

[40] In Norwegian called *lagmann*.

The local courts had appointed magistrates from 1591 onwards.[41] The original meaning of the word is 'sworn scribe'. He was first a professional scribe taking down court records, then after legal reforms in 1634 he was granted added responsibility, since he was now to judge together with the jury. In a new act of 1687, he replaced the jury altogether in minor cases.[42] Until 1660 the magistrate was appointed by the district governor, after the introduction of absolutism in 1660 by the king.[43] The chief magistrate was the scribe in Finnmark district.[44] From 1681 until 1687 the Bergen magistrate was given the civil administration of the district by the crown, and in fact took over the function as regional governor in Finnmark for a few years.[45] So in Finnmark the main judicial officers were the district governor, the magistrate, the bailiff and the Court of Appeal Judge.[46] When it came to the functioning of the courts in Finnmark, the geographical distance from central places further south should be paid attention to. Particularly in witchcraft trials this made itself strongly felt, as it might cause arbitrary judicial practice. The local courts could ignore existing legal procedure and laws and take rapid decisions on their own.[47]

The thirteenth-century national law of Norway stated that *maleficium* was a capital offence.[48] According to Hans Eyvind Næss, this statute did not seem to have been in use much until after the Reformation: 'As far as we know some time went by until death penalty in cases of witchcraft was generally accepted'.[49] The attitude to witchcraft as *crimen exceptum* was stated already in 1521–22.[50] Within contemporary jurisdiction, when there was a rumour that anybody had committed a serious crime, such as

---

[41] In Norwegian called *sorenskrivere*. Ref. Næss, 'Norway: The Criminological Context', 367.

[42] Willumsen, *Witchcraft Trials in Finnmark, Northern Norway*, 11.

[43] Willumsen, *Witchcraft Trials in Finnmark, Northern Norway*, 8.

[44] Næss, H. E., 'Fra tingskriver til dommer. Tiden 1591–1797', in Næss, *For rett og rettferdighet i 400 år. Sorenskriverne i Norge 1591–1991*, 45.

[45] Niemi, *Vadsøs historie*, 255.

[46] Sunde, *Speculum legale*, 170–172, 218–221; Næss, *For rett og rettferdighet i 400 år*, 23–43; Falkanger, A. T., *Lagmann og lagting i Hålogaland gjennom 1000 år* (Oslo, 2007), 77–94.

[47] Sörlin, P., *'Wicked Arts'*, 50; Monter, 'Scandinavian Witchcraft in Anglo-American Perspective', in Ankarloo and Henningsen, *Early Modern European Witchcraft*, 428; Johansen, J. Chr. V, *Da Djævelen var ude* (Odense, 1991), 164, footnote 5.

[48] This law is in Norwegian called *Landsloven*.

[49] Næss, 'Norway: The Criminological Context', 368.

[50] Cristian II's Clerical Law, in Danish Christian IIs Gejstlige Lov. Ref. Willumsen, *Trollkvinne i nord*, 56.

murder, the rumour was considered equal to an accusation. Witchcraft was considered to be such a serious crime.

The execution of witches started earlier in Denmark than in Norway; there were Danish cases already in the 1530s, and these continued also during the following decades. In these cases, however, the king and his council had tried to intervene in the procedures adopted, enacting that denunciations by witches should not be accepted as proof in any trial. In addition, new statutes said the use of torture should not be allowed until sentence was passed. These statutes date from 1547, 1558, and 1576.[51] Further, a harsher attitude towards witchcraft is clearly seen in legislation throughout the seventeenth century.[52] The demonological notions are clearest seen in the witchcraft decree of 1617, repeated in recess of 1643 and the Danish Law of 1683.[53]

The sterner practice on the European Continent regarding procedures in witchcraft cases seems to have influenced mid-sixteenth century Denmark and Norway. The judiciary's approach to witchcraft became more intransigent just before the turn of the century. In 1584 the king in Copenhagen responded to a letter sent by the Stavanger bishop. In this letter the bishop described the consultation of wise men and women, common in Norway, as a deadly sin against God.[54] White magic was also made a capital offence in the diocese of Stavanger.[55] By statutes of 1593 and 1594 this local criminal law was extended all over Norway.[56] These statutes stated that all those who were seeking or using ungodly sorcery should be sentenced to death without mercy.[57]

In 1604, the next code of laws was published, Christian IV's Norwegian Code of Laws, which again placed sorcery together with serious crimes. This code stated that such persons should not be forgiven, whether they

---

[51] Johansen, *Da Djævelen var ude*, ch. 13; Willumsen, *Trollkvinne i nord*, 56.

[52] Recesses of 1547 and 1558, statutes of 1593 and 1594, the law of 1604, the decree of 1617, recess of 1643, the Danish Law of 1683. Ref. Sunde, *Speculum legale*, 183–96; Jørgensen, *Dansk strafferet*, 390–411; Andersen, 'Danske Lov'.

[53] Willumsen, *Trollkvinne* (1994), 57; Alm, *Statens rolle*, 114, 117; Kallestrup, *Trolddoms-forfølgelser*, 73.

[54] Stavanger is located on the south-western coast of Norway. Ref. Næss, 'Norway: The Criminological Context', 368.

[55] This happened after a case was brought before the court which involved a district judge's consultation of wise men and women to cure his wife.

[56] Næss, *Trolldomsprosessene i Norge*, 78–80.

[57] In Danish, those who *befindis enten at søge og bruge eller at gjøre eller lade gjøre saadan uchristelig Trolddoms Handel, straffe paa Livet uden al Naade*. Ref. Willumsen, *Trollkvinne i nord*, 57.

were killed by the king's official or others they have committed this crime against.[58] Paying special attention to the northern districts of Norway, a letter sent to the district governor of Vardøhus in 1609 stated that Sami and Finnish people, who by nature were inclined to sorcery, should be sentenced to death without mercy.[59] Then there was the important decree of 1617, in which the 'right' witches were defined as those who had attached themselves to the Devil or who consorted with him. A clear demonological definition had found its way into the letters of the law.[60] The punishment for white magic and healing was exile from 1617 on.[61] The 1617 decree obviously had an impact on witchcraft persecutions in Norway.

William E. Monter describes the legal system in Scandinavia as a whole as characterized by accusatorial procedure. However, it is important to bear in mind that this was not the case for Finnmark.[62] The witchcraft trials there were partly conducted along the lines of inquisitorial trials, trials in which the judge was the one introducing the case and also the one who searched for proofs.[63] In fact, all the panics in Finnmark consisted of denunciation trials—where the case was started without accusations and without complaints.[64] For most of the period of the witch-hunt in Finnmark, the first and second instance court decided on verdict and sentence. It was not until 1686 that it was decided that death sentences passed in witchcraft trials should be submitted the king before execution.[65]

Jørn Øyrehagen Sunde says that there was a transition from a legal order to a legal system at the end of the fourteenth century, a development of the legal field governed by the state through borrowings from the rest of Western Europe. The legal order, in Europe and Norway, had had as its aim attractive and peaceful ways of solving conflicts as an alternative to violence. However, the state in the name of the king still had to handle crime, and the legal order established in the Middle Ages turned

---

[58] In Norwegian *slige folch skal ingen bod forgiffuis, huad heller de dræbis aff konnungens ombudsmand, eller anden de haffue brut imod.* Ref. Hallager, F. and Brandt, F., (eds.), *Kong Christian den fjerdes Norske Lovbog af 1604* (Christiania, 1855).

[59] This letter was also sent to the district governor in Nordland. Ref. Willumsen, *The Witchcraft Trials in Finnmark, Northern Norway*, 10; Willumsen, *Trollkvinne i nord*, 56.

[60] Willumsen, *The Witchcraft Trials in Finnmark*, 14.

[61] Næss, *Trolldomsprosessene i Norge*, 43.

[62] Monter, 'Scandinavian Witchcraft in Anglo-American Perspective', in Ankarloo and Henningsen, *Early Modern European Witchcraft*, 428.

[63] Knut Robberstad, *Rettssoga*, I (Oslo, 1976), 78.

[64] Robberstad, *Rettssoga* I, 78.

[65] Næss, *Trolldomsprosessene i Norge*, 281, 283.

out not to be adapted to this task.[66] The aim in Norway was to establish a legal system consisting of three instances: local, intermediate and central courts. What connected the three instances was the possibility of sending an appeal from an inferior to a superior court.[67] During this transition, magic became legally relevant, which was a pre-condition for the sixteenth- and seventeenth-century witchcraft persecution.[68] Use of circumstantial evidence and torture became common in witchcraft trials. The water ordeal was frequently used during the witchcraft trials in Finnmark.[69] So was torture. These means of pressure led to confessions and denunciations and escalation of trials. Sunde underlines that legal practice in seventeenth-century Finnmark should be considered within a continental context.

Clerical Conditions

Seventeenth-century Finnmark was a post-Reformation area: in Norway the Reformation took place in 1537, one year after Denmark. The old Norwegian Catholic clergy were replaced by Lutheran ministers, many of them of Danish origin. Most of these had studied theology in Copenhagen, and some in Wittenberg or at other German universities.[70] Rolf Schulte points to the connection between Germany and Denmark, as the dissemination of knowledge not only went in the direction to Denmark, but also in opposite direction, from Copenhagen to Schleswig-Holstein, wherein Danish influence occurred during the next generation.[71] Particularly the high authority within Danish theology, Niels Hemmingsen, attracted students from Schleswig-Holstein to study in Copenhagen under his catheter.

Hemmingsen's theses on witches appeared in Danish and Latin in 1575–76, and ten years later in German. According to Hemmingsen's teaching, the witches were real and they could cause rain and storm, and have a negative influence on male potency. He saw these evildoings as a result

---

[66] Sunde, *Speculum legale*, 183.
[67] Sunde, *Speculum legale*, 197.
[68] Sunde, *Speculum legale*, 183–84.
[69] One-third of those executed during the Finnmark witchcraft trials, were subjected to the water ordeal. Ref. Willumsen, *Steilneset. Memorial to the Victims*, 6. The water ordeal was prohibited in Denmark-Norway in the 1660s. This ordeal was for the first time rejected in Finnmark in 1653, by the Court Appeal Judge, cf. Sunde, *Speculum legale*, 188.
[70] Næss, 'Norway: The Criminological Context', 367.
[71] Schulte, *Hexenverfolgung in Schleswig-Holstein*, 22.

of a Devil's pact; a witch could not develop her own magical force, but received this from the Devil and was the Devil's servant. A person could not be a child of both God and the Devil.[72] Further, he believed that Satan could perform his deeds on earth through witches, and that women due to their lesser ability to believe in God, were easily tempted by the Devil. At the centre of his doctrine was the understanding of an individual pact. Thus there is no doubt that Hemmingsen saw the relation between the witch and the Devil as the core of the witch's power to do evil, or that his doctrine was founded on demonological grounds. However, he disbelieved some demonological features, thus following Luther. Hemmingsen denied the witches' Sabbath as well as the witches' ability to fly. In his interpretation there was no hidden army of the Devil's accomplices on earth. Hemmingsen was in favour of stronger persecution of witches. He claimed death sentence for all witches and the reason was given by the citation from the Old Testament—a witch should not be allowed to live.[73] He was appointed professor in 1553, but forced by the king to leave his position in 1579. Hemmingsen is frequently mentioned with a linking to the first Scottish witchcraft trials, because he had conversations with King James VI in Copenhagen in 1589. Opinions differ whether or not he managed to influence the king.[74] Even if Hemmingsen was dismissed from his professorship, his treatise on witches was influential and was used as standard lecture for students of theology for a long time. His follower at the University of Copenhagen, Jesper Brochmand, published a treatise on witchcraft in 1639, wherein he argued in favour of witches' meetings. However, this view had difficulties gaining acceptance because of his predecessor's strong position.

---

[72] Kallestrup, *I Pagt med Djævelen*, 85.

[73] Schulte, *Hexenverfolgung in Schleswig-Holstein*, 23.

[74] King James was in Copenhagen to bring home his bride. Ref. Willumsen, *Trollkvinne i nord*, (1994), 60; Maxwell-Stuart argues that Niels Hemmingsen, the leading contemporary Danish theologian—who, at the time of the Scottish king's visit, had been suspended from his job at the university and had withdrawn to Roskilde—did not believe in some of the main demonological points (such as the witches' ability to fly), and that the Scottish king did not bring demonological ideas back from Denmark. Ref. Maxwell-Stuart, P. G., 'The fear of the king is death: James VI and the witches of East Lothian', in W. G. Naphy and P. Roberts (eds.), *Fear in early modern society* (Manchester, 1997), 212–13; Goodare, 'Scottish Witchcraft in its European Context', 40; Goodate, J., 'Witchcraft in Scotland', in B. P. Levack (ed.), *The Oxford Handbook of Witchcraft in Early Modern Europe and Colonial America* (Oxford, 2013), 300–317, at pp. 304–305; Wormald, J., 'The Witches, the Devil and the King', in T. Brotherstone and D. Ditchburn (eds.), *Freedom and Authority: Scotland c. 1050–c. 1650* (East Linton, 2000), 165–180, at pp. 177–80.

The learned conception of witchcraft in seventeenth-century Denmark differed from ordinary people's view. The theologians did not distinguish between explicit and implicit Devil's pact; all persons practising witchcraft and magic were in pact with the Devil implicitly. The populace did not understand that white magic, or benevolent magic, had to do with a Devil alliance. However, in Denmark the peasants were the ones who had to report witchcraft suspects to the courts. Due to their understanding of witchcraft, they did not report practitioners of white magic. This was the reason why the witchcraft trials in Denmark did not grow to even larger proportions than in fact happened.[75]

In Denmark-Norway there was a centralised effort to standardize religious belief.[76] The consolidation of Lutheranism in the realm may be seen by formulations in post-Reformation bibles and religious scriptures promoted for use in churches. The first editions of post-Reformation Bibles may indicate certain attitudes to witchcraft and show that the state had a firm hand with the preaching of the church on this topic.[77] Hans P. Resen's edition of 1607 and Christian IV's Bible of 1633 were the first post Reformation Bibles used in the kingdom of Denmark-Norway. They do not show any significant changes from the older bibles in the formulations of Leviticus, chapter 20:27 or Deuteronomy, chapter 18:10–11, which are the places most important for views on witches.[78] The choice of correct doctrines from outstanding Danish theologians was of importance when ordinances were taken into official use. These ordinances played an important role for church preaching throughout the kingdom. Even if Finnmark was at the absolute periphery of Denmark-Norway, religious literature written by leading Danish theologians was in use in the churches there, for instance Danish sermon books by Niels Hemmingsen, Jesper Brochmand and Poul Andersen Medelby.[79] The same is true of psalm books by the Danes Hans Tommesen and Thomas Kingo. There is no doubt that religious literature from Denmark found its way to the far north. This means that through the church the common people in Finnmark learned about personal responsibility as the basis for a godly pact and the same as the basis for a pact

---

[75] Kallestrup, *I Pagt med Djævelen*, 86.
[76] Kallestrup, L. N., *Trolddomsforfølgelser og trolddomstro: En komparasjon af det post-tridentine Italien og det luthersk protestantiske Danmark i det 16. og 17. århundrede* (Aalborg University, Ph. D. thesis, 2007), 293.
[77] Grell, O. P., (ed.), *The Scandinavian Reformation* (Cambridge, 1995), 114–43, 129.
[78] *Biblia* (København, 1606), edn. by Hans P. Resen; *Biblia* (København, 1633).
[79] Willumsen, *Trollkvinne i nord* (1994), 60.

with the Devil. In addition, the image of the Devil as a frightening as well
as mighty person was conveyed.

Norwegian Witchcraft Trials

This section will deal with witchcraft trials in Norway as a whole. For the
Finnmark witchcraft trials in particular, a survey of research literature will
be given in the next chapter. For the whole of Norway, a source edition
worth mentioning is Norwegian Folklore Archives' collection of witchcraft
trials, which was digitized and published on-line in 2009.[80] This database
contains 984 cases, which includes all known witchcraft cases, including
slander cases, as well as a few cases related to scolding. Looking at the
different regions of Norway, substantial research has been carried out,
characterized by great variety as for approach and geographical distribution. I will start from the south-eastern part of Norway going towards the
west and north: Gunnar Knutsen has published a book on witchcraft trials in Østfold, the region close to Oslo, in 1998. The witchcraft trials in
Agder, on the south coast of Norway, have been studied by Terje Sødal.
A few witchcraft panics took place there, but they did not have the same
severity as the Finnmark panics. Rogaland, on the south-eastern coast, is
an area Hans Eyvind Næss has paid particular attention to in his doctoral
thesis about Norwegian witchcraft trials from 1982, and in his updated
version of the same. Ragnhild Botheim has performed a study of the cases
in Bergenhus district during the period 1566–1700. From the Bergen area is
also Nils Gilje's book about the famous trial of Anne Absalon Pedersdatter,
the wife of the Castle Priest at Bergenhus, a man who had studied in Wittenberg under Philip Melancton. Gilje has also written on demonizing of
popular magic. For the districts north of Bergen along the coast, Sogn and
Fjordane, Møre and Romsdal and Trøndelag, the area around Trondheim,
not much research has been done. From the information we have so far,
some witchcraft trials occurred, but the cases were lenient with regard
to sentence. Malefice seems to characterize these trials. The Trøndelag
cases started rather early, from 1571 till 1720.[81] For the district of Nordland,

---

[80] In Norwegian *Norsk folkeminnelags arkiv*.
[81] From Sogn and Fjordane 53 persons were accused, and 11 received death sentences.
From Møre and Romsdal 44 persons were accused of witchcraft, and 13 received death sentences. From the southern part of Trøndelag 45 were accused, and 12 death sentences were
passed. For North Trøndelag 21 persons were accused, and two received death sentences.
Ref. Hagen, *Dei europeiske trolldomsprosessane*, 92.

which was the neighboring district to Finnmark, the execution rate was high.[82] Torstein Stave has in his Master's thesis from 2012, dealing in particular with Vardøhus, included discussions of other parts of Norway.[83]

General factors related to witchcraft in Norway has been dealt with in Rune Blix Hagen's book *Hekser. Fra forfølgelse til fortryllelse*. The same is the case with Ellen Alm's and Mink Chan's Master's theses. Men in witchcraft trials are studied in Lars Petter Martinsen's and Birger Andreas Marthinsen's Master's theses, the latter also involving Iceland. By contribution by Hans Eyvind Næss and Gunnar Knutsen we see attempts to make a survey of the witch-hunt in Norway. Knutsen also reflects on the end of the hunt in Scandinavia. Rune Blix Hagen's book *Dei europeiske hekseprosessane* gives a historiographic survey of research on witchcraft trials in Europe, including a chapter on Norway. A contribution to witchcraft research in the Nordic countries, focusing on the Middle Ages, is Stephen A. Mitchell, *Witchcraft and magic in the Nordic Middle Ages*.[84]

---

[82] In Nordland, 21 persons were accused of witchcraft, and 16 of these received death sentences. Ref. Hagen, *Dei europeiske trolldomsprosessane*, 92.

[83] Willumsen, L. H., 'The Historiography of Witchcraft Research in Norway 1994–2011'. Ref. www.livhelenewillumsen.no; Næss, *Trolldomsprosessene i Norge på 1500–1600-tallet*; Næss, H. E., *Med bål og brann. Trolldomsprosessene i Norge* (Oslo, 2005). With focus on Agder, a book and articles have been written by Terje Sødal. Mink Chan has written on witchcraft trials in Hordaland, the region round Bergen. Also Botheim, *Trolldomsprosessene i Bergenhus len*, deals with Hordaland. Nils Gilje has written *Heksen og humanisten: Anne Pedersdatter og Absalon Pederssøn Beyer: en historie om magi og trolldom i Bergen på 1500-tallet*, [The witch and the humanist: Anne Pedersdatter and Absalon Pederssøn Beyer: a story about magic and witchcraft in sixteenth-century Bergen] in addition to 'Djevelen står alltid bak: Demonisering av folkelig magi på slutten av 1500–tallet' [The Devil is always behind: Demonizing of traditional magic at the end of the sixteenth century], in B. Askeland and J. F. Bernt (eds.), *Erkjennelse og engasjement* (Bergen, 2001), 93–107; Torstein Stave has in his Master's thesis from University of Tromsø (2012), *Da Lucifer kom til Vardøhus*, included discussions on demonological trials in Bergenhus, Rogaland, Agder, and Østlandet, the south-eastern part of Norway.

[84] Hagen, R. B., *Hekser* [Witches. From persecution to enchantment] (Oslo, 2003); Alm, E., *Statens rolle i trolldomsprosessene i Danmark og Norge på 1500-og 1600-tallet. En komparativ studie* [The role of the state during the witchcraft trials in Denmark and Norway in the sixteenth and seventeenth centuries. A comparative study] (Master's thesis, University of Tromsø, 2000); Chan, J. M., *Norske trolldomskonflikter i opplysningstiden* [Norwegian witchcraft conflicts in the age of enlightenment] (Master's thesis, University of Oslo, 2009). Martinsen, L. P., *Anklagede menn i trolldomsprosessene i Norge* [Accused men in Norwegian witchcraft trials] (Master's thesis, University of Oslo 2008); Marthinsen, B. A., *Trollmenn & galdramenn* [Sorcerers and men casting spells] (University of Trondheim, 2010). Næss has an article, 'Norway: the criminological context' in Ankarloo and Henningsen, *Early Modern European Witchcraft. Centres and Peripheries*, from 1993. Knutsen has an article, 'Norwegian witchcraft trials: a reassessment' in *Continuity and Change*, 2003; and same author, 'The End of the Witch Hunts in Scandinavia' in *Arv* (2006). Margit Løyland has written an article about witchcraft during the period of pietism in *Heimen* (2010). The

The main sources for the Norwegian witchcraft trials are court records
from local courts and Court of Appeal, and district accounts. The source
material is very unevenly preserved in different districts of Norway as for
completeness. The two districts with the best preserved material are Rogaland, round the town Stavanger, and Finnmark district in the north. The
trial period in Norway lasted mainly from around 1560s till around 1730
with few cases after 1700, the last one the trial against Johanne Nielsdatter
in Kvæfjord in 1695. In all districts of Norway persons were tried for witchcraft or for being connivances to witches. The core period of Norwegian
witchcraft trials was 1620–65. The number of accused persons was around
750–770, and out of these, around 310 persons were sentenced to death.[85]
As for gender, 80% of the accused were women, thus Norway is close to
the European mainstream. Of the around 300 persons sentenced to death,
250 were women.[86] In Norway, the persons who received death sentences
and were executed, were burned alive.

With regard to frequency, there are peaks and calmer periods during
the period of witchcraft trials in Norway, in the same way as in most other
European countries. We see an increase in witchcraft trials around 1620,
and even stronger in the early 1660s. There was a downward trend in the
number of witchcraft trials towards the end of the seventeenth century,
and very few cases after 1700.[87] So in an overall perspective the witchcraft
trials in Norway seem to fit in well with most countries in Europe.

Most witchcraft trials in Norway were centred on *maleficium*. There
were some demonic witchcraft trials in Bergen, Rogaland, Agder and Østlandet, the district around Oslo. However, these trials did not amount to
the numbers we find in the Finnmark witchcraft trials, nor did they reach
the same execution rate as we see in Finnmark.[88] The most frequent accu-

folklorist Ørnulf Hodne has published *Trolldom i Norge. Hekser og trollmenn i folketro og
lokaltradisjon* [Sorcery in Norway. Witches and sorcerers in folk belief and local tradition]
(Oslo, 2008). Mitchell's book was published in 2011.

[85] Næss has 860 accused persons, Hagen has 768 accused persons. Ref. Næss, *Trolldomsprosessene i Norge*, 16–17; Hagen, *Dei europeiske trolldomsprosessane*, 92.

[86] Hagen, *Dei europeiske trolldomsprosessane*, 92; Hagen, R. B., 'Witchcraft Criminality
and Witchcraft Research in the Nordic Countries', in B. P. Levack, *The Oxford Handbook of
Witchcraft*, 375–392, at p. 385.

[87] Næss, *Trolldomsprosessene i Norge*, 16; Ylikangas, H., Johansen, J. C. V., Johansson, K.,
Næss, H. E., 'Family, State and Patterns of Criminality', in Österberg and Sogner, *People
meet the law*, 90.

[88] Ref. Næss, *Trolldomsprosessene i Norge*, 222, 225; Sødal, T., 'Trolldomsprosessene på
Agder', *Heimen* 1 (2010), 17–23; Botheim, R., *Trolldomsprosessane i Bergenhus len 1566–1700*
(Master's thesis, University of Bergen, 1999), 91–94; Stave, *Da Lucifer kom til Vardøhus*, 94.

sation of witchcraft, in Norway as well as Denmark, was evildoing with sickness or death as a result. This could affect humans and animals, ships could be destroyed, crop could be destroyed, fire could be the result, bad weather could be the result, as could loss of luck. In addition, love magic and divination took place.[89] The type of evildoing practised was related to the local conditions. According to Næss, in Norwegian witchcraft trials except Finnmark, demonic pact trials amounted to 10%, *maleficium* and benevolent magic to around 45% each. There were peaks in malefice-accusations in the early 1640s and the early 1660s. There were peaks in the benevolent magic-accusations in the early 1620s and the early 1660s. More recent studies confirm that diabolism seems to have played a more prominent role in Finnmark than for the part of the country south of Finnmark.[90]

About one-fourth of those brought before the court for witchcraft were imprisoned over time, for some of them up to six months, and often under bad conditions.[91] There was a connection between panics, denunciations and diabolism. The majority of these cases were found in Finnmark. To be in rumour for witchcraft was often used as accusation during witchcraft trials. The water ordeal was in very few cases used south of Finnmark.[92] Use of torture after sentence was passed, which was legal in Norway, is documented all over the country, however, most often not more than one case in each district for the districts south of Finnmark. Also here the district of Finnmark turns out to come in a special position.[93]

---

[89] Næss, *Trolldomsprosessene i Norge*, 102.

[90] Næss, *Trolldomsprosessene i Norge*, 134, 136; Willumsen, *Trollkvinne i nord* (1994), 28–44, 68–73; Willumsen, *Steilneset. Memorial to the Victims*, 6–7, 11–101; Stave, *Da Lucifer kom til Vardøhus*, 98.

[91] For Norway as a whole, only thirteen attempts to flee from imprisonment are known. Ref. Næss, H. E., *Trolldomsprosessene i Norge*, 179.

[92] There were 30 water ordeals in Finnmark. Ref. Willumsen, *Steilneset. Memorial to the Victims*, 11–101. Stave has 40 water ordeals for the whole of Norway, whereof 8 from the districts south of Finnmark. Ref. *Da Lucifer kom til Vardøhus*, 114. However, two of the water ordeals mentioned by Stave as related to Finnmark, were only threaths of water ordeal, see Willumsen, *Steilneset, Memorial to the Victims*, 30, 33; Willumsen, *Witchcraft Trials in Finnmark*, 28, 38.

[93] Næss, H. E., *Trolldomsprosessene i Norge*, 192, 199.

CHAPTER NINE

FINNMARK—WHAT FIGURES CAN TELL

Witchcraft trials occurred throughout the whole of Norway. They were mostly characterized by *maleficium*, even if occurrence of trials containing diabolism to a minor degree are documented in areas of Norway south of the district of Finnmark, as shown in the previous chapter. With regard to Finnmark, a more severe character of the trials comes to the fore. The witchcraft trials in this district are more linked up to Continental Europe and Scotland than we find for trials further south in Norway. The statistics for Finnmark presented in this chapter are based on my Ph.D. thesis, wherein details of calculation procedures are found.[1]

Earlier Research and Source Editions

The Finnmark witchcraft trials have been studied by several scholars. Perhaps the most active witchcraft research in Norway the later years is related to this district. Studies of the Finnmark trials have been performed by Kirsten Bergh, Einar Niemi, Randi Rønning Balsvik, Liv Helene Willumsen, Ole Lindhartsen, Berit Roth Niemi, Rune Blix Hagen, and Torstein Stave. Kirsten Bergh wrote an article on this topic in 1960, very much based on primary records.[2] Studies by Niemi and Rønning Balsvik have been conducted as parts of local history series.[3] Einar Niemi has a comprehensive chapter on witchcraft trials in his history book about Vadsø, *Vadsøs historie* from 1983. In her history book about Vardø, *Vardø. Grensepost og fiskevær 1850–1950*, from 1989, Randi Rønning Balsvik writes about the witchcraft trials taking place there. I have myself worked on this topic since the early 1980s, written a Master's thesis in 1984 and published several books and articles about the witch-hunt in Finnmark.[4] In

---

[1] The only statistical treatment of the material from Finnmark is Willumsen's studies *Trollkvinne i nord*, 12–51, and *Seventeenth-Century Witchcraft Trials*, 91–110.

[2] Bergh, K., 'Til ild og bål', in G. I. Willoch, (ed.), *Vardøhus festning 650 år* (Oslo, 1960), 126–44.

[3] Niemi, *Vadsøs historie*, 219–28; Balsvik, *Vardø. Grensepost og fiskevær 1850–1950*, 33–36.

[4] Willumsen, *Trollkvinne i nord i historiske kilder og skjønnlitteratur* (University of Tromsø, Master's thesis, 1984), *Trollkvinne i nord* (Tromsø, 1994), 'Witches of the High North. The Finnmark Witchcraft Trials in the Seventeenth Century', *Scandinavian Journal of History*, xxii, no. 3 (1997), 199–221, 'Witches in Scotland and Northern Norway: two case

1994 I published *Trollkvinne i nord* [Witch in the North]. The book is the first research work pointing to the strong demonological elements during the Finnmark trials as well as to the connection between Scotland and Finnmark when it comes to demonological notions. Berit Roth Niemi has similarly pointed to the international context of the trials.[5] Ole Lindhartsen has focused on the increase in witchcraft trials after installation of a new district governor.[6] The last decade, Rune Blix Hagen has written several articles about the Finnmark witchcraft trials, particularly focusing on Samis. His research has been a valuable contribution to the knowledge of ethnicity and male sorcerers in Finnmark.[7] Torstein Stave has in 2012 written a Master's thesis, focusing on demonological ideas in the Finnmark witchcraft trials.[8]

They seventeenth-century court records are written in the gothic hand. Therefore transcribed versions of the records are of help to persons who do not read the gothic hand. Until quite recently, only a very few, and none complete, source editions of the Finnmark sources have been published. The first one is Hulda Rutberg's edited version of some of the court records from Finnmark, *Häxprocesser i norska Finnmarken*.[9] This book is not a verbatim transcription, compared to the original records many linguistic changes have been made. Still, it is valuable particularly because it contains the whole case of Karen Mogensdatter from 1626, where the main part of the record otherwise has been lost.[10]

Another source book is Hans H. Lilienskiold's manuscript: *Trolldom og ugudelighet i 1600-tallets Finnmark*, edited by Rune Blix Hagen and Per

studies', in A. Kruse and P. Graves, *Images and Imaginations. Perspectives on Britain and Scandinavia* (Edinburgh, 2007), 35–66; Willumsen, L. H., 'Children accused of Witchcraft in 17th Century Finnmark', *Scandinavian Journal of History*, 38:1, 18–41; Willumsen, L. H., 'Exporting the Devil across the North Sea—John Cunningham and the Finnmark Witch-hunt', in Goodare, *Scottish Witches and Witch-Hunters*.

   [5] *Varanger Årbok* (1989).
   [6] 'Lensherrer, heksejakt og justismord i Finnmark på 1600-tallet' [District Governors, witch-hunt and judicial murder in seventeenth-century Finnmark], in G. J. Valen, K. Skavhaug, K. Schanche (eds.), *Flytting og forandring i Finnmarks fortid* (Alta, 2002).
   [7] Among them are 'Sami Shamanism: The Arctic Dimension', *Magic, Rituals, and Witches*, i, no. 2 (2006), 227–33 and 'Female Witches and Sami Sorcerers in the Witch Trials of Arctic Norway', *Arv, Nordic Yearbook of Folklore*, vol. lxii (2006), 123–42; 'Forfølgelse av samiske trollfolk i Vest-Finnmark' [The Persecution of Sami sorcerers in West Finnmark], *Heimen. Lokal og regional historie*, 1 (2010): 43–45; 'The Sami—Sorcerers in Norwegian History. Sorcery Persecutions of the Sami', *Calliidlagadus* (Kárásjohka-Karasjok, 2012); 'Lapland Witches', in Golden, *Encyclopedia*, 625–27; 'Witchcraft Criminality and Witchcraft Research in the Nordic Countries, in Levack, *Oxford Handbook of Witchcraft*, 375–392.
   [8] Stave, *Da Lucifer kom til Vardøhus*.
   [9] In the series Svenska landsmål och svenskt folkeliv (Stockholm, 1918).
   [10] Willumsen, *Witchcraft Trials in Finnmark, Northern Norway*, 10.

Einar Sparboe. Lilienskiold was Regional Governor at Vardøhus in late seventeenth century. He copied many of the sentences related to witchcraft cases in local courts in Finnmark in a hand-written document.[11] Because he copied only the sentences, not the whole records, his manuscript is abbreviated and fragmentary compared to the original court records. His manuscript consists of 89 sentences, which is two-thirds of the number of persons accused of witchcraft in Finnmark. Lilienskiold's manuscript is important especially for the period before 1620, when ordinary court records are lacking.

The court records from the local courts in Finnmark for the period 1620–33 was published in 1987.[12] This edition contains transcriptions of all criminal cases during the period in question, in addition to register of place-names and persons' names. However, there are no word explanations. The most recent and only complete source edition is edited by myself, and is titled *Trolldomsprosessene i Finnmark. Et kildeskrift.*[13] This is a source-critical edition containing verbatim transcriptions of all witchcraft trial records from local courts in Finnmark from 1620 till 1692, kept in the Archives of Finnmark District Magistrate, in addition to facsimiles of all the court records, notes, glossary with word explanations and register. An English version was published in parallel, with the title *The Witchcraft Trials in Finnmark, Northern Norway.*

As part of the Steilneset Memorial to the victims of the Finnmark witchcraft trials in Vardø, opened in 2011, there is a Memorial Hall, housing a text exhibition. I have written the exhibition texts, one text for each of the 91 victims of the Finnmark witchcraft trials. The texts are based on original sources. These individual texts are published in a book, which appears in four languages; Norwegian, English, German and Finnish.[14]

Primary Sources

The most important primary sources documenting witchcraft trials in Finnmark consist of proceedings of court records from local trials, held in the court of the Finnmark District Magistrate. The court records exist from

---

[11] Lilienskiold's original document is kept in the Royal Library, Copenhagen, Thott's collection, no. 950,2°.
[12] Sandvik and Winge, *Tingbok for Finnmark 1620–33.*
[13] Published in Bergen, 2010.
[14] In English the title is: *Steilneset. Memorial to the Victims of the Finnmark Witchcraft Trials* (Oslo, 2011).

1620 onwards, throughout the whole period of witchcraft trials in Finnmark, with the exception of a lacuna for the period 1633–1647. This lacuna is partly filled by sources preserved in a different archive, namely copies of sentences in the archives of the Regional Governor of Finnmark.[15] The court records from Finnmark are unique as witchcraft sources, because they have such detail that we can follow the trial from an accused person enters the courtroom until sentence is passed. Due to their richness and detail, these documents offer a multi-layered potential for interpretation of the witch-hunt, particularly with regard to the accused persons' confessions. They are valuable sources for historical research. With regard to seventeenth-century court records from other parts of Norway, only the district of Rogaland has records from local courts which are almost fully preserved.[16] This situation as for sources is different for the rest of the Norwegian districts.[17]

In addition to the court records, the district accounts for Finnmark are primary sources for the witchcraft trials in the area. These are particularly valuable for the period before 1620, as other primary sources are lacking. Even if the information in these accounts is limited, these fiscal documents confirm that witchcraft trials took place and show the expenses that must be covered by the state for executing sentenced persons, and the state's income in liquidating accused persons' property.[18] Court records from the Court of Appeal complement the records from local courts for those cases passed on to the Court of Appeal.[19] The Court of Appeal Judge's main obligation was to hold Court of Appeals at Steigen in Nordland, where he had his seat. In addition, he held circuit courts in Finnmark every third year. King Christian IV made an effort to reform the judicial system, and set the various courts in Norway into a system where the local court acted as the first instance court and the Court of Appeal as the second instance court.[20] According to statute of 1590 the Court of Appeal was supposed to hear only second instance cases. However, there are several examples from the witchcraft trials in Finnmark that the Court of Appeal acted as a first instance court.[21]

---

[15] SATØ, AF, no. 2543.
[16] Næss, *Trolldomsprosessene i Norge*, 26.
[17] The term 'district', in Norwegian *len*, in the 1660s was changed to 'region', in Norwegian *amt*. Today, the term *fylke* is in Norwegian used to denote a county.
[18] RA, Lensregnskaper for Vardøhus len, Rentekammeret, 1600–92.
[19] SAT, Lagtingsprotokoll for Nordland og Finnmark, 1647–83.
[20] 'Instansbrevet' from 1590, Sunde, *Speculum legale—rettsspegelen*, 197–98.
[21] For instance Karen Edisdatter, 1620, SATØ, SF 6, fos. 10v–12v.

Gender, Frequency, and Panics

The percentage of women accused of witchcraft in Finnmark is 82.2. This is very close to the Scottish percentage, which is 83.9%. Compared to the rest of Europe the percentage of women in Finnmark witch trials is within the typical European range of between 75% and 85%.[22] The women accused of witchcraft in Finnmark, apparently represented an average of ordinary women with regard to social status and income.[23] They were old and young, married or not married, with or without children, had husbands with good income and high social status or poor husbands—all are included among those accused. We know that around two-thirds were or had been married, while having children was mentioned by only 5% of the women accused. Almost one-fifth of the total accused had moved in from regions further south. As Finnmark in the seventeenth century was gradually being populated by people from the rest of Norway, many women came to Finnmark as servants and settled there. Some of the accused confessed that they had learned witchcraft charms from housewives further south in Norway, where they had been employed formerly.[24]

135 persons were accused of witchcraft in the period 1600–92.[25] The chart below shows the frequency of witchcraft trials in Finnmark. There are three distinctive peaks in the period, denoting panics in 1620–21, 1651–52 and 1662–63.

The total number of persons accused of witchcraft was 4.5% of Finnmarks's average population, which is the highest frequency in any Norwegian county and extremely high compared to other European countries. With only 0.8% of Norway's population, the Finnmark county has 17%

---

[22] Exceptions include Normandy, Russia and Iceland, with respectively 27, 32 and 8% women. Ref. Levack, *The Witch-Hunt in Early Modern Europe*, 142.

[23] Willumsen, *Trollkvinne i nord*, (1994), 71.

[24] Willumsen, *Trollkvinne i nord*, (1994), 34; Willumsen, *Steilneset. Memorial to the Victims*, 73, 74, 76, 89.

[25] Hagen lists 138 persons accused for witchcraft in Finnmark for the period 1590–1692, *Dei europeiske hekseprosessane*, 92. Hagen has included two Sami men brought to trial in Utsjokk in Sweden in the 1590s. A bailiff from Finnmark, who knew the Sami language, a *lappefogd*, took part in these trials. Since Utsjokk is outside the area of Finnmark, these trials belong to Swedish witchcraft material. In addition one person, Anders Aal, 1654, is included in Hagen's list. This man was brought before the court in Loppen in West Finnmark, charged with adultery and violence. Sorcery was mentioned by one of the witnesses as an accusation, along with several other accusations. However, sorcery was never repeated by the bailiff as an accusation, like the rest of the points of accusation against Anders Aal. The verdict and the sentence did not mention witchcraft. This is not a witchcraft trial. Anders Aal was not sentenced for witchcraft, but for adultery and violence.

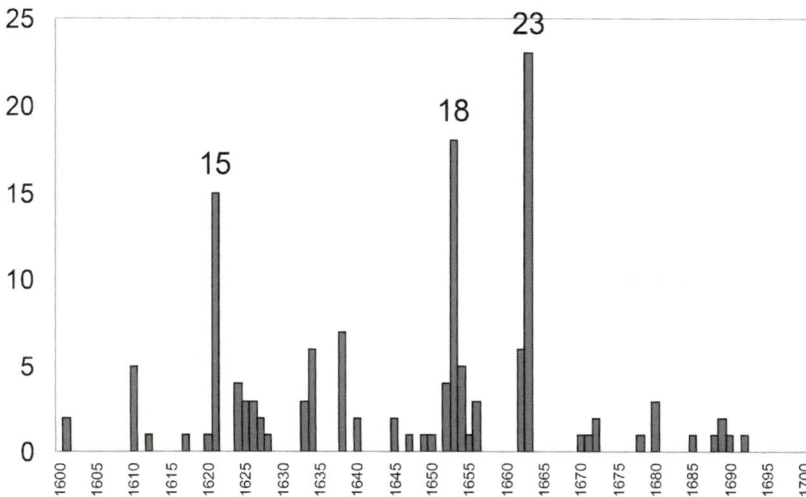

Chart 8: Witchcraft trials by year 1600–92, Finnmark.

of all Norwegian documented witchcraft trials and one-third of all death sentences in witchcraft trials.[26] Thus the witch-hunt must have had an enormous impact on the population in Finnmark.[27] When comparing the Finnmark witchcraft trials with those from Rogaland, a district with equally good coverage of court records as Finnmark, the high percentage of death sentences in Finnmark becomes conspicuous. In Finnmark 67% of the accused were executed. In Rogaland 22% of the accused were executed.[28]

A trend towards stronger persecution of witchcraft from around 1620 apparently started after the witchcraft decree of 1617. That year King Christian IV issued a decree 'About Witches and their Accomplices' that was used in both Denmark and Norway. In the Finnmark courts this decree is referred to on several occasions, the first time in 1620. In this decree, the concept of witchcraft is—for the first time in Danish-Norwegian legislation—related to a connection with the Devil. The most dangerous witches were those who were allied with the Devil. Use of charms is to be punished with banishment and 'forfeiture of real property'. The increased persecution during the 1620s might also be related to John Cunningham

---

[26] Næss, *Trolldomsprosessene i Norge*, 32.
[27] Lindhartsen, 'Lensherrer, heksejakt og justismord i Finnmark på 1600-tallet', in Valen, Skavhaug, Schanche, *Flytting og forandring i Finnmarks fortid*, 62–64.
[28] Næss, *Trolldomsprosessene i Norge*, 29, 247.

248 CHAPTER NINE

taking up the office of District Governor of Vardøhus in 1619. After Cunningham's death in 1651, Jørgen Friis took over as District Governor. Based on his frequent presence at local courts and his active participation in interrogation, Friis appears to have been a keen witch-hunter, in cooperation with the bailiff of East Finnmark, Hans Jensen Ørbech, and the depute bailiff Knud Jensen.[29] A new change at the administrative level occurred in 1660, when absolutism was introduced in Denmark-Norway. The District Governor was replaced by the Regional Governor, an installation which might possibly have contributed to triggering the panic of 1662–1663, with Christopher Orning as the leading witch-hunter. The number of witchcraft cases after 1663 decreased rapidly and there were no more panics.

To explain the concentration of trials during panic periods is in my view very important as part of the explanation of the European witch-hunt.[30] Gender and panics are strongly interrelated in Finnmark. We find that of the 111 accused females, 65 were accused in panic periods and 46 in non-panic periods. Of the 24 accused males, 2 were accused in panic periods and 22 in non-panic periods.[31] The different treatment of the genders is statistically highly significant.[32] The proportion of women accused of witchcraft was much higher in panic periods than in non-panic periods. Almost all men were accused in non-panic periods. Gender is demonstrated to be an important variable during panic years. Women cause panics to arise due to denunciations. There is an automatic and rapid accumulation of new suspects as a consequence of linked trials.[33]

The number of trials by gender and year in Finnmark is illustrated in Chart 9 below. The intensity in accusation of females throughout the witch-hunt is clearly seen to follow the panic years. The pattern of trials of men over the years is different from those of women. Most of the men were tried during the first half of the century, the majority before 1630. Men were accused of witchcraft either in single cases or in minor linked trials. Men were also tried after 1670, during the last period of the Finnmark

---

[29] Baptie, D. and Willumsen, L. H., 'From Fife to Finnmark. John Cunningham's way to the North', in *The Genealogist* (forthcoming); Willumsen, *The Witchcraft Trials in Finnmark, Northern Norway*; Willumsen, *Trollkvinne* (1994), 33.

[30] A panic in the Finnmark material is defined by me as more than seven linked trials.

[31] Willumsen, *Seventeenth-Century Witchcraft Trials*, 96.

[32] Chi-square 19.913. Ref. Willumsen, *Seventeenth-Century Witchcraft Trials*, 96.

[33] Implicit in the demonological type of witchcraft is a multiplying factor, which causes the escalation of trials during panics.

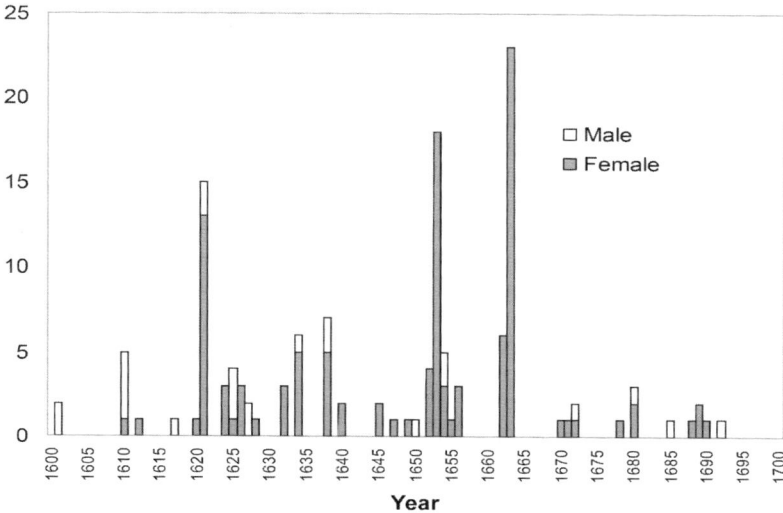

Chart 9: Number of trials by gender and year, Finnmark.

witch-hunt. The majority of women were tried between 1620 and 1663, mostly during panic years. In the largest panic, 1662–63, men were totally absent. The gender difference relating to panics is due to Devil's pact confessions and the use of torture, as will be seen later. The difference in frequency between women and men throughout the witchcraft trials corresponds with a heated climate during the five decades after 1620, when women were particularly exposed to witchcraft accusations. In addition to the obvious fact that for each accused man, five or six women were accused, it is a fact that women overall were treated differently from men. They were accused differently, they were interrogated differently, they confessed differently, and were sentenced differently from men.[34]

This observation, that women in witchcraft cases were treated differently from men, can be observed in different ways. Looking at frequency, type of trial and gender, clearly women were most frequently accused in panics, while men were accused in single trials between the panics. Also when one examines all linked trials in the material, not only the panics, the probability for a woman to be accused was much higher than that of a man.[35] So in fact women were accused differently than men; they

---

[34] Willumsen, *Trollkvinne i nord* (1994), 71–73.
[35] This correlation has been tested, and resulted in Chi-square 10.365. Ref. Willumsen, *Seventeenth-Century Witchcraft Trials*, 97.

were more involved in clusters of trials than men, be that panics or other linked trials.[36]

Type of Trial

Two types of trial were held in Finnmark in the period of the witch-hunt; local trials and Court of Appeal.[37] The Court of Appeal could act as a court of first as well as a court of second instance. The witchcraft cases by type of court and year are shown in Chart 10 below.

The majority of witchcraft suspects were tried before the local courts. Witchcraft cases were sent to the Court of Appeal particularly from the

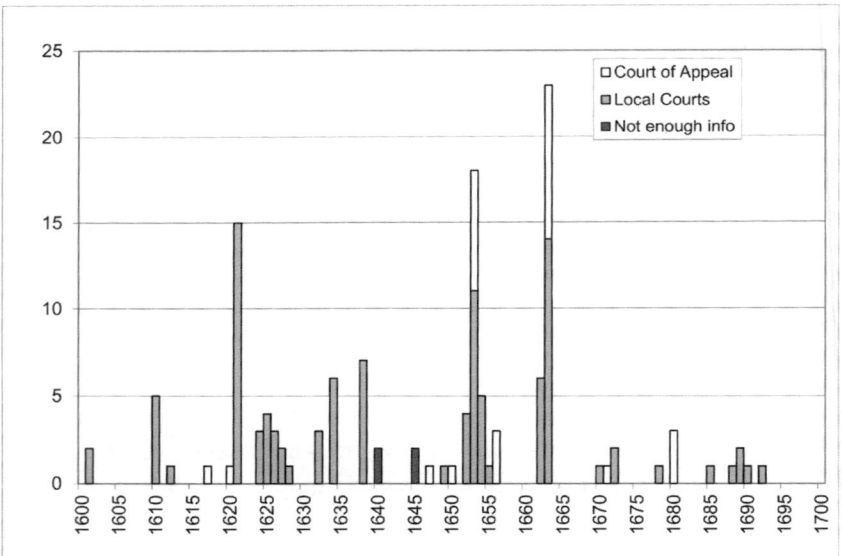

Chart 10: Witchcraft trials in Finnmark, by type of court and year.

---

[37] A variant of the local trial was the *ledingsting*. This was originally a local taxation court or administrative court. Some witchcraft trials in the 1620s were brought before this type of court: 5 cases in 1621, 2 in 1624 and 1 in 1626. The reason why witchcraft cases were brought before these courts was that the bailiff and magistrate filled several roles as officials in Finnmark.

late 1640s and the remainder of the period of witch-hunt. Only one very special case was deferred and sent to the King in Copenhagen.[38] The distance to Copenhagen is an important background when trying to understand and interpret the intensity and severity of trials before the local courts. The district governors, later the regional governors, were completely left to act on their own as far as activity in local courts was concerned. Disregard of accepted legal practice was common. For instance torture before verdict and sentence was used, although the practice was forbidden by law. It took a long time to send a message to Copenhagen by boat and more weeks before an answer could be expected in return. It would be difficult in practical terms for central authorities in Copenhagen to quell an emerging panic.

Cases sent to the Court of Appeal increased particularly in the 1650s and the 1660s, and might signal the end of the era of witchcraft panics in Finnmark. The role played by the Court of Appeal Judge for Nordlandene, Mandrup Pederssøn Schønnebøl, who held his office from 1648 until 1682, is especially important.[39] Aage Thor Falkanger maintains that Schønnebøl, because of his acquittal of a number of persons accused of witchcraft, had to face criticism.[40] The reason why many cases were sent to the Court of Appeal in 1663 was that the panic of 1662–63 included six small girls. These cases were considered too difficult for the local courts to judge. Therefore all the cases with children involved were passed on to the Court of Appeal. The possibility of using the Court of Appeal was limited due to the fact that this circuit court only assembled every third year in summer time, and the court was in session for only a few days at the court locations. If the jury knew that the Appeal Court Judge was coming to Finnmark just a few months later, difficult cases could easily be referred to him. However, if he was coming two years later, it was difficult to send on cases to the Court of Appeal.

During the Finnmark witchcraft trials, 83 women and 21 men were tried at local courts, while 24 women and 3 men were tried in the Court of Appeal. This means that 77% of the accused were tried in local courts, approximately four women for each man. The proportion in the Court of Appeal was eight women for each man.

---

[38] This was the case of Anders Poulsen, 1692.
[39] Falkanger, *Lagmann*, 148–53.
[40] He met with criticism from, among others, Regional Governor Hans H. Lilienskiold, who was in office from 1684 until 1701. Ref. Falkanger, *Lagmann*, 151.

Verdict and Sentence

As verdict and sentence are known in most witchcraft cases in Finnmark, the source material is valuable for calculations of an exact execution rate. The majority got the verdict guilty, very few were acquitted. Those who got the verdict guilty, were burned, beheaded, fined or banished. 88 persons were executed during the Finnmark witchcraft trials. Of these, the majority were burned, two were beheaded, and one person was executed by an unspecified method.[41] In addition three 3 people were killed before the end of their trial. Those killed before the trial ended were either tortured to death or murdered during custody. The number of those who lost their lives during the witch-hunt in Finnmark is 91. The result is that 67% of the accused were executed. For the rest of Norway, the percentage from district to another varied from 2% to 22%. The severity of the Finnmark trials compared to the rest of Norway is unquestionable.

Of non-capital sentences 11 people were fined, nine of them in local courts and two in the Court of Appeal. Eight cases were postponed. They all started in local courts. Usually these cases were postponed to a later session at the same court. The postponed cases were mainly from the periods 1620s and 1680s, representing a relatively early and a late stage of the witch-hunt and taking place in non-panic years. The acquittals occurred mainly during the 1662–63 panic. Afterwards there were acquittals in single cases in 1672, 1678 and 1680. This indicates that at the end of the witch-hunt, the risk of losing one's life when accused of witchcraft decreased.

The ratio of accused persons who received the sentence of execution was much higher in local trials than in the Court of Appeal. The chance of being executed was much higher when a person was brought before a local court compared with the Court of Appeal.[42] In contrast, one finds that acquittals were rare in local courts and frequent in the Court of Appeal. The chance of being acquitted in a local trial was significantly lower than in the Court of Appeal.[43] If a person in Finnmark managed to get his or her trial passed on to the Court of Appeal, the probability of acquittal increased enormously. This result also holds true for the rest of the Norwegian witchcraft trials.[44]

---

[41] Orig. *at miste liffuit*, meaning 'to lose one's life'; Goodare, 'The Finnmark Witches in European Context', in Andreassen and Willumsen, *Steilneset Memorial. Art. Architecture. History* (forthcoming).

[42] Chi-square 36.516. Ref. Willumsen, *Seventeenth-Century Witchcraft Trials*, 100.

[43] Willumsen, *Seventeenth-Century Witchcraft Trials*, 101.

[44] Næss, *Trolldomsprosessene i Norge*, 267.

The Demonological Element

There is a strong impact of demonology during the Finnmark witchcraft trials.[45] In spite of the remoteness and isolation, the strong influence of demonological elements found in witchcraft trials is similar in Finnmark and Scotland and many other European countries. The demonological element is important for the explanation of the high intensity and execution rate during the witchcraft trials in Finnmark. I make an operational distinction between explicit and implicit demonic pact confession. The term 'Implicit' is used to denote that demonic pact is implicitly understood from formulations in the court records. For the term 'Confessed Devil's pact', a marked confession of entering into a Devil's pact is given. Explicit Devil's pact confessions occur much more frequently in panic periods compared with non-panic periods.[46]

One of the features characterizing demonological trials is the multiplying effect of denunciations resulting in panics. It is therefore of importance to study how panics and demonology are related, both with regard to occurrence of demonic pact confessions in panic versus non-panic periods, the correlation between demonic pact confessions and panics,

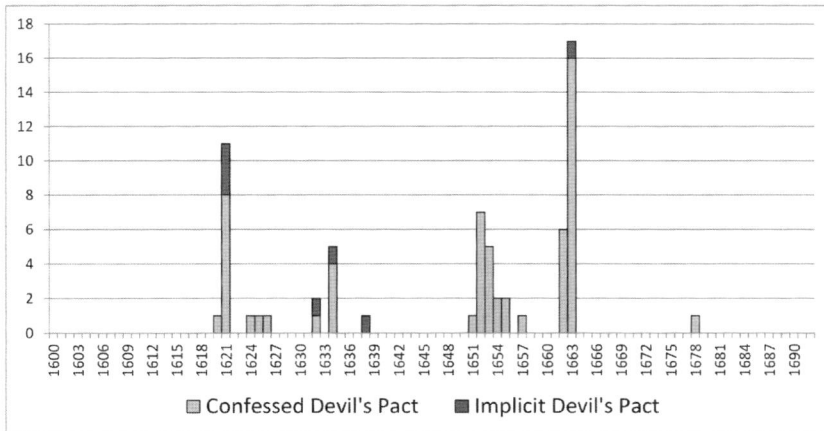

Chart 11: Devil's pact confession, Finnmark.

---

[45] Willumsen, *Trollkvinne i nord* (1994), 99.
[46] Willumsen, *Seventeenth-Century Witchcraft Trials*, 102.

and the correlation between demonic pact confessions, panics and women. The correlation between panics and demonology is statistically significant. Likewise is the correlation between panics, female and demonology significant. This demonstrates that in a panic period a demonological case was far more likely to occur than in a non-panic period and that a woman was much more likely than a man to deliver a demonological confession in a panic period than in a non-panic period. Thus my analysis supports a positive correlation between these factors.[47] It is also interesting to note that most of Devil's pact confessions in Finnmark were given at Vardøhus, where the majority of panics took place.

The rise of panics was dependent upon a multiplying factor. The reasons why the panics increase so rapidly is to be found in confessions of witches' meetings and confessions of collective witchcraft operations. The confessions in Finnmark contain the following places for witches' meetings: Lyderhorn, Balduolden, Vardbjerg, Dovre Mountain, Heckel Mountain, Domen and Lærvigen. These locations include well-known witches' mountains near and distant: Heckel Mountain,[48] Lyderhorn outside Bergen, Dovre Mountain in the south of Norway, Domen outside Vardø. The names of meeting places echo famous witches' mountains also mentioned in court records from other parts of Norway. Metamorphosis was included in the Finnmark confessions: shape-shifting to birds, whales and cats in order to obtain shapes appropriate to the sorcery activity.

Activities at witches' meetings in Finnmark confessions are singing, drinking, eating and Devil worship—often several of these at the same time. The Devil was the main person at the gathering; he provided the participants with food and drink and played for them.[49] Sex with the Devil was not an important issue in Finnmark and might only possibly be interpreted implicitly in one case when a woman confessed that she had to promise to serve Satan with her body.[50]

Several demonological features are mentioned in the Finnmark material, such as favour from the Devil when entering the pact, the Devil's mark and the names of personal demons, in Finnmark called *apostel*. These are the most prominent features in the Finnmark confessions. Favour from the Devil is often mentioned as part of the pact. Such favours might

---

[47] Willumsen, *Seventeenth-Century Witchcraft Trials*, 103.
[48] Heckel mountain probably refers to Hekla in Iceland. Ref. Grimm, J., *Teutoric Mythology*, 3 vols. III (London, 1883), 923.
[49] Willumsen, *Trollkvinne i nord* (1994), 28, 35–6, 40–2.
[50] Lisebet Nilsdatter, SATØ, SF 6, fo. 34v.

be the equivalent to the Scottish 'never want', money, luck regarding food and clothes, and luck regarding cattle. This range of favours points to the desire on the part of the women to have security and fulfilment of basic material needs. The Devil's mark is mentioned, but not often.[51] Names of demons found in these confessions are: Cax, Friis, Satan, Saclumb, Zakkerias, the Angel of Light, Asmudeo, Isach, Christopher, Dominicus, Mamo, Jermund, Abedom, Macome, Plister, Old Erich, Baris, Morten, Jacob, Peder, Samuel and Christen. Some of these are biblical names, some are common names and Old Erich is a common Norwegian euphemism for Satan.[52] The choice of demons' names shows the span between ordinary names and demonically influenced names in the witchcraft narratives.

In half of the Finnmark cases an accused person named other suspects as part of the confession. This fits into the pattern of Finnmark witchcraft trials as strongly marked by demonological features and characterized by panics. As will be seen in the qualitative analyses, there was a substantial network of denunciations during the panics, where each of the accused women mentioned several others who had participated at witches' meetings or in witchcraft operations.[53] When so many of the accused were brought to court because they were denounced by others, the character of a denunciation trial is emphasized; a case which began with a denunciation, without accusations and without complaints.[54] Ordinary legal requirements with regard to accusations and the burden of proof were set aside when the crime of witchcraft was dealt with.

An absolute majority of women confessed to the demonic pact in Finnmark. Direct confessions of the Devil's pact, as seen from chart 11 above, involved only women. Only one man confessed to an implicit demonic pact, saying that the Devil had taught him the craft. This suggests that the demonic pact in Finnmark was to an overwhelming degree a covenant between a female and the Devil.

Very few Samis confessed to the Devil's pact. When a Sami person confessed to the Devil's pact, this person was a woman and she was involved in a panic, as chart 12 shows.

[51] Mentioned in 11 of the confessions, in addition to 1 person having mentioned this in a previous trial. Ref. Willumsen, *Seventeenth-Century Witchcraft Trials*, 102.

[52] Rudwin, M., *The devil in legend and literature* (La Salle, 1973); Levack, *The Witch-Hunt*, 31.

[53] Willumsen, *Trollkvinne i nord*, (1994), 36, 41–2.

[54] Robberstad, *Rettsoga I*, 78.

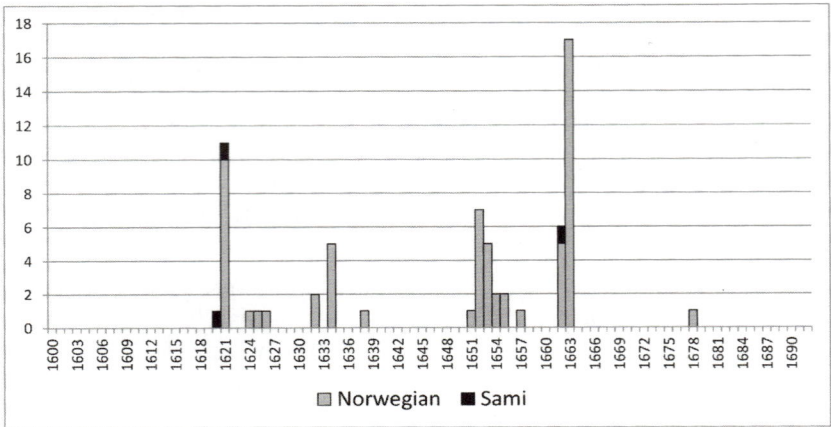

Chart 12: Devil's pact confession and ethnicity, Finnmark.

Torture

Use of torture is documented in the Finnmark witchcraft trials. The total occurrence of torture is difficult to unveil, as this piece of information is often 'hidden' in the sources. Torture before sentence was not permitted in Denmark-Norway. Torture after sentence was passed was permitted in order to obtain names of accomplices. This undoubtedly influenced documentation in the court records. Direct mentioning of torture occurs when use of torture openly is recorded. Implicit mention of torture may be exemplified by expressions as 'confessed willingly', 'confessed without torture' or 'confessed of own free will', used shortly after direct use of torture has been documented.

Torture led to the naming of accomplices and thus a sudden increase in the number of suspects. There is a significant correlation between torture and panics.[55] Likewise there is a positive correlation between torture and demonic pact confession.[56] This means that torture was frequently used before a demonic pact confession was delivered.

Several of the persons accused of witchcraft in Finnmark at first denied knowledge of witchcraft. During later interrogations they confessed. Such information can only be obtained by detailed study of court records

---

[55] Chi-square 7.079. Ref. Willumsen, *Seventeenth-Century Witchcraft Trials*, 105.
[56] Chi-square 18.947. Ref. Willumsen, *Seventeenth-Century Witchcraft Trials*, 105.

and shows a positive correlation between torture and initial denial of witchcraft.[57] This means that those individuals who first refused to confess were more likely to be tortured than those who confessed at once. The findings above support a hypothesis that torture caused panics and underline the harsh conditions during panic years.

The study of torture is extended by also focusing on gender. The correlation between panics, female and torture has been statistically tested. The result suggests that for women as a group, the proportion of those who were tortured was higher in panic periods compared to non-panic periods.[58] During panic periods several risks for women were intensified. In the first place, the risk of being accused was increased. Then the risk of being tortured was increased. Finally, there was a clear connection between those who were tortured and those who were executed.

The majority of cases of documented and implied torture were in local courts.[59] Even if the documentation of torture is scarce in the material, it is clear that both direct and indirect documentation of torture is linked mainly to local courts. The likelihood of being tortured was much higher for a person accused in a local court than for a person who got her or his case tried before the Court of Appeal.

Torture methods in Finnmark during the witchcraft trials were similar to those in several other European regions. Torture methods are documented in the court records from the local courts and the Court of Appeal. Among torture methods mentioned in Finnmark are the rack, red-hot tongs and 'sulphur on her breasts when she lay on the torture rack'. Moreover the women were periodically strapped down during their incarceration. It is recorded that Ingeborg, Peder Krog's wife, 'wore the iron collar and arm chains'.[60] Margrette Jonsdatter 'wore the prison on her body'.[61] Torture in Finnmark resulted in a couple of cases in death before sentence was passed, something which caused a reaction from people in Vardø. They sent a letter to the Regional Governor and required to have this incident investigated.[62] Torture methods will be dealt with in greater detail during the qualitative analyses.

---

[57] Chi-square 15.972. Ref. Willumsen, *Seventeenth-Century Witchcraft Trials*, 105.
[58] Chi-square 6.733. Ref. Willumsen, *Seventeenth-Century Witchcraft Trials*, 105.
[59] 37 out of 41 cases.
[60] SAT, Records of Court of Appeal 1647–1668, fo. 167.
[61] SAT, Records of Court of Appeal 1647–1668. fo. 161.
[62] Willumsen, *Trollkvinne i nord* (1994), 39.

Use of circumstantial evidence was frequent during the Finnmark witchcraft trials, particularly often the water ordeal was used. No district in Norway has more frequent use of the water ordeal than Finnmark.

As we see, most of the water ordeals were applied to Norwegian women. The two men who were tried by the water ordeal, were Sami. They were exposed to this ordeal before 1640, which corresponds with a focus on Sami male persons during the early period of the Finnmark witch-hunt.

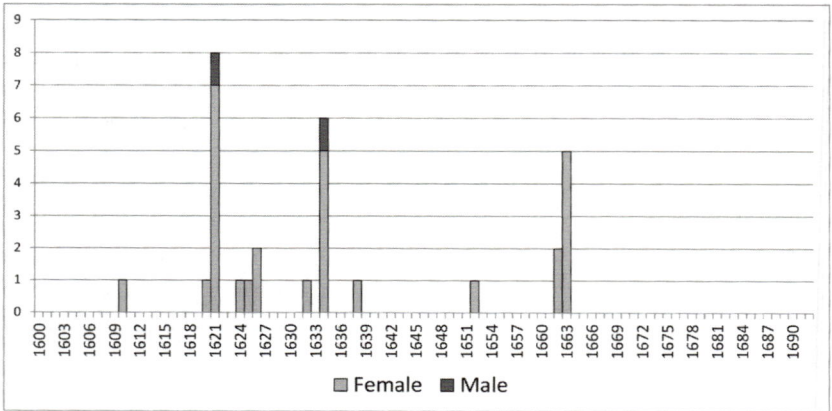

Chart 13: Water ordeal and gender, Finnmark.

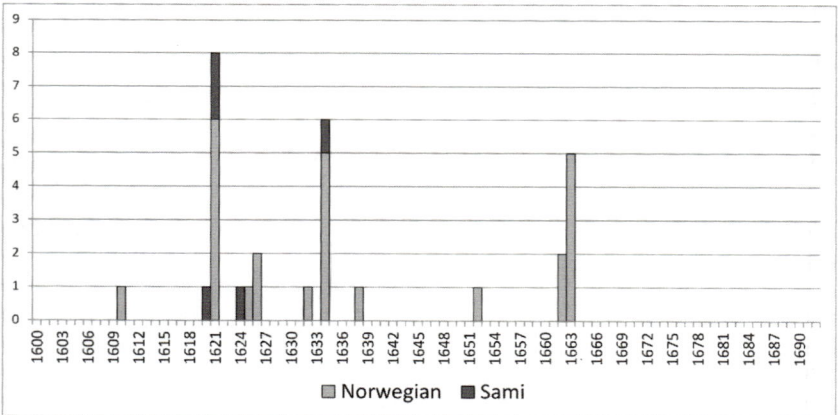

Chart 14: Water ordeal and ethnicity, Finnmark.

Ethnicity

King Christian IV paid special attention to Sami sorcery and focused on Finnmark as a place where sorcery was likely to take place. His letter from 1609 to District Governor Claus Gagge at Vardøhus, mentioned in the previous chapter, put sorcery in connection with 'Finns and Lapps' who, presumably by nature, were particularly apt to use magic. Witches should be judged and sentenced to be executed without mercy. Whoever was suspected of witchcraft should be banished from the district.[63] Here the term witchcraft is related to Sami practices of magic. So for the Finnmark district, ethnicity could possibly be influential on the witchcraft trials. Persons from both the ethnic groups Norwegians and Samis were accused during the witchcraft trials: 111 ethnic Norwegians and 24 ethnic Samis.

As seen from chart 15 below, the distribution of Sami persons accused of witchcraft in Finnmark is most distinct before 1640 and after 1670. The number of Samis during the panics in 1650s and 1660s is very low. The number of Samis follows the same pattern as for men in the material, something which is logical given the high percentage of men among the Samis accused.

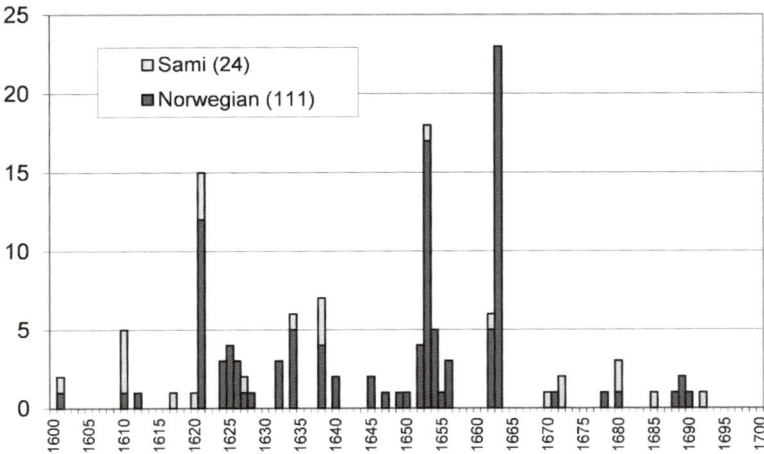

Chart 15: Frequency of ethnicity by year, Finnmark.

---

[63] Niemi, *Vadsøs historie*, 219; Willumsen, *Trollkvinne i nord* (1994), 73.

The Norwegian population was absolutely, and also relatively, more exposed to witchcraft accusations than the Sami population. Of the 135 accused persons, near 18% were Samis. This might be a bit unexpected, as the Samis had a reputation for sorcery all over Europe at the time. However, the explanation might be that traditional Sami sorcery was alleged to be an individual skill, displaying inherent magical power. The performers of Sami magic presented in contemporary books were all males. Authors like Olaus Magnus, Peder Clausssøn Friis and Johan Schefferus, whose books were published in 1555, 1632 and 1673 respectively, all portray Sami men—not Sami women—as exotic and pagan for a contemporary reading European audience.[64] The authors emphasize the superstition of the Samis and their ability to perform sorcery using a special type of Sami magic called *gand*,[65] and selling wind to sailors by binding three knots on a rope or a piece of cloth.[66] The distribution of females and males shows that eight Sami women and 16 Sami men were accused of witchcraft in Finnmark. In addition, among the males accused of witchcraft, the Sami men were in a majority. A Sami man was more likely to be accused of witchcraft than a Norwegian man. Among the women, Samis were only 7% of the women accused.[67]

Samis were little involved in panics. The data suggests that Sami persons were more strongly represented in isolated cases than in panics.[68] The proportion of Sami persons accused was higher during non-panic periods than during panic periods. This points to a view of Sami sorcery as an individual power and corresponds with the image of Sami sorcery found in contemporary learned Europe. A Sami sorcerer practised individual sorcery and was not seen as a member of a group of witches.

No doubt the Samis had a general reputation as cunning in sorcery. However, the reputation for sorcery in Finnmark at that time had a much wider range than the category ethnic Sami persons alone.[69] This suggests that also Norwegians might have had a reputation for sorcery. Of the Norwegian men accused of witchcraft, three out of four had such a reputa-

---

[64] Willumsen, *Trollkvinne i nord* (1994), 51–52; Magnus, *Historia om de nordiska folken*, orig. *Historia de Gentibus Septentrionalibus* (Rome, 1555); Friis, P. C., *Norriges Beskriffuelse* (Copenhagen, 1632); Schefferus, J., *Lapponia* (Frankfurt am Main, 1673).

[65] In Norwegian *gand* is the noun and *gande* is the verb denoting a curse falling upon a person due to Sami magic; Pollan, B., *Samiske beretninger* [Sami tales] (Oslo, 1997), 34.

[66] Willumsen, *Trollkvinne i nord*, 64–66.

[67] Willumsen, *Seventeenth-Century Witchcraft Trials*, 108.

[68] Chi-square 7.083. Ref. Willumsen, *Seventeenth-Century Witchcraft Trials*, 108.

[69] Willumsen, *Seventeenth-Century Witchcraft Trials*, 108.

tion. The situation for women is that Norwegian women and Sami women equally had a reputation for sorcery. So it seems that Sami men were in a special position as far as reputation was concerned, but among Norwegian men and Norwegian as well as Sami women accused, a reputation for sorcery was also very common.

Neighbourhood Disputes

In European witchcraft studies, neighbourhood disputes have been highlighted as an explanatory factor, frequently focusing on women's roles in local communities. The Finnmark witchcraft documents show that there is a correlation between neighbourhood witnesses and female accused. Likewise is there a correlation between neighbourhood witnesses and linked trials.[70] This means that neighbour witnesses were active during linked trials.

When it comes to the confessions, the pattern is a bit different. The occurrence of neighbourhood disputes given by the accused persons as a motive for performing sorcery is not overwhelming. Neighbour quarrels are mentioned as a reason for evil-doing in one-fourth of the trials with sufficient information. The connection between gender and neighbour quarrels as a motive for performing sorcery is not supported.[71] The likelihood of men and women accused of witchcraft mentioning neighbourhood quarrels as motives for performing sorcery is fairly equal.

Even if neighbourhood disputes are not often mentioned as direct motives for performing sorcery, no doubt disagreements related to daily living played a part in many witnesses' testimonies. It was dangerous at the time to fall out with neighbours, and often angry and threatening words from such a context were cited during a witchcraft trial and interpreted by witnesses and legal officials to have had mortal effect.

Folk Belief and Healing

The representation of folk belief in the Finnmark material is mostly related to weather magic, either wind was 'sold' to captains on ships or Sami spells, *gand*, were cast. Also frequent mentioned is magic performed

---

[70] Chi-square 12.289. Ref. Willumsen, *Seventeenth-Century Witchcraft Trials*, 109.
[71] Chi-square 0.826. Ref. Willumsen, *Seventeenth-Century Witchcraft Trials*, 109.

by conjuring up a storm in order to cause a ship-wreck. The latter type was often collective witchcraft performed by Norwegian women.[72] Half of the trials were related to this type of magic, thus the coastal location of the witchcraft trials in Finnmark is mirrored in the documents.

Fairies are mentioned only once in the Finnmark material, in a late trial in 1689.[73] It was not a prominent feature in folk belief in the north of Norway.

Benevolent magic played a minor role in the Finnmark trials. Healing was dealt with in the Danish-Norwegian laws at the time, as all types of magic from a theological interpretation had its origin in the Devil. At the very end of the sixteenth century and the beginning of the seventeenth century it was a capital crime, and after 1617 it was punished with exile. Healing is confessed to in 11 cases in Finnmark. Probably when healing was brought up during witchcraft trials, it was because this practice had been demonized and connected to the Devil.

Conclusion

The Finnmark witchcraft trials are special in a national as well as an international context. The material shows characteristic features due to geographical and ethnical conditions. The most conspicuous finding has to do with the influence of demonology on these trials. In a restricted area in the periphery of Europe, the highest percentage of witchcraft trials in Europe in relation to the population is found. This finding calls for attention. The material offers perspectives of interest for witchcraft research throughout Europe. The interaction between demonology, panics, type of trial and gender is convincing as an explanation for the sudden emergence of trials characterising the historical witch-hunt. The gender question, considered in isolation, is also prominent in this material, as a number of different approaches show that women were treated significantly differently from men.

---

[72] In close to half of the cases weather magic was confessed to directly; in 6 cases it was mentioned implicitly, i.e. in an earlier trial.
[73] Marite Nilsdatter, SATØ, SF 23, fos. 186v–187v.

CHAPTER TEN

FINNMARK—CLOSE-READINGS

This chapter contains close-readings of three cases from Finnmark district, each of them focusing on features of importance for the Finnmark trials; one case from the 1630s, one from the 1660s, and finally one from 1992, the end of the severe persecution. I have chosen for close-reading the trials of one adult woman, one girl, and one Sami man. In addition to this detailed studies of selected trials, I have chosen to write overviews of decades before and between these trials, thus covering the total period of witch-hunt in Finnmark. These overviews will to a larger extent than the statistical analyses in previous chapter deal with the contents of the witchcraft trials throughout the period of persecution, and thus broaden the information from the quantitative analyses.

The First Decades

The first two decades of witchcraft persecution in Finnmark, 1600–20, are characterized by few cases, a relatively high proportion of Sami men and cases located in West Finnmark. Of the nine persons accused, seven were men, and six out of these were Sami. A change in the climate towards witches seems to have developed around 1620. The first panic in Finnmark witchcraft trials was a reality in 1620–21. The change might have to do with the 1617 decree 'About Witches and their Accomplices',[1] when demonological ideas were taken into the legal definition of witches. It might also have to do with the installation of the Scotsman John Cunningham (c. 1575–1651). This panic was the first legal prosecution of witchcraft after Cunningham was appointed district governor of Vardøhus district in the spring of 1619.[2] During the panic of 1620–21, thirteen women were implicated. The main accusation concerned a shipwreck in 1617, when ten

---

[1] In Danish 'Om troldfolk og deres medvidere'.

[2] Willumsen, 'Exporting the Devil across the North Sea. John Cunningham and the Finnmark Witch-hunt', in Goodare, *Scottish witches and witch-hunters*; Willumsen, L. H. and Baptie, D., 'John Cunninghams karriere og bakgrunn', *Norsk slektshistorisk tidsskrift* 43:3 (2013), 159–176; Willumsen, L. H., 'Von Fife nach Finnmark—John Cunninghams Weg

[handwritten marginalia: "40 men lost on Christmas Eve"]

boats with 40 men from Kiberg and Vardø went down on the day before Christmas Day. After the start of the panic, alleged witches were transported to Vardøhus from Kiberg, Vadsø, Big and Small Ekkerø og Vardø accused of having caused the shipwreck.[3] The trial started in the fishing village of Omgang with the incarceration of Karen Edisdatter in May 1620.[4] She denounced several other women, which resulted in imprisonments the following year. In late April 1621, Kirsten Sørensdatter, living in the small fishing village of Kiberg, was imprisoned. Later the same year, on 9 August, a court meeting was held in Omgang, where Lisebet Nilsdatter was accused of witchcraft.[5] Court records are intact for four of the cases: Karen Edisdatter's, Kirsten Sørensdatter's, Lisebet Nilsdatter's and Mette Thorgiersdatter's. The fate of the other women is known through pieces of information in the regional accounts, where the crown's expenses for burning witches are registered. Twelve of the women in this panic received death sentences. One was released in expectation of a session of the local court the following spring.[6]

Persecution of witches in Finnmark during the 1630s and 1640s was characterized by relatively high activity during the 1630s (16 trials) and less during the 1640s (5 trials). These two decades show some new trends, compared with the decades before. Several women were tortured after the sentences had been passed. Also of interest is the idea that witches were organized into districts, heard in confessions during the 1630s. As for weather magic, the records show clearly that the women accused of witchcraft in this period performed the same type of magic otherwise attributed to Sami sorcerers. Witchcraft persecution in the 1630s suddenly increased and resulted in linked trials, as we shall see for the years 1632 and 1634.

Geographically the witchcraft cases were less clustered around Vardøhus Castle during these early decades than in the following decades. In addition, there was some witchcraft activity among the Samis further west, in the Porsanger area.[7]

---

nach Norden', in R. Voltmer (ed.), *Europäische Hexenforschung und Landesgeschichte—Methoden, Regionen, Vergleiche* (Trier, 2012, forthcoming); Hagen, 'At the Edge', 29.

[3] Niemi, *Vadsøs historie*, 221; Willumsen, *Trollkvinne* (1984), 28.
[4] SATØ, SF 6, fo. 10v–12v.
[5] Willumsen, *Trollkvinne* (1984), 30.
[6] Mette Thorgiersdatter, SATØ, SF 6, fo. 41r.
[7] Among them the Sami Sarve Pedersen, who was put to trial and executed in the year 1634. SATØ, AF, no. 2543, Domsutskrifter 1631–1670.

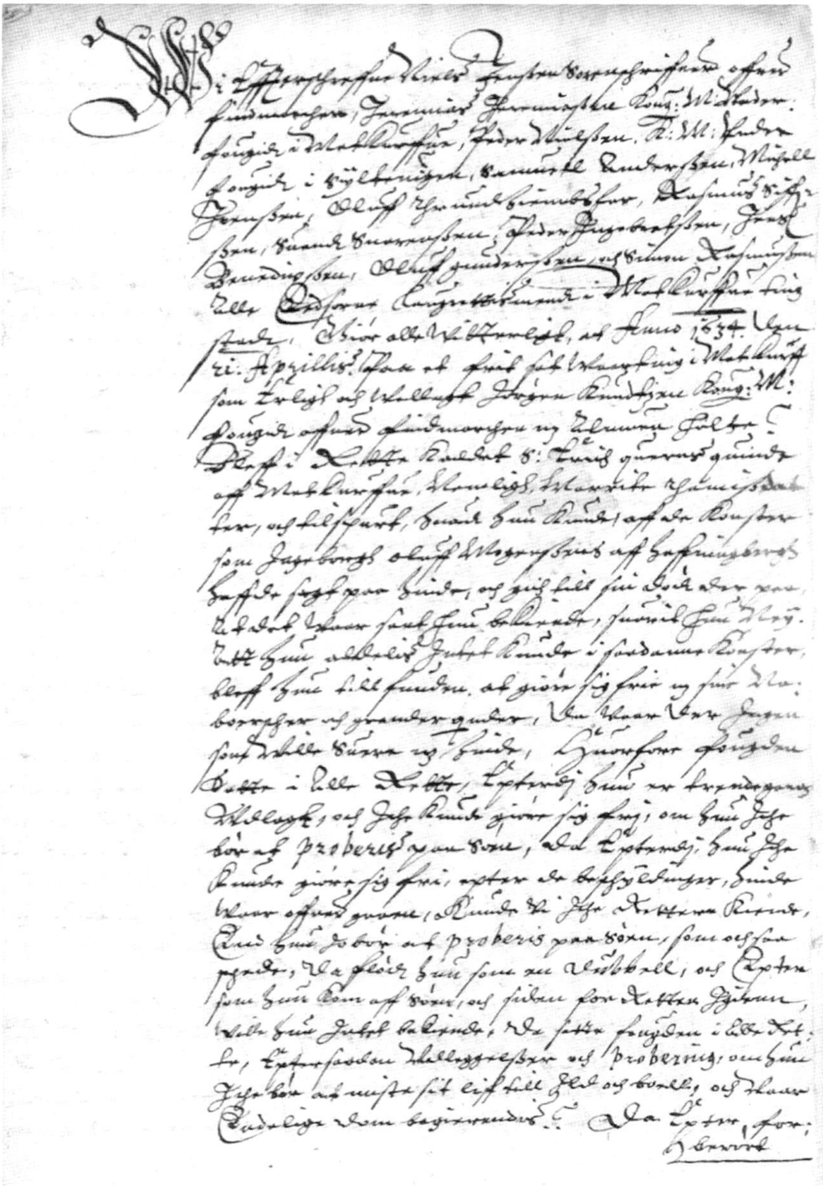

Figure 6: Court records Maritte Thamisdatter. SATØ, AF, no. 2543, Copies of sentences 1631–1670.

Maritte Thamisdatter, 1634

The trial of Maritte Thamisdatter is interesting in several respects. Her confession before the court gives a very good picture of the blending of traditional and demonological notions that seems to characterize the Finnmark as well as the Scottish cases. But most of all her trial is a crown example of how extremely locked a woman was as a witchcraft suspect before the court: the road leading to the stake was established from the very beginning, and there was no escape. In the same way as the trials from mainland Scotland, Orkney and Shetland have demonstrated with regard to severe methods of pressure used in order for the accused person to confess, the trial of Maritte Thamisdatter complements this picture. We see in Finnmark the same as in the Scottish cases; when a woman refused to confess, strong methods were taken in use to obtain the wanted confession. The case of Maritte Thamisdatter shows clearly how absolute helpless a woman was in such a situation. Even if her strategy from the beginning was one of denial of knowing witchcraft, extreme methods of pressure lead to complete breakdown of her own will, and she ended up confessing all that the witch-hunters wanted to hear.

As for reading the records, similarly to Scotland, this becomes clear by scrutinizing formulations in the records which at first glance do not seem to document torture. In addition to judicial torture, this trial allows us to focus on another means of pressure, the water ordeal, which was frequent in use during the Finnmark trials. Maritte Thamisdatter—and this was the same for several other women and men accused of witchcraft in Finnmark in this decade—underwent the water ordeal and was in addition subjected to torture.

The trial of Maritte Thamisdatter took place in Makkaur, a small village to the north-west of Vardø. Maritte was a married woman, the wife of Erich Quern in Makkaur.[8] She had been denounced by Ingeborg, Oluf Mogensen's wife from Hamningberg, a small village near Vardø. Maritte Thamisdatter first denied knowledge of witchcraft. It was used as an argument against her that she had been denounced three times. Being denounced more than once several times was used as an argument in court. In other trials one can see that the bailiff gave weight to denunciation by two witches who had

---

[8] *Quern* means *Kven*, referring to a minority people of Finnish stock that settled in North Norway from the sixteenth century onwards.

already been burned.[9] Maritte Thamisdatter was then offered the opportunity to clear herself of the accusations by using neighbours to swear an oath of compurgation for her, a court procedure often practised in Norway, and which we also saw in use in Shetland. The court records show that the bailiff tried to use his legal knowledge by moving step by step, collecting the required evidence in the case, and this was the first step. The voice of the law is heard in the rendering of the bailiff's words:

> She was told *to ask her women neighbours to clear her but none of them would swear an oath of compurgation,* for which reason the bailiff put to the entire court that she, having been denounced now, *for the third time,* and *having proved unable to clear herself of the accusations, should be tried by the water ordeal.* So *since she could not clear herself of the accusations levelled against her,* we had no other course than to order that she should be tried by the water ordeal, which was what happened.[10] [*My italics.*]

As she was unable to clear herself, the water ordeal was the next step. The type of 'evidence' given by the water ordeal was always the same—guilty for those who were floating. Heikki Pihlajamäki discusses why ordeals returned to use in early modern European witchcraft trials after they had been prohibited for several hundred years.[11] He argues that the English and Scandinavian judicial systems employed a logic wholly different to that of their continental counterparts:

> When the German and French inquisitors sought circumstantial evidence in witchcraft cases, their more peripheral colleagues in England and Scandinavia mostly left the accused at the mercy of the jurymen, nämndemän or compurgators. As we shall see, little place was left for the ordeals in these peripheral systems of evidence.[12]

Looking at Scotland and Finnmark, there was a jury in both areas. But circumstantial evidence was sought as well.[13] Pihlajamäki's argument could be accepted if one takes the mixed systems of criminal procedures into consideration, where inquisitorial as well as accusatorial features were found. The water ordeal was used in Scotland only in 1597.[14] Interestingly,

---

[9] For instance in the trial of Kirsten, Rasmus Siversen's wife, SATØ, AF, no 2543.

[10] SATØ, AF, no. 2543, Copies of sentences [*Domsutskrifter*] 1631–1670.

[11] '"Swimming the Witch, Pricking for the Devil's mark": Ordeals in the Early Modern Witchcraft Trials', *Legal History*, vol. xxi, no. 2 (2000), 35–58.

[12] Pihlajamäki, 'Swimming', 45.

[13] Levack, *Witch-Hunting in Scotland*, 20.

[14] Goodare, J., 'The Scottish Witchcraft panic of 1597', in Goodare, *Scottish witch-hunt in context*, 60.

the use of the water ordeal as well as witch-pricking are the two methods of obtaining proof in a witchcraft case which are emphasized by King
James VI in his *Demonology*. In Scotland witch-pricking was excessively
used in order to find out whether a suspected person was a witch, while
in Finnmark the water ordeal was frequently used. It thus seems that the
two areas had chosen to use one method each of the king's recommenda-
tions. In Finnmark 30 water ordeals took place out of 40 for the whole of
Norway. In a Scandinavian context, the Finnmark witchcraft trials seem
to be somewhat similar to the witch trials on the islands of Åland in Sweden, referred to by Pihlajamäki as trials where 'traces of continental practice reached Scandinavia as well'.[15] The Åland trials have been shown to
be largely the work of one man, the district court judge Nils Psilander.
He was strongly influenced by the witch doctrine and presided over the
court himself.[16] Pihlajamäki points out that Psilander's witch procedure
was clearly continental:

> Psilander and his court wanted the accused's confession in order to convict,
> and to obtain this they diligently sought sufficient circumstantial evidence
> to begin torture by thumb-screws. This circumstantial evidence, as in the
> continental doctrine, could appear in the form of denunciation or in witness
> statements. These 'rational' ways of obtaining evidence, were, however, often
> not sufficient and they needed to be complemented by other measures.[17]

For Psilander, the search for the Devil's mark was of special interest as
a type of measure that could help to obtain additional information, not
the water ordeal. But the parallel to the Finnmark trials is striking, not
least the analogy between the important roles apparently played by the
district court judge in Åland and the district governor at Vardøhus. Pihlajamäki argues that the water ordeal and the pricking test developed in
close contact with the learned theory of proof and that when the ordeals
were found in the peripheral regions of, for instance, Scandinavia, this
had to do with the learned law of proof and the progress the theory had
gained in that area. According to John L. Langbein the canon law of proof
'spread throughout Europe in the movement that is called the reception of Roman law'.[18] This law of proof consisted of three points: punishment requires full proof, two eyewitnesses or confession; circumstantial

---

Pihlajamäki, 'Swimming', 50; Stave, *Da Lucifer kom*, 74, 114.

Heikkinen, A., *Paholaisen liitoolaiset: Noita- ja magiakäsityksiä Suomessa 1600-luvun jälkipuoliskolla* (Helsinki, 1969), 208, 242.

Pihlajamäki, 'Swimming', 50–51.

Langbein, *Torture*, 3.

evidence bears only on whether or not to use torture; if full proof cannot be obtained, the accused must be released.[19]

Pihlajamäki's argument might be related to witchcraft trials in Scotland as well as in Finnmark due to the mixed systems of criminal procedures practised in both areas. Clearly traces of continental practice have been shown in the statistical analyses above. In this respect similarities with Åland witchcraft trials also come to the fore. The water ordeal was not considered as torture, but as a means of gathering evidence.[20] Often accused persons confessed when threatened by the water ordeal, both in Sweden and in Finnmark.[21] After the water ordeal had been applied, one often finds in the records from Finnmark remarks like 'as could be seen', which meant that the judicial officials, the jury as well as common people attending the court functioned as a kind of witnesses for this type of proof. In the case of Maritte Thamisdatter, she still refused to confess after the water ordeal. However, it seems that the bailiff considered the water ordeal as evidence in its own right, a test which was reliable and which made it possible to declare her guilty:

> She floated like a bob, and *since* she came out of the sea and stood before the court again still refusing to confess, the bailiff put to the court that *after such denunciations and tests* she should lose her life in fire at the stake, and he requested final judgment. Then, *on the grounds of the above, and since she has thrice been denounced for having taken part in casting spells on people and has been put to the water ordeal and thus found guilty,* we had no other course than to decide that she must lose her life in fire at the stake. [*My italics.*][22]

Maritte Thamisdatter's final fate was execution. This sentence was passed before Maritte Thamisdatter had confessed or denounced other women. It was therefore desirable to get more out of her, and torture was used: 'When sentence had been passed on the said Maritte, she was interrogated under torture and confessed *very little*'.[23] [*My italics.*] She started to confess during torture, but this was not enough. So far, we have heard a reliable scribe. But when it is said that the next day she confessed 'without torture', this is most likely a truth with modifications. After all, she was

---

[19] Langbein, *Torture*, 49–50.
[20] Pihlajamäki, 'Swimming', 35–58.
[21] Sörlin, *Trolldoms- och vidskepelseprocessarna i Göta hovrätt*, 54; Willumsen, *Steilneset. Memorial to the Victims of the Finnmark Witchcraft Trials*, 30, 33, 41, 85.
[22] SATØ, AF, no. 2543, Domsutskrifter 1631–1670.
[23] SATØ, AF, no. 2543, Domsutskrifter 1631–1670.

tortured the day before, and this must be seen in relation to her confession the following day. The remark 'without torture' from the hand of the scribe might also suggest that it was important in the formal document to hide that she was tortured anew. Certainly, at this point it was necessary to obtain more information from her. It is interesting to note that the jury when passing the sentence moves into the first person: *'we* had no other course', thus losing the objective perspective obtained by an impersonal manner of expression.

> But *on the second day, she confesses without torture* that she was with Ingeborgh from Haffningbergh in Wardøen, and she [Ingeborg] first taught her to tie knots on a piece of cloth, and put black, white and red stones in them. After that, she confesses that she was with Ingeborgh and two women from Kieluig. One of them, named Kirsten, was tall and middle-aged and in the likeness of a goose. The other, named Anne, was young, tall and fat and she was in the likeness of a duck. All of them cast a spell on Michel Lauritzen's boat.[24] As for the other things Ingeborgh had said about her in the *three denunciations*, she confesses it was all true. Moreover she says that *when the executioner*[25] *shaved off her eyebrows, Satan left her at once.* She confesses more, denouncing Marritte, Oluff Møring's wife, for having cast a spell on Anders Mand, from these parts, Matkurffue, and she tied three knots on a piece of cloth and *put three stones into them* and when he was rowing out to sea, she walked on the shore, throwing the stones after him, saying: *Off you go, never to return.* On that very day, the man drowned. She also reported that the said Maritte put a kid on the roof of Oluff Pouelsen's farmhouse, and that he had words with her about it, and shortly after, he lost an eye.[26] [*My italics.*]

This passage shows clearly the interweaving between traditional sorcery notions and demonological notions. Maritte Thamisdatter's repetition of being denounced three times is interesting as three is a magical number, often found in folklore and traditional oral tales. The number three appears again when she describes her sorcery ritual. Three knots on a piece of cloth is known from traditional practice of sorcery in Finnmark in the sixteenth century.[27] Putting stones inside a piece of cloth when casting spells on boats is known elsewhere from confessions during the Finnmark witchcraft trials. Also of interest is the image of the Devil leaving Maritte

---

[24] Orig. *jegt.*
[25] Orig. *mestermanden.*
[26] SATØ, AF, no. 2543.
[27] See for instance Olus Magnus' history book.

when her eyebrows were shaved off. This is an image not seen elsewhere in the Finnmark material, but it has connotations to demonology, as the *Malleus Maleficarum* mentions shaving. Most interesting is her rendering of the magic ritual and the magic words she used when casting the spell, affirming that magic formulas were dependent upon poetic devices and rhythm—a short and pointed saying, and again the stamp of orality is noticed. Maritte's belief in the magic words and rituals was shared by the scribe, as there are no distancing devices used in the text to signal doubt about the force of her craft. The attitude of the scribe towards what is written is confident, as when rendering the cause-and-effect connection related to the quarrel between Maritte and Oluf Poulsen and his loss of an eye shortly afterwards.

John H. Langbein has investigated crime in European legal systems from medieval times until well into the eighteenth century. He states that torture was part of the ordinary criminal procedure, 'regularly employed to investigate and prosecute routine crime before the ordinary courts. The system was one of *judicial torture*'.[28] [*Author's italics.*] According to Langbein 'judicial torture' was performed by officers of the state in order to gather evidence for judicial proceedings. 'The law of torture regulated this form of judicial investigation'.[29]

Related to the trial of Maritte Thamisdatter, it seems that the judicial climate similar to Finnmark was the judicial climate of Western Europe in the middle of the seventeenth century. The representatives of the law allowed torture after conviction if the aim was to find the conspirators. Langbein says that in French sources this type of torture was called '*torture préalable*', literally 'preliminary torture', in the sense of being preliminary to the execution of the capital sentence: 'The safeguards of the ordinary law of torture, such as the requirement of probable cause, did not exist. Torture préalable was regarded as much less objectionable than ordinary judicial torture'.[30]

Looking at the structure of Maritte Thamisdatter's trial, there is a strong increase in tension after the water ordeal, when she was first sentenced, afterwards tortured. It seems that her resistance was rapidly broken down. The torture was a turning point towards a confession, and when she had begun her confession, witchcraft operations and denunciations

---

[28] Langbein, *Torture*, 3.
[29] Langbein, *Torture*, 3.
[30] Langbein, *Torture*, 17.

were readily confessed. In addition to the confession quoted above, she confessed to having cast a spell on Oluf Poulsen, 'after which he presently got a backache, and it lasted quite a while, with cracks and contractions, so that he eventually had to go to bed for a fortnight and subsequently *had to use a staff on board his boat way into the spring fishing season*'.[31] [*My italics.*] This was the worst time of the year for a fisherman to get a handicap like a backache, as this was the time for the main fisheries. The motives for casting spells seem to be quarrels with acquaintances and neighbours, often about everyday affairs. The last person Maritte Thamis-datter denounced was Marette, the wife of Oluf Møring.[32]

> Moreover, she narrated that Marrite, too, cast a spell on the late Lauritz Taylor because he demanded payment for red fulled cloth for a skirt which Oluff Møring got in the past from the late Oluff Brat, the late Lauritz Taylor's servant. *This confession about what Maritte did was delivered in the said Maritte's face*, after which she was willing to meet her death and receive the sacrament upon it that what she confessed had happened just as has been related, something we confirm with the imprints of our signets here below.[33] [*My italics.*]

Confrontation between several of the accused persons in witchcraft trials was seen also in the Bute trials in Scotland. Denunciations could take place either in the face of another woman, like the above example, or with laying on of hands on the person denounced, which was also seen in Finnmark. This seems to increase the reliability of the denunciation and thus the chance of obtaining a confession. The voice of the scribe echoes the legal discourse, once more mentioning the sacrament she was going to receive and the confirmation of her confession. Then the next woman was brought to court, and she was also tortured.

During the 1640s six women were accused of witchcraft in Finnmark, four from the area around Vardø and two from the area around Vadsø. Five of them received death sentences, while the last was acquitted. She got her case tried before the Court of Appeal in 1650. Overall during the witchcraft trials in Finnmark, there was a greater chance for the accused person to be acquitted if the case was tried before the Court of Appeal than before the local court.

---

[31] SATØ, AF, no. 2543, Domsutskrifter 1631–1670.
[32] 'Møring' denotes the place he came from, Møre, a coastal area south of Trondheim.
[33] SATØ, AF, no. 2543, Domsutskrifter 1631–1670.

The 1650s

The 1650s were characterized by a panic in 1651–53 in which 14 women were implicated, and the linked trials of 1654–55 involving five women. In the first, the accused persons confessed to collective sorcery operations causing the shipwrecks of large boats steered by Bergen captains.[34] A Bergen citizen living in Vadsø, Lauritz Henrichsen Bras, played an important role in pushing the trials held in Vadsø, as pointed out and discussed by Einar Niemi.[35] His position and place of abode were related to the Bergen trade. Bras was an outfitter who supplied local fishermen with necessary fishing equipment.

From December 1651 till March 1653, 13 married women from Vadsø, Vardø, Ekkerøy, Andersby, Kiberg and Syltevik were imprisoned and sentenced to be burnt at the stake after having confessed about pacts with the Devil. Four of the women lived in Vadsø, three women lived in Vardø and the rest lived in small fishing villages near Vadsø and Vardø. Court sessions were held in Vadsø, Kiberg and Vardø, with the fort of Vardøhus as the centre of witch-hunting activity.[36] Ten of the death sentences were passed at Vardøhus, and three death sentences were passed in Kiberg.

The 1662–63 Panic

The 1660s were characterized by the largest panic during the Finnmark witchcraft trials, the 1662–63 panic. It involved around 30 people, all women; six of them were little girls. A Sami woman introduced the panic, as was the case in 1620–21. Three of the women were said to be mentors for other women. Seventeen of the women were married, five were still, or had been, servants, and two were born south of Finnmark. It was the most cruel of the panics in Finnmark, with extensive use of torture.

A common denominator with previous panics was that the implicated women lived in various parts of Varanger—seven of them in Ekkerøy, nine in Vadsø, six in Vardø, two in Kiberg, three in Andersby, and one in Makkaur, see Figure 7 below. Nevertheless, 17 of the women were questioned and tried at Vardøhus, whereas only two were tried in Vadsø and one in Kiberg. This means that Vardøhus castle played an important role

---

[34] Willumsen, *Trollkvinne i nord* (1984), 28.
[35] Niemi, *Vadsøs historie*, 223–25; Niemi, E., 'Hekseprosesser og økonomi', *Ottar*, no. 5 (2012), 9–25.
[36] Balsvik, *Vardø*, 20–33; Willumsen, *Steilneset. Memorial to the Victims*, 61–73.

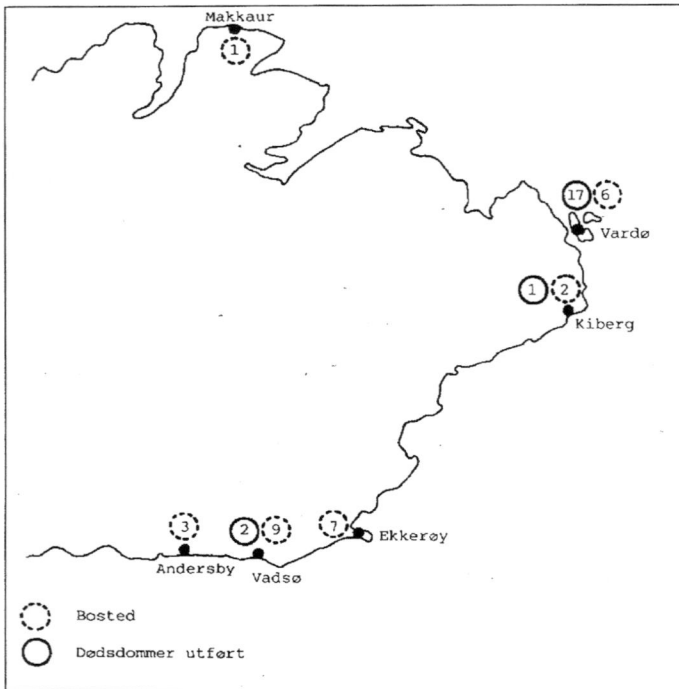

Figure 7: Place of living and place of trial 1662–63, Finnmark. Stippled circle denotes place of living and continuous circle denotes place of trial. Made by Liv Larsen.

during this panic, as the centre of interrogation and torture. Two persons died as a result of torture. The execution rate of this panic was 71 per cent, deaths under torture not included.

The principal collective operations confessed to by the witches in 1662–63 were driving away fish from the coast, evil spells cast on Jens Ottesen's and Marcus Erichsen's ships, and a conspiracy against the 'district lord'. In most cases when women confessed to having tried to harm ships by raising storms, they had done so while transformed into animals or birds. Jens Ottensen's ship was allegedly destroyed by a group of women sitting out at sea on an overturned barrel. Some of them had personal motives for this act, whereas Karen Olsdatter participated more or less because she wanted to assist the others, who would have her with them since they were wrathful against the captain.[37]

---

[37] SATØ, SF 10, fo. 276v.

Eight women confessed to having caused 'bad weather against Captain Marcus Erichsen and his ship (...) for the reason that (...) the said Barbra had not been paid in full for her trouble and for the rent'.[38] In other words, the other women displayed solidarity with Barbra and joined her because she felt she had been wronged. However, the women were unsuccessful with their spell on the boat. The evil-doing had to fail, 'for God was stronger than Satan'.[39]

The confessions give an interesting insight into the close connections between the accused women in a panic. The astonishing web of relations between the women during this panic is clearly shown in Figure 8 below.

The names around the circle denote all the women involved in the network of denunciations during the 1662–63 panic. I will draw the attention to the consistent use of denunciations by the women interrogated and the tight network of naming and contra-naming. When the arrow is pointing one way only, one woman denounced another woman. When an arrow points both ways, two women denounced each other reciprocally. This web of denunciation indicates that the women involved in the panic knew each other. The denunciations seem to hit in all directions. As severe torture was used during this panic, it is likely that a woman denouncing other women gave names of persons she knew. Being in a state of distress and pain, an interrogated woman probably saw the stage of denunciation as the last part of the interrogation. Still, this was an important point for the questioners to have fulfilled, in order for the panic to continue. This context taken into consideration, it is likely that the person who denounced others, chose to denounce persons among her acquaintants, old as well as young. The women who might possibly be denounced in such a situation, were in fact all women living in Vardø and Vadsø and in the vicinity of these villages. It is also likely that the confrontation in the courtroom between the ones who denounced and the ones who were being denounced, increased the tension and contributed to intensification of the panic.

A lesser project was undertaken by Margrette Jonsdatter, Solve Nilsdatter and Marie, the wife of Anders. This project was casting an evil spell on the sleigh of the previous district governor, Jørgen Friis, 'which had been dispatched to collect wood along the Russian coast'.[40] This evil

---

[38] SATØ, SF 10, fo. 273v.
[39] SATØ, SF 10, fo. 268r.
[40] SATØ, SF 10, fo. 260r.

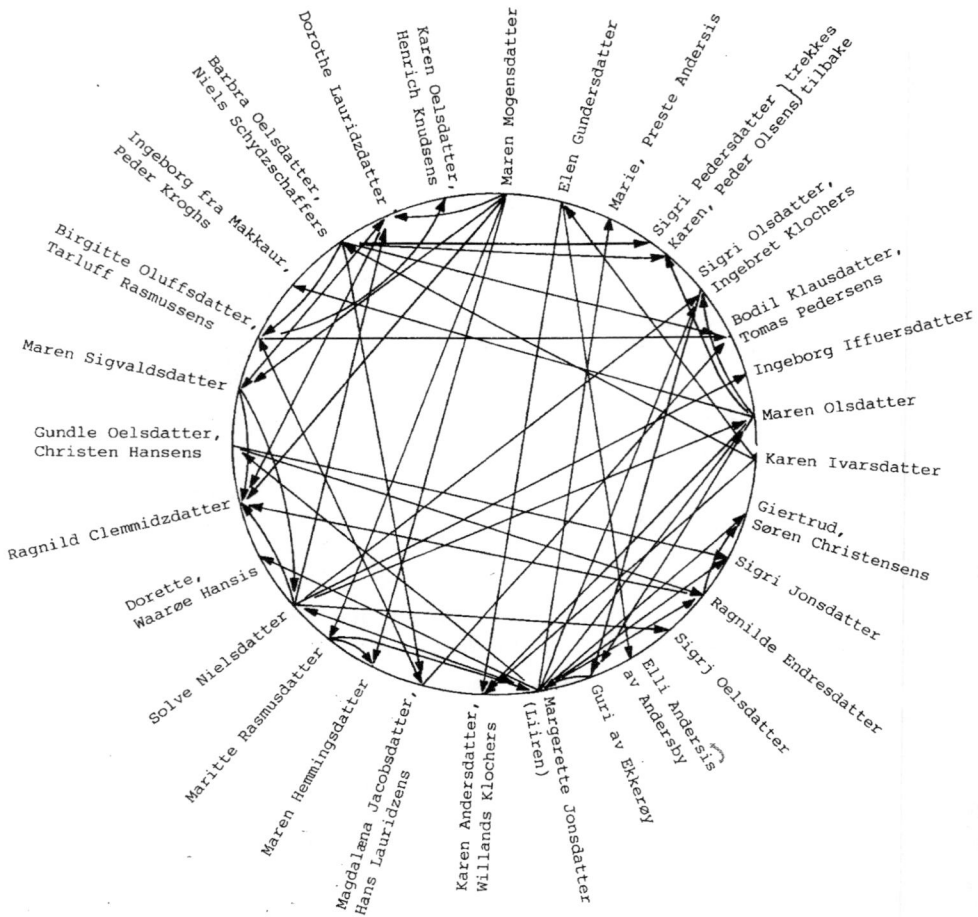

Figure 8: Web of denunciations 1662–63, Finnmark. Made by Liv Larsen.

spell was cast because Margrette Jonsdatter's ex-suitor was on this sleigh; 'Niels from the south had wooed her but not kept his word'.[41] This witch-craft operation, too, failed, because the people were in constant fear of God, but the sleigh was overturned.[42]

A collective operation which should be viewed in the light of the previous years' poor fishing, is the witches' undertaking to 'drive the fish away

---

[41] SATØ, SF 10, fo. 260r.
[42] SATØ, SF 10, fo. 260r.

from the coast, last Easter'.[43] Seven of the women confessed to having participated in this operation, which was allegedly carried out in the manner
described by Margrette Jonsdatter:

> And she also roundly denounced, before the court, the following person,
> Giertrud, Søren Christensen's woman from Krogen, saying that she was also
> there at the time, true enough[44] in her own likeness, and that she wore a
> black jacket, a red Bøffelbay[45] skirt, and also a red cap with golden lace, and
> white linen around her neck, and besides, she sat on the water, holding and
> surrounded by seaweed. Margrette says that she herself was in the likeness
> of a gull, while Gundle was in the likeness of a seal and Dorette, Waarøe
> Hans's wife, was in that of a porpoise, and Sigrij Jonsdatter was in that of a
> bluefin, and they were all holding stalks of seaweed with which they used
> their craft to drive the fish from the shore, and this they did around all
> the islands.[46]

From Margrette's description of Gjertrud a yearning for beauty in everyday
life comes to us. Gjertrud has turned into a beautifully garbed queen on
a throne surrounded by her subjects. Clothes such as the ones described
were presumably out of reach for these women. Yet, they serve to paint a
detailed picture of the ideal. The reasons for participating in this operation were, for Karen Olsdatter, that 'it annoyed them that some people
should have and catch more fish than others'[47] and for Birgitte Olufsdat-
ter, that 'she was angry with her master, for he from whom everybody
ordered their wares sold them dear, and kept the highest prices'.[48]

The last witchcraft operation in this chain was an attempt to cast an
evil spell on the district governor and his young lady 'because he had
treated them so harshly', as Solve Nilsdatter put it.[49] The tale, which was
corroborated by three of the children, the twelve-year-old Maren Olsdatter, the eight-year-old Ingeborg Iversdatter and her sister Karen Iversdatter, was indeed an odd one. Ellen Gundersdatter explained that the
district governor was visiting in Vadsø, where he passed the night in the
deputy bailiff's house. While he 'was in the sitting room in bed with his
beloved young lady', the witches would 'blow on him in the name of the

---

[43] SATØ, SF 10, fo. 260r.

[44] This is an idiomatic expression, in Norwegian *riktignok*.

[45] A soft, thick material of carded wool, loosely spun, wooly on one side, smooth on
the other, used also to make coats. Ref. Elstad, Å., *Moteløver og heimføingar: tekstilar og
samfunnsendringar i Øksnes og Astafjord 1750–1900* (Stamsund, 1997), 153.

[46] SATØ, SF 10, fos. 260r–260v.

[47] SATØ, SF 10, fo. 276r.

[48] SATØ, SF 10, fo. 275r.

[49] SATØ, SF 10, fo. 250v.

evil Satan. But since our good Lord Jesus and his holy angels were with and betwixt them, they were obstructed, so that their evil intention could not come to pass as they had planned'.[50] One of the other implicated persons, the small girl Karen Iversdatter, claimed they 'had wanted to kill the district governor with pins'.[51] Maren Olsdatter explained that 'they were obstructed because the district governor was for ever reading, praying for God's mercy'.[52] The same Maren claimed that Solve, Sigrid and Margrette were to blame for the pain in the district governor's leg and arm. Although we might be tempted to smile at this story, it seems clear that the district governor was so upset by what the women might be able to accomplish, that Solve Nilsdatter was arrested and put in chains, and the children's evidence was heeded. The little girls had understood, as is evident from their confessions, that whoever believed in God was protected against evil spells.

What might be considered a variant of a witches' meeting was a riotously party in Anders Pedersen's cellar on Christmas Eve. This event was referred to by several women in the panic. They drank beer from a ladle and Satan was there together with them. This must have been a merry party, indeed, with two of the women fighting with each other. One of them, Solve Nilsdatter, had too much to drink and 'fell twice or thrice on her way back led by the Evil One'.[53] Maybe the women's descriptions expressed their longing to let themselves go, like men, carousing and brawling all night.[54] Similar interpretations of witches' meetings are given by Larner and Roper. Larner underlines the element of disorder, Roper the dance as an 'interruption of the routine of town or village life'.[55] Roper stresses the sexual dimension of the dance: 'At the witches' dance, each witch appeared as part of a pair. Male or female, each witch had her own diabolic lover. Most witches described how the dance culminated in actual copulation between humans and devils, making the sexual dimension of the fantasy explicit'.[56]

All sentences convicting a person to be burnt at the stake during this panic were passed by one or more of the triumvirate: the district governor Christopher Orning, the bailiff of East Finnmark, Nils Sørensen Fiil,

---

[50] SATØ, SF 10, fo. 255r–255v.
[51] SATØ, SF 10, fo. 252r.
[52] SATØ, SF 10, fo. 246v.
[53] SATØ, SF 10, fo. 244v.
[54] Willumsen, *Trollkvinne i nord* (1994), 42.
[55] Larner, *Enemies*, 153; Roper, *Witch Craze*, 109–11.
[56] Roper, *Witch Craze*, 111.

and the deputy bailiff, Abraham Lockert. That their outlook was fanatical should be evident when the bailiff proposed that the children, too, should be burnt 'so that they stray no further into the Devil's snares, and so that other children should not be beguiled through them by the Devil's machinations'.[57] However, all the children were acquitted in the Court of Appeal.

In my discussion below I would like to draw attention to the following topics: new demonological ideas found in the sources from this decade, children among the accused persons, and the use of torture during the panic of 1662–63.

The Rhodius Couple and New Demonological Ideas

To a greater extent than any of the previous panics in Finnmark, this one might illustrate how the demonological notions came to the far north of Europe. During this panic, ideas from the intricate science of demonology percolate to the women's confessions, ideas that had never been mentioned in Finnmark so far. Such ideas include maternal child-sacrifice to the Devil—which is an echo of the *Malleus Maleficarum*[58]—the Devil's mark, the idea that the Devil fathered a woman's child, and the idea that a mother taught her eldest daughter witchcraft—learned demonological ideas known in Copenhagen and the rest of Europe. This panic is unique in the way that the introduction of new ideas to a restricted group of people, here the group of imprisoned women at Vardøhus castle, can be followed closely. The new demonological ideas were narrated within the walls of the castle and could easily be recalled and retold by the suspects in front of the court. These notions about the Devil were apparently regarded as interesting both by the interrogators and by the accused women. It may be noted that the number of demonological elements in the confessions increased from one year to the following, something which suggests that stories about the Devil were spread orally among the women and new elements were added to the narratives they knew of beforehand. The court records show that new ideas spread rapidly also outside the Castle walls, to the vicinity of Vardøhus. It is demonstrated how specific ideas were transferred from one geographical area to another. And it shows that

---

[57] SATØ, SF 10, fo. 257v.
[58] Behringer, *Witches*, 142. The Dominican inquisitor Kramer had claimed in his *Witches Hammer* that daughters were likely to become witches themselves, not by inheritance, but because the mothers devoted them to their master, the Devil.

introducing new notions was the work of one person. In fact, one can say that the ideological influence of one specific person had a triggering effect on the outset of this panic.

What happened was that a learned couple from the south of Norway, Ambrosius Rhodius and Anne Friedrichsdatter Rhodius, imprisoned at Akershus castle near Oslo, were transported to Vardøhus along the coast of Northern Norway during the winter months of 1662, just a few months before the panic started.[59] Together with them came another prisoner, the dismissed vicar Engebret Madsen. They were placed in one of the houses within the castle walls of Vardøhus. Ambrosius Rhodius was an astrologer and physician from Kemberg in Saxony.[60] He was considered to be politically dangerous because as a result of a vision in 1657 he had predicted the result of an ongoing war.[61] His wife was a grandchild of the private physician of Frederik II (1534–88). She was imprisoned after a severe disagreement with the governor and the mayor in Christiania, the capital of Norway, where they were living. The Rhodius couple was supposed to be a threat to the security of the kingdom. Among other restrictions they were not allowed to have access to paper and ink while imprisoned at Vardøhus, as it was feared that they would contact the Swedish government. Ambrosius Rhodius must have been one of the most erudite people in Finnmark at the time. With their education and former social standing the couple must have distinguished themselves from other prisoners.

It was Anne Friedrichsdatter Rhodius who would come to have a tremendous impact on the panic of 1662–63. Because the children suspected of witchcraft came to Vardøhus at a time when the castle was crowded with adult suspects, at least one of the children, Maren Olsdatter, had to stay in the same house as the Rhodius couple, which provided a good opportunity for Anne to influence her. Anne Rhodius also influenced other children suspected for witchcraft. In addition, she had her own key to the 'witches' hole'[62] and talked with women suspected of witchcraft imprisoned at Vardøhus. Two of the imprisoned women were pregnant, and she was asked to examine them, so she must have had a reputation as a person with some knowledge of medicine and health care. She played a prominent part in prison life and had considerable sway on the confes-

---

[59] Wessel, *Ambrosius*, 21. Wessel notes that a royal writ from Ivar Krabbe pronounced that they should be imprisoned in Vardøhus fort, having previously been kept in Akershus fort.
[60] Bergh, 'Til ild', 140.
[61] *Krabbekrigen* 1657–58 and *Revansjekrigen* 1658–60.
[62] One room at the castle was called The witches' hole, in Norwegian *Troldquindehullet*.

sions made by the suspects. According to imprisoned women and children, Anne was a most unpopular person amongst the prisoners. True enough, she was a prisoner herself, but she colluded with the wardens and prison authorities.[63] She may have sought to win favours from the district lord and his bailiff, probably to win release from her imprisonment.

The alleged plot against the district governor led to a confrontation between Anne Friedrichsdatter and several of the suspects at court. On 2 April 1663 Barbra, the wife of Nils the purveyor, denounced the wife and daughter of Peder Olsen, jury member, for witchcraft. Peder Olsen protested strongly, but Barbra said that Anne Rhodius and Maren had said this was true the day before. Then the two were sent for. During the confrontation Barbra and Maren were asked by Anne Rhodius whether she had told them to lie about anybody. They answered no. But when the district governor asked Maren if it was true that Peder Olsen's wife and daughter had been together with the other witches plotting against the district governor, she answered that it was true. However, this time the court did not believe Maren. They had probably become suspicious about the reliability of this child's testimony. From this episode it seems clear that Anne Friedrichsdatter knew the suspects and played an active role during the trials.

When the cases of the children were about to end in the local court, the bailiff put to the court whether the children should not be punished in fire at the stake, in order to prevent them from misleading other children. But the jury found these cases difficult to judge, and they were passed on to the Court of Appeal, which was due to be held in Finnmark in the summer of 1663. Among others Maren Olsdatter was questioned by the Court Appeal Judge during a session held on 25 June 1663. The same impression of Anne Friedrichsdatter as had come to the fore in the records of the local court was confirmed. During the sessions of the Court of Appeal, Anne Rhodius again played an active role, as she was frequently confronted with the suspects.[64] She was also said to have told a pregnant woman, Ragnilde Endresdatter, that Ragnilde was 'carrying not a child but a Devil'.[65] When Maren Olsdatter was questioned by the Court Appeal Judge, she had nothing to confess, but cried and recited some sections from the catechism. The Court Appeal Judge concluded that 'Ane Rhodi' had tempted her to

---

[63] Wessel, *Ambrosius*. Wessel believes Anna Rhodius had an 'unstable disposition'.

[64] For instance in the case of Magdelene Jacobsdatter, who finally was acquitted. SAT, LF 1647–1668, fos. 152–154.

[65] SAT, LF 1647–68, fo. 155.

lie about herself and others.[66] Finally all the children were acquitted by the Court of Appeal, so that those who had parents alive could learn from and obey their parents. For those who did not have parents alive, some of the neighbours out of Christian disposition had undertaken to care for the children as their own.[67]

However, the most comprehensive information about the influence of Anne Friedrichsdatter on those imprisoned for witchcraft is a written order from Ambrosius Rhodius to the district governor Frederic Schiort, presented on 8 October 1666.[68] The background for the order was this: Ambrosius Rhodius was pardoned by a letter from the King of 2 July 1666. Probably Anne Friedrichsdatter also hoped to be pardoned and would try to clear herself. Therefore Ambrosius Rhodius presented an order consisting of 29 itemized questions to be recited verbatim in court. The questions focused on what had been wrongly recorded about Anne Friedrichsdatter during the witchcraft trials. The purpose was to clear her of the complaints that had apparently been raised against her. After discussion of the questions in court it was concluded that Anne Friedrichsdatter had been very active in influencing the confessions of the suspected adults and children during the panic of 1662–63, trying to make them confess.[69] It was decided that she would remain in custody at Vardøhus.

Overall the role of Anne Friedrichsdatter during the 1662–63 panic is interesting in showing her intermediate position. On the one hand she was an outsider, a learned person from other levels of society than the suspects imprisoned at Vardøhus. On the other hand she was a woman and a fellow-prisoner. It seems that the authorities as well as the jury were tired of the Rhodius couple and all the extra work they gave the court and wanted to be left in peace. When the court had finished answering Rhodius' 29 itemized questions, a little sigh from the jury was entered into the records; they 'humbly request our merciful district governor to succour us people of small means so that we can disembarrass ourselves of Magister Rhodius and his wife's disruptive and uncalled-for questions'.[70] Ambrosius Rhodius left Vardøhus in June 1667 for Christiania. The same year he moved to his home town of Kemberg, where he remarried in 1675 and died in 1697, 90 years old, after having bequeathed a legacy in memory of

---

[66] SAT, LF 1647–68, fo. 151.
[67] SAT, LF 1647–1668, fo. 152.
[68] Schiort had been appointed district governor the same year.
[69] SATØ, SF 11, fos. 96v–114r.
[70] SATØ, SF 11, fo. 114r.

his release from Vardøhus castle. Anne Friedrichsdatter was alive in Vardø in 1672, when a new house for her custody at Vardøhus was mentioned as an item of expenditure in the district accounts.[71]

Maren Olsdatter, 1663

General

Six children were accused of witchcraft in Finnmark, all of them brought before the court in 1663.[72] I have chosen the case of one of them, Maren Olsdatter, for close-reading, due to several reasons. Firstly, it gives a good opportunity to examine the role of the scribe in witchcraft trials. Secondly, the voice of the law in such an unusual case as a trial against a child, comes to the fore. Thirdly, it is well fitted for examining contents as well as the narrative structures of the confession of a young person. Fourthly, it is a good example of the individualization of an accused person's voice. Fifthly, it underpins the transference of witchcraft ideas within an oral society and documents a rapid speed of transmission of witchcraft ideas.

Studies of children in witchcraft trials have been performed for various countries. Wolfgang Behringer, Rolf Schulte, Lyndal Roper, Alison Rowlands and Robert S. Walinski-Kiehl have written about child witches in Germany.[73] Diane Purkiss has studied incest in connection with Scottish witchcraft research.[74] In a European frame Sweden and Spain are often mentioned in connection with children in witchcraft cases. Gustav Henningsen and Gunnar Knutsen have treated children accused of witchcraft in Spain as part of broader studies. In the Swedish Blåkulla trials, a high number of children were called in as witnesses, a phenomenon which

---

[71] The entry was made by the then district governor Bjelke. Ref. Bergh, 'Til ild', 140.

[72] Willumsen, *Seventeenth-Century Witchcraft Trials in Scotland and Northern Norway*, 99.

[73] Behringer, W., 'Kinderhexenprozesse', *Zeitschrift für Historische Forschung*, 16 (1989), 31–47; Schulte, R., 'Ein Kinderhexenprozess aus St. Margarethen', 48–55 in *Wider Hexerey und Teufelswerk... ' Von Hexen und ihrer Verfolgung* (Itzehoe, 2000); Roper, L., "'Evil imaginings and fantasies": Child-witches and the end of the witch craze', *Past and Present*, no. 167, (2000), 107–139; Roper, L., *Witch Craze. Terror and fantasy in Baroque Germany* (New Haven, 2004), 196–221; Rowlands, A., *Witchcraft Narratives in Germany. Rothenburg 1561–1652* (Manchester, 2003), 16–26; Walinski-Kiehl, R. S., 'The devil's children: child witchtrials in early modern Germany', *Continuity and Change* 11(2) (1996), 171–189.

[74] Purkiss, D., 'Sounds of Silence: Fairies and Incest in Scottish Witchcraft Stories', in S. Clark (ed.), *Languages of Witchcraft: Narrative, Ideology and Meaning in Early Modern Culture* (New York, 2001), 81–98.

has been discussed in studies by Bengt Ankarloo, Per Sörlin, Per-Anders Östling, Maria Lennersand, Linda Oja and Jari Eilola.[75] As for discourse analyses related to child witches, the studies made by Rowlands, Roper, Sörlin, Eilola and myself are of interest.[76]

Maren Olsdatter, twelve years old, was denounced on 26 January 1663 by another child, Ingeborg Iversdatter, who was the first child accused of witchcraft in Finnmark. In her confession Ingeborg also mentioned the names of Solve Nilsdatter, Ingeborg, Guri from Ekkerøy, Liiren Margrete and Sigrid—all adults. Ingeborg said that on Christmas Eve she and Solve had crawled under the gate of the castle in the shapes of cats and set off for Kiberg, led and carried by the Evil One. Solve wanted Guri from Ekkerøy and Ingeborg to go with them, but Ingeborg said she did not know how they would get back and stayed behind. Margrete excused herself, saying she was heavy.[77] Eventually Solve and Ingeborg left on their own together with the Evil One. There they waited outside Anders Pedersen's cellar until the child Maren and Sigrid came from Vadsø. 'When they had arrived, they all went to the aforementioned Anders Pedersen's cellar, and while they were helping themselves to the contents of the barrels and drinking, the Evil One blew flames from the horn in his side, which lit up the cellar for them as he did so'.[78] This might be for amusement and entertainment; the Devil is often portrayed as a playful figure. So Maren's name was first introduced in connection with this special Christmas party.

---

[75] Ankarloo, B., 'Sweden: The Mass Burnings (1668–76)', in Ankarloo and Henningsen (eds.), *Early Modern European Witchcraft. Centres and Peripheries*, 295–96; Sörlin, P., 'The Blåkulla Story: Absurdity and Rationality', *Arv. Yearbook of Folklore*, 52 (1997), 131–152; Östling, P.-A., 'Blåkulla Journeys in Swedish Folklore', *Arv. Yearbook of Folklore*, 62 (2006), 81–122; Lennersand, M., 'Rättvik', 375–596 i Lennersand and Oja, *Livet går vidare*; Lennersand M. and Oja, L., 'Vitnande visionärer. Guds och Djävulens redskap i Dalarnas häxprocesser', in H. Sanders (ed.), *Mellom Gud og Djævelen. Religiøse og magiske verdenbilleder i Norden 1500–1800* (København, 2001), 177–184; Eilola, J., 'Lapsitodistajien kertomukset Ruotsin noitatapaukissa 1668–1676' [Child witnesses' stories in witchcraft trials in Sweden 1668–1676], E-journal *Kasvatus and Aika*, 3 (2009); Henningsen, G., *The witches advocate: Basque witchcraft and the Spanish Inquisition, 1609–1614* (Reno, 1980); Knutsen, *Servants of Satan and Masters of Demons*, 69, 91, 103–104, 119–124.

[76] In addition to the above mentioned research, see Willumsen, L. H., 'Barn anklaget for trolldom i Finnmark—en narratologisk tilnærming', in *Heimen*, 3 (2011); Willumsen, L. H., 'Cildren accused of witchcraft in 17th-century Finnmark', in *Scandinavian Journal of History*, 38:1 (2013), 18–41.

[77] This probably meant she was pregnant.

[78] SATØ, SF 10, fo. 244r.

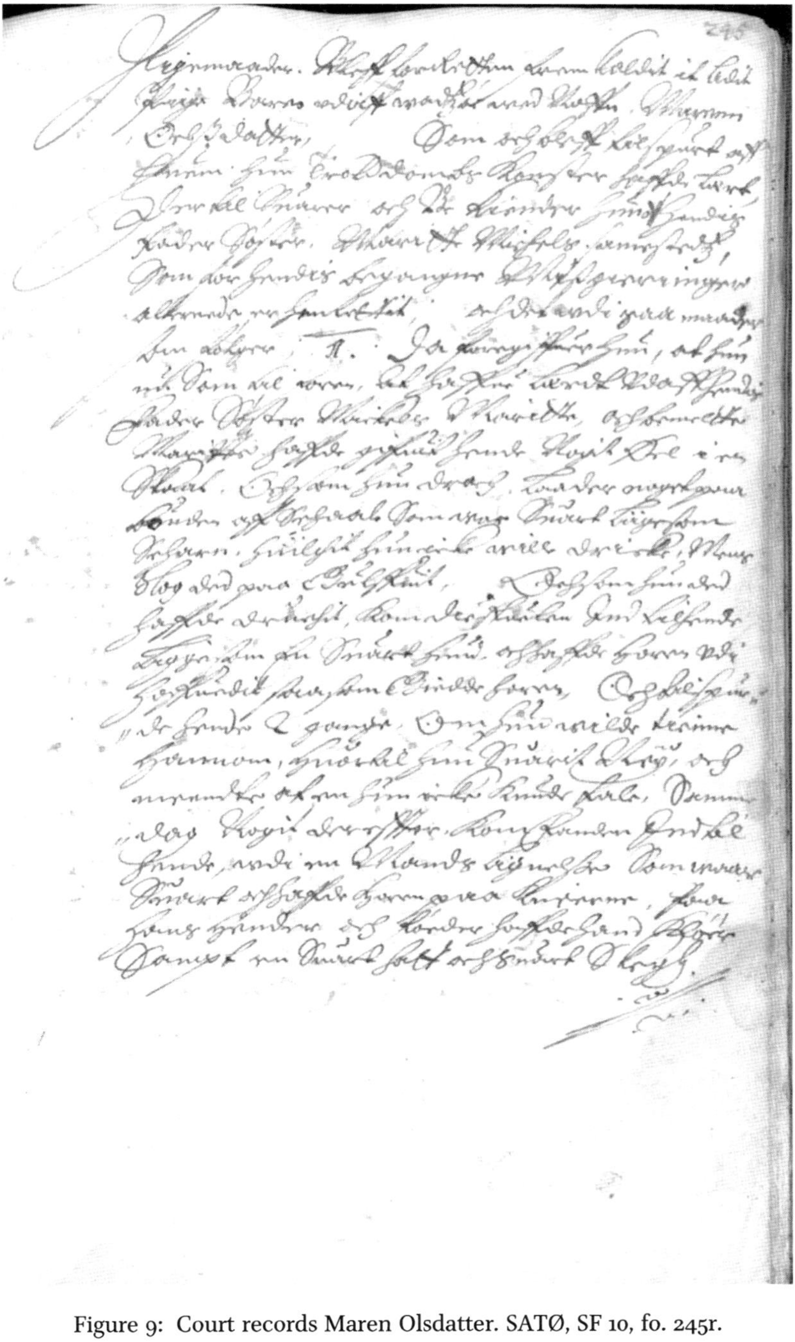

Figure 9: Court records Maren Olsdatter. SATØ, SF 10, fo. 245r.

The Voice of the Scribe

In the case of Maren Olsdatter, the main task of the scribe seems to have been inserting words of coherence like 'also' in sentences like 'she also confesses' and 'the little girl confesses'. The function of the scribe, in other words, was to keep the itemized confession together. Maren herself answered the questions posed to her in a fluent way. There was no need for the questioners to press her. She did not hesitate, nor did she show any despair, so there was nothing unusual about her way of confessing that might be of interest for the scribe. Thus he does not give any description of Maren or any evaluative comments on her behalf. His voice is withdrawn. Instead Maren's own voice may be clearly heard in her confession written down in the court records the same day as she was denounced.

On one occasion, however, the scribe shows scepticism as to whether Maren told the truth. When she persistently named Peder Oelsen's wife and daughter, contrary to the confessions of the other accused adults, the district governor

> *cautioned her to tell the truth if she wanted to be reckoned amongst God's children.* To which she answered, saying that it was certain that she and her daughter are witch people and that they had both been in the shapes of cats, as has been narrated, and that they were at the castle for that great convention and that she does not want to vilify them, *as the truth will always prevail in the end.* [My italics.][79]

The scribe found it appropriate to include the district governor's cautious remark in the records. The philosophical concluding remark of Maren, which functions as a kind of a threat, is also given space in the records, maybe to show that Maren's discourse was very insistent. The scribe is rendering the confession in an accurate way, keeping the oral features intact, thus letting the individual voice come to the fore, something which gives signals about a professional scribe, whose task it is to give a detailed account of what was said in the courtroom. His attitude to the told is not pointed out. This indicates that the scribe's attitude to the told is the same as the other judicial officials', which means he shared the fear of witchcraft which dominated at the time.

The Voice of the Accused

The voice of the accused is rendered by the scribe in just the same way as the voices of the adult persons who were questioned. The children do

---

[79] SATØ, SF 10, fo. 269r.

not seem to have been treated in a childish way or asked different questions to the grown-ups. Maren was probably asked the same questions about witchcraft as the adults.

Brought before the court, the first question was about her mentor, who had taught her. Maren confessed she had learned witchcraft from her mother and 'her father's sister, Maritte, Michel's wife from that same place, who has already been executed for her evil deeds'.[80] In demonological writing it is stressed how difficult it is to get rid of the Evil One once he has found a foothold in a family.[81] The notion that children were given[82] to the Devil by their mothers is found, for instance, in the confession of Ingeborg Iversdatter, in which she related about her sister Karen and herself, 'they both learnt it from their mother, for the Evil One was always with them in the past, and they cannot be rid of him, no matter how the priests work on them and try to convert them to Our Lord the Christ, he will never relinquish them, since they have been given to him by the mother'.[83]

Maren told how she acquired sorcery through a special drink, 'and the said Maritte gave her a little beer in a bowl, and as she was drinking, she saw something lying in the bottom of the bowl, something that was black as dirt,[84] something she refused to drink but poured out onto the floor'.[85] Black spots in drinks taken by witchcraft suspects have been documented in other records, and this has led to various suggestions, among others the ergotism theory.[86] According to this theory, it is maintained that those who gave confessions during witchcraft trials suffered from ergotism and hallucinated, for instance they felt they were flying through the air.[87] I do not think there is evidence for maintaining that ergotism could be a cause of confessions during witchcraft trials. In the fantastic narratives told by confessing persons, the element of explanation was central. Dark spots in drink or food could be seen as a convincing explanation for how they became able to perform witchcraft. The idea of the dark spots could easily

---

[80] SATØ, SF 10, fo. 245r.

[81] Cf. for instance Nicolas Remy: *Demonolatry* (London, 1930) chapter 3, orig. published 1595.

[82] In the records the Norwegian word *ofret* is used, which means sacrificed.

[83] SATØ, SF 10, fo. 257v.

[84] *Scharn*, in the original, what is cut off or secreted, for instance mouse droppings.

[85] SATØ, SF 10, fo. 245r.

[86] Alm, 'The Witch Trials of Finnmark, Northern Norway, during the 17th century: Evidence for Ergotism as a Contributing factor', *Economic Botany*, 57, iii (2003), 403–416.

[87] Goodare, 'Ergotism' in Golden, *Encyclopedia*, 4 vols., ii, 321–322.

be transferred from person to person, eventually being retold during a confession.[88] There are numerous examples during the witchcraft trials that specific notions are restricted to certain decades, in a way a passing fashion. The black spots could be looked upon as such an idea, making its entrance into the field of oral witchcraft belief and repeated within the witchcraft confessions during a restricted time period, which is exactly what we find in Finnmark during the panic of 1662–63.

Maren finished her drink, and 'the Devil came in to her as a black dog. And it had horns on its head, like goat horns'.[89] The appearance of the Devil, in Maren's description, is a common one. The image of the Devil as a creature with horns is widespread in oral tales and visual art. The notion of the Devil disguised as a dog is also frequent in folklore. But in her narrative about the Devil tempting her to be his servant, she also presented a more detailed portrait:

> And he asked her twice whether she would serve him, to which she replied, No, she did not believe a dog could speak. On that same day, a little later, the Devil came to her in the likeness of a man, black with horns on his knees. On his hands and feet there were claws, and he wore a black hat and had a black beard, and he asked her once again to serve him, but she kept her silence and refused to answer. Then he asked her once more to serve him for then he would give her money. Then she replied, Yes, and agreed to offer him her services.[90]

The images of the Devil were internalized among children as well as adults. Certainly sermons would have been important in introducing these notions into the local communities. Most common people at this time could neither read nor write. All types of material were transmitted orally, from governmental information to folklore. We clearly see the oral touch in Maren's narrative of temptation. The number three is well-known within folk tradition, and here we hear that the Devil first asked her three times, and not until the fourth time did she answer. The fact that the Devil offered her money seemed to be decisive. Taking into consideration that this is the voice of a child, it is interesting to see that in rendering this story, she maintained her autonomy vis-à-vis the Evil One, refusing several times to be his servant. She even revealed a sense of humour during her encounter with the Devil, telling him that she did

---

[88] Dark spots are not mentioned in S. Thompson (ed.), *Motif-index of Folk Literature* (Charlottesville, 2004).

[89] SATØ, SF 10, fo. 245r.

[90] SATØ, SF 10, fo. 245r–245v.

not believe a dog could speak. Maren had several fanciful elements in her confession, as was the case with the confessions of the other children as well. This is how Maren described a visit to hell:

> The Devil then told her that she should accompany him to Hell. She submitted to his demand and accompanied him to Hell, and she says that the route was very long, and when she got to Hell, she saw a very large lake in which a fire was burning, and the water was boiling, and the lake was full of people lying in the water, many of them flat on their faces, boiling. Now, the Devil had an iron pipe out of which he blew flames, saying that she should enjoy as much. The Devil also had a leg of ham which he dipped into the said water, bringing it up again at once, and now it was cooked. The said girl narrates that this lake was in a valley, and it was surrounded by a great darkness, and the people burning in the water, women and men alike, howled like cats, and then she saw these summoned women who had gone with her to Hell, the bell ringer's Sigrj from Kjberg in the likeness of a crow, a woman from Madkorffue by the name of Ingeborg, wearing crutches and in the likeness of a dove, Lirren from Waarøen, in the likeness of a long-tailed duck, Solwe from Andersby, in the likeness of an auk, Gurrj from Eckerøen, in the likeness of a fledgling cormorant. As for herself, she was in the likeness of a crow. When they had been in Hell for a while, they all went their separate ways, home.[91]

Such notions of Hell coincide with ideas that are common to this very day. Descriptions such as these may have seeped into popular beliefs through religious doctrine. Anyway, Maren must have been an observant child with a talent for story-telling, managing to bring into the narrative the detail about the Devil dipping a ham into the boiling water in hell. This might be a more innocent echo of the idea that the Devil boiled infant flesh in pots over the fire at Sabbaths.[92] This mild tone of the confessions in Finnmark is symptomatic, as the tone on the whole is less harsh than on the Continent. Maren also had a dramatic touch, adding to her description of the people boiling in hell, that many of them were lying flat on their faces in the water. But the Devil was a playful figure, and this aspect stands in contrast to the image of the people boiling. The Evil One entertained his guests, trying to create a merry atmosphere. Thus Maren was emphasizing both the agony of the boiling people and the laid-back attitude of the master of this place, playing on contrasts. She also managed to insert the location of Hell, lying in a valley surrounded by a great darkness—thus playing upon the well-known dichotomy between

[91] SATØ, SF 10, fo. 245v–246r.
[92] Roper, *Witch Craze*, 108.

the light of heaven and the darkness of evil forces. The whole narrative
is framed by literary devices as we know them from traditional oral tales:
first they left the human, recognizable world and at the end they went
back to their daily lives. As a whole, this description by a small girl tends
to strengthen the assumption that in orally transmitted stories, material
about the Devil and his kingdom was of great interest, and that children
were keen listeners to this type of stories. The image of Hell, however, the
children managed to remember and retell, as is seen in Maren's case.

Her confession also contained a story about a witches' meeting at the
Domen Mountain, not far from Vardø, where witches from the north
allegedly met:

> But somewhat later, on the eve of St Hans,[93] last year, these aforementioned
> women came to her and took her with them to Dommen. And there was the
> Devil with a red fiddle which he played for them, dancing with them. Solwe
> held his hand, the bell ringer's Sigrj held Solwe's hand, Lirren held Sigri's
> hand, little Maren held Liren's hand, Guren held this small child's hand and
> Ingeborg from Madkorff held Guren's hand. And when they had finished
> dancing, the Devil produced a small silver bowl and let them drink beer
> from it, saying that when they had served him, they would be remunerated
> with that very water which burned and boiled in Hell. And when they had
> made their arrangements and finished dancing with the Devil, each went
> back to her home led by the Evil One.[94]

This description emphasizes the joyfulness and sisterhood of the witches'
meeting, dancing in a ring, holding each other's hands. Drinking beer in
alehouses might be associated with something the women rarely did in
their daily lives. In this respect the witches' meeting seemed to represent
an opportunity for the women to live out wishes and desires. Still, this
was not an unpolished and utterly masculine event, on the contrary—a
certain refined touch can be seen, symbolized by the silver bowl.

Also traditional sorcery is mentioned in Maren's confession. Certain
rituals were related to stealing of milk from other people's cows. The
details in connection with this type of sorcery were mentioned in Maren's
confession:

> She also confesses and gives an account of how she learnt from her father's
> sister, on the eve of St Hans, before she was brought to Dommen, how to
> milk a cow. To this end, the father's sister gave her *a medium sized white
> horn*, which she tried out by milking Mortten Jensen's cow, *placing it on the*

---

[93] St John's Eve, a noted witchcraft time.
[94] SATØ, SF 10, fo. 246r.

cow's abdomen, saying that she wanted to milk *in the name of the Devil*. Then she got more milk than would fill a pail and after that, blood came out, and then the cow died. [*My italics.*][95]

Cows giving blood was a well-known indication that they had been bewitched. Still, it is interesting to note that the girl was so aware of the size of the horn to be used, where to place it on the cow and what to say in order to perform sorcery. Even the eve of St Hans is mentioned by Maren. Rendering all the details indicates that this was common knowledge among people and that she had heard oral stories about this practice. As for folkloric beliefs, Maren's confession is probably representative of the knowledge found among ordinary people, both those who were taken to court and accused of witchcraft and those who were not accused. Maren was in a situation during the questioning where all she had learnt about sorcery and witchcraft was activated.

The ability to transform themselves into different shapes was an element of demonology frequently confessed to in Finnmark. These shapes were used to perform sorcery and for witchcraft meetings. Maren was detailed about this element as well as the rest: 'She also confessed that she could turn herself into a cat, but only if the Devil brought her some cat's blood to smear over her body and the fur of a cat to coat herself with. When she had done so, she was a cat'.[96]

Naming other women was a compulsory element of a confession produced by the influence of leading questions. In her confession, Maren named five other women. All of them were accused of witchcraft and questioned later on. For one of these, Maren's denunciation had disastrous consequences.

> She also confessed that her father's sister taught two women in Omgang sorcery. She also confesses that she was with the bell ringer's Sigrj, who had her small child with her, and Solwe, in Anders Persen's cellar in Kjberg where they drank beer. The bell ringer's Sigrj poured it for them, and she placed her child on a barrel while she was tapping the beer and drinking it. Afterwards, they went to Rev. Hans's cellar in Waarøen and drank a bit there. After that, *the bell ringer's Sigrj and Solwe wanted to set fire to the castle*, but they couldn't get to it because the district governor was always reading the Bible and prayed to God for mercy, so they had to leave in shame. And the same girl child confesses that Solwe cast a spell upon the foot of the reverend's wife, Karen Rasmusdatter, but that they can get no power over

---

[95] SATØ, SF 10, fo. 246r–246v.
[96] SATØ, SF 10, fo. 246v.

Reverend Hans. Having done all this, they each went their separate ways,
home. [*My italics.*][97]

The confession thus far contained all the elements of interest to the witch-
hunters. One might think that this was sufficient and the questioning considered finished. But this was not the case. There was something more at
stake during this panic. The fact was that the district governor thought
that the witches had conspired against him. Maren mentioned in her
confession that after the visit to Anders Persen's cellar, Sigrid and Solve
wanted to set fire to the castle. However, they were prevented because of
the governor's trust in God. He also suspected the witches to have caused
pains in his arms and foot, and he wanted this confirmed. One item in
Maren's confession has to be seen within this frame.

> Moreover this little girl confesses how, two nights ago, she, Gurrj and Siigrj
> went to a place that was very dark, and Sigrj and the others requested from
> the wicked Satan a good bandage for the district governor's foot and arm so
> that it would heal, but the wicked one allegedly replied that they should not
> have it, for it would heal nobody, and they would not be let off anyway, and
> as for which of them had been the cause of the pains in the district gover-
> nor's foot and arm, the aforementioned girl Maren confesses that it appar-
> ently was Solwe and Siigrj, as well as that woman Margrette, who recently
> was incarcerated at the castle.[98]

Maren's confession about the object Solve had used in casting a spell on
the district governor created a possibility of showing this object to the
court, in order to strengthen Maren's confession.

> This same girl child Maren also gives an account of how Solwe allegedly
> had a piece of linen with black yarn held together with witchcraft, which
> she [*the child*] saw Solwe tucking into a hole in her [*prison cell*] wall. Her
> intention was allegedly to cast a spell on the district governor with it, and
> when this child saw it, the Evil One gave her [*Solwe*] the likeness of a cat.
> And this was all done because the district governor wanted to put Solwe
> in ball and chains, and when she finally was shackled, she threw away the
> bewitched thing, but *it was subsequently diligently searched for and found
> and presented before the court*, and it was just as this girl child has described
> it. [*My italics.*][99]

After Karen Iversdatter had confessed to a plot to kill the district governor with pins, Maren was brought in and maintained that this was true.

---

[97] SATØ, SF 10, fos. 246v–247r.
[98] SATØ, SF 10, fo. 247r.
[99] SATØ, SF 10, fo. 247r–247v.

She also confessed that after the district governor and his young woman[100] had left the castle and gone on a trip on the fjord, the young woman was left behind in Wadtzøe, and Lirren, who was imprisoned at the castle, contacted the Devil to ask for something with which to cast a spell on the young woman's head.[101]

Maren seems to have been accepted by the adult suspects as able to perform sorcery at the same level as a grown-up. Maren was an accomplice of Ellen Gundersdatter, who wanted to cast a spell upon her former mistress in Bergen: 'the Evil One wanted her and Ellen to go with him to Bergen, to the woman referred to, and the Wicked Satan was in the shape of a medium sized man dressed in black, and if she refused to go with him, he would take her anyway'.[102]

The voice of Maren, a child, does not differ much from the voices of the adult suspects. She answered leading questions thoroughly and knew how to colour her narrative with details. All the essential elements of a demonological witchcraft confession are present in her confession. She denounced other women, contributing to the continuance of the trials. And she gave important information about the conspiracy against the district governor, which was an important item during the panic of 1662–63. The women were accused of causing a shipwreck as well, but the accusations connected to the sickness of the district governor were important and, if possible, had to be proved. Maren's voice was strong and convincing as regards her participation in witchcraft.

The Voice of the Law

Since this was the first time children were accused during the Finnmark witchcraft trials, it is interesting to see how the legal authorities treated their cases. The local court considered the cases to be difficult:

> Furthermore, since these two children, Ingeborig and Maren, have so often confessed, at Waardøeshuus Castle, that they have learnt and practised witchcraft, and also since they are held at the Castle where the district governor repeatedly urges them, and the priest daily and assiduously admonishes them, to turn away from the Evil One and be converted to the ways of God in Heaven, to no avail, for they still, according to their own confessions, have the Evil One at their sides and cannot tear themselves away from him, and since, moreover, this little girl child Karen, who is the sister of Ingeborg,

---

[100] Orig. *Jomfru*, literally *virgin*; perhaps a very young bride.
[101] SATØ, SF 10, fo. 253r.
[102] SATØ, SF 10, fo. 255r.

who also, according to the latter's own confession, has learnt witchcraft, and they both saw it at their mother's, for the Evil One was always with them in the past, and they cannot be rid of him, no matter how the priests work on them and try to convert them to Our Lord the Christ, he will never relinquish them, since they have been given to him by the mother;

In view of such circumstances and of the clergymen's considerations, *His Royal Majesty's bailiff puts before the court whether they should not be punished with loss of life and prevented from learning more mischief from the Devil and enticing other children, at the whim of the Devil.*

Then, after indictment and responses, and in accordance with the circumstances of the case, and since the aforementioned children cannot deny having learnt witchcraft, according to their own lengthy confessions, which is self-evident, as has been recorded, and also *since they are but small under-age children who have not reached an age to make their own decisions, nor have they ever been to God's altar to receive the blessed sacrament, but are utterly ignorant, this is a difficult case to decide.* We therefore, in this case, know no other course than to decide and to judge that we, in this case, defer to a superior judge, our illustrious Court of Appeal Judge. [*My italics.*][103]

The argument for execution seems based on the children's alleged relation to the Devil and the danger of influencing other children. Their young age and lack of Christian knowledge weighs in the opposite direction. The same arguments were used by the presiding judge of the Court of Appeal, who acquitted all the children.[104] When the children's cases were tried before the Court of Appeal, they confessed that Anne Rhodius had persuaded them to lie about their mothers and to confess about pacts with the Devil.

Summing Up

The children's confessions at Vardøhus were taken seriously. Their denunciations led to imprisonments and executions. Anne Rhodius manipulated the children by tempting and threatening them, in fact she trained them in retelling demonological ideas, for instance where they had their Devil's mark. The role of the scribe, as it comes to the fore in Maren's case, is withdrawn. However, occasionally his own attitude penetrates the formal

---

[103] SATØ, SF 10, fos. 257v–258r.

[104] The children were acquitted from the accusation of witchcraft on 23 June 1663. Ref. Regional State Archives of Trondheim, LF 1647–1668, fos. 151–152. However, according to a document in the archives of the Regional Governor of Finnmark, the Court of Appeal Judge, Mandrup Scønnebøl, sentenced Maren Olsdatter for having lied on herself and others, to stay for some time at the penitentiary in Bergen. This is not entered into the Court of Appeal protocol and was probably not effectuated, as there is documentation that she lived in Vardø after 1663. Ref. SATØ, AF, no. 2543, Copies of sentences 1631–70.

language, showing that his fear of child witches as well as adult witches is strong. Features from oral discourse are preserved in the records, supporting the personalization of the various voices.

The voice of the law in this case is heard particularly in the verdict and sentence, where arguments come up for death sentence of children. It is clear that this was considered a difficult case, and therefore the local court could not take a final decision. After the cases were passed on to the Court of Appeal, there is no mentioning of guilt any more on the part of the children. From the wording of the Court of Appeal Judge, there was never a question of passing execution sentence on a child.

The contents and the structure of Maren's confession are similar to adults' confessions. Maren was asked the same range of questions, and she knew very well the answers to these questions. Her confession is structured like a narrative. Apparently these structures were important to remember the stories told.

Maren's voice was individualized, which particularly comes to the fore through orality stamps in her confession. For instance, in the story about the trip to Hell she used details which were absolutely her own creation. One of the adult women accused during this panic said that she was also on the trip to Hell, but she did not see the same details as Maren, indicating that this was an invention on the part of Maren. Other features of orality, for instance repetitions, occur frequently, for instance related to the ritual of learning witchcraft. Several scholars working with child witches, among them Jari Eilola, points to the fact that the children's narratives are complex and cannot as a rule be said to be produced only to satisfy the interrogators. Children's stories were not a direct repetition of what they heard from the adults.[105] Eilola maintains that the language in court records, next to spontaneous sermons, is closest to spoken language of all text corpuses from this period. Hence features of the local and the individual are prominent also in records from child cases, as we hear it in Maren's confession.

Oral transference of witchcraft ideas is documented in this case, when it is interpreted in a wider context. Demonological notions have been introduced in this society rather short time on beforehand by learned persons from the south of Norway. It is possible to find out the time span between the introduction of these notions and the retelling before the court. New ideas about witchcraft spread rapidly, also the ideas about children alleged to practice witchcraft. Stronger, even, than giving their children to the Devil, is another notion that was introduced by Anna Rhodius.

---

[105] Eilola, 'Lapsitodistajien', e-journal, not paginated.

Ragnilde Endresdatter, who was pregnant and gave birth to a child in prison, was exhorted by Anna Rhodius to confess. Ragnhild was threatened with every conceivable form of torture, but answered 'then I must lie about myself so that my life will end when I give birth to my child'. The answer she got from Ane M. Rodj[106] was: 'you are carrying not a child but a Devil'.[107] This is the only instance in the Finnmark material of the notion that the Devil had fathered a woman's child. The fact that such an allegation stemmed from a woman who had frequented learned circles is not surprising. There was a contemporary debate as to whether the Devil or demons could engender offspring, and if so, whether the offspring would be humans or demons.[108]

Both within a defined group of imprisoned persons at the castle as well as in the vicinity of Vardøhus the ideas of children in alliance with the Devil spread quickly. Also children listened to interesting 'news' of this type and they were able to learn the ideas and ready to accept these notions. The meetings between learned and popular culture in the villages was a continuous process, as pointed out by Sörlin.[109] The merging of ideas in the local communities was not the result of one meeting, but of many meetings.

Conclusion, 1662–63 Panic

With the panic of the early 1660s the period of witchcraft prosecution in Finnmark was close to an end. This was the last panic, and for the rest of the period of the witchcraft trials the number was only twelve. During the panic of 1662–63, new demonological ideas came to Finnmark. It has been possible to show that influence on the suspects from a learned person who knew demonology, Anne Friedrichsdatter Rhodius, resulted in witchcraft confessions containing ideas previously unknown in Finnmark. This suggests that the personal transference of demonological ideas was important. When new ideas were first planted in Finnmark, the situation was probably that a fusion between learned ideas and folkloric oral tradition took place.[110] This strengthens the assumption that government representatives from central Denmark-Norway with knowledge of demonological ideas played an important role in transferring these ideas

---

[106] Anne Magister Rhodius.
[107] SAT, LF Finnmark 1647–68, fo. 155.
[108] Broedel, H. P., *The Malleus Maleficarum and the construction of witchcraft* (Manchester, 2003).
[109] Sörlin, 'The Blåkulla story', 149.
[110] Briggs, *Witches*, 26.

to Finnmark in the first place when they entered important positions in the far north of Norway. The local communities were oral communities, and new ideas making their way into the mentality sphere were delivered from person to person in an oral manner. But the new ideas about the demonic pact, the witches' meeting, collective sorcery operations and shape-shifting had to be introduced to the common people in Finnmark by people from outside before these ideas could make their way into the existing mentality world of beliefs.

Children as suspects in witchcraft trials were found in Finnmark during the 1662–63 panic.[111] This finding is closely related to the new demonological ideas introduced during this decade, which stated that children could be dedicated to the Devil by their mothers and that the Devil could father a child. Children denouncing other persons during the Finnmark panic contributed to further imprisonments and deaths. Among those denounced by the children was Ingeborg, the wife of Peder Krog, one of the women tortured to death before sentence was passed on her. The fact that small girls were brought before the court suspected of witchcraft shows that the climate during this panic was more extreme than the earlier panics in Finnmark. When only girls, not boys, were accused, this corresponds with the absolute number of women during this trial. When demonological ideas were strengthened, the aspect of gender also came more clearly to the fore.

During the 1662–63 panic a variety of records from the local courts shows that torture was used to an extent and with a cruelty unknown before this date. An interesting finding—and a finding that could only be discovered through close-reading of the sources—is that indirect references may be a good indication of use of torture, for instance through expressions like 'confessed willingly' after torture had been documented applied. The same is found in a Swedish study by Bjørn Åstand.[112] Concealed ways of paraphrasing torture is also mentioned related to a study of witchcraft trials in Göta Court by Per Sörlin.[113] One has to read in the negative or 'between the lines' to find out what happened.

---

[111] Similarly to children witnesses during late witchcraft trials in Sweden. Ref. Ankarloo, B., 'Sweden: The Mass Burnings (1668–76), in Ankarloo and Henningsen, *Early Modern European Witchcraft*, 295–6; Östling, P.-A., 'Blåkulla Journeys in Swedish Folklore', in *Arv, Nordic Yearbook of Folklore*, lxii (2006), 81–122.

[112] Åstrand, B., *Tortyr och pinlig förhör—våld och tvång i äldre svensk rätt* (Umeå University, Ph.D. thesis, 2000), 116–18.

[113] Sörlin, P., *Trolldoms- och vidskepelseprocessarna i Göta hovrätt 1635–1754* (Umeå, 1993), 55.

The link between the influence of a specific person and the appearance of new demonological ideas in Finnmark during the early 1660s are findings of particular importance. Light is thrown not only on the transference of demonological ideas as such, but also on the time aspect. In this case it took only a few months from the new ideas being spread among those imprisoned to the same ideas being retold as part of confessions. Due to the scribe's very close rendering of the accused persons' discourse, the voices of the accused persons appear individualized.

Anders Poulsen, 1692

The Period 1664–92

The fires of the 1660s quickly burned out. The last decades of the witch trials in Finnmark were the 1670s, the 1680s and the 1690s. During the period 1670–1692 a total of 14 persons were accused of witchcraft in the district of Finnmark. Only one death sentence was passed. Four people were acquitted, one was fined, one was banished, two cases were postponed and not reopened, two were sentenced to confession in church, one person died during custody, one person was killed during custody, and in one case the sentence is not known. Overall the picture is quite different from the decades before 1670. The chances of acquittal, fine, banishment, or having the case postponed, increased dramatically. Linked trials no longer occurred. In short, accusations of witchcraft were not treated as severely as had been the case previously in the local courts of Finnmark.

The first witchcraft trial after the 1662–63 panic took place in Andersby, 1670, where a Sami woman, Sami Elli, was imprisoned. She died during custody; the cause of death is not known. Then in 1671, Magdelene Jacobsdatter from Andersby, who was involved in the 1662–63 panic, was acquitted. In 1672 there were two trials in West Finnmark, Maritte Gundersdatter from Hammerfest and Lange Mogens Zarasen from Øksfjord, resulting in acquittal and banishment. In 1678 Synnøve Johannesdatter was sentenced to death in Vadsø and two years later Kirsten Knudsdatter was acquitted in the same place. Then two trials in West Finnmark, against Karen Clemmitsdatter and Peder Gundersen, both 1680, resulted in acquittal and a fine. Five years later Gunder Tommersen was tried in Hammerfest; the sentence is unknown. In 1688 and 1689 two women were tried in Sandskjær for divination; Karen Nilsdatter and Birgitte Eriksdatter. Both cases were postponed and not reopened. In 1690 two women were tried in Kiberg, Karen Simensdatter and Maren Nilsdatter, and both

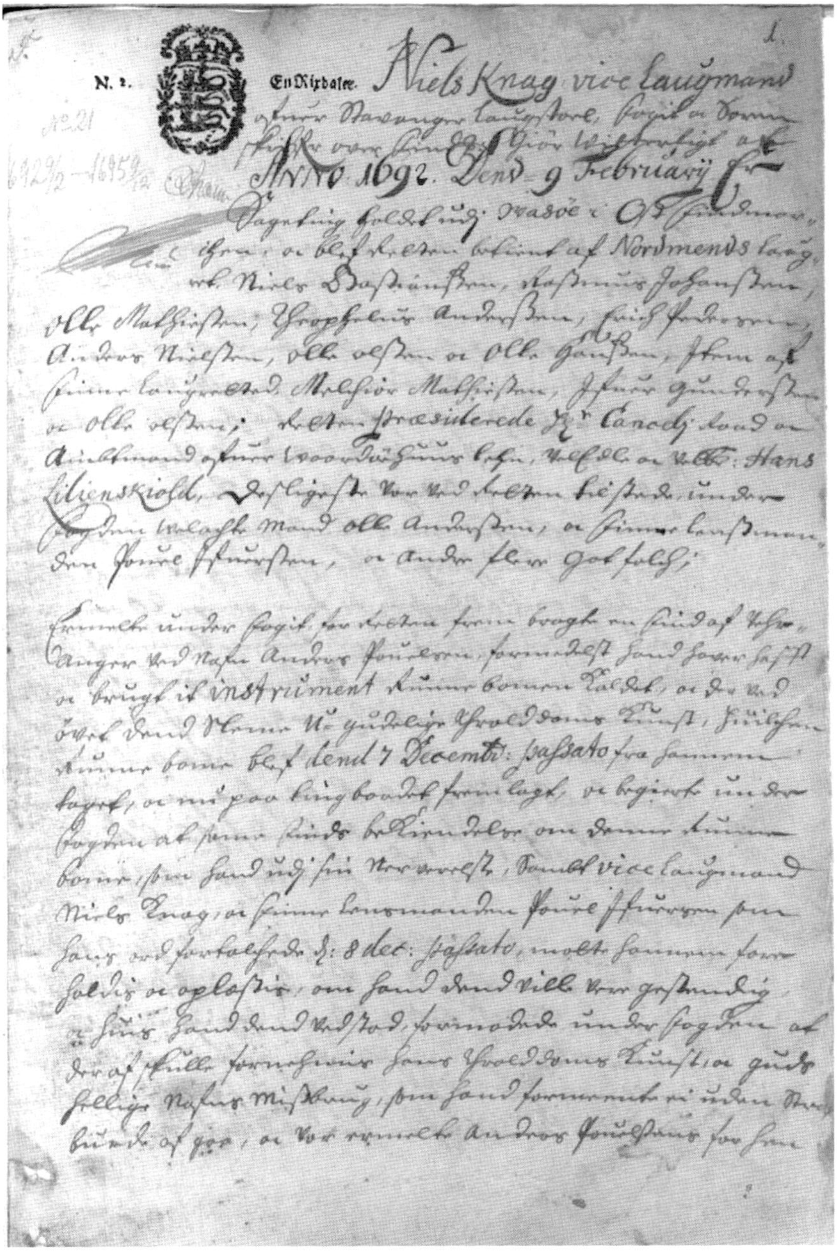

Figure 10: Court records Anders Poulsen. SATØ, SF 25, fo. 1r.

were sentenced to confession in church. Lastly, Anders Poulsen was tried in Vadsø in 1692. In the following I would like to focus on his trial.

The Trial

The trial of Anders Poulsen from Torne Lapland[114] in Sweden is indeed an unusual one. It has attracted attention from scholars and has been written about by among others Bergh, Niemi, Willumsen, Granquist and Hagen.[115] The existing scholarship so far has contributed in a valuable way to the exploration of Poulsen's case by focusing on his use of Sami magic, especially his use of the rune drum, as an authentic source of knowledge about Sami shamanism. The following analysis will add to the previous studies by a detailed discourse analysis as well as Poulsen's confession seen in the context of a criminal trial. Using a narratological approach enables me to examine the voice of Anders Poulsen in relation to the other voices heard during the trial, as well as to question the reliability of Anders Poulsen's confession.

Anders Poulsen was an old Sami shaman.[116] He possessed a rune drum, which was taken from him on 7 December 1691. He was interrogated 'in his chamber' about this drum and his confession was written down on 8 December.[117] The trial took place in Vadsø on 9 and 10 February 1692 under Deputy Appeal Court Judge[118] Niels Knag of Stavanger Court of Law, bailiff and magistrate of Finnmark.[119] The court was served by a jury of Norwegians and a jury of Samis and presided over by Herr Chancellery Secretary and Regional Governor of Waardøehuus District, Hans H. Lilienskiold. The trial was attended by the deputy bailiff, Olle Anderssen, and

---

[114] Orig. *Lapmarch*. Literally this word means in Norwegian 'The Sami field'. It is an area on the Swedish side of the border, around the lake Torneträsk and the river Torne river.

[115] Bergh, 'Til ild', 144; Niemi, *Vadsøs historie*, 346–349; Niemi, E., 'Anders Paulsen (Poulsen, Pouelsen)', in *Norsk biografisk leksikon* (Oslo, 1999), 84; Willumsen, *Trollkvinne i nord* (1984), 56–58; Granquist, K., 'Thou shalt have no other Gods before me, 13–21; Hagen, R., 'Harmløs dissenter eller djevelsk trollmann?', *Historisk tidsskrift*, no. 02–03 (2002) 319–46.

[116] The Sami word for shaman is *noaidi*.

[117] SATØ, SF 25, fo. 1r.

[118] This means that he had got the expectancy of the position.

[119] He possessed for some years the bailiff position as well as the magistrate position. As these two positions were connected with different aspects of the legal apparatus and the function of the legal official in the courtroom, his double position became problematic. Therefore the deputy bailiff had to run the case.

by the Sami constable[120] Pouel Iffuersen, who translated between Sami and Norwegian.

The Voice of the Law

The voice of the law is heard at the beginning and at the end of the trial, whereas the whole long middle section is the narrative of Anders Poulsen, almost a life story. Anders Poulsen was presented before the court by the deputy bailiff Olle Andersen

> on the grounds that *he has owned and used an instrument they call rune drum*,[121] with which he has practised that wicked and ungodly art of witch-craft. The said rune drum was taken from him on 7 December passato [*last*] and is now placed on the court table, and the deputy bailiff requests that this same Sami's deposition about this rune drum, which he made in his presence and that of the deputy appeal court judge, Niels Knag, and the Sami constable, Pouel Ifuersen, who interpreted his words on 8 December passato, should be put to him, and it is read out loud, so that it can be ascertained whether he abides by it, *and if so, the deputy bailiff assumes that it confirms his practice of witchcraft and the abuse of God's sacred name, something he claims should not go unpunished*, and the said Anders Pouelsen's previously made deposition, which is read to him now in court, is as follows. [*My italics.*][122]

This trial is different in several respects to the witchcraft trials referred to earlier. The only accusation against Anders Poulsen was that he had used the rune drum and thereby practised the 'ungodly art of witchcraft'. He had neither been denounced by another person, nor accused of having entered into a pact with the Devil, nor accused of any participation at a witches' meeting, nor accused of the deaths of humans or animals, nor accused of taking part in plots against the regional governor, nor accused of causing shipwrecks or being responsible for local disasters like chasing the fish from the shores or destroying the harvest. His art was an individual one, practised according to his personal knowledge of using the rune drum.

the only accusation is of using the rune drum

The voice of the law, in the words of the deputy bailiff Olle Andersen, reveals that the deputy bailiff himself considered Anders Poulsen's use of

---

[120] Orig. *lensmand*, an administrative official under the bailiff, at the lowest level of local administration in Norway. He represented the local police authority in Norway from the fourteenth century onwards.

[121] Orig. *Runne bomen.*

[122] SATØ, SF 25, fos. 1r–1v.

the rune drum ungodly and punishable. If Anders Poulsen abided by his previous confession, the deputy bailiff 'assumed' that this confirmed his practice of witchcraft and his abuse of God's name. The same depute bailiff 'claimed' that this practice should not go unpunished. The use of verbs reveals Olle Andersen's attitude towards the practice of Sami sorcery and the use of the rune drum. The denial of the pact of baptism is rewritten in this trial, the phrase 'the abuse of God's sacred name' echoing the common phrase from earlier decades, in which the legal discourse repeated that the confessing persons had given themselves from God to the Devil. Early in the trial words like 'devilish' and 'godless' were mentioned in relation to his mother: 'His immensely godless and devilish art, which he has learnt in the family, from his godless mother, a woman he says was not of the right faith in God in Heaven, like other people'.[123] This type of rhetoric becomes stronger towards the end of the trial, during the discussion of the verdict.

The account of the confiscation of the rune drum on 7 December is given in neutral language, although covering a dramatic situation, which must have been quite an event in the local community. In retrospect we learn what happened on 7 and 8 December, and it also becomes clear that Anders Poulsen did not speak Norwegian and therefore was dependent upon a translator during the interrogation. Anders Poulsen's rune drum is kept in the Sami Collections in Karasjok in Finnmark. It is a small, round drum, well-kept and with clear symbols, as seen in the illustration below, see Figure 11.

This drum is one of about 70 rune drums preserved today. It is described by E. Manker.[124] It is made of wood underneath and a reindeer hide is tightly pulled over it. The symbols are painted with bark colour.

The second time the rune drum is mentioned during the trial by the officials of the law, it is as an introduction to the detailed description of its construction and the imagery given by Anders Poulsen: 'The rune drum which is here present and which was made by him, according to his previous confession, *though he denies this now*, is quite worn by diligent use'.[125] [*My italics.*] During the interrogation on 8 December, Anders Poulsen admitted to having made the rune drum himself, but now, on 9 February, he denied this. The court still seems to have believed that he had made

---

[123] SATØ, SF 25, fo. 7v.
[124] Manker, E., *Die lappische Zaubertrommel*, ii (Uppsala, 1950) 430–40.
[125] SATØ, SF 25, fo. 2r.

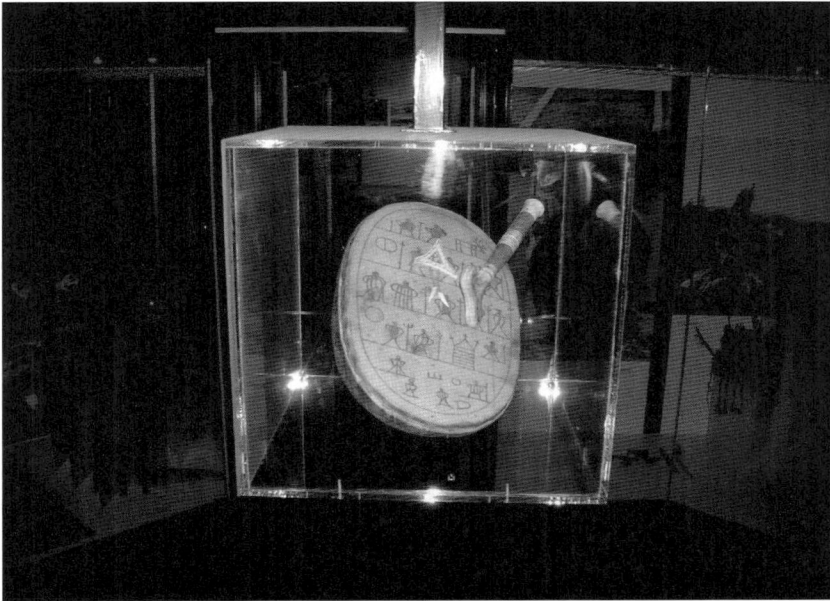

Figure 11: Anders Poulsen's rune drum, Finnmark.

the rune drum and that his denial was made in order to make his crime a bit milder. A comment from the court just before the detailed interpretation of the symbols of the rune drum starts makes it clear, however, that on 9 February Anders Poulsen again admitting to having made the rune drum himself, 'In the first row are, *now* that he has admitted to having made the drum himself...'. [*My italics.*][126]

As the description of the rune drum is rendered in indirect speech, the voice of the law can be heard in single words inserted in the sentences. For instance, the description of the figure of the *Engil*, belonging to the second row, is rendered in this way, 'The figure of a human, whom he calls Engil, *supposedly* the Holy Spirit'. [*My italics.*][127] The word 'supposedly' creates distance from the speech of Anders Poulsen on the part of the scribe, who uses a word that might have cast doubt on what Anders Poulsen was explaining. It is clear that the legal officials questioned Anders Poulsen's interpretation of the figures on the rune drum. The same expression is

---

[126] SATØ, SF 25, fo. 2r.
[127] SATØ, SF 25, fo. 3r.

used about the representation of a figure in the fourth row, manna: 'It is *supposed* to be the moon'.[128] Certainly a circle could have a lot of other interpretations, so the distancing word used by the scribe here is to the point. Another way on the part of the scribe to create distance from the story was to give a description of Anders Poulsen while he was drumming, 'all the while looking at his figures, and the ring danced up and down and he knocked with his hammer and uttered these words to the gods (...)'.[129] The sight of the shaman at work has for a while distracted the scribe from merely recording in an objective way. In addition he gives a glimpse of the situation in the courtroom, which must have been amazing, seen through his own eyes.

Traces of questions asked during the interrogation are seen throughout the whole confession, due to brief mentions of the questions. These echo the voice of the law, although indirectly. When Anders Poulsen had given his description of three figures in the third row representing the Christmas days, he was obviously asked if he had anything more to add, but answered that he 'would say no more about the days'.[130] We find another trace of a question after a description of the symbol of the moon in the fourth row: 'He would confess no more'. The last traced question during Poulsen's confession deals with lifting Sami spells: '*When asked* he says that when a Sami spell has been cast on someone (...)'. [*My italics.*][131] The traced questions suggest that the legal officials were eager to know as much as possible about the symbols on the drum, and in the courtroom they asked Anders Poulsen to add to his previous confession. In particular they were eager to know about the art of a Sami sorcerer, for instance lifting spells. But they were also interested in knowing about the dark effects of the rune drum, namely when the drum did not give answers implying luck and good fortune: 'But he will not *under any terms tell us* how the gods reply when the ring moves otherwise than in the same direction as the sun'. [*My italics.*][132]

Towards the end of the trial it becomes clear what the legal officials have really been looking for, while listening to Anders Poulsen. Before the verdict was delivered, the court went through the whole confession again and emphasized certain elements, especially that his art was a devilish art,

---

128 SATØ, SF 25, fo. 3v.
129 SATØ, SF 25, fo. 5r.
130 SATØ, SF 25, fo. 3v.
131 SATØ, SF 25, fo. 5r.
132 SATØ, SF 25, fo. 5v.

by which the figures of the drum 'induce him to believe, *at the devil's whim*, the acts and signs he asks about and looks for, which according to him are indeed confirmed by events'.[133] [*My italics.*] The figures in the fifth row are rendered by the court thus: 'in the fifth row he has a number of devils and the oldest devil's wife and the presumed instruments found in hell. In particular there is a devil who is supposed to represent disease, and he says it can kill humans, *and he worships many of these figures and symbols*'.[134] [*My italics.*] The court found his practice 'extremely punishable',

> particularly that he paints the holy trinity, God the Father, the Son and the Holy Ghost whom he by officiating with his incantations (...) and abuse so grievously profanes, scorns, desecrates and outrages, and that he recites the Lord's Prayer and makes the sign of the holy cross over himself and over the rune drum when preparing to play on it, and the reference he makes of his pictures as representations of God, God's created elements (...) and finally that he paints hell and the devils, and *he is particularly reluctant to explain the nature of his dealings with them*.[135] [*My italics.*]

The court had earlier stressed Anders Poulsen's reluctance to give details about the figures on the rune drum representing the Devil, as he himself had explained. Now these figures were seen as proving his godless and devilish art, which he had learnt from his mother. A distinction is being drawn between Samis who confess to Christianity and those who do not. Poulsen himself clearly did confess to Christianity. His son Christopher, who claimed to have conversations with Christ by talking with stones, is also mentioned as part of the family. The court found Anders Poulsen's art to be 'most outrageous, particularly in such desolate areas as these, where a great many people are unenlightened as to the true faith and worship of God, for which reason, many of them when subjected to something are far more prone to *seek advice from such witch people* than to turn to God in prayer and invocation'.[136] [*My italics.*] For the first time during the trial, the word 'witch' is used, and it is stated that is highly necessary to 'make a hideous example of suchlike godlessness'.[137] However, since such acts of worship of false gods 'as Anders Poulsen has voluntarily confessed to having practised and depended on, are not referred to in the statutes as punishable acts', the regional governor decided and found it advisable,

---

133 SATØ, SF 25, fo. 6v.
134 SATØ, SF 25, fo. 6v.
135 SATØ, SF 25, fo. 7v.
136 SATØ, SF 25, fo. 8r.
137 SATØ, SF 25, fo. 8r.

'after *my* having consulted with His Honour about the matter',[138] that the
case was deferred until a reply from the superior authorities in Copenhagen was forthcoming. The magistrate, Niels Knag, here enters the records
in the first person, which is very rare in this type of document. While the
court waited for a reply from Copenhagen, Anders Poulsen should be kept
in secure custody.

The court found that Anders Poulsen's property should be delivered
to the deputy bailiff, unless an adequate guarantee or bail was produced.
Subsequently an inventory, containing among other things reindeer and
reindeer sleighs, was presented to the court.

The answer from Copenhagen never reached Vadsø. On 22 February,
another hearing of the court took place in Vadsø, with regard to the killing
of Anders Poulsen on 11 February. He was killed with an axe by a mentally
disturbed person while he was asleep. The name of the murderer was Villum Gundersen, who had been working for the regional governor for a few
years. Gundersen admitted to the killing, and said 'there were no reasons
for this other than that he felt this same Sami was a sorcerer and that
he deserved to die'.[139] Witnesses were brought before the court, to testify about the killing. When questioned as to whether he felt guilty about
the killing and whether he deserved to die, he 'offered no sensible reply,
but was utterly silent'.[140] The heirs of Anders Poulsen, who demanded
death sentence for Villum Gundersen, did not receive any compensation
for their father, since he 'was a witchcraft practitioner and idol worship-
per who had forfeited his body to be burnt at the stake'.[141] This formulation, as it was heard in the voice of the law after Anders Poulsen's trial,
in my interpretation suggests that Anders Poulsen's practice was basically
looked upon as witchcraft, to be punished accordingly, even if Poulsen
was never convicted and his case was referred to Copenhagen.

The Voice of the Accused Person

The voice of Anders Poulsen is heard partly as the narrator of the document written on 8 December, read out loud in the court, and partly as a
commentator on this document. The written document contains information about his place of birth and his taxpaying both in Nordland and

---

138 SATØ, SF 25, fo. 8r.
139 SATØ, SF 25, fo. 11v.
140 SATØ, SF 25, fo. 14r.
141 SATØ, SF 25, fo. 14r.

in Finnmark, the two northernmost Norwegian regions.[142] He mentioned his many married children who lived in Finnmark, who paid tax to the king. Only one of his children, Christopher, was, according to him, a good doctor, though 'he did not know *the rune drum's art of doctoring*, but he could talk with stones, thereby obtaining answers to what he asked'. [*My italics.*][143] Anders Poulsen emphasized the taxpaying, both on his own and on his children's behalf. Even if his rune drum was taken from him and he knew that the interrogation had to do with his practice of the rune drum art, he seemed to have felt it necessary to introduce his confession by underlining that both he and his children had been lawfully paying taxes to the king.

In Anders Poulsen's own words, the art of using the rune drum is first referred to as the 'art of doctoring', later as 'wisdom':

> He says his age is a narrow century, which is five times twenty years, and that he derived his *wisdom* with the drum from his mother in his youth, and that when he first started learning, he was *wild and reckless*, though not reckless enough to harm any man, and *God promised him* that he would know good fortune all his life, but he said *he did not see God* when the promise was made to him; he only felt such thoughts in his chest while he was learning. [*My italics.*][144]

The whole range of words used by Anders Poulsen shows that he not only looked on the use of the rune drum as related to curing and healing, but that he included something wider when talking about the rune drum's doctorship. His mention of his son as a 'doctor', talking with stones to get the sought-for answers, and the doctoring connected to the rune drum, suggests that Anders Poulsen includes in the word 'doctoring' the rune drum's ability to give answers when questions are posed, so to speak the rune drum's ability to enable him to function as an oracle. This understanding of 'doctoring' denotes the rune drummer as someone having enormous authority.

Poulsen mentioned that he was 'wild and reckless' when he was learning the art of the rune drum, and later he said that his mother 'had been insane for nine years' when she learnt it.[145] Most probably Poulsen was referring to the experience of the trance that is supposed to be significant for the competence of a shaman. The use of the rune drum enabled the

---

142 In elderly Norwegian: *Nordlandene og Finmarken.*
143 SATØ, SF 25, fo. 1v.
144 SATØ, SF 25, fo. 1v.
145 SATØ, SF 25, fo. 1v.

drummer to enter a trance and go on a 'journey' to far away places to look for people, and to other 'levels of reality'. Wolfgang Behringer has called this separation of the soul from the body and its trip to certain places 'the constitutive element for any great shaman'.[146] According to Rita Pollan, a historian of religion who has been studying traditional Sami religion and culture, such a trip could take one and a half hours.[147]

Anders Poulsen describes his learning of the art of using the rune drum as directly related to God. In the same way as the accused witches during the earlier witch-hunt confessed that they gave themselves to the Devil and often got a promise from him that they would have something in return, Anders Poulsen said that God was the one promising him good fortune. When the name of God is mentioned early in his confession, it might be to underline that his art is not a devilish one, but a godly one, thus evading the idea that his use of the rune drum should be seen as witchcraft.

However, when he commented on his previous confession, he denied some of his former statements. About his mother, the one who had taught him, he said that 'she often spoke to God'.[148] But afterwards, when he named a person in Torne Lappmark, Anders Pedersen, as the one who had taught him and who had made his rune drum, Anders Poulsen said that 'the said Sami and his mother shared the same faith'.[149] Thus some contradictions are clear from the very beginning of Anders Poulsen's confession with regard to who taught him the use of the rune drum and who made the rune drum. These contradictions might suggest that he was trying to tell the deputy bailiff what the bailiff wanted to hear. It might also be that he confessed what he thought was appropriate for him to confess, to make the treatment in court less severe. The denial of the old Sami faith seems to have been particularly important for Anders Poulsen to underline, something that was repeated several times during his confession, related to himself and with an emphasis on Christian interpretation of the symbols in contrast to his mention of his ungodly mother.

The detailed rendering of the symbols of the rune drum is written in the records in indirect speech. What 'he says. . .' occupies most of the pages of the court records. It contains a long and detailed description of how the rune drum was made and an interpretation of all the symbols of the rune

---

[146] Behringer, W., *Shaman of Oberstdorf* (Charlottesville, 1998), 143.
[147] Pollan, *Samiske beretninger*, 22.
[148] SATØ, SF 25, fo. 2r.
[149] SATØ, SF 25, fo. 2r.

drum, five rows in all. In the first place, Anders Poulsen confessed that the symbols were painted with his blood; later he said they were painted with boiled water laced with alder bark. Most of the figures on the drum have Sami names. The rune drum is made from a pine tree that has been hollowed out so that it is a large, rounded, deep bowl, 'and he says it will not work unless it is made of pine'.[150] The skin of the drum head is reindeer skin, and it is decorated with two fox ears, a fox snout and a fox claw. When the rune drum is played with a hammer, a hollow triangle or ring[151] dances on the drumskin and eventually stops at one of the figures.

In the first row there are three symbols: the figure of a human called *Ilmaris*, who is tempest and bad weather, the figure of a human called *Diermis*, who is thunder, and the 'figure of a wild reindeer whom he calls *Gvodde*; it is a wild reindeer which, when God is prayed to, gives good fortune in the hunt of wild reindeer'.[152] Anders Poulsen repeated, when he was interpreting the symbols, 'When God is prayed to (...)'.[153] In the original historical document, 'God' is consistently written with a small initial letter. Presumably, the small 'g' implies that the scribe was rejecting the idea that it was the Christian 'God'. Due to the contents of Poulsen's confession, it seems that the God referred to here, is the One Christian God. And there is no doubt that the Christian tradition influenced Anders Poulsen's description of the symbols of his rune drum. However, the language of the rune drum as a religious language seems to have been flexible; new contexts and approaches made possible new interpretations of the drums' fixed structures and figures.[154] This might also be seen from the picture of Anders Poulsen's rune drum above. One of the religious insights Anders Poulsen pointed out in his confession was that God is almighty. God is in a position to delegate his power to his helpers, represented on the rune drum, but the helpers can act only on the command of God. The rune drum can be used for better or for worse, but the name of God is only mentioned in connection with the good effects of the rune drum:

> When God is prayed to, Diermis is helpful in that when there are floods and a lot of rain, he will call back the weather, and this *Diermis has no power unless God gives it to him*. He now also confessed that *Diermis can cause evil*

---

[150] SATØ, SF 25, fo. 2r.
[151] Orig. *dechel.*
[152] SATØ, SF 25, fo. 2v.
[153] SATØ, SF 25, fos. 2r–2v.
[154] Pollan, *Samiske beretninger*, 24.

and bad weather that damages ships and boats, but Diermis can also make
good weather again and prevent mishaps when God lets him. [My italics.][155]

Similarly, Anders Poulsen's comment on the figure of *Ilmaris* underlines
that when God is prayed to, *Ilmaris* is able to call back or drive away bad
weather that has been conjured. However, he is also able to make bad
weather, 'but he says it is *sinful* to ask for that'.[156] The use of the word
'sinful', which is a word frequently used in Christian discourse, suggests
that there is a border between good and bad use of the rune drum, even
if it might be used for both purposes. It is the same with the figure of the
wild reindeer—it may give good or bad luck. It 'gives good fortune in the
hunt for wild reindeer and when the rune drum is played. If the ring will
not dance for this reindeer, the one who asks for good hunting will not
get any reindeer, no matter how hard he tries'. Anders Poulsen's declarations are ambiguous. On one hand he underlines the blessings given
by God through the figures of the drum, the positive effects of practising
drumming, on the other hand he reveals that the drum might be used
for evil purposes.[157]

In the second row there are five figures. First a round circle pierced by a
line, called *Peive*, that is the sun, then a figure called the child *Jumal*, God's
child, or God's son the Christ. Then the figure of a human called *Juma-
Etziem*, God the father. Then the figure of a church, called *Dom Kirch*.[158]
At last the figure of a human, called *Engil*,[159] representing the Holy Spirit.
Even more than those on the first row, these symbols are interpreted by
Anders Poulsen as Christian symbols, although the legal officials seem to
doubt this frame of interpretation. The first symbol, *Peive*, the sun, is a
bit different from the others in this row, as it is related to the blessings
of good weather: 'When God is prayed to it will yield sunny and beautiful weather and fair air, particularly when the reindeer are calving and
when grain and grass are supposed to grow, and generally good weather
when this is asked for'.[160] The next four symbols in this row are religious
symbols with Christian connotations. These are all explained within the
framework of Christian discourse: God's son Christ absolves of all sin, God

---

[155] SATØ, SF 25, fo. 2v.

[156] SATØ, SF 25, fo. 2v.

[157] Another interpretation might be that he has developed his own quite sophisticated
theodicy, where *Diermis* guarantees good as well as evil.

[158] In Norwegian *domkirke*, in Swedish *domkyrka*, in German *Domkirche*.

[159] This word means in Norwegian 'angel'.

[160] SATØ, SF 25, fo. 2v.

the father 'castigates for all sins and other than that helps and provides, commands and punishes when asked to'[161] and *Engil*, supposedly the Holy Spirit. In the same row there is a symbol of a cathedral, which gives absolution, peace of mind and a Christian death, 'and whether you die or are alive, that same church will help'.[162] The language Anders Poulsen used to interpret the figures referred to the Christian trinity and mirrored central notions of the Christian Church: God as a strong, blessing and punishing father, Christ giving absolution of all sins, and the Holy Spirit: 'When prayed to he will absolve of all sin, so that you become a new and clean man, when he wants to help'.[163] The interpretation of the Holy Spirit is very much like the interpretation of the figure of Christ, so it might be that Anders Poulsen was not certain of the difference here. When describing the cathedral as giving absolution, peace of mind and a Christian death, several fields of Christian religious life are touched upon.

However, the ambiguity in this discourse comes to the surface again when a question possible to reconstruct from the discourse in the records, is answered by Anders Poulsen. The legal officials were apparently interested in knowing what kind of God he was worshipping. He answered that 'The God that is worshipped, *as has often been reiterated*, are those figures that he has painted, the deities, about whom he says his mother taught him'.[164] [*My italics.*] Anders Poulsen seems to have been of the opinion that he, during his confession, often had repeated what kind of God he had been worshipping, understood as the Christian God. But at the same time he referred to what his mother had taught him, a mother who was said not to share the Christian faith. The contradiction in Anders Poulsen's confession is a reason for becoming suspicious of his interpretation, even if he himself denied worshipping pagan gods.

The ambiguity and the blurred borders between different language levels become even more striking when Anders Poulsen interprets the figures' staffs, called *Juncher sabbe* or *Herr Sabbe*, painted on the rune drum. These were 'Juncher's staff' or 'the staff of great lords, for he says that just as the masters on earth hold staffs, so do these persons'.[165] Juncher—meaning a young nobleman—was a term used for the district governor at Vardøhus castle and a title Anders Poulsen certainly related to the highest

[*handwritten margin note:* the figures hold staffs like noblemen or governors]

---

[161] SATØ, SF 25, fo. 3r.
[162] SATØ, SF 25, fo. 3r.
[163] SATØ, SF 25, fo. 3r.
[164] SATØ, SF 25, fo. 3r.
[165] SATØ, SF 25, fo. 3r.

authority under the king. In Anders Poulsen's interpretation, these figures were actual human lords or government officials.

In the third row there are five figures: a human figure called St Anna, a figure of Maria, the mother of Christ, and three figures called *Julle*[166] *Peive, Julle Herr*, 'they are Christmas days, Christmas masters who rule over Christmas'.[167] For the first time some of the figures of the rune drum are interpreted as females. The first of the two figures, St Anna, he said was 'Mary's sister who assists Mary when she gives succour, but in other respects she can do nothing unless Mary wishes her to'.[168] Conventionally St Anne was Mary's mother. The second female figure is given various names by Anders Poulsen: Maria, *Jumal Enne, Jumal Ache*: 'This is Maria, the mother of Christ, God's wife, and when prayed to she will in particular help women in confinement, and she is conducive to absolution from sin and she is worshipped at God's side'.[169] Here we have two female symbols, the first one given a saint's name and the second being God's wife. This is certainly not in accordance with standard Protestant religious doctrine, and probably shows Anders Poulsen's lack of knowledge about these Biblical persons. However, to underline the function of the female symbols as helpers seems to be appropriate to the task of a shaman, a person who was often contacted in problematic situations. The fact that women were seen as suitable helpers for those who were in need, and especially in connection with confinement, probably reflected questions Anders Poulsen had often been asked about as a shaman, so this might be seen as an echo of his clients' questions.

About the figures representing the three Christmas days, Anders Poulsen explained:

> They are Christmas days, Christmas masters who rule over Christmas. Oucht Jule Peiv is the master of the first Christmas day, Gought Jule Peive is the master of the second Christmas day, Gvolme Jul Peive is the master of the third Christmas day. If anybody defiles these days, God will punish them, but if somebody honours them and then prays to God for something, then these days are exhibited to God and it will be submitted that so and so has honoured the days and that God will help for that very reason.[170]

---

[166] *jul* means Christmas in Norwegian.
[167] SATØ, SF 25, fo. 3v.
[168] Anne was Mary's mother. SATØ, SF 25, fo. 3v.
[169] SATØ, SF 25, fo. 3v.
[170] SATØ, SF 25, fo. 3v.

This explanation about keeping the Christmas holidays might or might not have been in accordance with the teaching of the church. God is described as blessing those who keep his commandments and punishing those who do not. But this might well be a mixture of several aspects.[171]

In the fourth row five figures are painted: a round circle representing the moon, the figures of two men going to church, the figure of the church he belongs to, and a figure of a man coming to church from the opposite direction. About the symbol of the moon, *Manna*, Anders Poulsen explained: 'When God is worshipped it shines brightly and the nocturnal weather will be fine even if there is a heavy cover of clouds'.[172] The other figures in the row represent the church,[173] persons going to church and giving to the church. The logic about giving to the church is interesting: 'Yet, he adds, nobody gives unless they receive help' and the kind of trouble he mentioned was related to reindeer and illness. Again the interpretation of the figures was influenced by the preaching of the church, that people should attend services and give money to the church.

In the fifth and last row there are seven figures—all of them have to do with the Devil: first a woman who is supposed to be the wife of the bound devil, the second a devil who kills people and who is disease, the third a figure of the devil 'who is on the loose now and rules in Hell and floats about in the world'.[174] The seventh figure, called *Hvenaales Gvolisis*, is 'a bound devil in chains, the one who was bound up when God created the world'.[175] Then the fourth, fifth and sixth symbols are drawn in the records, like this:

> 4 A figure that looks like this ⌊⌊⌋, which he calls Hilvet Tol, the flames of Hell, the fire that consumes people's souls in Hell.

> 5 A figure that looks like this ◌. which he calls Hilved Tarve Giedme, Hell's tar cauldron, in which people's souls in Hell are boiled.

> 6 A figure that looks like this ⌷, which he calls Hilvet Haufd, Hell's grave, into which all people who believe in the Devil are thrown, and God is the one to throw them.[176]

[171] In the Scottish withcraft trials in Aberdeenshire 1597, Andrew Man mentioned the word 'Christsonday', which resemble a bit Anders Poulson's rhetoric.

[172] SATØ, SF 25, fos. 3v–4r.

[173] Orig. *Kirche*.

[174] SATØ, SF 25, fo. 4r.

[175] SATØ, SF 25, fo. 4v.

[176] SATØ, SF 25, fo. 4v.

No doubt, the interpretation of these different devils was coloured by the Bible and the notions about hell and punishment after death found there, although here we hear that people's *souls* are consumed by the flames of hell and boiled in the tar cauldron of hell, not their bodies, and the image thus deviates from common visual representations of the boiling water of hell. There are several devils: one who is disease, one who is loose, for whom Anders Poulsen has no name, and one tied, and the explanation for how one of the devils escaped is very earth-bound: 'This devil escaped when God tied up the other devil, described below, and God was wearing iron shoes when he found this one and trampled on him so he disappeared in a great bog'.[177] During the explanation of the devils, Anders Poulsen touched upon God's creation of the world and the gruesome punishment in hell for those who believed in the Devil. There were no comments from the legal officials during this part of Anders Poulsen's interpretation of the rune drum symbols, even if the material about the devils must have been regarded as extremely important.

Anders Poulsen then continued by explaining how he used the hammer and the hollow ring, called Palm, to get 'answers' from the rune drum. When he used the hammer, the ring danced, and it mattered which way it danced around the drumskin. If the ring danced anti-clockwise, the person he was playing for would have bad luck, 'but if it gets so far down that it stops near them under the last line in the fifth row, God is angry with whoever he is playing for, and that person will have to pray a great deal to God before the ring will go back again, so that God shows him that he is a sinful person'.[178] As the last line in the fifth row deals with the torment of hell, this was obviously an unfortunate place for the ring to stop.

Then a very special event took place in court. Anders Poulsen picked up the rune drum and played the drum, 'having first crossed himself' and then made the sign of the cross over the drum, and recited the Lord's Prayer in the Karelian[179] language, before he continued with his own prayer. While drumming, he was looking at the figures and the ring and confessing the sins of the person he was pleading for.

He was afterwards asked whether he could lift a Sami spell, to which he answered that he could 'lift the spell with the aid of his gods and cast it on the one who cast the spell in the first place', and he demonstrated how

---

[177] SATØ, SF 25, fos. 4r–4v.
[178] SATØ, SF 25, fo. 5r.
[179] In this context the word means Finnish.

he did that. For the first time Anders Poulsen here mentioned his 'gods' in the plural. He demonstrated how he lifted spells, playing the drum until the ring landed on one of the devils in the fifth row. Then the spell released its hold on the person who was struck and shifted to the one who had cast the spell. He said he had helped many a person in Swedish Lapland, but nobody in Norway. In the same way he demonstrated how the ring danced to one of the devils if a thief should be punished, 'and then he plays for such a long time that God punishes the thief who has stolen, so that he withers and shrivels into no more than a dry tree'.[180] This part of Anders Poulsen's confession, where the traced question shows that he was particularly asked about his ability to lift Sami spells, has to do with the art of the shaman to use the drum in specific ways that Samis traditionally had a reputation for mastering. But even here, when finding a thief for instance, he underlined that God was the one who punished. He also said that by prayer to God, when he played the rune drum, 'he can provide good conditions for the reindeer so that wolves do not kill them, and good fortune in other ways. When helping women in confinement, he plays the rune drum, and he learns what is God's will when the ring dances on the rune drum'.[181] Anders Poulsen was very eager to show that he was only doing well with his playing, and he said that Christ had forbidden both him and his son to do harm. He claimed that he could get an answer from the drum when he held it high into the air, 'just as two persons do when they talk to each other'.[182]

The clearest indication of Anders Poulsen's fear comes at the end of his confession, where he declared that even if he could officiate in all the above-mentioned matters, 'he would not admit to having used or practised any of them here in this country, and he protested his innocence'.[183] He also stated that he had not forsworn God in heaven or his Christian faith, and when worshipping the depicted gods, he believed they were all God in heaven. And 'since the authorities objected to his using the rune drum, he would relinquish it now, and believe in God in Heaven just like other people'.[184] The last remark indicates that in spite of his frequent reassurance about his belief in the One Christian God, he still believed in the old traditional Sami religion.

---

[180] SATØ, SF 25, fo. 5v.
[181] SATØ, SF 25, fo. 5v.
[182] SATØ, SF 25, fo. 6r.
[183] SATØ, SF 25, fo. 6r.
[184] SATØ, SF 25, fo. 6r.

The next day Anders Poulsen was called to court again, and he abided by his previous confession. But he commented that when he learned the rune drum craft from his mother, he himself had not asked to learn. And he repeated once more that he had done no harm with his art and he only wanted to help people in distress.

The Reliability of Anders Poulsen's Confession

Is Anders Poulsen a reliable narrator? Most of his trial is a long narrative rendered in indirect speech, a narrative where his voice is heard, giving information about his life and about the rune drum. The information he gives of a biographical nature is presumably correct, but is the interpretation of the symbols of the rune drum correct seen in relation to the original use of the rune drum as part of the Sami traditional religion? First of all, his use of the rune drum, demonstrated in the courtroom, was certainly convincing. This was a man with long experience in rune drumming and one who showed emotions: with tears running down his cheek he lifted the rune drum up into the air and played it, so that all those present in court were able to see.[185] In addition, the occasions on which the rune drum was used were also probably correctly narrated. Several scholars have interpreted the court records of Anders Poulsen's trial as the most comprehensive contemporary source we have about Sami religious practice, especially the use of the rune drum, and one of the most important sources for the knowledge of Sami shamanism.[186] This might be true for the elements of the confession that have to do with symbols of nature: the sun, the moon, the tempest, the thunder and the wild reindeer. We also find in Anders Poulsen's confession interpretations related to reindeer keeping, hunting and other aspects of Sami traditional ways of life in the area of Nordkalotten.[187] No doubt this document is a fabulous source to the understanding of Sami culture and in particular the art of a Sami shaman. However, there is a question whether Anders Poulsen's confession as a whole can be taken at face value as far as information

---

[185] From a contemporary source by Niels Knag dated 15 December 1693 it becomes clear that Anders Poulsen was moved and shed tears in court, Appendix to Thott no. 1735, RLC.

[186] Niemi, E., 'Hans Hansen Lilienskiold—embetsmann, vitenskapsmann og opprører', in *Portretter fra norsk historie* (Oslo 1993), 61; Niemi, 'Anders Paulsen (Poulsen, Pouelsen)', 84; Rydving, H., *The End of Drum-time: Religious Change among the Lule Saami, 1670s–1740s* (Uppsala, 1995), 35–42; Hagen, *The Sami—Sorcerers in Norwegian History*.

[187] Nordkalotten means the areas in the very north of Norway, Sweden, Finland and Russia bordering to each other.

about the Sami traditional use of the rune drum is concerned. As the analysis above has shown, Anders Poulsen was trying to adjust the content of his confession to the doctrine of the Protestant church, a doctrine he did not know in detail. On the one hand, by use of repetition of standard religious phrases he tried to convince the court that the one God he worshipped was the Christian God. On the other, his abrupt changes from proclaiming belief in one God to proclaiming belief in several gods made his confession inconsistent and unreliable. His last remark in particular, promising that from now on he would believe in the right Christian God, showed that he had in fact belonged to the old Sami traditional religion his whole life, as had his mother before him. As other information about Sami religion and Sami magic during the sixteenth and seventeenth centuries (for instance Olaus Magnus' history) comes mostly from travellers going north who provide outsiders' views of Sami culture, it is difficult to obtain knowledge about what in fact were the attitudes of a Sami shaman towards Christianity and towards the old Sami religion at this time.

Anders Poulsen's interpretation of the rune drum symbols bears the stamp of ambiguity, and it is necessary to look at the separate figures to evaluate his interpretation. All the time he had to stress that when God was prayed to, he helped those who asked for help. He declared again and again that he used his rune drum for good purposes. Originally, all the symbols of the rune drum must have had an explanation in accordance with the old Sami religion, but the situation for Anders Poulsen when questioned by the court was that he had to interpret these symbols within the 'correct' frame, namely that of the Christian faith. Symbols of nature were easy to interpret within a frame he knew from his daily life, the blessings of good weather and the protection of reindeer from wolves. I think here he was close to the original Sami understanding of the symbols. The figures denoting the Trinity were also possible for him to interpret, even if he here had to draw on the knowledge he had from the preaching of the Christian church, not from the traditional Sami religion. It was also possible to explain the rune drum's ability to cause evil by using the image of God as a blessing god and a punishing god. The situation was the same for the figures denoting churches and the people seeking those churches. Probably the interrogators were more interested in the evil effects of the drum than in the good effects. The problems really started when he came to the fifth row and the devils turned up, demanding an explanation. Even if Anders Poulsen stressed that when the ring stopped here, it meant that the person in question was a sinful person and therefore would get his punishment, the authorities saw this as devil worship, even if the symbols denoting hell were described in Biblical terms. He did not use pagan terms, however; words like 'hell' and 'devil'—and 'devil worship' are at least as much Christian concepts. As a whole I think the elements of Anders Poulsen's confession should be differentiated and the interpretations considered as denoting aspects of the old Sami religion mixed with aspects of the Protestant Christian religion. Then it becomes clear that the confession is not a homogeneous one.

The reason for this is the very special context of his confession. Anders Poulsen was interrogated by officials of the law in a criminal trial. He did not know anything about the outcome. With the cruel witchcraft trials of the 1660s still in memory, he might have had reason to fear the verdict. Taking this into consideration, he was trying his best to convince the officials of the law that he believed in Christianity, that he was following the Christian commandments and that he was attending the sermons of the church. Therefore he was trying to interpret several of the figures of the rune drum as Christian religious symbols. His situation was difficult, having obviously lived a life in a culture clash between his own Sami background and Norwegian culture. The discourse of Anders Poulsen's confession is not consistent. He hesitates between different 'truths': for instance, who made the rune drum and where he learnt the art of the rune drum. He is unclear about the use of the drum, insisting upon the positive effects of the drumming when God is prayed to, while being evasive about who is the helper when the drum is used for causing bad events. The interpretations of the symbols of the rune drum would probably have been different if the context had not been a trial.

At the same time as the trial of Anders Poulsen took place in Vadsø, the trial of the Sami Lars Nilsson from Piteå Lappmark took place in Arjeplog in Sweden. Lars Nilsson used a rune drum and wooden figures. He was sentenced to the stake, and both the drum and the wooden figures were burned before he himself was burned.[188] Another case, from the Finnish Sami areas at the beginning of 1671, was the trial of Aikie Aikiesson from Kittka in Kemi Lappmark. He was accused of using the rune drum and singing a special Sami song called *joik*. The local court sentenced him to death, but on his way to the place of execution he died, allegedly due to the use of sorcery.[189] Information about other Sami rune drums which are

[188] Granquist, 'Du skal inga andra gudar hava Jämta mig', 71–88.
[189] The court records are found in Fellman, I., *Handlingar och uppsatsar angående finska lappmarken och lapparne*, vol. I (Helsingfors, 1910), 383–86.

preserved is given by (among others) Rendick Andersen from Foldalen. In 1723 he gave a description of a rune drum to the missionary Thomas von Westen, who was missionary among the Sami people in the region north of Trondheim as well as in Finnmark.[190] Works by (among others) Knud Leem in 1767, Jens Andreas Friis in 1871, Just Qvigstad from 1885 to 1929, Sigurd Agrell in 1934, T. I. Itkonen in 1956, Ernst Manker in 1950 and Louise Bäckman in 1975 all give important knowledge about the Sami rune drum.[191] However, all these descriptions are dated from the eighteenth and nineteenth centuries and are therefore difficult to compare with the description Anders Poulsen gave.

In the records from the trial of Anders Poulsen, a distanced attitude to the story is heard in the legal discourse, a voice displaying scepticism about what Anders Poulsen was narrating. As the above analysis has shown, this distance comes to the fore mainly in remarks about Anders Poulsen's contradictions and his reticence in explaining about the Devil in greater detail. The nature of the questions posed by the interrogators seems to indicate that they were seriously interested in all aspects of Anders Poulsen's knowledge and practice, but that they focused in particular on detailed knowledge about the devils painted on the drum and their powers.

The magistrate was certainly fascinated by Anders Poulsen's narrative and by his playing the drum. The description given of his drum-playing in court is full of amazement. It seems that the legal officials were more interested in hearing Anders Poulsen's voice than in exhibiting their own rhetoric, thus demonstrating a more open, listening and empathic attitude towards the accused person than that which can be traced in the records of the 1660s. Still, since the reliability of Anders Poulsen's confession may be questioned, his narrative does not necessarily give a complete picture of the knowledge and insights of an experienced Sami shaman.

---

[190] Jørkov, B., 'Den stærke tromme', *Siden Saxo*, no. 1 (2000), 9–17.

[191] Leem, K., *Beskrivelse over Finmarkens Lapper* (København, 1767); Friis, J. A., *Lappisk mytologi. Eventyr og Folkesagn* (Christiania, 1871); Quigstad, J., *Prøver af lappiske eventyr og folkesagn*, published together with G. Sandberg (Kristiania, 1885, 1887, 1888), *Kildeskrifter til den lappiske mytologi* (Trondheim, 1903), *Lappiske eventyr og sagn* (Oslo, 1927–29); Agrell, S., *Lapptrummor och runmagi* (Lund, 1934); Itkonen, T. I., *Heidnischer Religion und Späterer Aberglaube bei den Finnishen Lappen* (Helsinki, 1956); Manker, *Die lappische*; Bäckman, L., *Sájva: föreställinger om hjälp- och skyddsväsen i heliga fjäll bland samerna* (Stockholm, 1975).

PART FOUR

CLOSING

CHAPTER ELEVEN

COMPARISONS AND CONCLUSIONS

The Demonological Element

The importance of demonological ideas for the development of witch-craft trials in Scotland and Finnmark is an argument running through my study. As I see it, this ideological construct, which is the core of the cumu-lative concept of witchcraft, was crucial particularly for witchcraft panics to arise and to continue, a point clearly demonstrated in the total of ana-lyses above.[1] Various arguments have been used related to the introduc-tion of demonological ideas, particularly the demonic pact, in Scotland.[2] On one hand there is Christina Larner's argument that James VI imported the pact from Denmark to Scotland in 1590, when he went there to bring home his bride, princess Anne. In Denmark he had conversations with the Danish theologian Niels Hemmingsen, who had written an influential treatise on witchcraft.[3] On the other hand there is criticism of this view, among other arguing that the demonic pact was unimportant even after 1590.[4] In my view, there are unclear points related to the introduction of demonological ideas in Scotland, both with regard to date and geographi-cal links. What is certain is that the Devil's pact was known during the North Berwick trials 1590–91, when King James himself participated in interrogation of the accused.

In Finnmark, the first documented appearance of demonological notions is in the panic of 1620–21, just after the Scotsman John Cunning-ham entered office as district governor at Vardøhus in 1619.[5] Mention

---

[1] Larner, *Enemies*, 163.
[2] Willumsen, *Seventeenth-Century Witchcraft Trials*, 9–11.
[3] Goodare, J., 'The Scottish Witchcraft Act', *Church History*, lxxiv, no. 1 (2005), 58; Goodare, 'Witchcraft in Scotland', 304–05.
[4] Wormald, 'The Witches, the Devil and the King', 170–74; Cowan, 'Darker Vision', 125; Goodare, 'Scottish Witchcraft Act', 59; Maxwell-Stuart, 'Fear of the king', 211–13.
[5] In the rest of Norway, demonological ideas are documented in minor panics in the southern and western parts, but these never reached the intensity and rate of execution of the Finnmark trials. Ref. Willumsen, 'Historiography'; Næss, *Trolldomsprosessene i Norge*, 95; Sødal, 'Trolldomsprosessene på Agder', 17–23; Botheim, *Trolldomsprosessane i Bergen-hus len*, 91–94; Stave, *Da Lucifer kom*, 97–98.

should be made of demonological ideas coming into the laws of Denmark-Norway by a decree of 1617, wherein a demonological definition of a 'real' witch is entered. This decree might have had influence on witchcraft trials throughout Norway.

In the witchcraft records, demonological ideas most clearly come to the fore in the accused persons' confessions. Throughout, the females were in majority with highest number of demonological confessions. A spectre of demonological notions are found in the records, and the similarities in the rendered confessions in Scotland and in Finnmark are remarkable, taking in consideration that we are talking about regions located on either side of the Norwegian Sea.

When it comes to contents, the Devil's pact and its ritual is frequently mentioned in both areas. Also metamorphosis is documented in both Scotland and Finnmark, either in connection with witches' meeting or with sorcery operations. In Finnmark shape-shifting into whales, birds, cats and dogs is common, as seen demonstrated in the close-readings above. The same is the case with Scotland. Flying witches are found in Scotland as well as Finnmark.[6] Often one sees adjustment of witchcraft narratives to local conditions. In both Scotland and Finnmark metamorphosis was performed to adapt to natural surroundings. Another common element as for contents was participation in witches' meetings, which was frequently confessed to both in Scotland and Finnmark. In Scotland the witches did not go far away for witches' meetings, often the meetings were held at a field nearby. In Finnmark they frequently went to places of assembly located so far away that flying was the only possibility. Often food and drink and dancing were mentioned in connection with witches' meetings. There is a merriment related to these gatherings which might be seen as an expression of a break with daily routines and a longing for joy and amusement. The witches' gatherings in Scotland as well as Finnmark differed to a certain extent from the Continent. Even if there were wide variations on the Continent, some of the notions were special, with regard to other Sabbath features. For instance the Spaniards accused of witchcraft confessed to witches' Sabbaths including sexual orgies and baby-eating, confessions with more macabre content than those found in the Finnmark or in the Scottish material.[7] A reason for this might be the distance from central Europe as for these features.

---

[6] Goodare, 'Flying witches in Scotland', in Goodare, *Scottish Witches and Witch-Hunters*.

[7] Baroja, J. C., *The World of the Witches* (Chicago, 1961), 39–40; Knutsen, *Servants of Satan*, 6, 97; Monter, W., 'Witchcraft in Iberia', in Levack, The Oxford Handbook of Witchcraft, 273.

The impact of demonological ideas in witchcraft trials, and the problems arising from these ideas with regard to judicial procedure, is seen
not least from the fantastic elements embraced by demonology. These
notions are thought-provoking when it comes to the weight of proof
required by the court. When a suspected person was brought before the
court in a witchcraft case, the question of proof was a crucial one. The
crime of witchcraft was not just difficult to prove, it was impossible to
prove. The nature of witchcraft was not like crimes like theft or murder
when it came to the status of proof. Particularly the elements of metamorphosis and night flights were clearly non-realistic, and could only be
made likely by the accused person's own confession or by denunciations
or testimonies by accomplices. Hence the burden of proof was dependant
of making the accused person confess shape-shifting or flying through the
air, or accomplices saying they had seen her in this shape at a witches'
gathering on a mountain top or another distant place. To obtain such confessions and denunciations from down-to-earth peasant women, as most
of the accused were, forceful methods of pressure had to be taken into
use. In this light the use of torture might be seen as a necessity on the
part of the legal apparatus.

My analyses above provide rich evidence for the demonological element being present in primary sources in Scotland as well as in Finnmark.
Quantitative analyses of the Scottish material show a substantial numbers of demonic pact confessions. Particularly aspects of the pact ritual
point to inversion of religious motifs, underlining the demonic pact as an
individual agreement between the Devil and the witch. By contrast, the
notion of collective witchcraft comes to the fore through the confessions
of witches' meetings and collective witchcraft operations. The analyses
show correlations between torture, demonic pact confessions, panics and
females. The qualitative analyses show that Barbara Tomasdochter, Katherine Jonesdochter, Jonet Dynneis, Barbara Bowndie, Margaret Duchill,
Janet Morrison, Annabell Stewart and John Stewart all delivered demonological confessions, together displaying a wide spectre of ideas. Witch-
pricking, one of the methods emphasized in King James' *Demonology*, was
frequently used in Scotland to spot suspected witches.

For Finnmark the quantitative analyses show many similarities with
Scotland, in particular a strong impact of demonological confessions
with mention of rituals entering the pact. A difference between Scotland
and Finnmark is that in the Finnmark confessions we do not find carnal
dealings with the Devil. Parallell to Scotland, the quantitative analyses of
the sources from Finnmark show correlations between torture, demonic

pact confessions, panics and females. The qualitative analyses show a
wide range of demonological ideas confessed by Karen Edisdatter, Ingri,
Thorkild Andersen's wife, Maritte Thamisdatter, Bodelle Danielsdatter and
Maren Olsdatter.[8] Interesting is that the learned couple Rhodius imprisoned at Vardøhus Castle in 1662 brought with them specific demonological ideas and managed to circulate these ideas among the other people
imprisoned for witchcraft there. These ideas rapidly disseminated to the
areas outside the Castle Walls, and were retold in several of the confessions a few months after the arrival of the couple.[9] The Finnmark material
thus offers a very good illustration of the rapidity of dissemination of new
demonological ideas.

When comparing Scotland and Finnmark with regard to the demonological element, in specific the correlations between demonic pact confessions, panics and females become distinct. In addition a long row of
details related to entering the demonic pact, performing witchcraft and
participating at witches' meetings are similar; temptation to become the
Devil's accomplice, turning from God to the Devil, renouncing of Christian baptism, getting a new name, a new baptism, performing a ritual
when entering the pact, the Devil's offering of 'never want', the Devil
giving the power of evil-doing to the person entering the pact, collective
sorcery operations causing human and animal death or disease, dancing
and drinking at witches' meetings, shape-shifting into animals, birds or
whales. There is a difference between Scotland and Finnmark related
to the notion of sexual intercourse with the Devil. This aspect was not
confessed in Finnmark. Another difference is that in Finnmark there was
more weight on the mentor teaching witchcraft and the way one person
acquired knowledge about witchcraft than in Scotland. Likewise the pact
in Finnmark often included getting a demon as one's companion, called
Apostel. This fact points to demonological notions in Finnmark as slightly
different from Scotland as well as central Europe. There were local variations of demonological ideas in different areas of Europe. With regard to
Orkney and Shetland, where demonology did not get a very strong foothold, the notions of demonological character resemble the ones in mainland Scotland as well as Finnmark. Several of these notions are linked to

---

[8] The fact that children were involved resembles the Blåkulla trials in Sweden, but in
Sweden the children were witnesses to a greater extent than being accused. Ref. Ankarloo,
'Sweden', 295–96.
[9] Willumsen, 'Children accused of Witchcraft in 17th-century Finnmark', 23, 30, 33.

coastal areas and the sea. The idea of shape-shifting into a whale is similarly found in Shetland and Finnmark. The idea of weather magic is similarly found in the coastal areas of mainland Scotland, Orkney, Shetland and Finnmark. Hence some specific demonological notions seem to be shared within all regions in this study. A common feature in the confessions in question is also the merging between demonological and folkloric ideas coming to the fore during interrogation.

My argument is that demonological ideas were of vital importance for the initiating and developing of the early modern witch-hunt. When these ideas got such tremendous impact, it has to do with the urge to press forth demonological confessions on the part of the suspects and the judicial procedures subsequently followed. My analyses, quantitative and qualitative alike, strongly support the close connection between torture, demonic pact confessions and panics, thus explaining how the panics arose. Once a person confessed to a witches meeting, this person also gave the names of other persons participating at the same meeting, which corresponded to a fear among legal and clerical officials of an ungodly, hidden army of the Devil's accomplices existing on earth. In the regions in question torture was applied and the accused persons were asked leading questions, focused on specific demonological elements. The close-readings of documents from Scotland and Finnmark convincingly show the importance of the demonic pact for the development of panics. The analyses have given evidence that demonic pact confessions often were given in response to leading questions from the interrogators and after various types of torture. How often leading questions were applied the sources cannot uncover. The technique of asking specific questions was important in leading the interrogation towards a demonic pact confession. However, the accused person seemed to know the narratives about the Devil before they were brought into the courtroom and responded to leading questions with long and detailed confessions. In Finnmark the connection between local trials and demonic pact confessions is evident. This connection is more difficult to prove in Scotland, which is probably accidental, due to the range of sources which have survived. However, because the correlation between local trials and panics is equally strong in Scotland and in Finnmark, this strengthens the probability that the demonological element being decisive also in Scotland for the panics arising.

The link between magic and the demonic pact was a very dangerous one, as practice of all kinds of magic was seen as the Devil's work during the period of the witch-hunt. I find it convincing to see the demonic pact in the light of period-specific demonological notions and religious preaching in the post-Reformation era.[10] Knowledge of demonological ideas rapidly spread to the populace via church preaching and information from witch-craft cases, and these notions were known by the peasants at an early stage of the witch-hunt. This knowledge was probably due to assimilation of demonological ideas in the local communities. The emphasis placed during the interrogation on rituals related to the pact signals a parallel to the ritual of baptism. The demonological ideas in the confessions give insight into the accused person's knowledge of detailed demonology. The data support an emphasis on post-Reformation religious elements, in terms of a personal relationship between an individual and God as contributory to the demonological confessions.[11] Also of interest is the Protestant view of the Holy Communion as symbolic, and the inversion of religious motifs touched upon through the denial of baptism.[12] This inversion is clearly an important aspect of the demonic pact and probably contributed to a kind of solemnity attached to the description of entering the pact.

In order for witchcraft panics to arise, there must be a link between an individual pact and a collective element. This multiplier effect is recognizable in the notion of the witches' meeting or witches' sabbath. Accused individuals confessed that they had attended a witches' meeting, which led to denouncing other people attending the meeting. These persons were interrogated in turn, giving rise to panics, which is demonstrated in Scotland as well as in Finnmark.

The Role of the State

To what extent the state was responsible for witchcraft trials has been frequently focused and debated in witchcraft research. The role of the state could be related to politics as exercised in the realms or to the influence the state had in the legal arena. The term politics, which covers a multitude of meanings, will be used here in accordance with Levack's definition, 'to identify all those considerations of governance that may have impelled

---

[10] For instance the Danish theologian Niels Hemmingsen's scriptures are good examples of how demonic pact was interpreted by him, with some elements included and some excluded.

[11] Among other underlined by Christina Larner. Ref. Larner, *Enemies*, 25.

[12] Levack, *Witch-Hunting in Scotland*, 46; Larner, *Enemies of God*, 153; Clark, S., 'Inversion, misrule and the meaning of witchcraft', *Past and Present*, no. 87 (1980), 98–127.

central or local authorities to inaugurate or encourage witch-hunts, sustain them once they had begun or at least allow them to continue'.[13] The importance of witchcraft trials as judicial operations is not possible to disregard. The state's role in witchcraft trials is closely interwoven with legislation and the functioning of the courts as well as the church. In addition, periods of political unrest which in turn influenced the outbreak of panics during witch-hunt were certainly influenced by the state.[14] The role of the state is reflected in an overall jurisdiction responsible for the passing of laws and their enforcement, by the decision for a criminal trial to be held, and the actual witchcraft trials held.

In Scotland, the witchcraft statute of 1563 brought witchcraft within the jurisdiction of the secular courts, whereas punishment for witches before the Reformation was carried out by church courts.[15] Research so far has given comprehensive and detailed information about the role of the state and the governmental framework during the Scottish witch-hunt.[16] Attention has been paid to Scottish witch-hunting as a centralised operation due to the Privy Council's monopoly position with regard to appointing commissions for trying witches in local courts.[17] Witch-hunting in Scotland has also been seen 'as a local affair that the central government tried to control, regulate and eventually eliminate, but not always with complete success'.[18]

The question of state interference in witchcraft trials is closely linked to the question how freely the local courts operated. Whether the judiciary system was little centralized, so that trials mainly were conducted in the localities, is a complex discussion. In Scotland, the local kirk courts, created after the Reformation of 1560, were often the first to identify a person suspected of witchcraft. Often this person was interrogated by the kirk session or presbytery to obtain a confession. This confession was then used to apply to the Privy Council for a warrant, or commission, to try witches. It was necessary with such a warrant to start a local trial, so in this respect the state has decisive power as for initiating a formal trial.

---

[13] Levack, *Witch-hunting in Scotland*, 3.
[14] Larner, *Enemies of God*, 198.
[15] Goodare, 'Witch-hunting and the Scottish state', 124–25.
[16] Goodare, 'Framework for Scottish Witch-Hunting', 240; Levack, *Witch-hunting in Scotland*, 240–50.
[17] Goodare, 'Witch-hunting and the Scottish state', 122, 139; 'Framework for Scottish Witch-Hunting', 248.
[18] Levack, *Witch-hunting in Scotland*, 144.

Also other centralized ways of initiating trials were found.[19] However, Commissions of Justiciary came to dominate the witch-hunt after 1590. It has been argued that the high percentage of witchcraft trials held at local courts reflects this tendency, also seen in Europe in general: 'A final precondition of the great European witch-hunt was the ability of local courts and subordinate tribunals to operate with a certain amount of independence from central political and judicial control'.[20] This strong autonomy in the functioning of the local courts holds true for Scotland as well as Finnmark, as has been amply demonstrated in the analyses above.

In my opinion there is evidence for an interaction between central and local legal authorities in witchcraft cases, both in Scotland and in Finnmark. The involvement of the Privy Council counts for a certain degree of activity from the central authorities in Scottish witchcraft cases. In Finnmark, there was a unified pressure from local and central legal representatives, in addition to pressure from individuals with socio-economical influence in the community, to initiate and continue witchcraft trials. To which extent state interference influenced the witchcraft trials in areas in question, appear very clearly in the quantitative analyses above. For Scotland, the relative frequency of central and mixed central-local trials throughout the period of witch-hunt, shows that during the last third part of the witch-hunt, mixed central-local trials were more frequent. With central representatives present during the trials the rate of acquittal increased. This is a good indication that active state interference after 1670 contributed to the end of the trials. This analysis is also interesting because the information related to type of trial in SSW is very strong, as we know for the majority of cases what type of trial occurred. Hence the figures are absolutely reliable and the calculations show strongly significant results. The same is the case for Finnmark. From good quantitative data the analyses show clearly that when a number of trials during the last period of witchcraft trials were sent from the local courts and brought before the Court of Appeal, the rate of acquittals increased and the end of the witch-hunt came close.

With regard to state interference on the part of the monarch, active attempts to prosecute witches were made by the kings in Scotland as well as in Denmark-Norway. The policy of both kingdoms had as its aim cleansing the country of ungodly persons. In addition to this national agenda,

---

[19] Levack, *Witch-hunting in Scotland*, 19; Goodare, 'Witchcraft in Scotland', 303–307.
[20] Levack, *The Witch-Hunt in Early Modern Europe*, 93.

the monarchs felt personally the threat of witches, or at least believed in the evil-doing of witches. In Scotland, King James VI was an active witch-hunter in his early years as king. The intensive witch-hunt at the beginning of the 1590s was inaugurated as a direct result of the initiative of King James VI. He was personally involved in the interrogation during the 1590–91 North Berwick trials, as he thought he had experienced the power of witchcraft himself and that the fetching of his Danish bride was allegedly delayed by cooperation between Danish and Scottish witches.[21] This illustrates the active role of the monarch in witch-hunting and the power of the king to put such a hunt on his political agenda.

Use of torture was a field wherein the state through the issuing of warrants from the Privy Council had power to decide. Steps were taken centrally to reduce application of torture in the 1660s.[22] The fundamental importance of the Witchcraft Act for the Scottish witch-hunt must be emphasized. Privy Council's issuing of Commissions of Justiciary to try witches in local courts has been seen as a manifestation of central power. Another example of state intervention is seen in distribution over time of types of trial, demonstrated in my quantitative analyses of Scottish cases, shows a stronger central control towards the end of the witch-hunt due to actions taken centrally to re-introduce circuit courts.[23]

In the same way as with Scotland, the Finnmark witchcraft trials were initially influenced by the king. When travelling north to Finnmark and Kola in 1599, the Danish-Norwegian King Christian IV became aware of the region as one liable to sorcery due to the Samis living there.[24] He felt threatened by alleged Sami sorcery on this voyage.[25] He also stated that his aim was to cleanse the area in the north of witches. An indication that Christian IV paid special attention to the northern area and the persons there cunning in sorcery can be seen by a letter to the district governors of Vardøhus and Nordland in 1609, which obliged the district governor to look to that those persons who were found guilty in using sorcery,

---

[21] Goodare, 'The Framework for Scottish Witch-Hunting', 240; Levack, *Witch-hunting in Scotland*, 35.

[22] Levack, *Witch-hunting in Scotland*, 137.

[23] Levack, *Witch-hunting in Scotland*, 137.

[24] Grubbe, S., 'Kongens sjøreise', in R. B. Hagen and P. E. Sparboe (eds.), *Kongens reise til det ytterste nord* (Tromsø, 2004), 77; Hagen, R., 'The King, the Cat, and the Chaplain' in Klaniczay, G. and Pócs, É., *Communicating with the Spirits* (Budapest, 2005), 246–63.

[25] Niemi, E., 'Christian 4s Finnmarksreise i 1599', *Årbok for Foreningen til norske fortidsminnesmerkers bevaring* (1988), 34; Grubbe, 'Kongens sjøreise', 77.

should be sentenced to death without mercy.[26] The king wanted to have district governors at Vardøhus Castle with a will to persecute witches and to implement the king's policy with regard to trade and taxation in Bussesundet in Finnmark. The starting point of the witch-hunt in Finnmark around 1600, which is seen in the quantitative analyses, is simultaneous with Christian IV's interest in this region. Later on during the period of witch persecution, the panics coincide to a large extent with the shift in instalment of district governors.[27]

Comparing the Scottish and the Finnmark material with regard to the role of the state, via the state in person, one finds that during the initial phase of the witch-hunt in both regions the monarchs were active. In both areas the kings were active in hunting witches both as part of an official policy and as a result of personal fear.

The qualitative approach to the documents illuminates the role of the state particularly through the analyses of the voice of the law. As shown in the analysis of the central trial of Margaret Wallace, 1622, elaborate defence pleadings could be seen as interest in the topic on the part of the legal professionals. References to secular as well as clerical laws were repeated several times in the course of the trial. Efforts to keep standards of normal legal procedure might be seen as reflections of state policy towards the crime of witchcraft. The case of Margaret Duchill shows the cooperation between the presbytery and secular legal officials for obtaining a warrant for waking. By leading questions the interrogators managed to turn traditional sorcery in direction of demonology, as seen in the case of Janet Morrison. Evidence points to legal practice as dominated by demonology.

In Finnmark, direct relations between local courts and central legal authorities with regard to sentences in witchcraft trials were non-existent. There were no central trials among the cases, even if the last case, in 1692, was sent from the local court in Finnmark to Copenhagen for final decision. This was a deed of necessity, because the Norwegian Law of 1687 stated that death penalties in witchcraft cases should be sanctioned by the king. The Court of Appeal was an intermediate court. The Court Appeal Judge was much more restrictive with regard to death sentences than the local legal officials at Vardøhus. The quantitative analyses of the Finnmark sources demonstrate clearly that the trials conducted at the

---

[26] Niemi, *Vadsøs historie*, 219; Willumsen, *Trollkvinne i nord* (1994), 57.
[27] Lindhartsen, 'Lensherrer', 61.

ACTA BOREALIA

NORDIC JOURNAL OF CIRCUMPOLAR SOCIETIES

February 19, 2015

Dear Marion:

Thank you for agreeing to review the book *Witches of the North: Scotland and Finnmark* for our journal *Acta Borealia*. The review should be up to about 2000 words, but you can go a bit over if necessary. The top line of the submission can be in this format:

BOOK REVIEW

Witches of the North: Scotland and Finnmark. Liv-Helene Willumsen. Leiden: Brill, 2013, 394 pp., ISBN 978-90-04-25291-2.

You can write in your name and correspondence address, with email, at the end of the review.

Information on *Acta Borealia* can be accessed here:

The journal is edited in Tromsø, Norway, and published by Taylor & Francis in England.

Please feel free to contact me if you have any questions.

Bryan C. Hood
Co-editor, Acta Borealia
Department of Archaeology and Social Anthropology
Faculty of Humanities, Social Science and Education
University of Tromsø – The Arctic University of Norway
9037 Tromsø
Norway
E-mail: bryan.hood@uit.no

Court of Appeal followed another pattern than those conducted by the local courts as for rate of execution and acquittals. The qualitative analyses show that the legislation of the kingdom was adhered to during the trials through judicial practice: the compurgatory oath, and torture after sentence, which was legal in Denmark-Norway, as mentioned earlier. In-depth studies demonstrate a link between legislation and demonological notions.

In addition, both regions demonstrate state control and influence on legislation and judicial practice. Similarities are laws passed directed towards the persecution of witchcraft and statutes making torture possible in certain contexts. The practice of circuit courts with representatives from central legal authorities or legal authorities at a higher level than the local court, exemplified by the Norwegian Court of Appeal Judge, is also a similarity. Mixed central-local courts in Scotland might be seen in parallel with the circuit Court of Appeal in Finnmark. In both regions a stronger intervention from central authorities or from a legal official at a higher level than the local court resulted in a decrease of executions towards the end of the witch-hunt.[28] In total the state played an important role during the witchcraft trials, mainly because of legislation and judicial practice in both kingdoms. However, as will be seen below, in my view the local courts similarly played a very important role.

With regard to Orkney and Shetland, there are indications that the distance from mainland Scotland diminished the state power in witchcraft cases. Due to particular historical development of the judiciary for Shetland in particular, with permission to use Norse laws up to 1611, which means after the period of witch-hunt has started, a feeling of autonomy towards the Scottish state might have influenced the development of witch trials in direction of preventing the huge panics. The strong fear of the Devil's allies never seems to get the grip of governmental officials in the same way as in mainland Scotland and Finnmark. Hence the pressure for witchcraft persecution did not occur to the same extent.

The Local Courts

The role of the local courts is very important when it comes to compare Scotland and Finnmark, as the majority of witchcraft trials were local

---

[28] See Knutsen, G. W., 'The End of the Witch Hunts in Scandinavia', in *Arv. Nordic Yearbook of Folklore*, lxii (2006), 159.

trials in both regions. As first instance courts, they play a decisive role
not only due to the majority of trials taking place there, but also due to
the fact that this arena turns out to be the place where a lot of crucial features of the historical witch-hunt merge and get effect. I would here like
to discuss some points related to the local courts which should be given
high priority when it comes to possible explanatory potential as for early
modern witchcraft trials.

Several witchcraft scholars have pointed to differences in legal procedure as part of the reason why persecution of witches in Europe varied
so much in extent, intensity and contents of the trials.[29] One perspective
to be taken into account is the change from accusatorial to inquisitional
judicial procedure. It is important for the analyses of witchcraft trials that
Finnmark as well as Scotland had mixed systems of criminal procedure
in which some Roman elements were received and others rejected. Both
areas adopted some features, but not all, of a mature inquisitorial system.
There is a clear connection between the use of inquisitorial procedure
and panics arising. As for Scotland, the provisions of the 1587 Act marked
the introduction of an important element of inquisitorial procedure. The
private accuser was replaced by an officer of the court and the prosecution of the crime performed by officials rather than private persons.[30]
This moderation of accusatorial procedure has been exemplified in the
close-readings above. However, trial by jury was maintained, and private
persons still were accusers in many cases. As for Scandinavia, the witchcraft trials took on a distinctive character in each country, and the judicial
procedures varied.[31] Large panics took place in Sweden, wherein inquisitorial procedure was followed.[32] In Denmark, the accusatorial procedure was
kept, hence there were no large panics arising. In Norway, while criminal
cases normally were conducted according to accusatorial procedures, in
witchcraft trials inquisitorial procedure was used, particularly in panics.[33]
Judiciary procedure in witchcraft trials in Norway was arbitrary and not

[29] Sörlin, 'Wicked Arts', 46; Larner, *Witchcraft and Religion*, 35–67; Levack, *The Witch-hunt in Scotland*, 19–21; Ankarloo, *Trolldomsprocesserna*, 60ff; Næss, *Trolldomsprosessene i Norge*, 160–63; Birkelund, M., *Troldkvinden og hennes anklagere* (Århus, 1983), 13–17.
[30] Levack, *The Witch-hunt in Scotland*, 19–20.
[31] Ylikangas, H., Johansen, J. C. V., Johansson, K. and Næss, H. E., 'Family, State, and Patterns of Criminality', 89.
[32] Birkelund, *Troldkvinden*, 14; Ankarloo, *Trolldomsprocesserna*, 246ff.
[33] Næss, 'The Criminological Context', 375.

in accordance with the legal statutes.[34] The country applied a mixture of Norwegian, Danish and Continental criminal procedure. There was a brutalization of judicial procedure in the seventeenth century, which particularly might be seen in witchcraft trials.[35] This is supported by my qualitative text readings, which show that the local court's adoption of inquisitorial procedural methods resulted in demonological confessions and subsequent executions.

Related to arbitrary judicial procedure was the use of torture. There is no doubt that torture was used illegally in local courts in Finnmark and likewise in mainland Scotland, which might contribute to explain the intensity of the witch-hunt.[36] Torture was used frequently in Scottish criminal cases; the Privy Council had to intervene to stop judicial torture in witchcraft cases in the second half of the seventeenth century.[37] In Finnmark too, torture was certainly decisive for the bulk of confessions, practised in the local courts as long as the panics went on. Similarly methods of pressure which were not defined as torture, like the water ordeal in Finnmark and witch pricking in Scotland, were in addition highly responsible for confessions. Use of torture in Scotland and Finnmark only occasionally were entered into the court records. However, the close-readings of court records turn out to be important, as detailed reading on several occasions make it possible to read between the lines. The qualitative analyses have shown for both countries with clarity how quickly the accused person's resistance is broken down during interrogation, and even how the accused person's language dissolved. Hence the records from local courts in both areas underpin the argument that arbitrary legal procedure was an important part of the reason why witches were persecuted and executed.

The potential of local courts to act on their own is one of the perspectives which should also be paid attention to when explanations of witchcraft trials are sought.[38] Both in Scotland and Finnmark we find that the

---

[34] For instance this could be the impartiality of the witnesses. Næss, *Trolldomsprosessene i Norge*, 161, 163, 184, 263.

[35] Næss, *Trolldomsprosessene i Norge*, 281.

[36] Levack, 'Judicial Torture in Scotland during the Age of Mackenzie', 49, 185–98.

[37] In authorising the trial of Margareth Guthrie in 1664, the council found it necessary to specify that her confession should be voluntary. In 1669 the Aberdeen burgh council openly admitted that torturing the accused had been the ordinary practice in witchcraft cases. Ref. Levack, *Witch-hunting in Scotland*, 140.

[38] This perspective comes to the fore in Ankarloo and Henningsen, *Early Modern European Witchcraft*.

local courts might be placed far from central legal authorities. This is of
vital importance. In Scotland, a long distance between local courts and
central judicial authorities might be the case for the northern regions,
including Orkney and Shetland. In Finnmark, on the margin of Europe,
any contact with Christiana[39] or Copenhagen by boat was several weeks
away, a long time to wait for decisions. As for the circuit Court of Appeal,
sessions were held in Finnmark only every third year. It is thus clear that
the chance of having cases brought before the Court of Appeal, most often
was minimal. The judicial officials in local courts knew that there would
be no control from superior authorities. Probably this made it easier for
them to take side-steps from legal judicial procedure. William E. Monter
describes Finnmark as a 'terrible remote region'.[40] This remoteness might
be one of the reasons why 17% of all Norwegian witchcraft trials took
place there and one-third of the total sentences of execution in Norwegian witchcraft cases were passed there.

Comparing northern regions of Scotland and Finnmark, witchcraft trials developed in different ways. The explanation might be sought in the
functioning of the courts, particularly for Scotland the interaction between
local courts and the Privy Council. In order for the Scottish local courts to
have commissions of Justiciary issued, a dossier of documents from preliminary examination was required to convince the Privy Council. A suspect was first questioned by the kirk session or the presbytery in order to
get a confession, and this pre-trial confession was very important for the
chance of obtaining a warrant from the Privy Council. Thus the initiative
to start a local trial was taken well in advance of the trial. While in Scotland there was a delay before a witchcraft trial formally was brought before
the court, from the point of time a person was brought into the searchlight for practising witchcraft, in Finnmark there was no such delaying
first step. The whole trial was started and carried through in the ordinary
court system.[41] During the panics, a person could be denounced, brought
before the court and sentenced to death in the course of a couple of days,

---

[39] Oslo, founded in the eleventh century and capital from 1314, was the name until 1625, Christiania was the name of the capital of Norway until 1877, then Kristiania until 1897, then Christiania until 1925, afterwards Oslo.

[40] Monter, 'Scandinavian Witchcraft in Anglo-American Perspective', in Ankarloo and Henningsen, *Early Modern European Witchcraft*, 427.

[41] Ylikangas, H., Johansen, J. C. V., Johansson, K. and Næss, H. E., 'Family, State, and Patterns of Criminality', 90.

even one day. This difference in the functioning of the courts between the regions dealt with, I consider to be decisive, and can explain the different development and intensity of the witch-hunts in these regions. Due to the immediate start of a witchcraft trial in Finnmark during the panic periods, in addition to arbitrary judicial procedure and the speed of carrying through each trial, a panic got a tremendous drive. Hence the initial phase of a witchcraft trial from my findings above is seen to be a crucial factor. A major explanation of different developments in the regions in question is found within the court system itself, due to differences in the functioning of the courts. For mainland Scotland, the lack of a delaying first step in local courts obviously would have led to a much higher number of trials than the number in fact was.

The quantitative analyses above show an astonishing similar pattern in Scotland and Finnmark with regard to the correlation between local courts, females, torture, demonic pact confessions, denunciations, panics and execution rate. This solid connection is my main argument for claiming that the attention should be directed towards the local courts to find explanations for the witch-hunt in Scotland and Finnmark. It has been demonstrated beyond doubt in the analyses that the demonological element has permeated the witchcraft trials in ways that turned out to have tremendous effect in the local courts. The pressure to hold these trials came in both regions from the local elites; in Scotland from the kirk and the courts in alliance; in Finnmark mostly from legal officials at the local courts, but also from Bergen merchants living in the Finnmark fishing villages. The urge to continue and multiply a trial also was found in the local courts and was successful due to eager witch-hunters, for example the district governors in Finnmark, and the use of torture with subsequent demonological confessions. The total analyses of frequency of cases, panics versus non-panic periods, the occurrence of torture, the number of accused denounced by others, types of trials and executions, all point towards the local courts as the main arena for the witch-hunt in both regions. A simple fact is that most witchcraft cases were local. In these courts the legal officials would decide the procedures during the trial: the witnesses brought before the court, the interrogation in court, and the potential use of torture. The panics arose in local courts. The majority of accused persons denounced by others were found in local courts. The local legal authorities had a lot of influence on the finalizing of a trial. Execution sentences were mostly passed in local courts. In sum this weight of evidence shows that local courts during the seventeenth-century witchcraft trials in Scotland and Finnmark were particularly dedicated to their task of witch-hunting.

The qualitative analyses in both regions support the findings from the quantitative analyses that there was a deadly connection between local courts, women, torture, Devil's pact confession, panics and sentence of execution. The analyses of the voices of the accused give a revealing image of what happened in the courtroom. Use of torture and the multiplying effect of demonology contributed to the significant pattern. In both countries there is evidence that persons died during torture, before sentence was passed. It seems clear when comparing local courts with the Court of Appeal in Finnmark that the local courts were less prohibitive as for use of torture than the Court of Appeal. In Scotland, when mixed central-local trials took over, torture was no longer documented during witchcraft cases. Use of leading questions to obtain confessions is frequently documented. The interrogations demonstrate the purposefulness of the witch-hunters in local courts with regard to extracting demonic pact confessions including witches' meetings. Interrogation became increasingly efficient as decades went by.

The several parallel results from the quantitative and qualitative analyses performed gives evidence that the mechanisms of demonology in cooperation with use of torture in local courts had a tremendous effect on the witchcraft trials in Scotland as well as Finnmark. There is evidence in the material for particular cruelty during panics to obtain denunciations and confessions. The use of torture seems to have been crucial in this connection. This finding supports the argument that the combination of pressure from local courts to initiate demonological trials and use of torture to press forth confessions and denunciations during interrogation are very important explanatory factors for the witchcraft persecution in the two regions in question. The initiation of trials in the regions in question also account for the interesting difference between the development of witchcraft trials in Finnmark and the northern regions of Scotland, including Orkney and Shetland. It should also be pointed out that we find similarities due to mixed systems of criminal procedures in both areas, with use of jury and at the same time application of methods for seeking circumstantial evidence. A judicial practice combining accusatorial as well as inquisitorial features contributed to the severity of the witch-hunt in Scotland as well as Finnmark. This procedural similarity in Scotland and Finnmark probably heightened the rate of execution during the witchcraft trials in both areas.

The Role of the Church

Scotland and Finnmark were both post-Reformation areas in the seventeenth century. In the period after the Reformation, Christianity had become a political ideology in the sense that a degree of education was required for its content to be absorbed. Common people were effectively Christianized for the first time. The crucial factors with regard to the European witch prosecutions were, according to Christina Larner, 'the rise of nation states and the development of a personal religion among the peasantry'.[42] It was necessary to the governing elite that the individual subjects of the kingdom adhered to the correct version of Christianity. In this way the legitimacy of the regime was demonstrated, and certain views prevailed with regard to witchcraft. This interpretation has been supported by many witchcraft scholars, as it is based on several of the specific time-limited factors in the historical setting of seventeenth-century witchcraft persecution and offers a convincingly logical chain of reasoning.

The notion of the Devil as portrayed in demonological books crept into religious scriptures and church preaching. In Scotland, post-Reformation bibles manifested the official policy and carried the stamp of what the state legitimized. The role of the state with regard to witch-hunting can be seen through the involvement of bishops, who were 'central government's agents in the locality',[43] the informal encouragement of witch-hunting through networks of general assemblies of the church, and the presbyteries' involvement in witch-hunting. In Scotland the kirk frequently took the first step to interrogate a person suspected of witchcraft to make her or him confess.

In Denmark-Norway the influence of the state on matters related to witchcraft might be seen similarly with regard to the consolidation of Lutheranism in the realm. The Reformation meant that royal power was strengthened and the aim of central authorities was to standardize religious belief.[44] Through formulations in post-Reformation bibles

---

[42] Larner, 'When is', 54.
[43] Goodare, 'Witch-hunting and the Scottish state', in Goodare, *The Scottish witch-hunt in context*, 132.
[44] Kallestrup, *Trolddomsforfølgelser og trolddomstro: En komparasjon af det posttridentine Italien og det luthersk protestantiske Danmark i det 16. og 17. århundrede*, 293; Tamm, D., Johansen, J. C. V., Næss, H. E., Johansson, K., 'The law and the Judicial System', 27.

and through religious scriptures promoted for use in churches, the state had a firm hand with the preaching on the topic of witches.[45] Leading Danish theologians had marked and strong views on witchcraft—one of the most known was Niels Hemmingsen, another was Jesper Brochmand. Even if witchcraft was under secular jurisdiction after the Reformation, and the first years interpreted in terms of malevolent practice, around 1600 the religious aspect of witchcraft got the upper hand and all kinds of practice of witchcraft, sorcery and magic was looked upon as a crime. The view of the church was that every contact and communication with evil forces involved a pact with the Devil, either implicit or explicit. In addition, all magic was the work of the Devil, even benevolent magic was made demonic and criminalized.[46] All witches and sorcerers had via their conviction and their deeds attached themselves to the Devil; the post-Reformation Danish theologians considered this to be idolatry. The legal understanding of witchcraft was identical with the theological.

Even if Finnmark was at the absolute periphery in the union of Denmark-Norway, religious literature written by outstanding Danish theologians was in use in the churches there.[47] The choice of correct doctrines from these theologians was of importance when ordinances were taken into official use. These scriptures played an important role for church preaching throughout the kingdom. The existence of Danish sermon books by theologians like Niels Hemmingsen, Jesper Brochmand and Poul Andersen Medelby in the churches of Finnmark is documented.[48] The first editions of post-Reformation Bibles may indicate attitudes to witchcraft due to specific formulations used.[49] The same is true of psalm books by Hans Tommesen and Thomas Kingo. There is no doubt that religious literature from Denmark found its way to the far north. This means that through the church the common people learned about personal responsibility as the basis for a godly pact and the same as the basis for a pact with the Devil. It also means that the populace met the idea of the Devil as a figure who was fighting to get hold of human souls.

The role played by the church is one of marked differences between the witch-hunt in Scotland and Finnmark. The situation was different

---

[45] Grell, *The Scandinavian Reformation*, 114–43.
[46] Kallestrup, *I pagt med Djævelen*, 82.
[47] Willumsen, *Trollkvinne i nord* (1994), 60.
[48] Willumsen, *Trollkvinne i nord* (1994), 60.
[49] Grell, *The Scandinavian*, 129.

particularly with regard to the church's interference in pre-trial witchcraft cases. In Finnmark, the church itself did not act to take the initiative in interrogation. While the kirk in Scotland in most cases was active during the first steps of a witchcraft trial, in Norway the whole trial took place in the courtroom. Close-readings of sources from both Scotland and Finnmark have shown that the ministers had two functions in witchcraft trials: Participation during interrogation and preparation of sentenced persons before their deaths. In Scotland the ministers were active with regard to preparing a dossier of documents to be sent to the Privy Council in order to have a warrant issued for trying a witch. The close-reading of the Bute document has thrown light on the active roles of the kirk session, the minister and some of its members. Part of the questioning of Janet Morrison had to do with her activity as a trusted cunning person. A connection between Janet Morrison's healing activity and the suspicion of witchcraft was established by the kirk session when they used her healing activity as a threat that she would be charged as a 'witch'. As soon as the word 'witch' is used, a link was made to demonology. The scribe, probably the minister, did not question this connection, nor did he question the necessity of having the accusations against Janet Morrison treated further on in the judicial system. This attitude on the part of the scribe shows how deep the fear of witchcraft was during this period.

However, there was not the same eagerness from the church in Norway as from the kirk in Scotland as for trying witches. The reason why the kirk in Scotland took an active part in the pre-trial stage, might be found in the field of interaction between kirk and judiciary. From the primary sources of kirk sessions, presbytery and courts it is clearly seen that a witchcraft suspect was first reported and questioned within the context of the kirk, before the Privy Council was approached and before a formal trial was initiated. This is supported by the close-readings above. Further, the close-readings have shown that the handing over of the case from the kirk to the judicial apparatus took place rather late in the trial process, for instance when permission for torture was needed. So the Scottish sources show that the kirk was actively involved in the crucial steps of a witchcraft trial, namely the first report on a person being suspected of practising witchcraft and the pressing forth of confessions. As for Orkney and Shetland, these regions seem to have had the same tight interaction between kirk and judiciary in witchcraft trials as the rest of Scotland. This has been demonstrated for instance in the analyses of the cases of Barbara Bowndie and Marion Pardoun above. It becomes also clear from the trial of Barbara Bowndie, who was tried in Orkney, that the delay in the proceeding of the trial that is caused by the necessity of fetching information about her from the judiciary related to her previous stay in Shetland, in addition to the necessity of getting admission for torturing her, has contributed to postponing her trial. Whether or not her trial was also ended due to these events, the sources do not tell, as her name does not appear again in the court records. In any case, it seems that the judicial procedures in Scotland tend to create a delay in the speed of court preocedure, as long as the letters of the law are followed, and this may be an advantage to the accused person. Here the geographical distance to Edinburgh might be decisive, as it was easier to get permissions from the Privy Council both for trying witches and for torture in the neighbouring areas to Edinburgh.

The difference between Scotland and Norway clearly had to do with the fact that witchcraft accusations in Norway were brought immediately before the court and the full case further handled there. The whole procedure of dealing with suspected witches was one handled by the courts in Denmark-Norway. There was no formal interrogation by ministers of the church in Norway as the first step of a witchcraft trial. However, when studying court records from Finnmark and from other regions of Norway, it is clear that ministers, together with judicial officials, have been involved in the questioning of suspects after they had been imprisoned for witchcraft. This could be both before they were brought to court the first time and between court sessions, if the suspect was brought before the court several times. Hence the minister had a function during the informal questioning almost parallel to the function of the judicial officials, within the context of a legal trial.[50] Information about this participation on the part of the ministers is not rendered openly in the sources. It often comes to the fore in courtroom discourse via the voice of the accused person. Thus there is indication that in Norway the ministers took part in questioning of the suspect outside the courtroom in the pre-trial as well as trial phase. However, this questioning was carried out under the auspices of the justiciary and rarely rendered in the records.

The minister's function in preparing the accused persons before their deaths seems to be similar in Scotland and Finnmark. In both countries those sentenced to execution received the last rites.[51] Thus the religious understanding of witchcraft characterizes the last act of the trial; this crime is a sin against God, still there is the prospect of salvation. The minister

---

[50] See Alver, B., *Mellem mennesker og magter* (Oslo, 2008).
[51] Willumsen, *Trollkvinne i nord* (1994), 62–63.

is the last person to talk with the accused witches, the last to come close to their despair and agony. Thus he probably was experienced as a nearer person by the accused than the judicial officials in court. In the small villages where witchcraft trials took place, the human factor is important to take into account, also when it comes to the role of the church. In Nordic countries at the time, the social elites were small; neither the nobility nor the clergy amounted to more than a few per cent of the total population.[52] In the Finnmark villages this élite consisted of very few persons, the governmental officials and the ministers. Probably the officials were the more powerful. At Vardøhus the district governor must have been a mighty person, the one appointed by the king to take the lead in the handling of witchcraft accusations. He could initiate and drive forth the trials, but he could not take care of the alleged witches' souls. For the preaching in Finnmark as well as Scotland, being based on post-Reformation scriptures, the notion of a personal relation to God was prominent, and had its effect after a trial had come to its end in the courtroom.

Ethnicity

Certain characteristics were attributed to the two ethnic groups living in the north of Scotland, the Highlanders, and the north of Norway, the Samis. They were in many respects regarded as exotic people, something which may be noted by the illustration below, where we see a Scot, presumably a Highlander, a Sami person and a person from Latvia. They were presented as users of magic during Gustava Adolfus' seven years' war, portrayed as peculiar persons coming out of the wild.[53]

It is clear that in both countries the two minority groups the Highlanders and the Samis were looked upon by the majority groups the Lowlanders and the Norwegians as strange and mystical. With regard to sorcery, these ethnic groups were clearly established as 'the others' within their respective countries and within a European setting: King James' *Demonology* mentions that the Devil 'commonly counterfeits God among the ethnics' (pagans).[54] The Samis are described by King Christian IV as a

---

[52] Österberg, E. and Sandmo, E., 'Introduction', in Österberg and Sogner (eds.), *People Meet the Law. Control and conflict-handling in the courts. The Nordic countries in the post-Reformation and pre-industrial period* (Oslo, 2000), 13.

[53] Williamson, A. H., 'Scots, Indian and Empire: The Scottish politics of civilization, 1519–1609', *Past and Present*, no. 150 (1996), 55.

[54] Normand and Roberts, *Witchcraft*, 419 (*Daemonologie*, Book 3, ch. 5).

people who by their nature were inclined to sorcery.[55] The Highlanders and the Samis were 'those' living in the North, being more cunning in and liable to sorcery than people living other places. In Norway, early ecclesiastical law mentioned Finnmark as a place where people went to 'ask for prophecies'.[56] For the district of Finnmark, the cultural encounter between different ethnic groups and their spheres of mentalities resulted in a reputation for sorcery spread all over Europe related to the Samis, a reputation that had effect on the seventeenth-century witch-hunt. This type of encounter between two ethnic groups had greater effect in Norway than in Scotland as for witchcraft trials.

There are different views on the question to which extent Highland witches were involved in the witch-hunt. Christina Larner maintains that when it comes to geographic density, the northern and western Highlands, as well as the Hebrides, had no witchcraft trials. She characterized this blank area as 'Gaelic speaking'.[57] Robin Briggs maintains that these same areas, together with Wales, and Ireland, should be labelled 'light or no persecution'.[58] It has likewise been maintained by Ronald Hutton that the Highlanders hardly were represented among the accused witches.[59] On the contrary, it has been argued by Lizanne Henderson and Lauren Martin that witchcraft persecution took place in the Highlands as well as the Lowlands. Even if witch trials were fewer in Gaelic-speaking areas than otherwise, a number of Highlanders were touched by the persecution.[60]

There is no doubt that some of the Scottish witchcraft trials comprised Highlanders, for instance the Bute trials of the early 1660s, the Inverness trials of the 1660s and the Cromerty trials.[61] Lizanne Henderson and Edward J. Cowan say:

---

[55] Formulations used in King James IV's *Demonology* and in a royal letter of sent by King Christian IV to the district governor of Vardøhus in 1609. Ref. Willumsen, *Trollkvinne i nord*, 57.

[56] In the Eldre Borgarting Kristenrett (Ecclesiastical Law) we find in two different places stated that it is an irreparable crime if a person goes to Finnmark to seek prophesies. Ref. *Norges Gamle Lover*, Vol. I:362. The other instance is in *Norges Gamle Lover*, Vol. I:372.

[57] Larner, *Enemies of God*, 81.

[58] Briggs, *Witches and Neighbours*, xi.

[59] Hutton, 'Witch-Hunting in Celtic Societies'.

[60] Henderson, L., 'Witch Hunting and Witch Belief in the Gàidhealtachd', 95–118; Martin, L., 'Scottish Witchcraft Panics Re-Examined', 127–129.

[61] A Highland woman, Margaret McClain, is mentioned as mentor. 'You answeres a Highland woman learned you called Margaret McClain.' She has asked the man accused to renounce his baptism. Another panel: 'Ane Highland woman learned her, did she renounce her baptism; the pannal answered, she did quhat she bade her'. Ref. RPC, 3rd series, xiii (1686–89), 250, 261.

Figure 12: A Laplander, a Latvier, a Scot. StB Ulm, Einblattdruck 231.

While trials did take place in Gaelic-speaking regions, witch panics were
fewer though the precise reasons for this are unknown. It is possible that
Gaelic society enjoyed a higher level of toleration of the occult and so managed to retain a certain level of acceptance or, perhaps large parishes and
the fewer number of kirk sessions in the Highlands decreased the chances
of major outbreaks of panic.[62]

Henderson and Cowan point to toleration of the occult and a less active
and less organized church as possible reasons for the fewer panics in the
Gaelic-speaking regions. However, single trials took place in the Highlands. This tendency of having Highland witches tried on an individual
basis might be related to a folkloric belief system wherein the practice
of sorcery was seen as an individual art, not as a collective phenomenon.
Additional influential factors resulting in few witchcraft trials in the Highlands could be the functioning of the courts and the geographical distance to the Privy Council in Edinburgh, a distance that obviously created
a delay in starting a trial. The Highlands apparently had to wait longer
than Lothian and Fife areas for receiving a warrant to try witches locally.
It might also be that the language was an obstacle, as it was necessary
to have both ministers and judicial officials with knowledge of Gaelic in
order to deal with these questions in the Highlands.

There is documentation in SSW that both women and men of Gaelic
origin were accused in witchcraft trials. Some of these lived in the Highlands. Some had moved out from the Highlands and lived in central areas
of the Lowlands. A difference appears between those who lived in the
Highlands and those who had moved to the Lowlands. Several of those living in the Lowlands were accused in panic years, which means they might
have been accused on equal level with other inhabitants of the community due to the heated atmosphere during a panic, and not because they
were Highlanders. Most of those of Gaelic origin were tried before 1650.
There is not a high execution rate among those persons of Gaelic origin
registered by SSW. To sum up: The group of Gaelic origin was exposed to
witch trials, but not to a very high degree. They do not seem to be a main
target for witchcraft persecution in Scotland.

A somewhat different picture appears for Finnmark. Here it turns out
that the ethnic group of Samis had an influence on the outbreak of the
witchcraft persecution as well as mattered when it came to gender distribution among the persons accused of witchcraft. Sami men were reputed

---

[62] Henderson and Cowan, *Scottish Fairy Belief,* 121.

for magic throughout Europe by 1600, due to presentations in well-known history books. Authors like Olaus Magnus, Peder Clausssøn Friis and Johan Schefferus, whose books were published in 1555, 1632 and 1673 respectively, portray Sami men as exotic and pagan for a contemporary reading European audience.[63] The authors emphasize the superstition of the Samis and their ability to perform sorcery using a special type of Sami spells called *gand*,[64] in addition to selling wind to sailors by binding three knots on a rope or a piece of cloth and playing the rune drum.[65] In fact, the Samis as an ethnic group was conspicuous within the European field of magic, much more so than the Scottish Highlanders. Therefore the first two decades of witchcraft persecution in Finnmark focused on Sami men, and the king in Copenhagen issues letters to the district governors of the north so that they should be aware of this danger and take the challenge of persecuting these people seriously.

The gender question is interesting with regard to the Samis accused of witchcraft. The distribution of males in total in the Finnmark material shows that among the accused, the Sami men were in a majority, as 67% of the males were Samis. Hence a Sami man was more likely to be accused of witchcraft than a Norwegian man. Among the women, however, Samis are only 7% of the women accused. This means that within the group of women, mostly Norwegians were accused.[66] The number of Samis was most distinct before 1640 and after 1670. During the panics of 1650s and 1660s, very few Samis were involved. The explanation might be that traditional Sami sorcery was alleged to be an individual skill, displaying inherent magical power. Therefore the Samis were stronger represented in isolated cases than in panics. This points to a view of Sami sorcery as an individual art and corresponds with the image of Sami sorcery found in contemporary learned Europe. A Sami sorcerer was not seen as a member of a group.[67] On the contrary, Norwegian women were

---

[63] Willumsen, *Trollkvinne i nord* (1994), 51–52; Magnus, *Historia om de nordiska folken*; Friis, P. C., *Norriges Beskriffuelse* (Copenhagen, 1632); Schefferus, J., *Lapponia* (Frankfurt am Main, 1673).

[64] Pollan, *Samiske beretninger*, 34.

[65] Willumsen, *Trollkvinne i nord* (1984), 64–66.

[66] Willumsen, *Trollkvinne i nord* (1984), 30–55; Willumsen, L. H., 'Den historiske trollkvinne i nord', Ottar, no. 5 (2012), 12–18.

[67] The connection between ethnicity and panics shows that the proportion of Sami persons accused was higher during non-panics periods than during panic periods. Chi-square 7.083. Ref. Willumsen, Seventeenth-Century Witchcraft Trials, 108.

strongly represented in panics and were focused during the middle period of the Finnmark witch-hunt.

In Finnmark, reputation for sorcery was not restricted to the Samis alone, it also comprised Norwegians. The connection between ethnicity and reputation for sorcery shows that such a reputation at the time had a much wider range than ethnic Sami persons alone. Also among the Norwegian women accused, a reputation for sorcery was very common.[68]

If we compare the Samis with the Highlanders, a few factors of interest appear. Firstly, both Highlanders and Samis were exposed to the witch-hunt. Most of the Sami persons were not prosecuted in panics, but instead in single cases for traditional sorcery.[69] When demonological ideas took over, the Samis were no longer targeted. This emphasis on individual sorcery among the Samis is the same as we see in the Highland cases. It seems that the Highlanders as well as the Samis were less involved in demonic trials than the respective countries ethnic majority groups.

However, with regard to gender, there is a difference between the two countries. For women, the Highlanders and Samis were not explicitly targeted during the witchcraft persecution. For men, the situation was that Sami men were specially exposed to witchcraft persecution, whereas male Highlanders were not. My interpretation is that due to the reputation Sami men had throughout Europe as well versed in sorcery, they attracted attention as witchcraft suspects. The fact that they inhabited Finnmark might have contributed to the start of the witch-hunt there. The conviction that Sami witch people lived in the north may have increased the suspicion with regard to potential witches living in these areas, be that also Norwegian witches.

Neighbourhood Disputes

The role of the local community and the social setting of witchcraft accusations have been considered important since the influential studies of Keith Thomas and Alan Macfarlane in the early 1970s. A more recent study inspired by sociology and anthropology is Robin Briggs's *Witches & Neighbours*.[70] With reference to a specific case in his sources, Briggs says, 'here again the accusations and confrontations seem to have occurred between

---

[68] Chi-square 0.242. Ref. Willumsen, Seventeenth-Century Witchcraft Trials, 108.
[69] Willumsen, *Trollkvinne i nord* (1994), 66.
[70] Oxford, 2002.

women, with negligible male input before the trial itself'.[71] Briggs is arguing that aggression and competitiveness by women were primarily expressed in relation to other women; 'direct quarrels between men and women were rather less common, outside the family itself'.[72] The predominance of women in neighbourhood disputes in Scotland tends to support Briggs' interpretations of a community as 'feminine society'. Lauren Martin maintains that witch-hunting was partly grounded on everyday relations and practices, partly an expression of mass panic and religious fanaticism.[73] It is important to discuss the role of women and how they functioned in communities. However, it is equally important to bear in mind when discussing neighbourhood disputes the fact that these disputes were brought before the court as crimes. This could never have happened unless everyday conflicts were exploited within a legal framework which used such disputes as a means of pressing serious accusations. When it comes to women's role in society, Raisa Maria Toivo has pointed out that a good deal of the problematic related to women had a corresponding problematic in the lives of men, a fact that should be remembered with regard to interpretation of neighbourhood conflicts.[74]

My qualitative analyses above have displayed that socio-economic relations created tension in communities and increased opportunities for witchcraft persecution. Close-reading of the source material from Scotland and Finnmark shows that pressure arising from socio-economic tension in the community influenced the witch-hunt. This comes to the fore in witnesses' testimonies. In addition, conflicts of socio-economic origin were often given by the accused person as motives for casting spells. In Finnmark the local economy was founded on dependency of the Bergen merchants, which resulted in long-term debts and harsh living conditions, a fact which is displayed in the witchcraft documents.[75] The question is how much socio-economic conditions could have contributed to initiation of witchcraft trials as well of continuation of such trials.

In Robert Briggs' witchcraft study from Lorraine the nature of witchcraft persecution is interpreted as a social and political phenomenon. He argues that 'multiple local variations resulted from a complex and unpredictable

---

[71] Briggs, *Witches*, 231.
[72] Briggs, *Witches*, 233.
[73] Martin, L., 'The devil and the domestic: witchcraft, quarrels and women's work in Scotland' in Goodare, *Scottish witch-hunt in context*, 89.
[74] Toivo, 'Women at Stake Interpretations of Women's Roles in Witchcraft', *Arv, Nordic Yearbook of Folklore*, lxii (2006), 187–202, at p. 199.
[75] Niemi, E., *Vadsøs historie*, i, 224.

interaction between popular and elite ideas about witchcraft'.[76] The continual existence of witchcraft in the local communities is underlined:

> Witchcraft was about envy, ill-will and the power to harm others, exercised in small face-to-face communities which, although they could often contain such feelings, found it almost impossible to disperse them. Those involved relied heavily on the cunning folk and their counter-magic, alongside a range of social and political pressures, to deal with suspect neighbours.[77]

To what extent do my findings support this argument? For Scotland, the quantitative analyses show evidence that neighbourhood disputes were mentioned as motives for witchcraft accusations in all types of trials. There is no indication that neighbourhood disputes increased during panic periods. The qualitative analyses show in detail how these conflicts came into being and strongly support an interpretation of the sources in which the beginning of a witchcraft trial often was accidental; the consequence of some angry words related to daily life might have a disastrous result. The eagerness to testify about these conflicts shows that the witnesses considered these motives relevant for the case. The testimonies bear the stamp of retrospectively making a link between word uttered and a tragic event happening afterwards.

The Finnmark material demonstrates similar findings. The quantitative analyses give evidence that quarrels with neighbours were part of a broad range of motives mentioned by witnesses. However, it is important to bear in mind that the majority of cases in Finnmark were denunciation cases, not accusation cases, thus paying little attention to motives. Denunciations of suspected persons seemed to go in all directions within social networks with regard to those denounced, and were often delivered after severe pressure. Still, the qualitative analyses show that hasty quarrels often came up due to disagreements in house-hold work or deeper tensions founded in socio-economic relations. Clues that could substantiate an explanation of the witch-hunt on socio-economic grounds could be that the period 1500–1650 in Finnmark was one moving from expansion to stagnation.[78] The seventeenth century was characterized by bad periods in fisheries and several severe shipwrecks. Bergen merchants living in Vadsø played an important role in initiating witchcraft trials, due to economic losses related to shipwrecks allegedly caused by witches and fear

---

[76] Briggs, *Witches*, 345.
[77] Briggs, *Witches*, 344.
[78] Balsvik, *Vardø*, 20–33; Niemi, *Vadsøs historie*, 69–230.

that the merchants would lose control over the local fishermen.[79] Alleged witches were seen as scapegoats for the disasters that struck local communities.[80] Common people frequently brought complaints before the local courts related to bad fisheries and poverty, so that they could not manage to pay their taxes.[81]

A theory according to which 'social strain' was the cause of the persecutions was initially introduced by Marwick in 1965[82] about conditions in England, and later followed up by Thomas and Macfarlane[83] in studies of English trials. The essence of the theory is that accusations of witchcraft are linked with profound changes in the social texture, applied to English conditions from 1550 to 1650. As argued by Larner, these conditions did neither explain the start of the witch-hunt nor the end of the witch-hunt and did not necessarily have relevance for other countries than England. Discussions on this topic have been actualized also for Norway and Scotland.[84] However, the Finnmark sources do not substantiate the supposition that responsibility for the have-nots has been shifted during the period at hand. The fact that the district governor occasionally had to interfere by providing food simply because he alone was in a position to do so did not mean that the principle of neighbourliness had been abandoned. There is no evidence in the sources from Finnmark of refused charity related to begging. In the analyses from Shetland above, it seems that begging comes in as a factor paid attention to at the very end of the witch-hunt, which may have to do with the official handling of poor relief, how this should be dealt with. Economic problems might have caused a strain in the population, but the sources do not contain evidence that this could be the only explanation neither to the witch-hunt in Finnmark nor in Scotland.[85]

The explanation of the historical witchcraft trials must be based on a concept of witchcraft which was not a continual one. The analyses in this study have pointed to the demonological notions, which were limited in time, as essential when it comes to explain the beginning and the sudden

---

[79] Niemi, *Vadsøs historie*, 69, 108, 221–5; Niemi, 'Hekseprosesser og økonomi', 20–23.
[80] Willumsen, *Trollkvinne* (1984), 87; Niemi, *Vadsøs historie*, 221–5.
[81] Willumsen, *Trollkvinne* (1984), 86.
[82] Marwick, M. G., *Sorcery in its Social Setting* (Manchester, 1965).
[83] Macfarlane, A., *Witchcraft in Tudor and Stuart England* (London, 1970), 200–6; Thomas, K., *Religion and the Decline of Magic* (London, 1971), 561–7.
[84] Larner, C., 'Crimen Exceptum. The crime of Witchcraft in Europe', in *Witchcraft and Religion* (Oxford, 1984), 48–53; Næss, *Trolldomsprosessene i Norge*, 353–5, 358; Goodare, J., *The Government of Scotland* (Oxford, 2004), chs. 9 and 11.
[85] Willumsen, *Trollkvinne i nord* (1994), 66.

increase of witchcraft trials. Witches were accused and burnt in Europe during a limited time-span, and neither socio-economic tensions nor the occurrence of continuant neighbourhood disputes in the local communities can explain or account for the upsurge of witchcraft trials during the historical witch-hunt.

The Spoken Word

The culture of seventeenth-century peasants was predominantly an oral one. An oral discourse differs in many ways from a written one and leads to the development of certain structural features in order to help the remembrance and retelling of stories.[86] Several of these structural devices are found in the confessions of witchcraft trials, indicating that the confessions were influenced by the oral field. The same was true of the testimonies of witnesses. Orality put its stamp on courtroom discourse. A study focusing on the transition from oral to written narratives is made by M. T. Clanchy.[87] He mentions the strong foothold of the narrator in thirteenth-century legal procedures in England. The narrator was a professional teller of tales in the vernacular, 'but his tales were legal pleadings and not romances in the modern sense'.[88] He made formal claims and pleadings on the litigant's behalf. 'The narrator was a layman, expert in oral pleadings, whereas the attorney was often a cleric and expert in written ones'.[89] The two functions remained distinct. The narrator spoke on the behalf of the litigant, and was thus an extension of the latter's faculty of speech, but he was not appointed 'to win or lose', as the attorney was. The function of the narrator in older legal procedure is interesting to bear in mind when working with narratology within a legal context, as the old 'legal' narrator left his stamp upon the legal proceedings just as a scribe did in seventeenth-century written legal documents. Clanchy emphasizes that a long time after the art of writing documents had begun to be practised, the emphasis on hearing remained strong. This did not mean that the contents stemmed directly from oral tradition, but that reading continued to be conceived in terms of hearing rather than seeing.[90] Even if Clanchy's material is from an earlier period than the seventeenth century,

---

[86] Ong, *Orality and Literacy. The Technologizing of the Word*, 11.
[87] *From memory to written record. England 1066–1307* (Oxford, 1993).
[88] Clanchy, *From memory*, 274.
[89] Clanchy, *From memory*, 274.
[90] Clanchy, *From memory*, 268.

the situation to a certain extent parallels seventeenth-century Scotland and Finnmark.[91]

The oral dimension is in my view central for our understanding of witchcraft confessions. Probably narratives about the Devil were found interesting at the time and were transmitted rapidly in the oral arena. Adam Fox has shed light on the relationship between oral, manuscript and printed media among those at the lower levels of society. He found that the speed of the transmission of rumours and news within certain oral networks was high in late sixteenth- and early seventeenth-century England.[92] In the same way the spoken word was important in passing on demonological notions to illiterate peasants and the common people as a whole. This rapid transmission of demonological 'news' has been clearly demonstrated in the analysis of the Finnmark panic of 1662–63 and the trial of Maren Olsdatter above.

The confession was fatal for the result of a witchcraft trial. It was fatal because of the demonological contents confessed. Therefore the question arises how the accused persons could be familiar with demonological ideas. My assumption is that in an early phase of the witch-hunt, demonological ideas were introduced by the learned elite and circulated in the communities in question and were fused with already-known popular narratives. When imprisoned and interrogated during witchcraft trials the accused individuals retold the narratives they had heard about the Devil, the sabbath and the pact.

The confessions in witchcraft cases to a large extent give access to oral demonological narratives about the Devil known among common people. Even if leading questions focusing on demonological elements were used during interrogation, there is a rich amount of narrative motifs and images in the confessions that could only stem from the accused persons. The leading questions were so to speak responded to on the part of the accused by a spectre of already known narratives, wherein the core came from the oral field. The reason why we have these demonological narratives preserved today is that they found their way into the kirk sessions and the courtrooms, where they were written down as proof of a 'crime'— often to be read aloud for an audience as part of judicial proceedings.

In an oral society the spoken word was absolutely necessary for ideas about the Devil to spread and develop. When the confessions were so rich

---

[91] See also Kryk-Kastovsky, 'Historical Courtroom Discourse'.
[92] Fox, 'Rumour', 597–620.

and flourishing in language as has been demonstrated from both Scotland and Finnmark, I take it that the knowledge of these ideas to a large extent were known by the accused before the trial. Exposed to torture during interrogation it was a question of *knowledge* in response to leading questions. In Scotland's case the belief in the world of the fairies is demonstrated among other places in the Barbara Bowndie case. However, it was when the fairies were demonized by the interrogators in the courtroom that the situation for Barbara became dangerous.[93]

In the Scottish sources there is a good example of assimilation of demonological narratives in the villages—stories being told about witches' meetings. In the case of Barbara Bowndie we hear about the dancers from Munes and get information about how many years it was since the story started to be told among the peasants in the community. This reveals that the peasants were aware of these types of stories and knew how many years they had been in circulation. The Finnmark analyses show the speed of specific demonological ideas being introduced, retold and disseminated inside as well as outside the walls of Vardøhus Castle in the early 1660s. New ideas of this kind spread rapidly according to interest among common people.

The qualitative analyses have further shown that the confessions both in Scotland and in Finnmark have a strong oral accent; structured by easily remembered syntactic expressions and characterized by easily remembered images. The linguistic richness and all the details in the confessions are arguments that the accused persons knew these notions well before they were imprisoned. Not in any case is seen a short 'Yes' or 'No' in response to the interrogator's questions. Instead a long and detailed confession is given. In both areas words in vernacular are recorded, just as the scribe heard the word pronounced orally, a fact which underlines that the scribe was eager to preserve in writing the individualized and differentiated voices. I see the recorded courtroom discourse as a way of acquiring knowledge about the mentality of the period. The contents of the accused persons' confessions are preserved, particularly when it comes to narrative motifs. The total of analyses supports an introduction and oral transmission of demonological narratives in the villages, notions which in turn were reproduced in confessions during witchcraft trials.

---

[93] See also Roper, *Witch Craze*, 121; Briggs, *Witches*, 339.

Folk Belief

The analyses in this study have demonstrated details and nuances of folk belief through the analyses of the voice of the accused and the voices of the witnesses, illustrating that the belief in working magic was profound among the peasants.[94] Sorcery as a 'material' crime is demonstrated in the use of physical objects.[95] Woven into these notions are demonological ideas as exemplified in the qualitative analyses above. Both Scotland and Finnmark are areas with rich folk traditions and with ethnic minority groups for whom traditional narratives are documented, however, primarily at a later stage.[96] For instance were in-depth studies of Sami mythology and folklore carried out from the 1880s onwards by Just Qvigstad.[97]

What becomes clear when looking at aspects of folk belief as they come to the fore during interrogation and confessions in witchcraft trials is a common denominator for the two areas Scotland and Finnmark: demonizing of folk belief took place in the courtrooms. The knowledge common people accused of witchcraft had of folklore, was exploited by the interrogators during interrogation and connected to the stage of evil and the Master of evil.

This holds true for the Finnmark sources, as we have seen in the qualitative analyses of the records of Marrite Thamisdatter, Maren Olsdatter and Anders Poulsen. In the confession of Marrite Thamisdatter we clearly see the interweaving between traditional and demonological notions. She was three times denounced, which is a magical number, known from folk tales and legends. She confessed to tying knots on a piece of cloth, putting red, white and black stones in the knots, in order to raise wind and cause a ship-wreck. This method may be recognized from Sami magical practice in order to raise wind for sale to sailing ships. In addition Marrite used a

---

[94] See also Kieckhefer, *European Witch Trials*; Thomas, K., *Religion and the decline of magic* (New York, 1971); Ginzburg, C., *Ecstacies: deciphering the Witches' Sabbath* (New York, 2001).

[95] Kallestrup, *Trolddomsforfølgelser*, 291; Alver, *Mellem mennesker og magter*, 163.

[96] Goodare, 'Scottish Witchcraft in its European Context', in Goodare et al. (eds.), *Witchcraft and Belief*, 26–50; Miller, J., 'Men in Black: Appearances of the Devil in Early Modern Scottish Witchcraft Discourse', in Goodare et al. (eds.), *Witchcraft and Belief*, 144–65.

[97] Brita Pollan has later on edited Qvigstad's works. Ref. Qvigstad, J. and Sandberg, G., *Lappiske eventyr og folkesagn* (Kristiania, 1887); Qvigstad, J., *Kildeskrifter til den lappiske mytologi* [Sources to Sami Mythology], (Trondheim, 1903); Qvigstad, J., *Lappiske eventyr og sagn I/IV* [Sami fairy tales and stories], (Oslo, 1927–29); Pollan, B., *Samiske beretninger*, (Oslo, 1997, 2005).

formula when casting spells on boats, orally delivered mastery of sorcery. She used words to strengthen her magic, convinced that these magic words were powerful. However, during the interrogation these features are related to evil forces and thus made very dangerous. Maren Olsdatter confessed to stealing milk by putting a horn under the animal, a typical feature known within folk belief. This is during the questioning connected to demonological notions, with the result that elements of folk belief are considered equally dangerous with demonic elements. In his confession, Anders Poulsen tried to manoeuvre between a Shaman's traditional performance and knowledge and Christendom. He tried to avoid that his shamanistic practice should be interpreted as idolatry, and described as a devilish practice. But in vain. His knowledge was seen as belonging to the Evil One.

Going to Scotland, fairy belief was a characteristic feature of national folklore. As the quantitative analyses have shown, confessions containing fairy belief is in the Scottish material scattered throughout the whole period of the witch-hunt. There was no upheaval during panic years, so the belief in fairies seems to have existed like an undercurrent while witchcraft trials took place. Men and women in equal proportions confessed to fairy belief. This belief may provide a good example for what happened in the crossing field between folk belief and demonology during a witchcraft trial. Belief in fairies and the second sight of the Highlanders have been pointed to as manifestations of the belief in another world.[98] This belief would fit in easily with the notion of witches' metamorphoses and flights to remote Sabbath places.[99] When the world of the fairies is brought into the questioning of a witchcraft case, it becomes demonized, as seen in the interrogation of Barbara Bowndie. The interrogator showed an interest in what Barbara knew about the fairies. Her story was not a story of evil. However, her story became, by the interrogator, related to evil forces. Folk belief was attached to demonology and was then regarded a dangerous crime. The questioner looked to that this was effectuated during the interrogation.

Ronald Hutton has posed the question whether the Highlanders were more reluctant to try witches than the Lowlanders, with the result few trials in the Highlands. He argues that the belief in fairies and the

---

[98] Hunter, M., 'The Discovery of Second Sight in Late 17th century Scotland', *History today* (2001), 48–53; Black, Introduction to Campbell, *The Gaelic Otherworld* (Edinburgh, 2005).

[99] Campbell, *Witchcraft and the Second Sight in the Highlands and Islands of Scotland*; Macgregor, A., *Highland Superstitions* (Stirling, 1922); Hunter, 'The Discovery', 48–53.

understanding of fairies is different from Lowland Scotland to the Celtic societies, including in the Celtic region the Highlands of Scotland and also Orkney and Shetland. He maintains that the Highlanders believed the fairies were fierce and dangerous creatures, while the Lowlanders had a different view.[100] Henderson argues that fear of fairies was found among the Scots as well as among the Highlanders and the contents of this belief did not differ between the Lowlands and the Highlands.[101] This is also in accordance with Laurence Normand and Gareth Roberts' argument. They maintain that folkloric features, which originally were regarded as good by the peasants by 1590, came to be regarded as evil. Any relationship between human and fairies was seen as an evil one. This change happened due to learned demonological influence, from the 1570s onwards, particularly through church preaching, and is seen as a general development in Scotland.[102] I think the change occured later than 1590. Looking at the Bowndie case, may be such a change took place gradually throughout the first half of the seventeenth century. My quantitative analyses show that a variety of aspects of fairy belief were activated in the Lowlands as well as the Highlands during the entire period of witch-hunt. Among the aspects are elfshot, fairy blast and changeling, features pointing to fairies as scaring and dangerous creatures.[103] This supports the argument that fairies and elves had some evil aspects attributed to them. My qualitative analysis, for instance the case of Barbara Bowndie, clearly shows the demonizing of fairy belief which took part during the interrogation of a person suspected for witchcraft.

In the Finnmark witchcraft trials, fairies were mentioned in only one case, in 1689.[104] Within the range of notions that could be related to folk belief in the Finnmark witchcraft cases, the belief in fairies is not dominant at all. Belief in fairies was very rarely brought onto the agenda in witchcraft trials. Thus fairy belief is a field where the two countries display different patterns.

However, what we see in both Scotland and Finnmark is that accused persons' confessions are influenced by folk belief. The interrogators deliberately try to get hold of what the accused person knows about aspects

---

[100] Hutton, 'Witch-hunting in Celtic societies', 44–71; see also Hutton, R., 'Anthropological and historical approaches to witchcraft: Potential for a new collaboration?', *The Historical Journal*, 47, 2(2004), 413–34.

[101] Henderson, 'Witch Hunting and Witch Belief in the Gàidhealtachd', 95.

[102] Normand, and Roberts, *Witchcraft in early Modern Scotland*, 80.

[103] Willumsen, *Seventeenth-Century Witchcraft Trials*, 297–298.

[104] Birgitte Eriksdatter, SATØ, SF 23, fos. 3v–5v.

of folk belief in order to connect this to the demonic field. Knowledge of folklore is exploited by the judicial officials in the courtroom by connecting it to the demonological notions, which in turn can be considered evil and dangerous. Thus, the real danger is not folk belief, but the efforts of the legal officials to turn folk belief into something demonic. The underlying fear of the representatives of the law comes to the surface in their eagerness to discover the Devil's allies. When folk belief can be used to create a link to the demonic, it is exploited in that way.

The Superstitious North

Because people living in Scotland and Finnmark were supposed to be very superstitious and powerful in the art of magic, this created fear further south. In addition, both regions were allegedly related to evil forces. In the Middle Ages, it was believed that the entrance to the purgatory and to hell was to be found on desolate, frightening places, and this belief lasted for centuries. The last archbishop of Norway, Erik Walkendorf, wrote in 1520, after a voyage to Finnmark, that according to the opinion of many persons, souls were cleaned for the filth of souls in hidden cliff caves in Finnmark. This could be born witness to by his men, who had heard unhappy and terrifying voices from these cliff caves.[105] King James' treatise on witchcraft mentions Lapland, Finland, Orkney and Shetland as parts of the world 'where the devil findes greatest ignorance and barbaritie'.[106] Likewise Olaus Magnus' history book from 1555 stresses the Samis's magic performance. In addition, he suggests that the Devil is located in the North, thus giving an impression of the North as a mysterious and frightening place.[107] Olaus Magnus' book was the most prominent description in the sixteenth and seventeenth centuries of the Nordic peoples, and it was influential among a learned European audience. But Olaus Magnus's gaze was from outside; he had never been to the north himself, but based his description on other sources. Thus this image of the north of Norway was an image portrayed by an outsider—an exotic impression of the northern areas. Magnus was also cartographer, and

---

[105] Bergh, 'Til ild og bål'.
[106] Cf. Normand and Roberts, *Witchcraft*, 414 (*Daemonologie*, Book 3, ch. 3); 419 (*Daemonologie*, Book 3, ch. 5).
[107] *Historia de Gentibus Septentrionalibus* (Roma, 1555), *Historia om de nordiska folken* (Malmø, 1982).

a similar portrayal of the northern areas as mysterious and dangerous comes to the fore in his famous map Carta Marina (1539).

The specific ethnic conditions in Scotland and in Finnmark influenced the witchcraft trials in Finnmark to a larger extent than those in Scotland. While Sami men clearly were focused in Finnmark, the male Highlanders were not to the same extent in focus during the witch-hunt in Scotland. As for women, neither Sami nor Highland women were particularly exposed. The portrayal of Sami men—not Sami women—as exotic and pagan for a contemporary reading European audience, included also religious practice. The Samis were looked upon as a pagan people, due to their old nature religion, and missionaries were sent to work among them. Seventeenth-century source material related to Sami religious practise was written down by male missionaries. Harald Rydving points to the fact that in the source material for indigenious Sami religion, there is an imbalance between how men's and women's religious customs and ideas are described. Even if Sami men's religion and Sami women's religion contrasted and complemented each other, the sacrificial cult presented in the sources above all dealt with an aspect of the Saami men's religion.[108] The one-sidedness of the descriptions was due to the fact that it was not possible for the male missionaries to get acquainted with women's religious world.[109] Several other studies focusing on Sami encounters with the Swedish state, religious change and the image of the Devil in the north, support this view.[110] The fact that Sami men dominated the written presentations given of magic as well as religious practice among the Samis, is most likely the explanation for Sami men being focused during the witch-hunt, whereas Sami women were not.

Two different concepts of sorcery were at stake in seventeenth century Finnmark: Sami sorcery was an individual art, whereas demonological witchcraft was mainly a collective phenomenon. In the sources from Finnmark there is a clear split in the material between the accusations towards and the confessions of the Samis on the one hand, and the accusations and confessions of the Norwegians on the other hand. Sami sorcery is

---

[108] Rydving, H., 'Saami responses to Christianity. Resistance and change', in J. K. Olupona, *Beyond primitivism. Indigenous religious traditions and modernity* (New York, 2004), 103.

[109] Rydving, 'Saami responses', 103.

[110] Rydving, *The End of Drum-time*; Davidson, P., *The Idea of North* (London, 2005); Fur, G., *Colonialism in the Margins: Cultural Encounters in New Sweden and Lapland* (Leiden, 2006).

part of an old tradition, and performed on an individual basis. This type
of sorcery was not learned from the Devil. Therefore Sami persons were
mainly represented in single cases. Contrary to this was the demonological concept of ideas, where witchcraft was obtained through the pact with
the Devil and where witches' meetings and collective sorcery operations
were important aspects.

The understanding of special ethnic groups being liable to sorcery might
have had an impact on the start and end of witchcraft persecution in Finnmark. This does not seem to have been the case for the Highlanders. One
explanation could be that the Sami practice of sorcery was better known
in contemporary Europe than the Highlanders' practice and thus influenced the treatment of the various ethnic groups related to witchcraft
trials. A second explanation could be that the traditional religion of the
Samis was regarded as a greater obstacle to the implementation of post
Reformation religion than was the case for the Highlanders, consequently
bringing witchcraft persecution of this ethnic group onto the agenda of
the state.

If ideas about the superstitious north intensified the witch-hunt in
Scotland or Finnmark, this might have to do with the understanding of
witch-hunters both centrally and locally placed that the areas in question
were more likely to be inhabited by witches than were other areas. Due
to indications in the sources concerning certain attitudes on the part of
the witch-hunters, it seems that attitudes grounded in the states' political
ambitions to cleanse these countries of witches, especially in liable areas,
have had different consequences in Scotland and Finnmark. In Finnmark,
attitudes towards the Samis seem to have contributed to intensifying
the witch-hunt related to men. The 'superstitious north' ideas did affect
the witch-hunt in Finnmark by strengthening the alertness on the part
of the authorities towards male witches to be found there. In Scotland,
attitudes towards the Highlanders do not seem to have had the same
consequences.

The Personal Factor

Witchcraft trials arose in some areas and not in others. So far no single
witchcraft analysis or study has managed to come to terms with this
enigma. Even neighbouring communities might have completely different
developments with regard to witchcraft persecution, as can be seen from

trials in central Europe.[111] So the basic questions are: What kind of triggering factors originated the witchcraft trials, and what kind of sustaining factors kept the trials alive during the period of the witch-hunt? All the above-mentioned factors are important, but they are not in themselves enough to explain why Scotland and Finnmark suffered severe witch-hunts, because these factors would be functional in places where witchcraft persecution took place as well as where witch-hunt did not occur. So first we have to look for a triggering factor that originated the witch-hunt. Secondly, we have to look for a sustaining factor able to wake the witch-hunt into life after a dormant period with few trials. In both these cases I think the personal factor is the decisive one. There must be one or several individuals in positions which enable him or them to start the witch-hunt and similarly for the continuation of trials.

The personal factor has been pointed out by scholars such as Golden, Voltmer and Pihlajamäki as crucial for initiating and putting a stamp on a witchcraft panic.[112] In Scotland and Finnmark the personal factor was distinctive with regard to influence on the early stages of the witch-hunt. James VI's visit to Denmark related to the introduction of demonological ideas in Scottish witchcraft trials has been discussed.[113] What is clear is that King James came back from Denmark to Scotland in April 1590 and c. 1591 wrote an early draft of his manuscript for *Demonology*. The origin of demonological ideas in Finnmark is easier to trace, as they occur in the court records shortly after John Cunningham was installed as district governor in 1619. There is a high probability that specific notions were brought to Finnmark by him and set in circulation locally from the top downwards.

The personal factor can be seen in relation to personal threat as well as official practice. The witch-hunt in both areas studied here really took off when powerful people felt they were personally threatened by witches. We see this in the case of James VI and the North Berwick witches; in the case of an alleged plot against the district governor and his wife in

---

[111] Volmer, R., 'Hexenjagd im Territorium der Reichsabtei St Maximin vor Trier', 227–71; Voltmer, R., 'Hexenverfolgungen im Maas-Rhein-Mosel-Raum', 153–187; Rummel, W. and Voltmer, R., *Hexen und Hexenverfolgung in der Frühen Neuzeit*, 34–57, 74–83; Pihlajamäki, 'Swimming', 50–51.

[112] Golden, 'Satan in Europe'; Voltmer, 'Hexenjagd', 241–42.

[113] It is a possibility that Chancellor Maitland, who went with King James on the voyage to Denmark, might have brought back demonological ideas.

Finnmark in 1663; in the case of a Bergen merchant in Vadsø who felt his ships as well as his family members to be under threat.[114] The closer the consequences of witches' activity came to the private sphere, the more the person in question panicked. The personal factor related to individuals in office is exemplified in the case of Janet Morrison. The witch-hunters in Bute seem to be closely connected with the leading members of the local church and the persons possessing authority within the bureaucracy of the burgh. In Finnmark, there is evidence that the district governors and the bailiffs personally influenced the witch-hunt. There was a need for governors to manifest their power after they entered office, which may be reflected in the witchcraft panics which followed the installation of each new district governor. The same is seen related to the Scottish panics in 1649 and 1661, which both took place after new regimes came to power. Similarly we have seen an increase in witchcraft trials in Orkney and Shetland after changes in administration of the legal field were carried through. Thus state policy and personal ambition went hand in hand. It will hardly be possible to tell exactly what kind of ideas the government officials carried with them, but judged from the results of their practise, their implementation of demonological ideas was effective.

As for Finnmark, my argument is that ideas related to the European doctrine of demonology was closely related to the personal factor and that individual persons strongly influenced the introduction and spread of these ideas in Finnmark. The carrying of new demonological notions to the north happened simultaneously with new governmental installations. Most likely introduction of demonological ideas to the local communities may be seen in connection with information from court sessions and church sermons reaching the local people. News passed on from the local courts or from church services must have been interesting for fellow villagers. However, the initial phase where the demonological ideas were first put forth, seem to depend upon particular persons with knowledge of these European ideas, like John Cunningham in the 1620s and the Rhodius couple in the 1660s. Thus the importance of the personal factor should not be overlooked when working with transference of ideas about witchcraft in the early modern period. The remote location of Finnmark within Europe made the personal influence from each individual official potential strong.

---

[114] Levack, *Witch-hunting in Scotland*, 37; Willumsen, *Trollkvinne i nord*, 42.

The Scottish Connection

This last factor is a further development of the 'personal factor' discussed above. I will argue there was a direct link between the Scottish and the Finnmark witchcraft trials—a link I will call 'the Scottish connection'.[115] My argument is based on the installation of John Cunningham as district governor in Finnmark in 1619 as well as linguistic evidence in the sources.

The first real outburst of witchcraft panics in Finnmark came in the 1620s, the year after John Cunningham's instalment as district governor. Cunningham was a Scotsman recommended by the Scottish king—'by our request and recommendation'—to serve the Danish king.[116] He was employed in the service of Christian IV in 1603. Cunningham led one naval expedition to Greenland in 1605, when Mount Cunningham, Cunningham's Fjord and Christian IV's Fjord got their names.[117] He also participated in an expedition to Greenland in 1606, that time not as leader. He was known to be a decisive and strong leader. His appointment as the king's servant in the north had to do with the king's ambitions to strengthen the northern border areas, to lead a more aggressive fiscal policy with stricter taxation, and to extend Vardøhus Castle.[118] There were few restrictions on Cunningham in his office in Finnmark, which gave him a free hand in his dealing with witchcraft trials.

John Cunningham of Barns in Fife is a key person when it comes to understand the initial phase of demonological trials in Finnmark. John Cunningham must have heard about the North Berwick trials in 1590–91. Born in c. 1575 he was a youth when these trials took place. The estate of Barns was located near the village of Crail, from where he could see over to North Berwick. Even if the accused persons were tried in Edinburgh, these trials must have been well known in the vicinity of North Berwick, among high and low of the population. It would be impossible to live in Crail not knowing about alleged witches allied with the Devil being persecuted. During these trials, the Scottish King James VI participated in the interrogation of suspected witches. Cunningham knew the Scottish

---

[115] Willumsen, *Trollkvinne i nord*, 73.

[116] Meldrum, R. M., (ed.), *Letters from James I to Christian IV, 1603–1625* (Washington, 1977), 41.

[117] Egede, H., *Grønlands Nye Perlustration eller Naturel-Historie* (Copenhagen, 1742); *Dictionary of Canadian Biography* (Toronto, 1966), i, 243.

[118] Hagen, H., 'At the Edge of Civilisation. John Cunningham, lensmann of Finnmark 1619–51', in A. Mackillop and S. Murdoch (eds.), *Military Governors and Imperial Frontiers c. 1600–1800* (Leiden, 2003), 30.

king, who was an eager witch-hunter and the only European monarch to publish a demonological treatise. This work was published in 1597, a publication well known all over Scotland. In addition, John Cunningham must have been aware of witch-hunting in towns near Crail in Fife in 1597, as well as the large 1597 Aberdeen panic.[119] All in all, John Cunningham certainly knew about witchcraft persecutions as well as the Devil's snares before he entered the service of the Danish king in 1603.[120] Travelling north to Finnmark and to Vardøhus Castle, Cunningham was just in time to influence judicial officials, jury members and peasants before the outbreak of the first panic. In the same way as King James, he was himself active in the questioning the suspected witches and contributed to bring demonological notions into the interrogation.[121] There is no evidence in the records that demonological ideas were known before 1620 in Finnmark. When looking at the whole period of witchcraft persecution in Finnmark, a change towards demonology took place in 1620, corresponding with Cunningham's arrival.

The most important evidence in my study supporting the connection between Scotland and Finnmark are two extraordinary linguistic findings. The first is a place-name, Balduolden or Ballvolden. This place-name appeared in the records from witchcraft trials in 1621, then continued to be mentioned in the records for a few years afterwards. It has neither been mentioned as place-name in Vardø before nor after. Balduolden is a descriptive noun, the first part denoting a ball, the latter part denoting a piece of grassland or turf. The idea was that witches were gathering at a piece of grassland near the village. During the first Finnmark panic several accused women from Vardø confessed to have attended witches meetings' at Balduolden in Vardø.[122]

We find exactly the same image of witches' meeting at a Ball-Ley in the Scottish material, thus connecting the use of the word in Scotland

---

[119] Goodare, 'Scottish witchcraft panic', 57.

[120] Willumsen, L. H. and Baptie, D., 'John Cunninghams karriere og bakgrunn', *Norsk slektshistorisk tidsskrift*, 43:3 (2013), 161; Willumsen, L. H., 'Exporting the Devil across the North Sea—John Cunningham and the Finnmark Witch-Hunt', in Goodare, Scottish Witches and Witch-Hunters.

[121] It is documented in the court records that John Cunningham was present during the trials of Karen Edisdatter, 1620; Kirsten Sørensdatter, 1621; Mari Jørgensdatter, 1621; Oluf Mogensen, 1625; Thorben Olsen, 1625; Jacob Pedersen, 1625; Birgete, Christopher's wife, 1632; Lisbet, Oluf Nilsen's wife, 1632; Ingeborg Jørgensdatter, 1634; Kirsten, Rasmus Sivertsen's wife, 1634.

[122] For instance the trial of Kirsten Sørensdatter in 1621, SATØ, SF 6, fo. 29a.

and Finnmark.[123] As shown in the analyses of Barbara Bowndie's case, she confessed that the witches used to meet at the Ball Ley. This is a word denoting the same as Balduolden. The word was in ordinary use in Scotland at this time.[124]

The connection between Ballvolden and Ball Ley is very interesting. It is a word with a specific meaning, due to the identical first part of the word, Ball.[125] This word display similarity as for phonetic sounds as well as for meaning. In Danish orthography, the first part of the word could be written 'Ball' or 'Bald', while the second part could be written 'Volden/ Uolden/Vollen/Uollen', denoting an open field or a slope or a piece of land. In Scotland 'Ball' could only be rendered 'Ball'. But Ley could be rendered with several realizations, like 'lee', 'ley', 'lay'. A person who knew both Scottish and Danish, like John Cunningham, could easily translate Ball-Ley to Ballvolden simultaneously in the courtroom. The scribe wrote down what he heard pronounced. It was a direct transfer from one language to another of a place-name. It is the particular meaning of the first part which makes the word interesting as for the comparative argument I make. The meaning of Ball is literally a ball to play with, as has been argued within place-name research.[126] In Scotland and Orkney they had a famous ball-game in the seventeenth century, which is referred to. The similarity of meaning in two countries is most likely connected with another by a human being who was present during the trial and participated in the interrogation, so that he could bring the Ball Ley into the questioning of the accused. When these words with identical meaning and used in the same semantic context is documented in demonological witchcraft cases in the two areas on either side of the Norwegian Sea, this cannot be accidental.

In the Scottish material, there is also used other words to denote the grassland where the witches allegedly met. Margaret Duchill confessed that Elisabeth Blak came to her and took her to the 'crofts of Alloway',

---

[123] Ball-ley, Ball-grene and Balgrene are variants of the same word. The word means a green on which ball-games are played. Ley means a tract of open grass-land, meadow or pasture, found chiefly as second element in Scottiash place-names from an early date. The word also means land which has been left untilled for some time and allowed to return to grass used as pasture. Ref. DOST, 12 vols., i, 176.

[124] Ball-grene is mentioned in Pitcairn's *Criminal trials* in records from 1611, located to the Edinburgh area, 'the Reidhous was vpone the Ball-grene, playing with him'. Ref. Pitcairn, *Criminal Trials*, iii, part I, 214.

[125] It is not a general rendering of a word like 'Tanzenplatz', which is found for instance in German witchcraft material, denoting a place for dancing and feasting.

[126] Nils Hallan, 'Balvolden (Baluolden)', *Håløygminne* 14, pp. 276–87.

where the Devil came to them. A 'croft' is a piece of enclosed land, or small field, used for tillage or pasture.[127] The word croft has the meaning small, enclosed field.[128] Witches' meeting at the 'cuning yaird' is also mentioned in connection with Duchill.[129] The word means a rabbit-warren, also attributed to hillis land.[130] So the witches in Scotland often gathered in fields nearby the villages.

Another language image found in both areas is the one of a woman being 'admiral' for the other witches in a group. In Finnmark we find the image in the case of Kirsten Sørensdatter in 1621, where she is said to be the 'admiral' for the rest of a group.[131] The same image is used in the North Berwick trials, and the word admiral is used in exactly the same way.[132] Here the function of being a leader of a group of witches is described by the same expression, namely a word related to the sea military system. The image that a witch is officer for other witches in a group, is used in some witchcraft trials, in Norway as well as in Sweden. However, we do not have any examples of the use if an identical word admiral in the same witchcraft context in two different countries. The linguistic findings in the material cannot be overlooked. They point to very interesting similarities between the two regions in question. In my view it is likely that these notions were brought to Finnmark by John Cunningham as part of the demonological element being introduced by him.

Conclusion

This study has compared witchcraft trials in two European regions. It has explored tendencies in the entire source material as well as highlighted discourse and language in individual witchcraft documents. Several explanatory reasons for the witch-hunts in the two regions have been illuminated, in total supporting the view that the historical witchcraft trials was a very complex phenomenon.

---

[127] BL, Egerton MS 2879, fo. 8v.
[128] *DOST*, 12 vols., i, 747, e. g. 1600, 'All and haill the fauld and croft of land', ref. *Misc.* Spalding, c iv, 268.
[129] BL, Egerton MS 2879, fo. 6r.
[130] DOST, 12 vols., i, 775. Cuning, cunning means a rabbit. The word is frequently documented during the sixteenth and seventeenth centuries, e.g. 1625, 'The landis of Cassakes (...) with the salmond fishings and cunyngars of the samyne lands', Reg. Great S., 332/2; 1638, 'There are rich cuningars almost in every isle', Aboyne Rec., 281, 1693.
[131] SATØ, SF 6, fo. 27r. A similar image is found in Sweden, cf. Svennungsson, L. M., *Rannsakingarna om trolldom i Bohuslän 1669–1672* (Uddevalla, 1970), 59, 89.
[132] In the trial of Euphame McCalzane, 1591. NAS, JC 2/2, fo. 224r.

Quantitative and qualitative analyses have completed each other. In my view, the statistical analyses are important to provide a basis for the close-readings and the final interpretations of the whole material. As for the qualitative analyses, a narratological approach to witchcraft research is considered a fruitful approach as long as it is seen in connection with other contemporary historical sources. A close-reading of a historical document with the intention of carrying through a discourse analysis, making the voices of the different participants as distinct as possible, may contribute to clarity as for interpretation of the document as a whole. The two analytical approaches to the material, quantitative and qualitative, have in completion demonstrated the fruitfulness of a broad interpretative effort as well as the complexity of the historical witch-hunt as a phenomenon. Today, researchers of witchcraft trials agree about the complexity of the trials. New light may be thrown on this topic from several methodological angles as well as from several fields of research. The aim will still be a better understanding of this dark period of history.

My study is a comparison between two European areas. A set of factors constituted the analytical framework for comparison between the two areas. My analyses have confirmed that several of these factors were influential on the actual witchcraft trials; the demonological element, the state, the laws, the church, ethnicity, pressures from local courts, torture, personal influence from legal and clerical officials, assimilation of demonological ideas in an oral society, ideas about the superstitious north, connection between the regions based on linguistic coalescence in demonological imagery, as we see in the images of the Ball-Ley and a woman being admiral for a group of witches. The remaining factors, neighbourhood disputes and folk belief, are more difficult to relate to the period of witch-hunt as explanatory reasons, even if they have been dealt with in the analyses. Folk belief is not in itself an explanation for witchcraft persecution, but it became dangerous when it was demonized during interrogation. Neighbourhood disputes were mentioned as motives for casting spells, but these cases became dangerous only when they were brought before the court. The comparison has shown that witches in Scotland and Finnmark share many features with each other. Still they have their cultural distinctiveness intact. My conclusion is that a co-existence of several factors working in the same direction, influencing different levels of society, prepared the ground for the witch-hunt to start and to continue.

The question of gender runs through my study. Most analyses of the material show that women were treated differently from men. The

study has shown the vulnerability of women and the impossibility of
being treated in a neutral way once she was imprisoned. Records report
women's everyday lives: loyalty towards other women, disputes with
other women, anxiety for lack of food, loss of animals and sickness. But
ordinary women living their ordinary lives—for most of the accused
females were in that category—would never had to fear being burned
unless there was a formal system to catch denunciations and push for trials. This insecurity had an effect on them all, young and old, married and
unmarried. Therefore the characterization of women accused of witchcraft as victims is appropriate and the explanation for the gender bias is
to be found in the ideological sphere.

A comparative study of this kind is a contribution to witchcraft research
in Scotland and in Norway. However, the study will hopefully also contribute to the field of witchcraft research in general, offering analyses and
findings from two European areas with severe witchcraft persecution.

BIBLIOGRAPHY

Primary Manuscript Sources

Manuscript in private hands, Bressay
Proceedings against Marion Pardoun, 1644, in possession of John and Wendy Scott, Gardie
  House, Bressay, Shetland

National Library of Denmark, Copenhagen
Lilienskiold, H. H., 'Troldom oc anden ugudelighed udi dette seculo sig hafuer tildragen
  blant fin som Nordmand' [Sorcery and Ungodliness which has happened in this century
  among Sami as well as Norwegian], Thott's collection, 950,2°

Edinburgh City Archives, Edinburgh
Edinburgh Town Treasurer's Accounts, iv, (1612–23)

National Archives of Scotland, Edinburgh
Books of Adjournal, JC2/6
Circuit Court Books, JC10/4
Stirling Presbytery records, CH2/722/6
Rothesay Kirk Session Book, CH2/890/1

Orkney Library and Archive, Kirkwall
Marwick Collection, D31/4/4
Orkney Presbytery Records, CH2/1082/1

British Library, London
Egerton MS 2879

Riksarkivet, Oslo [National Archives of Norway]
Lensregnskap for Vardøhus len, Rentekammeret [District Accounts for Vardøhus District,
  The Exchequer], 1600–92

Regional State Archives of Tromsø, Tromsø [Regional State Archives of Tromsø]
Amtmannen i Finnmarks arkiv [The Archives of the Regional Governor of Finnmark],
  no. 2543, copies of sentences 1631–70
Sorenskriveren i Finnmarks arkiv [The Archives of the Magistrate of Finnmark], no. 6,
  Records of court proceedings 1620–27
Sorenskriveren i Finnmarks arkiv [The Archives of the Magistrate of Finnmark], no. 10,
  Records of court proceedings 1654–63
Sorenskriveren i Finnmarks arkiv [The Archives of the Magistrate of Finnmark], no. 25,
  Records of court proceedings 1692–95

Regional State Archives of Trondheim, Trondheim [Regional State Archives of Trondheim]
Lagtingsprotokoll for Nordland og Finnmark [Court records Court of Appeal for Nordland
  and Finnmark], 1647–68

Shetland Museum and Archives, Lerwick
Shetland Presbytery Records, CH2/1071/1

Primary Printed Sources

J. H. Ballantyne and B. Smith (eds.), *Shetland documents 1580–1611*, (Lerwick, 1994), xix
R. S. Barclay (ed.), *The Court Book of Orkney and Shetland 1612–1613* (Kirkwall, 1962)
P. H. Brown et al. (eds.), *The Register of the Privy Council of Scotland*, 38 vols. (Edinburgh, 1908–70)
J. Cameron and J. Imrie (eds.), *Justiciary Records of Argyll and the Isles, 1664–1705*, 2 vols., (SS, 1949–69)
G. Donaldson (ed.), *Court Book of Shetland 1615–1629* (Lerwick, 1991)
G. Donaldsen (ed.), *The Court Book of Shetland 1602–1604* (Edinburgh, 1954)
Fellman, I., *Handlingar och uppsatsar angående finska lappmarken och lapparne*, i, (Helsingfors, 1910)
R. Hagen and P. E. Sparboe (eds.), H. H. Lilienskiold, *Trolldom og ugudelighet i 1600-tallets Finnmark* [Sorcery and Ungodliness in seventeenth-century Finnmark] (Tromsø, 1998)
J. R. N. MacPhail (ed.), 'Papers related to Witchcraft 1662–1677' in *Highland Papers*, 4 vols. (SHS, 1914–34), iii, 3–30
R. Pitcairn (ed.), *Criminal Trials in Scotland, 1488–1624*, 3 vols. (Edinburgh, 1833), iii, part I
Records from the Earldom of Orkney, 1299–1614, vii, 2nd series (SHS, 1914)
H. Sandvik and H. Winge (eds.), *Tingbok for Finnmark 1620–33* [Records of Court Proceedings for Finnmark 1620–1633] (Oslo, 1987)
T. Thomson and C. Innes (eds.), *The Acts of the Parliaments of Scotland*, 12 vols. (Edinburgh, 1814–75)
J. M. Thomson et al. (eds.), *Registrum Magni Sigilli Regum Scotorum* (Register of the Great Seal of Scotland) (Edinburgh, 1882–)

Secondary Sources

Aaslestad, P., *Pasienten som tekst*, (Oslo, 1997)
Agrell, S., *Lapptrummor och runmagi* (Lund, 1934)
Alm, E., *Statens rolle i trolldomsprosessene i Danmark og Norge på 1500– og 1600–tallet. En komparativ undersøkelse* [The role of the state during the witchcraft trials in Denmark and Norway in the sixteenth and seventeenth centuries. A comparative study] (Master's thesis, University of Tromsø, 2000)
Alm, T., 'The Witch Trials of Finnmark, Northern Norway, during the 17th century: Evidence for Ergotism as a Contributing Factor', *Economic Botany*, 57, iii (2003), 403–16
Alver, B. G., *Mellem mennesker og magter. Magi i hekseforfølgelsernes tid* [Between human beings and forces. Magic in the time of witchcraft persecution] (Bergen, 2008)
Alver, B. G., *Heksetro og trolldom* [Witchcraft beliefs and sorcery] (Oslo, 1971)
R. L. Andreassen and L. H. Willumsen (eds.), *Steilneset Memorial. Art, Architecture, History* (Stamsund, 2013)
Ankarloo, B., 'Sweden: The Mass Burnings (1668–76), in B. Ankarloo and G. Henningsen (eds.), *Early Modern European Witchcraft. Centres and Peripheries* (Oxford, 1993), 295–96
Andersen, B., *'Danske Lov' 1683* [Danish Law of 1683] (København, 2003)
Anderson, P. D., *Black Patie* (Edinburgh, 1992)
——, *Robert Stewart. Earl of Orkney, Lord of Shetland* (Edinburgh, 1982)
P. J. Anderson (ed.), *Officers and Graduates of University and King's College, Aberdeen* (Aberdeen: New Spalding Club, MVD–MDCCCLX)
Ankarloo, B., 'Sweden: The Mass Burnings (1668–76)', in B. Ankarloo and G. Henningsen (eds.), *Early Modern European Witchcraft. Centres and Peripheries* (Oxford, 1993)
B. Ankarloo and G. Henningsen (eds.) *Early Modern European Witchcraft. Centres and Peripheries* (Oxford, 1990)
L. Apps and A. Gow (eds.), *Male Witches in Early Modern Europe* (Manchester, 2003)

Asbjørnsen, P. C., *Norske Huldre-Eventyr og Folkesagn* [Norwegian Nymph Tales and Legends], (Christiania, 1845–48)

Asbjørnsen, P. C. and Moe, J., *Norske Folkeeventyr* [Norwegian Fairytales] (Oslo, 1841–44); *Norske Folkeeventyr* [Norwegian Fairytales] (Christiania, 1852); *Norske Folkeeventyr* [Norwegian Fairytales] (Oslo, 1871)

Åstrand, B., *Tortyr och pinlig förhör—våld och tvång i äldre svensk rätt* (Umeå Univerity, Ph. D. thesis, 2000)

Bal, M., *Narratology. Introduction to the Theory of Narrative* (Toronto, 1997)

Balsvik, R. R., 'Religious beliefs and witches in contemporary Africa', in R. L. Andreassen and L. H. Willumsen (eds.), *Steilneset Memorial. Art. Architecture. History* (Stamsund, 2013)

———, *Vardø. Grensepost og fiskevær 1850–1950* [Border post and fishing village], (Vardø, 1989)

Baptie, D., *A lairdship lost: the Mowats of Balquholly, 1309–1736* (Edinburgh, 2000)

Barclay, R. S., 'Introduction', in R. R. Barclay (ed.), *Court Books of Orkney and Shetland 1614–1615* (Edinburgh, 1967)

———, *Orkney Testaments and Inventories, 1573–1615*, Scottish Record Society (1977)

Baroja, J. C., *The World of the Witches* (Chicago, 1961)

Behringer, W., *Hexen und Hexenprozesse* (München, 1995)

———, *Hexenverfolgung in Bayern, Volksmagie, Glaubenseifer und Staatsraison in der Frühen Neuzeit* (München, 1987)

———, 'Kinderhexenprozesse', *Zeitschrift für Historische Forschung*, 16 (1989), 31–47

———, *Shaman of Oberstdorf: Chonrad Stoekhlin and the Phantoms of the Night* (Charlottesville, 1998)

———, *Witches and Witch-Hunts* (Cambridge, 2004)

———, 'Zur Geschichte der Hexenforschung', in S. Lorenz (ed.), *Hexen und Hexenverfolgung in deutschen Südwesten*, Aufsatzband, Volkskundliche Veröffentlichung des badischen Landesmuseums Karlsruhe, b. 2 (Ostfildern, 1994), 93–146

Bereday, G. Z. F., *Comparative Method in Education* (New York, 1964)

Bergh, K., 'Til ild og bål', in G. I. Willoch, (ed.), *Vardøhus festning 650 år* (Oslo, 1960), 126–44

Bever, E., *The Realities of Witchcraft and Popular Magic in Early Modern Europe* (Basingstoke, 2008)

The Bible (Geneva, 1560)

Biblia (København, 1606), edn. by Hans P. Resen

Biblia (København, 1633)

Birkelund, M., *Troldkvinden og hennes anklagere* (Århus, 1983)

Black, R., 'Introduction', in R. Black (ed.), *The Gaelic Otherworld* (Edinburgh, 2005)

Bloch, M., 'Towards a Comparative History of European Societies', in F. C. Lane and J. C. Riemersma (eds.), *Enterprise and Secular Change. Readings in Economic History*, (London, 1953); German version, 'Für eine vergleichende Geschicte der europäischen Gesellschaften', in P. Schöttler (ed.), *Aus der Werkstatt des Historikers. Zur Theorie und Praxis der Geschichtswissenschaft* (Frankfurt, 2000), 122–167

Botheim, R., *Trolldomsprosessene i Bergenhus len*, 1566–1700 [Witchcraft trials in Bergenhus district] (Master's thesis, University of Bergen, 1999)

Braembussche, A. von der, 'Historical explanation and comparative method: towards a theory of the history of society', *History and Theory*, vol. 28, no. 1 (February 1989), 1–24

Briggs, R., *Witches and Neighbours. The Social and Cultural Context of European Witchcraft* (Oxford, 2002; orig. New York, 1996)

Broedel, H. P., *The Malleus Maleficarum and the construction of witchcraft* (Manchester, 2003)

Bulloch, J., *Scottish notes and queries*, Series Two, Vol. VII (Aberdeen, 1906)

Bäckman, L., *Sájva: föreställinger om hjälp- och skyddsväsen i helige fjäll bland samerna* (Stockholm, 1975)

Bäckman, L., 'Types of Shaman: Comparative Perspectives', in Bäckman, L. and Hultkrantz, Å., *Studies in Lapp Shaminism* (Stockholm, 1978), 62–90

Båkte, V. A., 'Den samiske befolkning i Nord-Norge'. Artikler fra Statistisk Sentralbyrå nr. 107 (Oslo, 1978)

J. Cameron and J. Imrie (eds.), *The Justiciary Records of Argyll and the Isles 1664–1705*, 2 vols. (SS, 1949–69)

Campbell, J. G., *Witchcraft and the Second Sight in the Highlands and Islands of Scotland* (Glasgow, 1902)

Chan, M., *Norske trolldomskonflikter i opplysningstiden* [Norwegian witchcraft conflicts in the age of enlightenment] (Master's thesis, University of Oslo, 2009)

——, 'Trolldom som realitet eller overtro? Trolldomskonfliktene i Hordaland på 1700-tallet', *Heimen* 1, (2010), 51–63

Clanchy, M. T., *From memory to written record. England 1066–1307* (Oxford, 1993)

Clark, S., 'Inversion, misrule and the meaning of witchcraft', *Past and Present*, no. 87 (1980), 98–127

——, 'Protestant Demonology: Sin, Superstition, and Society (*c.*1520–*c.*1630)', in B. Ankarloo and G. Henningsen (eds.), *Early Modern European Witchcraft. Centres and Peripheries* (Oxford, 1993), 45–82

——, *Thinking with Demons: the idea of witchcraft in early modern Europe* (Oxford, 1997)

——, 'Witchcraft and Magic in Early Modern Culture', in B. Ankarloo, S. Clark and W. Monter, *Witchcraft and Magic in Europe* (London, 2002), 97–169

Clouston, J. S., *History of Orkney* (Kirkwall, 1932)

Cohen, E. S., 'Back Talk: Two Prositutes' Voices from Rome *c.* 1600', *Early Modern Women: An Interdisciplinary Journal*, vol. 2 (2007), 95–126

——, 'Between Oral and Written Culture: The Social meaning of an Illustrated Love Letter', in B. Diefendorf and C. Hesse, *Culture and Identity in Early Modern Europe (1500–1800): Essays in Honour of Natalie Zemon Davis* (Michigan, 1993), 181–201

Cohn, D., *Transparent Minds. Narrative Modes for presenting Consciousness in Fiction* (Princeton, 1983)

——, *The Distiction of Fiction* (Baltimore, 1999)

Cohn, N., *Europe's Inner Demons* (London, 1993)

Cordey, A. L., *Witch-hunting in the Presbytery of Dalkeith, 1649 to 1662* (University of Edinburgh, M. Sc., 2003)

Cowan, E. B., 'The Darker Vision of the Scottish Renaissance: the Devil and Francis Stewart', in I. B. Cowan and D. Shaw (eds.), *The Renaissance and Reformation in Scotland. Essays in Honour of Gordon Donaldson* (Edinburgh, 1983)

Craigie, W. A., *Dictionary of the Older Scottish Tongue*, 12 vols. (Chicago, 1931)

Dalyell, G., *The Darker Superstitions of Scotland* (Edinburgh, 1834)

Daum, W., Riederer, G. and H. von Seggern, 'Fallobst oder Steinschlag: Einleiende Überlegungen', in H. Schnabel-Schüle (ed.), *Vergleichende Perspectiven. Perspectiven des Vergleichs*, (Mainz, 1998), 1–21

Davidson, P., *The Idea of North* (London, 2005)

O. Davies and W. de Blécourt (eds.), *Beyond the Witch Trials. Witchcraft and Magic in Enlightenment Europe*, (Manchester, 2004)

——, 'Introduction: beyond the witch trials', in Davies and de Blécourt, *Beyond the witch trials*, 1–8

Davis, N. Z., *Fiction in the Archives. Pardon Tales and their Tellers in Sixteenth Century France* (Cambridge, 1987)

Dictionary of Canadian Biography (Toronto, 1966)

Dillinger, J., *"Böse Leute". Hexenverfolgungen in Swäbish-Österreich und Kurtrier im Vergleich* in G. Franz and F. Irsigler (eds.), Trierer Hexenprozesse. Quellen und Darstellungen, band 5 (Trier, 1998)

——, *"Evil people". A comparative study of witch hunts in Swabian Austria and the electorate of Trier* (London, 2009)

——, 'Trier, Electorate of', in Golden (ed.), *Encyclopedia*, 4 vols., iv, 1135–36

Donald, P., *An Uncounselled King. Charles I and the Scottish Troubles* (Cambridge, 1990)

Donaldson, G., 'The Scots Settlement in Shetland', in D. J. Withrington (ed.), *Shetland and the Outside World 1469–1969* (Oxford, 1983), 8–19

Doty, K. L., 'Telling tales. The role of scribes in constructing the discourse of the Salem witchcraft trials', *Journal of Historical Pragmatics*, vol. 8, no. 1 (2007), 25–41

Doty, K. L. and R. Hiltunen, 'I will tell, I will tell', *Journal of Historical Pragmatics*, 3: 2 (2002), 299–335

Durrant, J., 'Why Some Men and Not Others', in Rowlands (ed.), Witchcraft and masculinities, 100–120

Egede, H., *Grønlands Nye Perlustration eller Naturel-Historie* (Copenhagen, 1742)

Eilola, J., 'Lapsitodistajien kertomukset Ruotsin noitatapaukissa 1668–1676' [Child witnesses' stories in witchcraft trials in Sweden 1668–1676], E-journal *Kasvatus and Aika*, 3 (2009)

Elstad, Å., *Moteløver og heimføingar: tekstilar og samfunnsendringar i Øksnes og Astafjord 1750–1900* (Stamsund, 1997)

Falkanger, A. T., *Lagmann og lagting i Hålogaland gjennom 1000 år* [Court of Appeal Judge and Court of Appeal in Hålogaland during 1000 years] (Oslo, 2007)

Favret-Saada, J., *Deadly Words: Witchcraft in the Bocage* (Cambridge, 1980)

Ferber, S., 'Possesion and the sexes', in Rowlands (ed.), Witchcraft and Masculinities, 214–238

Fergusson, R. M., 'The Witches of Alloa', *SHR*, iv (1908), 40–48

Ferraiuolo, A., 'Pro exoneratione sua propria conscientia: magic, witchcraft and church in early eighteenth-century Capua', in Davies and de Blécourt, *Beyond the witch trials*, 26–44

Fludernik, M., *The fictions of languages and the languages of fiction: the linguistic representation of speech and consciousness* (London, 1993)

——, *Towards a 'Natural' Narratology* (London, 1996)

Fox, A., *Oral and Literate Culture in England, 1500–1700* (Oxford, 2000)

——, 'Rumour, News and Popular Political Opinion in Elizabethan and Early Stuart England', *The Historical Journal*, 11:3 (1997), 597–620

Foyster, E. and C. A. Whatley, *A History of Everyday Life in Scotland, 1600 to 1800* (Edinburgh, 2010)

Friis, J. A., *Lappisk mytologi. Eventyr og Folkesagn* (Christiania, 1871)

Friis, P. C., *Norriges Beskriffuelse* (Copenhagen, 1632)

Fur, G., *Colonialism in the Margins: Cultural Encounters in New Sweden and Lapland* (Leiden, 2006)

Gaskill, M., 'Masculinity and Witchcraft in Seventeenth-Century England', in Rowlands (ed.), Witchcraft and Masculiniteis, 171–190

——, 'Reporting murder: fiction in the archives in early modern England', *Social History*, Vol. 23, No. 1 (1998), 1–29

——, 'Witches and Witnesses in Old and New England', in Clark (ed.), *Languages of Witchcraft*

Genette, G., *Fiction & Diction* (Ithaca, 1993), orig. *Fiction et diction* (1991)

——, *Narrative Discourse. An Essay in Method* (Paris, 1983), orig. *Discours du récit*

——, *Narrative Discourse Revisited* (Ithaca, 1988), orig. *Nouveau discourse du récit* (1983)

Gibson, M., *Early modern witches: witchcraft cases in contemporary writing* (London, 2000)

——, *Reading Witchcraft: stories of early English witches* (London, 1999)

——, *Witchcraft and society in England and America, 1550–1750* (New York, 2003)

——, *Women and witchcraft in popular literature, c.1650–1715* (Aldershot, 2007)

Gilje, N., 'Djevelen står alltid bak": Demonisering av folkelig magi på slutten av 1500-tallet" ['The Devil is always behind': Demonizing of traditional magic at the end of the sixteenth century], in B. Askeland and J. F. Bernt (eds.), *Erkjennelse og engasjement: minneseminar for Davis Roland Doublet (1954–2000)* (Bergen, 2002)

——, *Heksen og humanisten: Anne Pedersdatter og Absalon Pederssøn Beyer: en historie om magi og trolldom i Bergen på 1500-tallet*, [The witch and the humanist: Anne Pedersdatter and Absalon Pederssøn Beyer: a story about magic and witchcraft in sixteenth-century Bergen] (Bergen, 2003)

Ginzburg, C., *Ecstacies: deciphering the Witches' Sabbath* (New York, 2001)

Godske, C. L., *Statistikk i forskning og praksis* (Oslo, 1966)

R. M. Golden (ed.), *Encyclopedia of Witchcraft. The Western Tradition*, 4 vols. (Santa Barbara, 2006)

——, 'Satan in Europe: The Geography of Witch Hunts', in M. Wolfe (ed.), *Changing Identities in Early Modern France* (Durham, 1997), 216–47

'Gongferd, feigd og spøykjeri. Framsynte folk', *Bøfjerding*, (1981), 54–57

Goodare, J., 'The cult of the seely wights in Scotland', *Folklore*, 123 (2012, forthcoming)

——, 'Ergotism', in Golden (ed.), *Encyclopedia*, 4 vols., ii, 321–322

——, 'Flying witches in Scotland' in J. Goodare (ed.), *Scottish Witches and Witch-Hunters* (Basingstoke, forthcoming)

——, 'The Finnmark Witches in European Context', in R. L. Andreassen and L. H. Willumsen, *Steilneset Memorial. Art, Architecture, History* (Stamsund, 2013)

——, 'The Framework for Scottish Witch-Hunting in the 1590s', *SHR*, 81 (2002), 240–50

——, *The Government of Scotland* (Oxford, 2004)

——, 'Men and the witch-hunt in Scotland', in A. Rowlands, (ed.) *Witchcraft and Masculinities in Early Modern Europe*, 149–170

——, 'Pricking of suspected witches', in Golden (ed.), *Encyclopedia*, 4 vols., iii, 930–2

——, 'The Scottish Witchcraft Act', *Church History*, lxxiv, no. 1 (2005), 39–67

——, 'The Scottish witchcraft panic of 1597', in J. Goodare (ed.), *The Scottish witch-hunt in context* (Manchester, 2002), 51–72

——, (ed.), *The Scottish witch-hunt in context* (Manchester, 2002)

——, 'Scottish Witchcraft in its European Context', in J. Goodare et al. (eds.), *Witchcraft and Belief in Early Modern Scotland* (Hampshire, 2008), 26–50

—— (ed.), *Scottish witches and witch-hunters* (Basingstoke, forthcoming)

——, *State and Society in Early Modern Scotland*

——, Martin, L., Miller, J. and L. Yeoman, 'The Survey of Scottish Witchcraft', www.arts .ed.ac.uk/witches (archived January 2003, accessed February 2007)

——, 'Witch-hunting and the Scottish state', in J. Goodare (ed.), *The Scottish witch-hunt in context* (Manchester, 2002), 122–45

——, 'Witchcraft in Scotland', in B. P. Levack, *The Oxford Handbook of Witchcraft in Early Modern Europe and Colonial America* (Oxford, 2013), 300–317

——, 'Women and the witch-hunt in Scotland', *Social History*, xxiii (1998), 288–307

Gowing, L., *Domestic Dangers. Women, Words and Sex in Early Modern London* (Oxford, 1996)

——, 'Language, power and the law: women's slander litigation in early modern London', in J. Kermode and C. Walker (eds.), *Women, crime and the courts in early modern England* (London, 1994), 26–47

Granquist, K., 'Du skal inga andra gudar hava jämta mig', in B.-P. Finstad (ed.), *Stat, religion, etnisitet* (Tromsø, 1997), 71–88

——, 'Thou shalt have no other Gods before me (Exodus 20:3). Witchcraft and Superstition trials in 17th- and 18th century Swedish Lapland' in P. Skiöld and K. Kram (eds.), *Kulturkonfrontation i Lappmarken* (Umeå, 1998), 13–21

O. P. Grell (ed.), *The Scandinavian Reformation* (Cambridge, 1995)

Grew, R., 'The Case for Comparing Histories', *The American Historical Review*, vol. 85, no. 4 (1980), 763–778

Grimm, J. and W., *Kinder- und Haus-Märchen* (Berlin, 1819–22)

Grimm, J., *Teutoric Mythology*, 3 vols. III (London, 1883)

Grubbe, S., 'Kongens sjøreise', in R. B. Hagen and P. E. Sparboe (eds.), *Kongens reise til det ytterste nord. Dagbøker fra Christian IVs tokt til Finnmark og Kola i 1599* [The king's voyage to the uttermost north. Diaries from Christian IV's travel to Finnmark and Kola in 1599] (Tromsø, 2004)

Gaasland, R., 'Fra narratologiens tidligste år' [From the earliest years of narratology], in E. Arntzen and R. Gaasland (eds.), *Teorismer* (Tromsø, 1995)

Hagen, R. B., 'At the Edge of Civilisation. John Cunningham, lensmann of Finnmark 1619–51', in A. Mackillop and S. Murdoch (eds.), *Military Governors and Imperia(Frontiers c.1600–1800* (Leiden, 2003)

——, *Dei europeiske hekseprosessane* [The European witchcraft trials] (Oslo, 2007)

——, 'Female Witches and Sami Sorcerers in the Witch Trials of Arctic Norway', *Arv, Nordic Yearbook of Folklore*, lxii (2006), 123–42

——, 'Harmløs dissenter eller djevelsk trollmann?', Historisk tidsskrift, no. 02–03 (2002), 319–46

——, 'The King, the Cat, and the Chaplain' in Klaniczay, G. and Pócs, É., *Communicating with the Spirits* (Budapest, 2005), 246–63

——, 'Sami Shamanism: The Arctic Dimension', *Magic, Rituals, and Witches*, vol. i, no. 2 (2006), 227–33

——, 'The Sami—Sorcerers in Norwegian History. Sorcery Persecutions of the Sami' (Kárasjohka/Karasjok, 2012)

——, *Hekser. Fra forfølgelse til fortryllelse* [Witches. From persecution to enchantment] (Oslo, 2003)

——, 'Witchcraft Criminality and Witchcraft Research in the Nordic Countries', in Levack (ed.), *The Oxford Handbook of Witchcraft*, 375–392

Hall, A., *The Meaning of Elf, and Elves, in Medieval England* (University of Glasgow, 2005)

F. Hallager and F. Brandt (eds.), *Kong Christian den fjerdes Norske Lovbog af 1604* (Christiania, 1855)

Hansen, L. I. and Olsen, B., *Samenes historie fram til 1750* [The History of the Samis until 1750] (Oslo, 2004)

Harris, R. L., 'Janet Douglas and the Witches of Pollock', in S. R. McKenna (ed.), *Selected Essays in Scottish Language and Literature* (Lewington, 1992), 97–124

Haupt, H-G. and Kocka, J., 'Historischer Vergleich: Methoden, Aufgaben, Probleme. Eine Einleitung', in H.-G. Haupt and J. Kocka (eds.), *Geschicte und Vergleich. Ansätze und Ergebnisse international vergleichender Geschichtsschreibung* (Frankfurt, 1996)

Heikkinen, A., *Paholaisen liitoolaiset: Noita- ja magiakäsityksiä Suomessa 1600–luvun jälkipuoliskolla* [Allies of the Devil] (Helsinki, 1969)

Henderson, L., *Supernatural Traditions and Folk Beliefs in an Age of Transition: Witchcraft and Charming in Scotland, c.1670–1740* (Ph. D. thesis, University of Strathclyde, 2004)

——, 'Witch Hunting and Witch Belief in the Gàidhealtachd', in J. Goodare, L. Martin and J. Miller (eds.), *Witchcraft and Belief in Early Modern Scotland* (Basingstoke, 2008), 95–118

Henderson, L. and Cowan, E. B., *Scottish Fairy Belief* (East Linton, 2004)

Henningsen, G., *The Witches' Advocate. Basque Witchcraft and the Spanish Inquisition* (Reno, 1980)

E. Henryson (ed.), *Actis and Constitutionis of the Realme of Scotland* (Edinburgh, 1566)

D. Herman (ed.), *Narratologies. New Perspectives on Narrative Analysis* (Ohio, 1999)

Hibbert, S., *A Description of the Shetland Islands* (Edinburgh, 1822)

Hodges, J. L. Jr. and Lehmann, E. L., *Basic Concepts of Probability and Statistics* (San Fransisco, 1964)

Hodne, B., *Kjærlighetsmagi. Folketro om forelskelse og erotikk* [Love magic. Folk belief about love and erotics] (Oslo, 2012)

——, *Mystikk og magi i norsk folketro* (Oslo, 2011)

Hodne, Ø., *Trolldom i Norge. Hekser og trollmenn i folketro og lokaltradisjon* [Sorcery in Norway. Witches and sorcerers in folk belief and local tradition] (Oslo, 2008)

The Holy Bible (London, 1611), authorised version

Hughes, P., 'Witch-Hunting in Scotland 1649–1650', in Goodare (ed.), *Scottish Witches and Witch-Hunters*, ch. 5 (Basingstoke, forthcoming)

Hossack, B. H., *Kirkwall in the Orkneys* (Kirkwall, 1900)

http://www.arts.ed.co.uk/witches, SSW project by Julian Goodare, Lauren Martin, Joyce Miller and Louise Yeoman, (archived January 2003, accessed February 2007)

Hultkranz, Å., 'Means and Ends in Lapp Shamanism', in Bäckman, L. and Hultkrantz, Å., *Studies in Lapp Shaminism* (Stockholm, 1978), 40–62

Hunter, M., 'The Discovery of Second Sight in Late 17th century Scotland', *History today* (June, 2001), 48–53

——, *The Occult Laboratory: Magic, Science and the Second Sight in Late 17th Century Scotland. The Secret Commonwealth and Other Texts* (Woodbridge, 2001)

Hutton, R., 'Anthropological and historical approaches to witchcraft: Potential for a new collaboration?', *The Historical Journal*, 47, 2(2004), 413–34

——, 'Witch-hunting in Celtic societies', *Past and Present*, 212 (2011), 43–71

Itkonen, T. I., *Heidnischer Religion und Späterer Aberglaube bei den Finnishen Lappen* (Helsinki, 1956)

Jacobsen, J. C., *Danske Domme i Trolddomssager i Øverste Instans* (Cbh. 1966)

Johansen, J. V., *Da Djævelen var ude… Trolddom i det 17. århundredes Danmark* (Viborg, 1991)

Johnstone, J. F. K., *Fasti Academiae Mariscallanae Aberdonensis: selections from the records of the Mariscal College and University, 1593–1860*, (Aberdeen: New Spalding Club, 1889–1898)

Johnstone, N., *The Devil and Demonism in Early Modern England* (Cambridge, 2006)

Jørgensen, P. J., *Dansk strafferet fra Reformationen til Danske Lov* (København, 2007)

Jørkov, B., 'Den stærke tromme', *Siden Saxo*, no. 1 (2000), 9–17

Kallestrup, L. N., 'Maleficium ò "abuso di sacramento"?', *Dansk Historisk Tidsskrift*, cii, no. 2 (2002), 282–305

——, *Trolddomsforfølgelser og trolddomstro: En komparasjon af det posttridentine Italien og det luthersk protestantiske Danmark i det 16 og 17. århundrede* (Ph. D. thesis, University of Aalborg, 2007)

——, *I pagt med Djævelen. Trolddomsforestillinger og trolddomsforfølgelser i Italien og Danmark efter Reformationen* (København, 2009)

Kieckhefer, R., *European Witch Trials. Their Foundations in Popular and Learned Culture, 1300–1500* (London, 1976)

Kiil, A., *Når bøndene seilte* [When the peasants sailed] (Oslo, 1993)

Kittang, A., 'Merknader til nokre grunntema i narratologien', in Kittang, A., *Sju artiklar om litteraturvitenskap* (Oslo, 2001), 77–96

Kivelson, V. A., 'Witchcraft in Russia', in G. N. Rhyne and J. L. Wieczynski (eds.), *The Modern Encyclopedia of Russian and Soviet History*, vol. 55 Supplement: Witchcraft in Russia (Zvenigorod, 1993)

Kjeldstadli, K., *Fortida er ikke hva den engang var* [The past is not was it once used to be] (Oslo, 1999)

Knutsen, G. W., 'A central periphery? Witchcraft trials in south-eastern Norway' in S. Sogner (ed.), *Fact, fiction and forensic evidence: the potential of judicial sources for historical research in the early modern period* (Oslo, 1997), 63–74

——, 'The End of the Witch Hunts in Scandinavia', *Arv, Nordic Yearbook of Folklore*, lxii (2006), 143–64

——, 'Norwegian witchcraft trials: a reassessment', *Continuity and Change*, vol. xviii, no. 2 (2003), 185–200

——, *Servants of Satan and Masters of Demons. The Spanish Inquisition's Trials for Superstition, Valencia and Barcelona, 1478–1700* (Turnhout, 2009)

——, *Trolldomsprosessene på Østlandet. En kulturhistorisk undersøkelse* (Oslo, 1998)

Kryk-Kastovsky, B., 'Historical courtroom discourse', *Journal of Historical Pragmatics*, 7:2 (2006), 213–245

——, 'How bad is "bad data"? In search for the features of orality in Early Modern English legal texts', *Current issues in unity and diversity of languages. Collection of papers selected from the CIL 18, held at Korea University in Seoul on July 21–26, 2008*. Seoul; The linguistic society of Korea

——, 'Representations of Orality in Early Modern English Trial Records', *Journal of Historical Pragmatics* vol. 1, no. 2 (2000), 201–230

J. G. Kyd (ed.), *Scottish Popular Statistics including Webster's analysis of population 1755* (Edinburgh, 1952)

Lambrecht, K., *Hexenverfolgung und Zaubereiprozesse in den schlesischen Territorien* (Köln, 1995)

Labouvie, E., 'Hexenforschung als Regionalgeschichte. Probleme, Grenzen und neue Perspektiven', in G. Wilbertz, G. Schwerhoff and J. Scheffler (eds.), *Hexenverfolgung und Regionalgeschichte. Der Grafschaft Lippe im Vergleich*, Studien zur Regionalgeschichte, b. 4 (Bielefeld, 1994), 45–60

——, *Zauberei und Hexenwerk. Ländlicher Hexenglaube in der frühen Neuzeit* (Frankfurt am Main, 1991)

Langbein, J., *Torture and the Law of Proof* (Chicago, 2006)

Larner, C., 'Crimen Exceptum. The Crime of Witchcraft in Europe', in Larner, C., *Witchcraft and Religion. The Politics of Popular Belief* (Oxford, 1984), 48–53

——, *Enemies of God: the witch-hunt in Scotland* (Oxford, 1981)

——, 'James VI and I and Witchcraft' in A. G. R. Smith (ed.), *The Reign of James VI and I* (London, 1973)

——, 'Was witch-hunting woman-hunting?', *New Society* (8. Oct. 1981), 11–13

C. Larner, C. H. Lee and H. McLachlan (eds.), *A Source-Book of Scottish Witchcraft* (Glasgow, 1977)

Leem, K., *Beskrivelse over Finmarkens Lapper* [Orig. Beskriffuelse offuer Finmarkens Lapper] (København, 1767)

Lennersand, M., 'Rättvik' in M. Lennersand and Oja, L., *Livet går vidare: Älvdalen och Rättvik efter de stora häxprocesserna 1668–1671* (Gidlund, 2006), 375–596

Lennersand, M. and Oja, L., 'Vitnande visionärer. Guds och Djävulens redskap i Dalarnas häxprocesser', 177–184 i H. Sanders (ed.), *Mellom Gud og Djævelen. Religiøse og magiske verdenbilleder i Norden 1500–1800* (København, 2001)

Levack, B. P., 'The decline and end of Scottish witch-hunting' in Goodare (ed.), *Scottish witch-hunt in context*, 166–181

——, 'Judicial Torture in Scotland during the Age of Mackenzie', SS *Miscellany*, iv (2002), 185–98

——, 'The Great Scottish Witch Hunt of 1661–1662', *Journal of British Studies*, xx (1980), 90–108

——, (ed.), *The Oxford Handbook of Witchcraft in Early Modern Europe and Colonial America* (Oxford, 2013)

——, 'Themes of Recent Witchcraft Research', *Arv, Nordic Yearbook of Folklore*, lxii (2006), 7–32

——, 'Torture', in Golden (ed.), *Encyclopedia*, 4 vols., iii, 1129

——, 'Introduction', in B. P. Levack (ed.), *New Perspectives on Witchcraft, Magic and Demonology*, 6 vols., ii, *Witchcraft in Continental Europe* (New York, 2001), pp. vii–ix

——, *Witch-hunting in Scotland. Law, Politics and Religion* (New York, 2008)

——, *The Witch-Hunt in Early Modern Europe* (3rd edn., London, 2006)

——, *Witchcraft in Continental Europe: Local and Regional Studies* (New York, 1992), ix–x, in Witchcraft, Magic and Demonology, B. P. Levack (ed.), vol. 5

Lindhartsen, O., 'Lensherrer, heksejakt og justismord i Finnmark på 1600-tallet' [District Governors, witch-hunt and judicial murder in seventeenth century Finnmark], in G. J. Valen, K. Skavhaug and K. Schanche (eds.), *Flytting og forandring i Finnmarks fortid* (Alta, 2002), 58–71

Lorentz, C., 'Kausale Erklärungen in der Geschictswissenschaft (3): Das vergleichende Erklärungsmodell', in Lorentz, C., *Konstruktion der Vergangenheit. Eine Einführung in die Geschichtstheorie* (Köln, 1997), 231–284. Orig. *De constructie van het verleden. Ein inleiding in de theorie van de geschiedenis* (Amsterdam, 1987), new editions 1990, 1994
——, *Konstruktion der Vergangenheit. Eine Einführung in die Geschictsteorie* (Köln, 1997)
Low, G., *Tour through Orkney and Shetland* (Kirkwall, 1789)
Lynch, M., *The Early Modern Town in Scotland* (London, 1987)
Løyland, M., 'Tankar om trolldom i pietismens tid', *Heimen* 1 (2010), 5–14
Macdonald, S., 'Devil in Fife witchcraft cases' in Goodare, *Scottish witch-hunt in context*
——, 'Torture and the Scottish Witch-hunt: A Re-examination', *Scottish Tradition*, 28 (2002), 95–114
——, *The witches of Fife. Witch-hunting in a Scottish Shire, 1560–1710* (East Linton, 2002)
Macfarlane, A., 'To Contrast and Compare', *Social Dynamics and Complexity. Working Papers Series*, Institute for Mathematical Behavioral Sciences, University of California (Irvine, 2006)
——, *Witchcraft in Tudor and Stuart England* (London, 1970)
Macgregor, A., *Highland Superstitions* (Stirling, 1922)
J. Macha, E. Topalovic, I. Hille, U. Nolting and A. Wilke (eds.), *Deutsche Kanzleisprache in Hexenverhörprotokollen der Frühen Neuzeit*, Auswahledition 1 (Berlin, 2005)
Macha, J., 'Redewiedergabe in Verhörprotokollen und der Hintergrund gesprochener Sprache', in S. Krämer-Neubert and N. R. Wolf (eds.), *Bayerische Dialektologie. Akten der Internationalen Dialektologischen Konferenz 26.–28. Februar 2002*, Schriften zum Bayerischen Sprachatlas 8, (Heidelberg, 2005), 171–178
C. S. Mackay (ed.), Henricis Institoris, o.p. og Jacobus Sprenger, o.p., *Malleus Maleficarum*, I–II (Cambridge, 2006) Magnus, O., *Historia om de nordiska folken* (Malmø, 1982), orig. *Historia de Gentibus Septentrionalibus* (Roma, 1555)
Manker, E., *Die lappische Zaubertrommel*, ii (Uppsala, 1950)
Martin, L., 'The Devil and the domestic: witchcraft, quarrels and women's work', in J. Goodare (ed.) *The Scottish witch-hunt in context*, 73–89
——, 'Scottish Witchcraft Panics Re-examined', in Goodare et al. (eds.), *Witchcraft and Belief in Early Modern Scotland*, (Hampshire, 2007), 119–43
——, 'Witchcraft, quarrels and women's work' in J. Goodare (ed.), *The Scottish witch-hunt in context*
Martin, L. and Miller, J., 'Some Findings from the Survey of Scottish Witchcraft', in J. Goodare et al. (eds.), *Witchcraft and Belief*, (Hampshire, 2008), 51–70
Martinsen, B. A., *Trollmenn & galdramenn* [Sorcerers and men casting spells] (Master's thesis, University of Trondheim, 2010)
Martinsen, L. P., *Anklagede menn i trolldomsprosessene i Norge* [Accused men in Norwegian witchcraft trials] (Master's thesis, University of Oslo, 2008)
Marwick, M. G., *Sorcery in its Social Setting* (Manchester, 1965)
Maxwell-Stuart, P. G., *An abundance of witches. The Great Scottish Witch-Hunt*, (Gloucestershire, 2005)
——, 'The fear of the King is death: James VI and the witches of East Lothia', in W. G. Naphy and P. Roberts (eds.), *Fear in early modern society* (Manchester, 1997)
Maxwell-Stuart, P. G., *Satan's Conspiracy: Magic and Witchcraft in Sixteenth-Century Scotland* (East Linton, 2001)
——, 'Scotland' in Golden (ed.), *Encyclopedia*, 4 vols., iv, 1019
McDonald, S. W., 'The Devil's mark and the witch-prickers of Scotland', *Journal of the Royal Society of Medicin*, xc (1997), 507–11
Mchale, B., 'Free indirect discourse: a survey of recent accounts', *PTL.: A Journal for descriptive poetics and theory of literature*, no. 2 (1978), 249–287
P. McNeill and R. Nicholson (eds.), *An Historical Atlas of Scotland c.400–c.1600* (St Andrews, 1975)
R. M. Meldrum (ed.), *Letters from James I to Christian IV, 1603–1625* (Washington, 1977)

Melville, R. D., 'The Use and Forms of Judicial Torture in England and Scotland', SHR, 2 (1905), 225–48

Miller, J., *Cantrips and Carlins: Magic, Medicine and Sociey in the Presbyteries of Haddington and Stirling, 1600–1688* (Ph. D. thesis, University of Stirling, 1999)

——, 'Devices and directions: folk healing aspects of witchcraft practice in seventeenth century Scotland', in J. Goodare (ed.), *The Scottish witch-hunt in context* (Manchester, 2002) 90–95

——, *Magic and Witchcraft in Scotland* (Musselburgh, 2004)

——, 'Men in Black: Appearances of the Devil in Early Modern Scottish Witchcraft Discourse', in J. Goodare et al. (eds.), *Witchcraft and Belief in Early Modern Scotland* (Hampshire, 2008), 144–65

Mitchell, S. A., *Witchcraft and magic in the Nordic Middle Ages* (Philadelphia, 2011)

——, *Witchcraft and Magic in the Nordic Middle Ages* (Philadelphia, 2011)

W. E. Monter (ed.), *European Witchcraft* (New York, 1969)

——, 'Geography of the witch hunts,' in Golden, *Encyclopedia*, ii, 413

——, 'Scandinavian Witchcraft in Anglo-American Perspective', in Ankarloo and Henningsen (eds.), *Early Modern European Witchcraft*

——, 'Witch Trials in Continental Europe 1560–1660', in Ankarloo, B, Clark, S. and W. Monter (eds.), *Witchcraft and Magic in Europe. The Period of the Witch Trials* (London, 2002)

——, 'Witchcraft in Iberia', in Levack (ed.), The Oxford Handbook of Witchcraft, 268–282

Muchembled, R., 'Foreword', in Golden (ed.), *Encyclopedia*, 4 vols., i, p. xxvii

The New Statistical Account of Scotland, vol. xv (Edinburgh, 1845)

Nennonen, M., 'Witch Hunts in Europe: A New Geography', *Arv, Nordic Yearbook of Folklore*, lxii (2006), 165–85

Nielssen, A. R., 'Fra storvær til småbruk. Den geografiske ekspansjonen i den norske bosetting i Finnmark ca 1570–1700', *Heimen* no. 2 (1986)

Niemi, B. R., *Varanger årbok* (1989), 158–185

Niemi, E., 'Anders Paulsen (Poulsen, Pouelsen)', in *Norsk biografisk leksikon* (Oslo, 1999)

——, 'Christian 4s Finnmarksreise i 1599', *Årbok for Foreningen til norske fortidsminnesmerkers bevaring* (Oslo, 1988), 17–38

——, 'Hans Hansen Lilienskiold—embetsmann, vitenskapsmann og opprører' in *Portretter fra norsk historie* (Oslo, 1993)

——, 'Hekseprosesser og økonomi', *Ottar*, no. 5 (2012), 19–25

——, *Vadsøs historie*, i (Vadsø, 1983)

L. Normand and G. Roberts (eds.), *Witchcraft in Early Modern Scotland* (Exeter, 2000)

Næss, H. E., 'Norway: The Criminological Context', in Ankarloo and Henningsen (eds.), *Early Modern European Witchcraft*

—— (ed.), *For rett og rettferdighet i 400 år Sorenskriverne i Norge 1591–1991* [For law and justice during 400 years] (Oslo, 1991)

——, 'Forbrytelse og straff', in L. Marthinsen (ed.), *Tingboka som kilde* (Oslo, 1990)

——, 'Fra tingskriver til dommer. Tiden 1591–1797' in Næss (ed.), *For rett og rettferdighet i 400 år*.

——, 'Lagtingsprotokoller—gullgruber med feller' [Court records from the Court of Appeal—gold mines with traps], *Heimen* no. 1 (1984), 59–67

——, *Med bål og brann* (Oslo, 2005)

——, 'Norway' in Golden (ed.), *Encyclopedia*, 4 vols., iii, 838Næss, H. E., 'Sorenskriverenes tingbøker fra 1600–1700-tallet som historisk kildemateriale' [The seventeenth and eighteenth-centuries magistrates'court records as historical sources], *Heimen* no. 4 (1981), 781–795

——, *Trolldomsprosessene i Norge på 1500–1600-tallet. En retts- og sosialhistorisk undersøkelse* [Witchcraft trials in Norway during the sixteenth and seventeenth centuries. A legal- and socioeconomical study] (Oslo, 1982)

Onega, S. and José Á. G. Landa, Introduction to Gérard Genette: 'Voice', in S. Onega and J. Á. G. Landa (eds.), *Narratology* (London, 1996)

Ong, W., *Orality and Literacy. The Technologizing of the Word* (London, 1988)
Österberg, E. and Sandmo, E., 'Introduction', in E. Österberg and S. Sogner (eds.), *People Meet the Law. Control and conflict-handling in the courts. The Nordic countries in the post-Reformation and pre-industrial period* (Oslo, 2000)
Östling, P.-A., 'Blåkulla Journeys in Swedish Folklore', in *Arv, Nordic Yearbook of Folklore*, vol. lxii (2006), 81–122
Peterkin, A., *Rentals of the Ancient Earldom and Bishopric of Orkney*, No. II, The Rentale of King and Bishoppis Lands of Orkney 1595 (Edinburgh, 1820)
Pihlajamäki, H., ' "Swimming the Witch, Pricking for the Devil's mark": Ordeals in the Early Modern Witchcraft Trials', *Legal History*, xxi, no. 2 (2000), 35–58
Pollan, B., *Samiske beretninger*, [Sami stories] (Oslo, 1997)
——, *Samiske sjamaner. Religion og helbredelse* [Sami shamans. Religion and healing] (Oslo, 1993)
Purkiss, D., 'Sounds of Silence: Fairies and Incest in Scottish Witchcraft Stories', 81–98 in S. Clark (ed.), *Languages of Witchcraft: Narrative, Ideology and Meaning in Early Modern Culture* (New York, 2001)
——, *Troublesome Things. A History of Fairies and Fairy Stories* (London, 2000)
——, *The Witch in History* (London, 1996)
Qvigstad, J., *Kildeskrifter til den lappiske mytologi* [Sources to Sami Mythology] (Trondheim, 1903)
——, *Lappiske eventyr og sagn I/IV* [Sami fairy tales and legends], (Oslo, 1927–29)
Qvigstad, J. and Sandberg, G., *Lappiske eventyr og folkesagn* (Kristiania, 1887)
Rafnsson, M., *The Witch-hunts in Iceland* (Hólmavik, 2003)
Remy, N., *Demonolatry* (London, 1930), orig. published 1595
Riis, T., *Should Auld Acquaintance Be Forgot: Scottish-Danish Relations, c.1450–1707*, 2 vols. (Odense, 1988)
Robertsen, J. D. M., *The Kirkwall Ba'. Between the Water and the Wall* (Edinburgh, 2005)
Robberstad, K., *Rettssoga*, I (Oslo, 1976)
——, 'Udal Law', in D. J. Withrington (ed.), *Shetland and the Outside World 1469–1969* (Oxford, 1983), 49–68
Rogers, C., *Social Life in Scotland. From Early to Recent Times*, 3 vols. (Edinburgh, 1886)
Roper, L., ' "Evil Imaginations and Fantasies": Child-Witches and the End of Witch Craze', *Past and Present*, no. 167 (2000), 107–139
——, *Witch Craze. Terror and fantasy in Baroque Germany* (New Haven, 2004)
Rowlands, A. (ed.), *Witchcraft and Masculinities in Early Modern Europe* (Hampshire, 2009)
——, *Witchcraft narratives in Germany: Rothenburg, 1561–1652* (Manchester, 2003)
Rudwin, M., *The devil in legend and literature* (La Salle, 1973)
Rummel, W., *Bauern, Herren und Hexen. Studien zur Sozialgeschichte sponheimischer und kurtrierischer Hexenprozesse (1574–1664* (Göttingen, 1991)
——, 'Hexenprozesse in Raum von Untermosel und Hunsrück. Raumkulturelle und Soziokulturelle Dimensionen', in K. Freckmann (ed.), Sobernheimer Gespräche I.: *Prozesse in Raum* (Bonn, 1993), 83–92
Rummel, W., and Voltmer, R., *Hexen und Hexenverfolgung in der Frühen neuzeit* (Darmstadt, 2008)
Rushton, P., 'Texts of Authority: Witchcraft Accusations and the Demonstration of Truth in Early Modern England', in S. Clark (ed.), *Languages of Witchcraft. Narrative, Ideology and Meaning in Early Modern Culture* (New York, 2001)
Ryan, W. F., 'The Witchcraft Hysteria in Early Modern Europe: Was Russia an Exception?', *The Slavonic and East European Review*, vol. 76, no. 1 (1999)
Rydving, H., *The End of drum-time: Religious Change among the Lule Saami, 1670s–1740s* (Uppsala, 1995)
——, 'Saami responses to Christianity. Resistance and change', in J. K. Olupona (ed.), *Beyond primitivism. Indigenous religious traditions and modernity* (New York, 2004), 99–107

Sandmo, E., *Tingets tenkemåter* (Oslo, 1992)

Sandvik, H., 'Tinget i Finnmark 1620–33' [The court in Finnmark 1620–1633], *Heimen* no. 4 (1987), 232–242

——, *Tingbøker. Avskrivning og registrering* (Oslo, 1989)

Schefferus, J., *Lapponia* (Frankfurt am Main, 1673)

Schulte, R., 'Der dänische Reformator: Niels Hemmingsen', in *Hexenvervolgung in Schleswig-Holstein* (Heide, 2001)

——, *Hexenverfolgung in Schleswig-Holstein 16.-18. Jahrhundert* (Heide, 2001)

——, 'Ein Kinderhexenprozess aus St. Margarethen', 48–55 in *Wider Hexerey und Teufelswerk...' Von Hexen und ihrer Verfolgung* (Itzehoe, 2000)

——, *Man as Witch. Male Witches in Central Europe* (Basingstoke, 2009)

Schwerhoff, G., 'Hexerei, geschlect und Regionalgeschicte', in G. Wilbertz, G. Schwerhoff and J. Scheffler (eds.), *Hexenverfolgung und Regionalgeschichte. Der Grafschaft Lippe im Vergleich*, Studien zur Regionalgeschichte, b. 4 (Bielefield, 1994), 325–353

Schieder, T., 'Möglichkeiten und Grenzen vergleichender Methoden in der Geschichtswissenscahft', in *Geschicte als Wissenscahft* (München, 1968)

Scott, H., *Fasti Ecclesiae Scoticanae: the Succession of Ministers in the Church of Scotland from the Reformation*, 8 vols. (Edinburgh, rev. edn., 1915–50)

Scott, W., *Minstrelsy of the Scottish Border*, 2 vols. (Edinburgh, 1802)

Sewell, W. H., 'Marc Bloch and the Logic of Comparative History', *History and Theory*, vol. 6, no. 2 (1967), 208–218

Sinclair, G., *Satan's invisible World Discovered* (Edinburgh, 1685)

Smith, B., 'Gibbets and gallows. Local rough justice in Shetland, 800–1700', paper presented at the conference 'Recent developments in North Atlantic Studies', arranged by Northern Studies and Aberdeen University, Aberdeen 13–15 April 2007

——, ' "Lairds" and "Improvement" in the 17th and 18th century Shetland', in T. M. Devine (ed.), *Lairds and improvement in the Scotland of the enlightenment* (Stratchclyde, 1978), 11–20

——, *Toons and Tenants* (Lerwick, 2000)

——, 'Shetland, Scandinavia, Scotland, 1300–1700: The changing nature of contact', in G. G. Simpson, (ed.), *Scotland and Scandinavia 800–1800*, (Edinburgh, 1990), 25–37

Sogner, S., 'Rettsprotokollene som kilde til mentalitet og kultur i europeisk historieforskning', in L. Mathinsen (ed.), *Tingboka som kilde*, 7–18

——, 'Trolldomsprosessene i Norge på 1500-1600-tallet', Norveg, no. 25 (1982), 155–182

Solberg, O., *Forteljingar om drap—kriminalhistorier frå seinmellomalderen* [Narratives about murder—criminal stories from the late Middle Ages], (Oslo, 2003)

Stave, T., *Da Lucifer kom til Vardøhus* (Master's thesis, University of Tromsø, 2012)

Sternberg, M., 'Ordering the Unordened: Time, Space and Descriptive Coherence', *Yale French Studies*, lxi (1981), 60–88

——, 'Telling in Time (1): Chronology and Narrative Theory', *Poetics today*, no. 4 (1990), 901–48

Stewart, W. G., *Popular Superstitions and Festive Amusements of the Highlanders* (Edinburgh, 1979), orig. published 1923

M. Summers (ed.), *The Malleus Maleficarum of Heinrich Kramer and James Sprenger* (New York, 1971). *Malleus Maleficarum* was originally published in 1486

Sunde, J. Ø., *Speculum legale—rettsspegelen* [Speculum legale—the mirror of the law] (Bergen, 2005)

Svennungsson, L. M., *Rannsakingarna om trolldom i Bohuslän 1669–1672* (Uddevalla, 1970)

Swales, J. K. and McLachlan, H. V., 'Witchcraft and the status of women: a comment', *British Journal of Sociology*, xxx, no. 3 (1979) 349–58

Sødal, T., 'Trolldomsprosessene på Agder' [Witchcraft trials in Agder], *Heimen*, no. 1 (2010), 15–33

Sörlin, P., 'The Blåkulla Story: Absurdity and Rationality', *Arv. Yearbook of Folklore*, 52 (1997), 131–152

——, *Trolldoms- och vidskepelseprocessarna i Göta hovrätt 1635–1754* (Umeå, 1993)
——, *'Wicked Arts'. Witchcraft and Magic Trials in Southern Sweden, 1635–1754* (Leiden, 1999)
Tamm, D., Johansen, J. C. V. and Næss, H. E., 'The Law and the Judicial System', in E. Österberg and S. Sogner (eds.), *People Meet the Law. Control and conflict-handling in the courts. The Nordic countries in the post-Reformation and pre-industrial period* (Oslo, 2000), 27–56
N. W. Thomas (ed.), *County Folk-Lore. Examples of printed folk-lore concerning the Orkney & Shetland Islands*, collected by Black, G. F., vol. 3 (London, 1903)
Thomas, K., *Religion and the Decline of Magic* (London, 1971)
S. Thompson (ed.), *Motif-index of Folk Literature* (Charlottesville, 2004)
Thomson, W. P., 'The Eighteenth Century Church in Orkney', in H. W. M. Cant and N. H. Firth (eds.), *Light in the North: St. Magnus Cathedral Through the Centuries* (Kirkwall, 1989)
——, *History of Orkney* (Edinburgh, 1987)
Tilly, C., 'Big Structures, Large processes, Huge Comparisons', Ann Arbor University of Michigan, CRSO Working Papers 195 (1983)
——, *Big structures. Large processes. Huge comparisons* (New York, 1984)
Toivo, R. M., 'Discerning voices and values in the Finnish witch trial records', *Studia Neophilologica*, 1 (2012)
Toivo, R. M., 'Marking (dis)order: witchcraft and the symbolics of hierachy in late seventeenth- and early eighteenth-century Finland', in O. Davies and W. de Blécourt (eds.), *Beyond the witch trials. Witchcraft and magic in Enlightenment Europe* (Manchester, 2004)
——, *Witchcraft and Gender in Early Modern Society* (Hampshire, 2008)
——, 'Women at Stake: Interpretations of Women's Roles in Witchcraft', *Arv, Nordic Yearbook of Folklore*, lxii (2006), 187–202
Topalovic, E., ' "Ick kike in die Stern vndt versake Gott den Herrn". Versprachligung des Teufelspaktes in westfälishen Verhörsprotokollen des 16./17. Jahrhunderts', *Augustin Wibbelt-Gesellschaft. Jahrbuch 20*, 69–86
Trusen, W., 'Der Inquisitionsprozess: Seine historische Grundlagen und frühen Formen', *Zeitschrift der Savigny-Stiftung für Rechtsgeschichte 105, Kanonische Abteilung 74* (1988), 168–230
Tønnesson, J., *Hva er sakprosa* (Oslo, 2008)
Vitoux, P., 'Le jeu de la focalisation', *Poetique*, no. 51 (1982), 359–368
Voltmer, R., 'Die Hexenverfolgungen in Raum des Erzbistums Trier (15.–17. Jahrhundert)—Strukturen und Deutungen', in B. Schneider (ed.), *Kirchenreform und Konfessionsstaat 1500–1800*, vol. 3 in M. Persch and B. Schneider, *Geschicte des Bistums Trier*, (Trier, 2010)
——, 'Hexenjagd im Territorium der Reichsabtei St Maximin vor Trier', in W. Reichert, G. Minn and R. Voltmer (eds.), *Quellen zur Geschicte des Rhein-Maas-Raumes* (Trier, 2006), 227–71
——, 'Hexenverfolgungen im Maas-Rhein-Mosel-Raum', in Irsigler, F., (ed.), *Beziehungen, Begegnungen und Konflikte in einem europäishen Kernraum von der Spätantike bis zum 19. Jahrhundert* (Trier, 2006)
——, 'Netzwerk, Denkollektiv oder Dschungel?', *Zeitscfift für historische Forschung*, 34:3 (2007), 486–87
——, 'St Maximin, Prince-Abbey of ', in Golden (ed.), *Encyclopedia*, 4 vols., iv, 1082–3
——, 'Vom getrübten Blick auf frühneuzeitlichen Hexenverfolgungen—Versuch einer Klärung', *Gnostika. Zeitschrift für Wissenscahft und Esoretik*, no. 11 (2006), 45–58
——, 'Witch-Finders, Witch-Hunters or Kings of the Sabbath? The prominent Role of Men in the Mass Persecutions of the Rhine-Meuse Area (Sixteenth-seventeenth Centuries)', in A. Rowlands (ed.), Witchcraft and Masculinities in Early Modern Europe, 74–99
Vorren, Ø., 'Bosetning og ressursutnytting under veidekulturen og dens differensiering. *Finnmarksvidda natur—kultur*, NOU, 18 A. (Oslo, 1978)

Walinski-Kiehl, R. S., 'The devil's children: child witch-trials in early modern Germany', *Continuity and Change* 11(2) (1996), 171–189

Walker, C., 'Crime, Gender and Social Order in Early Modern Chesire', (Ph. D. Diss., University of Liverpool, 1994)

——, 'Women, theft and the world of stolen goods', in J. Kermode and C. Walker, *Women, crime and the courts in early modern England* (London, 1994), 95–97

Wasser, M., 'The Privy Council and the Witches: The Curtailment of Witchcraft Prosecutions in Scotland, 1597–1628', *The Scottish Historical Review* Volume 82, 1, no. 213 (2003), 20–46

Welskopp, T., 'Stolpersteine auf dem Königsweg: methodenkritische Anmerkungen zum internationalen Vergleich in der Gesellschaftsgeschichte', *Archiv für Sozialgeschicte*, 35 (1995), 339–367

——, 'Vergleichende geschicte', in Europäische Geschicte Online (EGO), hg. vom Institut für Europäische Geschichte (IEG), Mainz European History Online (EGO), published by the Institute of European History (IEG), Mainz 2010-12-03

Werner, M. and Zimmermann, B., 'Beyond comparison: Histoire croisée and the challenge of reflexivity', *History and Theory* 45 (2006), 30–50

Wessel, A. B., *Ambrosius Rhodius, en til Finmarken forvist læge i det 17de aar hundrede* (Kirkenes, 1929)

Whyte, I. D., *Scotland before the Industrial Revolution* (Essex, 1995)

Wiesner-Hanks, M., 'Gender' in Golden (ed.), *Encyclopedia*, 4 vols., ii, 407

Wilby, E., *The Visions of Isobel Gowdie: Magic, Witchcraft and Dark Shamanism in Seventeenth-Century Scotland* (Eastborne, 2010)

Williams, M., 'The Witch's Familiar, Past and Present', *New Age*, May 1 (2000)

Williamson, A. H., 'Scots, Indian and Empire: The Scottish politics of civilization, 1519–1609', *Past and Present*, no. 150 (1996), 46–83

Willumsen, L. H., 'Barn anklaget for trolldom i Finnmark—en narratologisk tilnærming', *Heimen* vol. 48, no. 3 (2011), 257–78

——, 'Children accused of witchcraft in 17th-century Finnmark', *Scandinavian Journal of History*, 38:1(2013), 18–41

——, *Dømt til ild og bål. Trolldomsprosessene i Skottland og Finnmark* (Stamsund, 2013)

——, 'Exporting the Devil across the North Sea. John Cunningham and the Finnmark Witchhunt', in Goodare, J., *Scottish Witches and Witch-Hunters* (Basingstoke, forthcoming)

——, 'Den historiske trollkvinne i nord', *Ottar*, no. 5 (2012), 12–18

——, 'A Narratological Approach to Witchcraft Trials: A Scottish Case', *Journal of Early Modern History*, 15 (2011), 531–60

——, 'Narratologi som tekstanalytisk metode' [Narratology as text-analytical tool], in M. Brekke (ed.) *Å begripe teksten* (Kristiansand, 2006), 39–72

——, 'From court records to exhibition texts', in R. L. Andreassen and L. H. Willumsen (eds.), *Steilneset Memorial. Art, Architecture, History* (Stamsund, 2013)

——, *Seventeenth-Century Witchcraft Trials in Scotland and Northern Norway* (Ph D thesis, University of Edinburgh, 2008)

——, *Steilneset. Memorial to the Victims of the Finnmark Witchcraft Trials* (Oslo, 2011)

——, *Trolldomsprosessene i Finnmark. Et kildeskrift* (Bergen, 2010)

——, *Trollkvinne i nord* [Witch in the North] (Tromsø, 1994)

——, *Trollkvinne i nord i historiske kilder og skjønnlitteratur* [Witch in the North in historical sources and literature] (Master's thesis, University of Tromsø 1984)

——, 'Witches in Scotland and Northern Norway: two case studies', in A. Kruse and P. Graves, *Images and Imaginations. Perspectives on Britain and Scandinavia* (Edinburgh, 2007), 35–66

——, 'Witches of the High North. The Finnmark Witchcraft Trials in the Seventeenth Century', *Scandinavian Journal of History*, xxii, no. 3 (1997), 199–221

——, 'John Cunninghams karriere og bakgrunn', *Norsk slektshistorisk tidsskrift* 43:3 (2013), 159–176

Willumsen, L. H. and Baptie, D., 'From Fife to Finnmark. John Cunningham's Way to the
    North', *The Geneologist* (forthcoming)
——, 'Von Fife nach Finnmark—John Cunninghams Weg nach Norden', in R. Voltmer,
    (ed.), *Europäische Hexenforschung und Landesgeschichte—Methoden, Regionen, Vergle-
    iche* (Trier, 2013)
Withers, C. W. J., 'Gaelic in Scotland before 1609' in *Gaelic in Scotland 1698–1981. The geo-
    graphical History of a Language* (Edinburgh, 1984), 16–41
——, *Caelic Scotland. The Transformation of a Culture Region* (London, 1988)
D. J. Withrington (ed.), *Shetland and the outside world 1469–1969* (Oxford, 1983)
Wormald, J., *Court, Kirk, and Community. Scotland 1625–1625* (London, 1981)
——, 'The Witches, the Devil and the King' in Brotherstone, T. and D. Ditchburn, *Freedom
    and Authority* (East Linton, 2000), 165–180
Worobec, C. D., *Possessed. Women, and Demons in Imperial Russia* (De Kalb, 2001)
Wrightson, K. E., 'Kindred adjoining kingdoms: An English perspective on the social and
    economical history of early modern Scotland', in R. A. Houston and I. D. Whyte (eds.),
    Scottish Society 1500–1800 (Cambridge, 1989), 245–60
Ylikangas, H., Johansen, J. C. V., Johansson, K. and Næss, H. E., 'Family, State and Patterns
    of Criminality', in Österberg and Sogner (eds.), *People meet the law. Control and conflict-
    handling in the courts. The Nordic countries in the post-Reformation and pre-industrial
    period* (Oslo, 2000)

INDEX OF OLD NAMES

In Index of Old Names, accused persons' names from original sources are arranged by first name, whereas names of official persons are arranged by surname.

THEMATIC INDEX

INDEX OF AUTHORS